MW00830947

A Dictionary of New Mexico
and Southern Colorado Spanish

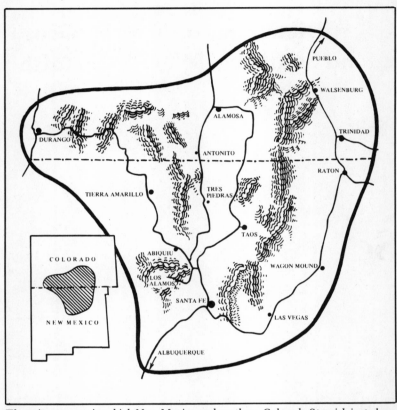

The primary area in which New Mexico and southern Colorado Spanish is spoken.

A
DICTIONARY
OF
NEW MEXICO
AND
SOUTHERN COLORADO
SPANISH

Rubén Cobos

MUSEUM OF NEW MEXICO PRESS
SANTA FE

All things to nothingness descend,
Grow old and die and meet their end;
Man dies, iron rusts, wood goes decayed,
Towers fall, walls crumble, roses fade . . .
Nor long shall any name resound
Beyond the grave, unless 't be found
In some clerk' book; it is the pen
Gives immortality to men.—*Anonymous*

The publication of this volume has been supported in part
by a grant from the National Endowment for the Humanities.

Copyright © 1983 the Museum of New Mexico Press
Post Office Box 2087
Santa Fe, New Mexico 87503

10 9 8 7

Printed in the United States of America.
All rights reserved.

Library of Congress Cataloging in Publication Data

Cobos, Rubén.
  A dictionary of New Mexico and southern Colorado Spanish.

  Bibliography: p.
    1. Spanish language—Provincialisms—New Mexico—Dictionaries.
2. Spanish language—Provincialisms—Colorado—Dictionaries. 3. Spanish
language—Etymology—Dictionaries. I. Title.
PC4829.N4C6   1982   467'.9789   82–22528
ISBN 0–89013–141–4 (clothbound), ISBN 0–89013–142–2 (paperback)

Designed by Glen Strock.

CONTENTS

PREFACE

The lexical items contained in this work come from towns and villages of the upper Rio Grande in northern New Mexico and southern Colorado. A dialect of Spanish has been spoken uninterruptedly since the end of the seventeenth century in New Mexico, and since the middle of the nineteenth century in southern Colorado.

I have been in direct contact with the Spanish spoken in these areas since coming from Mexico into New Mexico some fifty years ago. It was as a student at Menaul, a Presbyterian school for Spanish-American boys in Albuquerque, New Mexico, that I first became acquainted with New Mexico Spanish as spoken by my classmates. Those young men came to Menaul from homes in Santa Fe, Chimayó, Española, El Rito, Peñasco, Taos, Mora, Chama, and other towns in New Mexico, and from Antonito, Conejos, La Jara, Alamosa, Fort Garland, San Luis, Walsenburg, Trinidad, La Junta, and other towns in Colorado.

Since the early 1940s, with the help of my students at the University of New Mexico and the cooperation of villagers in their sixties, seventies and eighties, I have recorded a large body of New Mexico and southern Colorado Indo-Hispanic folklore materials on magnetic tape. Included in this collection are hundreds of personal interviews and countless examples of *corridos* and *inditas* (local ballads), children's games and songs, folktales, *chistes* (anecdotes), jokes, home remedies, recipes, narratives dealing with local events, proverbs, riddles, songs, *versos* (rimed quatrains), and witch stories and accounts of witchcraft. These materials gave me the majority of terms. Many items, also, come from literary works touching on New Mexico history, customs and life in general in this area (see *Bibliography*).

I have excluded common household words in daily use (such as *agua*, water; *burro*, donkey; *caballo*, horse) which are readily recognized as standard Spanish. I have included words which have local acceptations superimposed on their original meanings, a shift of accent, or definite semantic variations not present in their standard Spanish counterparts.

The spelling of entries in this work is based on current rules of Spanish orthography and accentuation. Alphabetization, likewise, follows standard Spanish practices. The letters ch, ll and ñ occur after c, l and n respectively, and have separate, individual sections in the dictionary.

Pronunciation of local Spanish is akin to that of northern Mexico, and both differ from Castilian Spanish pronunciation with respect to c, z, ll, and y.

> c, z: c before e and i, and z in a final position or before a, o, u, have the sound of English s in assess, assets, professor (*centavo* [*sentáƀo*], *cinco* [*sínko*], *zacate* [*sakáte*], *zoquete* [*sokéte*], *azul* [*asúl*], *capaz* [*kapás*], *luz* [*lús*]).
> ll, y: ll and y are pronounced like English y in yes, yet (*calle* [*káye*], *caballo* [*kaƀáyo*], *pollo* [*póyo*], *ayer* [*ayér*], *joyo* [*xóyo*]).

For the pronunciation of Spanish vowels and consonants (except as noted above), I suggest the pronunciation aids in the pages preceding the Spanish section of *Appleton's New Cuyás English-Spanish, Spanish-English Dictionary* (see *Bibliography*).

I wish to thank my communicants for their help in clarifying lexical meanings with which I was not completely familiar. I am eternally grateful to my wife, Ella M. Cobos, for letting me use her collection of Indo-Hispanic folklore materials. I also want to thank Mrs. Elvira García Cobos, RN, PhN, for her invaluable contributions of vocabulary items used in Indian and Hispanic folk-medicine in Taos county. Likewise, I am most grateful to those students at the University of New Mexico (1944-1976) who helped me in contacting and scheduling interviews with their parents or relatives, or who interviewed those persons themselves as part of their class assignments in my courses in Southwest Indo-Hispanic folklore. I would also like to thank the staff at the Museum of New Mexico Press, James Mafchir, publisher, Sarah Nestor, editor, and Martha Baca, who with her specialized knowledge of regional and archaic terms provided many valuable editorial suggestions and additions.

INTRODUCTION

The Spanish spoken in rural areas of New Mexico and southern Colorado can be described as a regional type of language made up of archaic (sixteenth- and seventeenth-century) Spanish; Mexican Indian words, mostly from the Náhuatl; a few indigenous Rio Grande Indian words; words and idiomatic expressions peculiar to the Spanish of Mexico (the so-called *mexicanismos*); local New Mexico and southern Colorado vocabulary; and countless language items from English which the Spanish-speaking segment of the population has borrowed and adapted for everyday use. New Mexico and southern Colorado Spanish, quite uniform over the whole geographical area, has survived by word of mouth for over three hundred and eighty years in a land that until very recent times was almost completely isolated from other Spanish-speaking centers.

Basically Spanish in its morphology and syntax, New Mexico and southern Colorado Spanish is an offshoot of the Spanish of northern Mexico, especially with respect to usage and pronunciation. This is understandable, since New Mexico was an integral part of New Spain (Mexico) from 1540 to 1821 and a part of Mexico from that year until 1850, when it became a territory of the United States.

Archaic Spanish

The original settlers who came to New Mexico in 1598—to the *Nueba México,* as the land was called at that time—brought with them a sixteenth-century Spanish that was fundamentally rural Castilian, mixed with the speech of Andalusians, Asturians, Basques, and Galicians (see Espinosa, *Estudios*). Words such as *luvia* <Sp. *lluvia* [*lúƀia*], flash flood; *mantelina* <Sp. *mantellina* [*manteḷína*], a short cloak worn by women; *pelizcar* <Sp. *pellizcar* [*peḷiƟkár*], to pinch; *pelizco* <Sp. *pellizco* [*peḷíƟko*], pinch; and *turra* <Sp. *zurra* [Ɵúra], beating, which betray a European Spanish pronunciation, and the use of expressions such as *¡A redo vaya!*, Good heavens!; *en silla de manos*, regally; *¿La gracia de su merced?*, Your name, please?; *¡Bal, ni que juera el rey!*, Gee, as if he were a king!, testify to the presence in New Mexico of a continental type of Spanish during colonial times.

The following are a few examples of the archaic sixteenth- and seventeenth-century vocabulary that constitutes an integral part of New Mexico and southern Colorado Spanish: *alverjón*, peas; *arrollar*, to lull to sleep; *camalta*, bed; *el celebro*, the mind; *cientopiés*, centipede; *cudicia*, greed; *¡Curre!*, Run!; *culantro*, coriander; *desafuciado*, discouraged; *dispertar*, to awaken; *dispierto*, awake; *empeloto*, stark naked; *húmido*, humid; *iyendo*, going; *jogata*, fire; *lumbricias*, worms; *mushas*, front part of the face; *ñervos*, muscles; *ñudo*, knot; *relós*, timepiece; *rétulo*, sign; *rostro*, trace, track; *turco*, gypsy.

In addition to the above, in sporadic areas of New Mexico and southern Colorado the local speech contains certain phonological speech mannerisms that date from the sixteenth and seventeenth centuries. These peculiarities have been thoroughly studied by A. M. Espinosa, Sr., E. C. Hills and others (see *Bibliography*). Among the speech mannerisms are (1) the aspiration of f, h, s, and related s sounds (za, zo, zu): *jui* (*fui*); *jogata* (*fogata*); *jervir* (*hervir*); *jumo* (*humo*); *jumadera* (*humareda*); *caja* (*casa*); *No je.* (*No sé.*); *rajón* (*razón*); *quijás* (*quizá*); *ajul* (*azul*); (2) diphthongization of some stressed words: *cai* (*cae*); *Cain* (*Caín*); *pais* (*país*); *tapao* (*tapado*); *alzao* (*alzado*); *paraiso* (*paraíso*); and (3) the pronunciation of a paragogic i sound at the end of infinitives and oxytones ending in l, n, r, and s: *papeli*, *¿Acuáli?*, *¿Quiéni?*, *Beleni, A veri, beberi, Taosi, despuesi.* This paragogic sound is usually added to words that appear isolated or at the end of a breath group. As stated above, these speech mannerisms appear only in certain sporadic areas and are not widespread.

What is widespread and very typical of local Spanish both in New Mexico and southern Colorado are the following. First, the disappearance of the second person plural verb form in all conjugations (the *vosotros* form): *lonchar* (present) *loncheo, loncheas, lonchea, lonchamos, ———, lonchean;* (preterit) *lonché, lonchates, lonchó, lonchamos, ———, loncharon;* (imperfect) *lonchaba, lonchabas, lonchaba, lonchábanos, ———, lonchaban.* (See *cambeo, coser, juir, oler,* and *vide.*) Second, the change of the verb endings in the second person singular of the preterit from Standard Spanish *-aste, -iste, -iste* either to *-ates, -ites, -ites* or to *-astes, -istes, -istes: hablé, hablates (habastes), habló; comí, comites (comistes), comió; viví, vivites (vivistes), vivió.* (The corresponding Standard Span-

ix

ish forms are: *hablaste, comiste, viviste*.) Third, the transfer or substitution of the first person plural ending *-emos* of the second conjugation to the same person in the third conjugation: *bebo, bebes, bebe, bebemos, ———, beben; vivo, vives, vive, vivemos* (St. Sp. *vivimos*), ———, *viven*. This is true of all third conjugation verbs: *muremos* (Sp. *morimos*), *sintemos* (Sp. *sentimos*), *salemos* (Sp. *salimos*), etc. The gentle folk use the ending *-emos* to express present time and the *-imos* ending for past time. (*Todos los días venemos*. We come every day. *Ayer no venimos*. We did not come yesterday.) Fourth, the shift of accent and the substitution of the form *-nos* for the verb endings *-emos, -amos, -amos* of the Standard Spanish forms in the first person plural of the present subjunctive: (Local Spanish) *háblenos, bébanos, vívanos*; (Standard Spanish) *hablemos, bebamos, vivamos*. ('*M papá no quiere que háblenos*. My father doesn't want us to talk.) The particle *-nos* also replaces the Standard Spanish endings of the first person plural of the imperfect indicative: (Local Spanish) *hablábanos, bébanos, vivíanos*; (Standard Spanish) *hablábamos, bebíamos, vivíamos*. Fifth, the loss of intervocalic *-d* at the end of past participles of *-ar* verbs (*buscar, hablar, tomar*, etc.) and in adjectives derived from these verb forms: *buscao* (Sp. *buscado*), *hablao* (Sp. *hablado*), *tomao* (Sp. *tomado*).

Náhuatl vocabulary

As the Spanish language spread throughout central New Spain during the course of the sixteenth century, it adopted many words from the Indian dialect, particularly from the Náhuatl. Most of this vocabulary referred to items related to the culture of the Aztecs and for which the Spaniards had no equivalents in their tongue (*metlacahuitl*, pole for hanging skins, *nexectic*, ashen colored, *tenamaxtli*, trivet, *tequesquitl*, efflorescent). Many of these terms are no longer household words in the Spanish of Mexico; if they are used, they have undergone pronunciation changes that make them quite different from their sixteenth-century originals. In New Mexico and southern Colorado, however, most words retained from the Náhuatl of Oñate's day are still pronounced very much as they were spoken by the early seventeenth-century settlers (*shocoque* <Náhuatl *xococ* [*šokók*], sour; *tinamaishte* <Náhuatl *tenamaxtli* [*tenamáštli*], trivet; *nesha* <Náhuatl *nexectic* [*nešéktik*], yellowish). We must point out that the adjective *nexectic* meant ashen-colored to the Aztecs and that it was applied to corn tortillas that turned grayish due to an excess of lime used in the boiling of the corn. In New Mexico and southern Colorado the term *nesha* is applied to the color of the flour tortilla that turns yellowish due to the use of too much baking powder in the preparation of the dough.

The following entries exemplify the vocabulary from the Náhuatl that has been retained by New Mexicans and southern Coloradoans from their seventeenth-century ancestors: *chichincle,* fawner; *chimal,* shield; *chincual,* a kind of diaper rash; *guajalote* (confused with *ajalote*), salamander; *jumate,* dipper; *metlacahuitl,* pole for hanging hides out to dry; *nesha,* yellowish; *shocoque,* sour, spoiled; *tapeshte,* a type of hayloft; *tazol,* straw; *tazolera,* shed for storing hay, straw, etc.; *tequesquite,* crude bicarbonate of soda; *tinamaishte,* trivet.

Words such as *nesha, shocoque* and *tinamaishte,* which locally retain the sixteenth-century palatal fricative sound of x [š], may date from a transition period when Spanish x was changing from palatal to velar. Other terms (*jacal* <Náhuatl *xacalli* [*šakáli*], *jícara* <Náhuatl *xicalli* [*šikáli*], and *jumate* <Náhuatl *xumatli* [*šumátli*]) had already changed the Náhuatl palatal fricative [š] to a velar [x] by the time they came into New Mexico.

Rio Grande Indian vocabulary

As life went on in New Mexico during the seventeenth, eighteenth and nineteenth centuries, the colonists, particularly those establishing their *rancherías* (groups of ranches) near the Rio Grande Indian pueblos, acquired a few local Indian words pertinent to plants, articles of dress, housing, foods, topography, etc., which they incorporated into their language. The list of these terms is very short, due primarily to the lack of an extended social contact between the Spaniards and their Indian neighbors. One must remember that by the Laws of the Indies the Spaniards were forbidden to establish themselves within the limits of the Indian settlements. It was only for purposes of mutual protection against nomadic marauders that a few Spanish villages (San Gabriel, Don Fernando de Taos, Peña Blanca, and one or two others) were founded near those of the Indians.

The following is a list of Indian terms that have figured in the everyday language of New Mexicans of Spanish descent: *aguapá,* cattail; *cacona,* turquoise ornament; *cachinas,* ceremonial dolls; *comanche, comancha* (also, *cumanche, cumancha*), Comanche; *conchelle,* dressed buffalo skin; *coi* or *coye,* underground cellar; *coyaye,* rattlesnake weed; *cuncoso,* having sediment, coffee grounds or crumbs; *cunques,* coffee grounds or crumbs; *chaquegüe,* a kind of mush; *chiguata,* squaw or woman; *chigüil,* dale; *chimajá,* parsley; *chimayó,* obsidian flake; *guayabe,* a kind of paper-thin bread; *kiva,* ceremonial chamber; *oshá,* wild celery; *pagué,* a medicinal plant used in the making of tea; *pergate,* nipple or teat; *pujacante,* Comanche Indian witch doctor; *tano,* inhabitant of Galisteo, New Mexico (the Tano Indians had a settlement in the vicinity of present-day Galisteo); *teguas,* Indian buffalo-skin sandals; *topil,* cane or rod of authority; *tosayes,* sun-dried strips of pumpkin.

Toward the end of the nineteenth century (in the early eighties and nineties), American agriculture, small industries and the railroad attracted thousands of Mexican *braceros* or farmhands to New Mexico, Colorado, Texas, and other states of the Southwest. The Mexican newcomers brought with them the Spanish of Mexico—a Spanish basically Castilian in construction but definitely influenced and enriched by countless terms and idiomatic expressions of the various Indian dialects of that country. By the first decade of the twentieth century, "Mexican Spanish" began to show its influence on the colonial type Spanish of the New Mexicans and southern Coloradoans. Contributing to this was the mobility of the Mexican immigrants working on the railroad in various parts of northern New Mexico and southern Colorado and in Colorado's rich carrot, potato and sugar-beet fields. Another very important factor was the literary impetus given to Mexican Spanish language and culture by Mexican nationals residing permanently throughout the Southwest. These people established clubs and libraries where books written in Spanish could be checked out and read. The same Mexican citizens published literary works, jokes, riddles, stories, folktales, and ballads and printed local and national news, so that Mexicans throughout the area would be well informed even though they did not know English. The bilingual Americans of Spanish descent profited greatly by this dissemination of Mexican language and culture.

The following items are typical of the Mexican Spanish vocabulary that has come into New Mexico and southern Colorado in the course of the last hundred years: *arrancado*, broke, penniless; *la arranquera*, the depression; *bolillo*, white citizen of the United States (the designation *bolillo* is synonymous with *gringo*, but *bolillo* is equivalent to the Indian word *paleface*; it compares the skin color of an American to that of the small, French-style Mexican breakfast roll called *bolillo*); *cócano*, turkey (the words *ganso* and *torque* are far more common in northern New Mexico and southern Colorado); *cuate*, pal; *chamacos*, kids (*la plebe* is a more common term); *chapulín*, grasshopper; *chiple*, spoiled child; *diantre*, imp; *enlame*, slime; *guangoche*, burlap; *güilanchar*, to pamper or spoil a child; *joto*, homosexual; *mayate*, Black; *mero*, almost, exactly; *papalote*, kite; *petaquilla*, trunk; *pirujo, piruja*, homosexual; *tápalo*, shawl; *tepocate*, tadpole; *trastes*, dishes; *trastero*, cupboard; *tucero*, prairie-dog hole or mound; *tuza*, prairie dog; *zacate*, grass; *zacatito*, lawn; *zapeta*, diaper; *zoquete*, mud.

Typical regional vocabulary

The lack of a continuous, day-to-day contact with the people of Mexico throughout the seventeenth, eighteenth and nineteenth centuries, together with a dearth of books, dictionaries and other reading materials, stagnated and impoverished the Spanish of the colonists. Many times these people could not recall the name of a particular article and had no recourse but to coin a new term. It is wonderful to observe how resourceful the New Mexicans were in developing their purely local nomenclature. This was done most naturally on the basis of their senses, especially their keen observation of the color, shape and general appearance of the objects under consideration. The foul smell of the stinkbug, for example, suggested the name *perrodo* <Sp. *pedorro*, flatulent. The Mexican word for stinkbug (*pinacate*) seems to have come too late for its adoption in New Mexico. Because of its stripes (Sp. *rayas*), the chipmunk was called *rayús* or *ratón rayús*. The bat, which has the appearance of a mouse, was given the designation *ratón volador* (flying mouse) because of its ability to fly. The Germans seem to have had the same idea in naming their bat *fleder maus* (winged mouse)! Crutches are designed to fit (when needed) under one's armpits. The Spanish term for armpit is *sobaco*, and the local populace readily came up with the name *sobaqueras* (those what-you-may-call-'em that fit under one's armpit). Again, as in the case of the stinkbug, the Spanish designation for crutches (*muletas*), brought into the area by Mexican immigrants, came too late to be adopted locally. Northern New Mexicans tried some berries in the mountains and, finding them to taste somewhat sour, gave them the name of *agritos* <N. M. Sp. *agro*, sour. Southern Colorado Hispanos, likewise, called the red gooseberries *aguaditas* (the watery ones) for lack of a more precise name.

The following entries give an idea of local or regional New Mexico and southern Colorado Spanish: *aguapiedra*, carbonate of lime; *alejo*, shabby; *alegrís*, homemade rouge; *amarre*, mock arrest during a dance; *estar arrendando*, to be famished; *atrotear*, to incite; *basa* (*hacer basa*), to cut up or misbehave; *bau* (*dar bau*), to please or give in to another's whims; *caladas*, waves on one's hair; *calave*, skeleton; *calote*, plaster cast; *callado*, illegitimate child (illegitimates are also referred to as *"de los pajaritos del monte,"* "[gift] of the birds of the woods"); *compostura*, cornice or crown decoration on a *trastero*; *comprender*, to hire or to employ; *cuerpo*, blouse; *cuipas*, shavings of juniper bark; *champes*, rosehips; *chifonete*, a kind of clown; *desorillo*, rough pine slab; *dominita*, a kind of scapular used to ward off evil or disease; *empelillado*, an adjective applied to a horse or donkey weak from eating nothing but tender grass; *encuerdo*, muscle twist; *engüerado*, rotten (egg); *forcha*, mason's hawk; *guachas*, lies; *ispiado*, sore (from split hooves); *lavastín*, calcimine; *mataseca*, name of an indoor game for children; *melacera*, shed where syrup is made; *mulero*, bootlegger; *ocupar*, to need; *palomita*, butterfly, moth; *pelilludo*, an adjective applied to a donkey or horse with the use of only one of its testicles; *perfición*, resemblance; *pichete*, large mole or birthmark; *pingo*, tilted, or with one leg shorter than the other or others; *pinta*, penitentiary; *pintarse*, to leave; *pitijuyo*, a kind of weevil; *poros*, nostrils; *quedada*, old maid, spinster; *rabiate*, a long line of things; *raíces*, red beets; *salado*, cursed; *varillero*, hawker, peddler; *ucioso*, mischievous.

Borrowings from English

When New Mexico became a territory of the United States in 1850 and very soon after the various non-Pueblo Indians were pacified, Americans from the East and Middle West started moving into southern Colorado and New Mexico. These *americanos* (as they were then and still are called), brought with them a new language filled with words, phrases and idiomatic expressions that the natives learned and adopted, Hispanicizing these terms and pronouncing them as closely as they could to the English originals. English greetings such as howdy, how do you do, and how do you do, suh came out of the mouths of Hispanos as *jare, jarirú* and *jariusa*, respectively. Baking powder and yeast powder, which had been used previously, were Hispanicized into *bequenpaura* and *espauda, espabre* and *espaura*. Through metathesis (the transposition of letters or sounds in a word), undoubtedly, the endearing English term, sweetheart, produced the local entry, *güisa*, meaning sweetheart, girl friend, and good-looking, as an adjective. The masculine form of this noun resulted in *güiso*, for boyfriend, and handsome, as an adjective. Another endearing expression, honey, gave us *jane* [*xáne*]. This word, in turn, created the verb *janear*, to look for girls. The expression, how much?, was Hispanicized into *jamache*, which, in turn, gave us *jamachar*, to talk turkey.

Many words for which the natives had no equivalents were adopted and used as though they had always been part of the local speech. Some of these terms are easily recognized, especially when they are spoken: *atomobil*, automobile; *cloche*, clutch; *flate*, flat; *gaselín*, gasoline; *garache*, garage; *telefón*, telephone; *güinchil*, windshield; *reque, requera, requearse*, wreck, wrecker and to have a wreck, respectively. Words such as *atomobil, gaselín, garache, saxofón*, and *telefón* retained their pronunciation and stress as in English because it was directly from oral English (and not from Spanish) that they were first heard. When Spanish terms such as *automóvil, gasolina, garaje, saxófono*, and *teléfono* came into the area just before the First World War, it was hard for the people to adjust to the pronunciation of the *"mexicanos de México"!*

The following vocabulary will give an idea of how extensively New Mexican and southern Coloradoans borrow terms and expressions from English: *aseguranza*, insurance; *bequenpaura*, baking powder; *bísquete*, biscuit (the word *galleta* is more common); *bloque*, block, the head; *buen tiempo*, good time; *cacombra*, cucumber; *cambiar de mente*, to change one's mind; *chanza*, perhaps; *¡Chite!*, Shit!; *clas*, class, kind; *coconate*, coconut; *contesta*, contest; *copa*, cup, as of coffee; *correr*, to run for public office; *corretear*, to correct (school papers, etc.); *craqueado*, cracked; *crismes*, Christmas; *crochar*, to crochet; *cruque*, crook; *cuque*, cookie; *cute*, coat, especially an overcoat; *cutilio*, cotillion; *daime*, dime; *cuara*, quarter; *nicle*, nickel; *pene*, penny; *dejar saber*, to let (one) know; *descargar*, to discharge, as from the armed services; *dompe* and *dompear*, dump, to dump; *dona*, doughnut; *enlistarse*, to enlist; *escrache*, *de escrache*, by scratch; *escuela alta*, high school; *espauda* or *espaura*, baking powder; *esperar niño*, to be expecting; *fecha*, date or rendezvous; *flirtear*, to flirt; *florería*, flower shop; *gérmenes*, germs; *granma, granpa* or *granpo*, grandma, grandpa; *greira*, grater; *greve*, gravy; *grique*, Greek; *gauche*, watchman; *ingenio*, engine, motor; *jaira*, harrow; *librería*, library; *línea*, line, persuasive speech; *lonchar, lonche*, to lunch, lunch; *magacín*, magazine; *menejador*, manager; *mistear*, to miss; *los mompes*, the mumps; *mope, mopear*, mop, to mop; *mula*, corn liquor; *nodriza*, nurse; *nodrizo*, male nurse, orderly; *pinates*, peanuts; *polbero*, pallbearer; *pope*, puppy, dog; *rentar*, to rent, lease; *rusio*, Russian; *sobrechuses*, overshoes; *taite*, tight, stingy; *tichear*, to teach; *trampe*, bum, hobo, tramp; *troca, troque, troquear, troquero*, truck, to truck, truck driver; *yela*, jelly; *yonque*, junk.

These elements, then (and I repeat them here in reverse order) —borrowings from English, local and regional vocabulary, words and idiomatic expressions peculiar to the Spanish of Mexico, indigenous Rio Grande Indian terms, Mexican Indian vocabulary (mostly from the Náhuatl), and archaic sixteenth- and seventeenth-century Spanish—make up the Spanish dialect of northern New Mexico and southern Colorado.

It must be pointed out at this juncture that in our day, in the 1980s, the dialect is losing its struggle for existence because English is the official language of the area (notwithstanding state constitutional articles or amendments to the contrary—especially in New Mexico). The Hispano population in the region lives in an Anglo-oriented environment where all facets of daily living (commerce, education, entertainment, local and national news communications, politics, etc.) use English for their expression. When Hispanos discuss the latest news, politics or items having to do with entertainment in Spanish, they borrow and use with their Spanish many English words for which they have no equivalents in their dialect. Terms and expressions such as average rainfall, ballpoint pen, bowling tournament, belt buckle, closed circuit, corduroy pants, dividend, faucet, frostless refrigerator, ice-cream cone, ice maker, insurance premium, jumper cable, magnet, microphone, pencil sharpener, premium gasoline, unleaded gasoline, quilt, reversible sweater, schedule, skiing, spark plug, speedometer, special delivery letter, station wagon, stock market, subpoena, summons, volts, watts, windshield sticker, and thousands of others, which the average English-speaking person uses frequently, are typical of this borrowed vocabulary.

In the face of such Spanish language deficiencies, the Hispanos in this region of the Southwest are inevitably shifting to English as their most important medium of communication. It is only the older citizens who still use Spanish, however deficient it may be. Most young Hispano parents in their twenties and thirties are no longer speaking Spanish to their children. If these young people know Spanish themselves, they find it very difficult and inconvenient to transmit it to their offspring. And often children, especially in the company of their Anglo-American playmates, find it embarrassing for their parents to address them in Spanish!

As a result of this state of things, and particularly as the older Spanish-speaking citizens join their colonial ancestors, it is very likely that by the turn of the twenty-first century English and Mexican Spanish will have completely replaced the archaic local Spanish dialect. That this has not happened so far in the hundred and thirty years or so since the English language came into the region, testifies to the strength of the language of Cervantes.

Rubén Cobos
Professor emeritus
University Of New Mexico

USE OF THE DICTIONARY

The elements in an entry consist of: the word (occasionally followed by pronunciation if this varies from the norm), the part of speech (abbreviated), the derivation (in brackets), definition(s), idiomatic phrases which incorporate the word, examples of usage (in parentheses), and extended examples from literature and the oral tradition (indented and translated, with sources given).

Although accents are not generally used on capital letters in Spanish, they are occasionally retained in the dictionary as aids to pronunciation when this is necessary.

Epigraphs at the headings of letters are traditional Colorado and New Mexico Spanish proverbs.

The following abbreviations and phonetic symbols are used in the dictionary:

Abbreviations

adj.	adjective	bot.	botany
adv.	adverb	cf.	compare
Am.	American	Col.	Colonial
astron.	astronomy	Colo.	Colorado
aug.	augmentative	conj.	conjunction

contr.	contraction	Mod.	Modern
derog.	derogatory	mus.	music
dim.	diminutive	N.M.	New Mexico
Eng.	English	no.	northern
euph.	euphemism	ornith.	ornithology
excl.	exclamation	pl.	plural
f.	feminine	poet.	poetic
fig.	figurative(ly)	Port.	Portuguese
Fr.	French	prep.	preposition
i.e.	that is	pres. part.	present participle
imp.	imperative	pron.	pronoun
indef.	indefinite	pt. part.	past participle
int.	intransitive	q.v.	which see
interj.	interjection	reflex.	reflexive
interr.	interrogative	so.	southern
It.	Italian	Sp.	Spanish
Lat.	Latin	St.	Standard
lit.	literally	SW	Southwest(ern)
m.	masculine	Terr.	Territorial
med.	medical	trans.	transitive
met.	metathesis	var.	variant
Mex.	Mexican	vars.	variants
milit.	military	vb.	verb
min.	mineralogy		

Phonetic symbols

[ƀ]	fricative b between vowels	[ļ]	l as in million
[ç]	ts sound in colonial Spanish	[š]	sh as in shoe
[č]	ch sound as in China	[Ɵ]	approximate th sound as in thin
[đ]	fricative d between vowels	[x]	h sound as in hue
[ǥ]	fricative g between vowels		

A Dictionary of New Mexico
and Southern Colorado Spanish

Amor de lejos es pa los pendejos.
Love at a distance is for fools.

abajar, *vb.* [<Col. N.M. Sp. *abaxar*] *int.*, to descend, to come or go down; *trans.*, to lower. (*Abaje la güeja.* Lower your head.)

abaldonado, -da, *adj.* [<N.M. Sp. *abaldonar*] abandoned, forsaken; neglected. (*Este probe muchito lo dejaron abaldonado.* This poor child was left abandoned.)

abaldonar, *vb.* [<Sp. *abandonar*] *trans.*, to abandon, to forsake; to neglect. *Abaldonar* is explained in Aurelio M. Espinosa, *Estudios* I, 177–178, as a case of dissimilation.

abatanado, -da, *adj.* [<Mex. Sp. *abatanado*] snarled, tangled, applied to hair, yarn, etc.

abridor, *m.* [<Sp. *abridor*] opener; *abridor de jarros,* can opener. Cf. Sp. *abridor de latas.*

abrigo, *m.* [<Sp. *abrigo,* wrap, overcoat] *abrigo de abajo,* winter underwear.

abrir, *vb.* [<Sp. *abrir*] to open. (*Ya está abriendo.* The sky is now clearing.) *Re-flex.*, to open up suddenly or hit; to spread out, as a disease; *abrirse de seco, -ca,* to be parched. (*Esta tierra ya se abre de seca.* This land is almost parched.) *¡Abranse!* Get out of the way!

abuelo, *m.* [<Sp. *abuelo,* grandfather] bugbear; name of one of the dancers in the *Matachines,* q.v.

Santa Claus was still unknown in those days. The ***abuelo*** (bug-a-booman) took his place, although he was a stern old man dreaded by the children. Dressed in an old, shabby, patched suit and patched hat, the ***abuelo*** went around the *luminarias* cracking his long whip, sending the boys home on the run. He followed some of them into their homes and made them kneel down and say their prayers. If they did not know their prayers, he gave them a good scolding and told them to stay home and learn them. (Cleofas M. Jaramillo, *Shadows of the Past*)

3

abuja

abuja, *f.* [<Sp. *aguja*] needle; syringe; hand of a clock or watch. N.M. and so. Colo. Hispanos confuse the consonants b (v) and g: *burrión* <Sp. *gorrión, gomitarse* <Sp. *vomitarse, guñuelo* <Sp. *buñuelo,* etc.

abujerar, *vb.* [<Sp. *agujerear*] to pierce, to bore, to make holes.

abujero, *m.* [<Sp. *agujero*] hole; *ajuero* (<Sp. *agujero*) is a more common term.

abujeta, *f.* [<Sp. *agujeta,* a kind of latchet with metal tips] hairpin; bobby pin. *¡Abujetas!* Watch out! (slang).

abularia, *f.* [<N.M. Sp. *albularia<arbolaria*<Sp. *herbolaria,* herbalist] female folk healer. See also *albolaria, ambularia, arbolaria, arbularia.*

acabo, *adv.* [<Sp. *al cabo*] anyway; at any rate.

acafetado, -da, *adj.* [<Sp. *café,* coffee-colored] brown, brownish.

acamorrado, -da, *adj.* [<Mex. Sp. *encamorrado*] drowsy.

acariciarse, *vb.* [<Sp. *acariciar,* to caress] to pick one's eyebrows.

acarralado, -da, *adj.* [<Sp. *acarralado,* with a thread skipped (weaving)] thread-worn, threadbare.

acatar, *vb.* [<Sp. *acatar,* to respect] to notice; to realize; to occur to one. (*No acatamos.* It did not occur to us.)

aceite, *m.* [<Sp. *aceite,* oil] *aceite de castor,* castor oil; *aceite de lámpara,* kerosene; *aceite de olivo,* olive oil; *aceite mexicano* or *volcánico,* volcanic oil, a patent liniment.

acentellado, -da, *adj.* [<Sp. *centella,* flash of lightning] in a hurry; lightning fast. (*Salió de aquí acentellado.* He left here like a flash of lightning.)

acirgüelado, -da, *adj.* [<SW Sp. *cirgüela,* plum] doped up; in a stupor (slang).

acompañador, *m.* [<Sp. *acompañar,* to accompany] in N.M. Penitente flagellation rituals, the accompanying brother who aids a flagellant. See *hermano salido a luz.*

acompañamiento, *m.* [<Sp. *acompañamiento,* retinue] group of attendants at a Penitente's deathbed, wake or funeral procession; retinue at a *casorio* or wedding.

aconforme, *adv.* [<Sp. *conforme*] according to; in proportion to. Aurelio M. Espinosa, *Estudios* I, 240–241, cites this entry as an example of prothesis.

acoordinar, *vb.* [<Sp. *coordinar,* to coordinate] to train (dogs, horses, etc.).

acuál, *int. pron.* [<Sp. *cuál*] which, which one. (*¿Miras aquella ánsara? ¿Acuál?* Do you see that wild goose? Which one?) N.M. and so. Colo. Sp. confuses *cuál* (accusative) with (*a*) *cuál* (dative).

acha, *f.* See *hacha.*

achachurrado, -da, *adj.* [<Sp. *achuchurrado,* crushed] wrinkled (clothes) or dented (car fender).

achantarse, *vb.* [<SW Sp. *chante*<Eng. shanty] to get married; to "shack up" (slang).

achapanecada, *adj.* [<N.M. and so. Colo. Sp. *chapaneca*] applied to a woman with heavy makeup. Also, *chapaneca, máscara, payasa, pintureteada.*

achicharronado, -da, *adj.* [<Mex. Sp. *achicharronado<chicharrón,* crackling] wrinkled, dented.

achinar, *vb.* [<Sp. *achinar?,* to intimidate] *achinársele el cuerpo a uno,* to get goose flesh.

achón, *m.* See *hachón.*

achucharrado, -da, *adj.* [<Sp. *achuchurrado,* crushed] dented, wrinkled.

achucharrar, *vb.* [<Sp. *achuchurrar,* to crush] to dent, to wrinkle.

adelante, *adv.* [<Sp. *adelante,* farther off] *pa adelante,* pregnant. (*Ella está pa adelante.* She is pregnant.)

¡Adevina!, *interj.* [<N.M. Sp. *adevinar*<Sp. *adivinar*] Guess! Guess what!

adevinador, *m.* [<N.M. Sp. *adevinar,* to guess, to foretell] fortune-teller; soothsayer. Cf. Sp. *adivino.*

adevinancia, *f.* [<Sp. *adivinanza*] riddle.

4

Also, *adivinancia, adevinanza.*

adevinar, *vb.* [<Sp. *adivinar*] to foretell; to guess.

adevino, *m.* [<Sp. *adivino*] fortune-teller, soothsayer; palmist.

¡Adió!, *interj.* [<Mex. Sp. *¡Adió!*] Of all things! The very idea! Cf. Sp. *¡No faltaba más!*

adobe, *m.* [<Sp. *adobe*] adobe brick; also, the specially prepared mud from which adobes are made.
Like his Spanish forebears and his Pueblo neighbors, the New Mexican uses mud to build his house. *Adobe,* he calls it, a term of Moorish origin to which our word "daub" is related. (Roland F. Dickey, *New Mexico Village Arts*)

adonaime, *m.* [<Eng. iodine] tincture of iodine.

afijar, *vb.* [<Sp. *fijar*] to fasten, to fix. *¡Afíjate!* Brace yourself! Watch it! You just watch!

afloja-tuerca, *m.* [<Sp. *aflojar,* to loosen, and *tuerca,* nut] wrench.

agacharse, *vb.* [<Mex. Sp. *agacharse*] to consent; to hush a thing maliciously; to look the other way.

agachón, -na, *adj.* [<N.M. Sp. *agacharse*] permissive.

agachón, *m.* [<N.M. Sp. *agacharse*] cuckold.

agarrada, *f.* [<Mex. Sp. *agarrada*] dispute; quarrel; fight.

agarrar, *vb.* [<Mex. Sp. *agarrar*] to take; *int.,* to go in a certain direction. (*¿Par' 'onde agarró?* Which way did he go?) See also *ganar.*

agarrón, *m.* [<N.M. Sp. *agarrar*] dispute, quarrel; fight, scuffle.

agorís, *m.* [<unknown origin] berry of the juniper tree.

agradar, *vb.* [<Sp. *graduarse*] to graduate.

agradecido, -da, *adj.* [<Sp. *agradecer,* to be grateful for] hardy, said of plants, shrubs, etc. (*Esta planta es muy agradecida.* This is a very hardy plant.)

agringado, -da, *adj.* [<Mex. Sp. *gringo,* an Anglo American] said of a Mexican American acculturated into Anglo-American society.

agringarse, *vb.* [<N.M. Sp. *gringo*<Mex. Sp. *gringo,* foreigner, Anglo-American] to act and talk like an Anglo-American.

agrito, *m.* [<Sp. dim. of *agrio,* sour] bot., a three-leaf plant with small red berries.

agro, -ra, *adj.* [<Col. N.M. Sp. *agro* (Molina)] sour, acid.

agua, *f.* [<Sp. *agua*] water; *cortarle 'l agua a alguno,* to put a stop to someone's actions or activities; *de agua, adj.,* gay, homosexual (slang).

aguachinado, -da, *adj.* [Sp. *aguachinado,* flooded] said of plants suffering from an excess of water.

aguachinarse, *vb.* [<Sp. *aguachinar,* to flood (land)] said of a plant that withers or dies from an excess of water or humidity. (*Ya esta matita se aguachinó.* This little plant is ruined.)

aguachistarse, *aguachinarse,* var.

aguadearse, *vb.* [<Mex. Sp. *aguadearse*] to become physically weak.

aguaditas, *f. pl.* [<Mex. Sp. *aguada?,* said of fruits without taste] red gooseberries.

aguado, -da, *adj.* [<Mex. Sp. *aguado,* weak] physically weak; wishy-washy.

aguador, *m.* [<Sp. *aguador,* water carrier] ditch boss (Las Cruces, N.M.). In northern New Mexico and southern Colorado the term for ditch boss is *mayordomo de 'cequias.*

aguapá, *f.* [<Tewa *'Awap'a*] bot., Cattail. Cf. Sp. *espadaña.*

aguapiedra, *f.* [<Sp. *agua,* water, and *piedra,* stone] carbonate of lime formed by the mineral content of water.
Aguapiedra, found in caves, is a deposit that, supposedly has been formed by the mineral content of water so that long narrow stone-like

deposits, resembling a bone on one side and a stone on the other, are produced. (Leonora S.M. Curtin, *Healing Herbs of the Upper Rio Grande*)

aguarismo, *m.* [<Sp. *guarismo,* cipher] any one of the numerals or numerical characters; *sin aguarismo,* countless.

¡Aguate! (*A'guate*), *interj.* [SW Sp. slang *¡Aguate!*] Be careful! Watch out! (slang).

agüelo, *m.* [<Sp. *abuelo*] grandfather; bogeyman; one of the characters in the folk dance, *Los Matachines.*

agüerado, -da, *adj.* [<Mex. Sp. *güero* (*huevo güero*)] rotten (applied to eggs). See also *engüerado.*

¡Aguila! (*A'guila*), *interj.* [<Mex. Sp. *¡Aguila!*] Look out! Watch out! *Ponerse águila,* to be aware or on the lookout; *ser una águila,* to be astute, sharp.

aguinaldo, *m.* [<Col. N.M. Sp. *aguinaldo*] a gift (candy, cookies, fruit, etc.) given to children on the Epiphany, when the birth of Christ was celebrated. On the evening of the sixth of January, children went from house to house asking for *aguinaldos.*

> *En Belén nació Jesús*
> *que es hijo de María,*
> *los señores como usted*
> *dan **aguinaldo** este día.*
> Jesus was born in Bethlehem
> The son of Mary;
> Gentlemen like you
> Give presents on this day.
> (N.M. Sp. *verso popular*)

agüitado, -da, *adj.* [<Sp. *cuitado*<*cuitas*] sad, dejected; mad, as a result of frustration.

agüitarse, *vb.* [<Sp. *acuitar,* to afflict] to become frustrated or angry.

agüite, *m.* [<N.M. Sp. *agüitarse*] dejection; frustration. *¡Qué agüite!* How frustrating! What a bummer! (slang).

aigre, *m.* [<Sp. *aire*] air; *dar aigre una persona a otra,* to resemble; *en tanto que el aigre,* right away, in a jiffy; *mal aigre,* bad air which often causes a slight paralysis.

aigriento, -ta, *adj.* [<N.M. Sp. *aigre,* air] windy; stormy.

aigrio, -a, *adj.* [<Sp. *agrio*] sour; unfriendly; introverted.

aigro, -gra, *adj.* [<Sp. *agrio*] sour; acrid.

aigrón, *m.* [<N.M. Sp. aug. of *aigre,* air; wind] gust of wind; windstorm.

aigroso, -sa, *adj.* [<N.M. Sp. *aigre*] stormy; windy.

ajalote, *m.* [<Mex. Sp. *ajolote*<Náhuatl *axolotl,* salamander] tiger salamander.

ajamachar, *vb.* [<Eng. at how much?] to haggle (about prices, etc.). See also *jamachar.*

ajitado, -da, *adj.* [<Sp. *ahitado*<*ahitarse,* to stuff oneself] stuffed or suffering from indigestion.

ajitarse, *vb.* [<Sp. *ahitarse*] to become upset, particularly when eating greasy or oily food, butter, etc.

ajito, *m.* [<Sp. *ahíto,* indigestion] indigestion; repletion.

ajo, *m.* [<Sp. *ajo*] garlic. *¡Mal ajo!* Confound it!

ajolote, *m.* [<Mex. Sp. *ajolote*] tiger salamander. See also *guajalote.*

ajondar, *vb.* [<Sp. *ahondar*] to make deeper; to deepen.

ajuera, *adv.* [<Sp. *afuera*] out; outside.

ajuerado, -da, *adj.* [<N.M. Sp. *ajuero,* hole] full of holes; perforated.

ajuerar, *vb.* [<Sp. *agujerear*] to make holes; to perforate.

ajuereño, -ña, *adj.* [<N.M. Sp. *ajuera*] outsider; from another place.

ajuero, *m.* [<Sp. *agujero*] hole; perforation.

> *Redondito,*
> *redondón*
> *sin **ajuero***
> *y con tapón.*
> Somewhat round,
> Quite a bit round,
> Without a hole,
> And with a cork.
> (*La calabaza, The Pumpkin,* N.M. Sp. riddle)

ajumado, -da, *adj.* [<Sp. *ahumado,* blackened with smoke] black; blackened; smoked. Cf. Sp. *tiznado.*

ajumar, *vb.* [<Sp. *ahumar,* to blacken with smoke] to cure with smoke (hams, etc.); to blacken with smoke. (*A la mejor cocinera se le ajuma l' olla.* Everyone can make a mistake.)

ajuyentado, -da, *adj.* [<Sp. *ahuyentado,* driven away] said of the person who stays away from his friends and relatives; scared, driven away; alienated.

ajuyentar, *vb.*[<Sp. *ahuyentar,* to drive away] to scare away, to drive away; *reflex.,* to stay away from friends or relatives; to become alienated.

ala, *f.* [<Sp. *ala*] wing; *alas caidas,* downhearted, depressed; *cortarle las alas a uno,* to cut or put down; *dar alas a uno,* to encourage, to incite; *pegarse ala,* to boast, to brag.

alabado, *m.* [<Sp. *alabar,* to praise] a kind of religious hymn of praise to God, the Virgin or the saints.

alacrado, -da, *adj.* [<Sp. *pt. part.* of *lacrar,* to injure the health of] injured, hurting; in bad physical condition; ailing, afflicted, disease-ridden.

alambre, *m.* [<Sp. *alambre*] wire; wire screen door; *ponerse en 'l alambre,* to get drunk.

alambrón, *m.* [<Sp. aug. of *alambre*] large, heavy wire; telephone call.

álamo, *m.* [<Sp. *álamo,* poplar] cottonwood tree.

alanés, *m.* [<Sp. *alanés*] a kind of stag. See also *venado alanés.*

alante, *adv.* [<Sp. *adelante*] ahead; forward, onward.

alargarse, *vb.* [<Sp. *alargar*] to raise a bid; to increase.

alazán, *m.* [<Sp. *alazán,* sorrel (horse)] elk; *venado alazán,* elk; *adj.,* sorrel.

alba, *f.* [<Sp. *alba*] dawn, daybreak; a kind of morning song of praise to the dawn.

Cantemos 'l alba,
ya viene el día
daremos gracias,

¡Ave María!
Let's sing to the dawn
The day is breaking;
We shall give thanks,
Hail Mary!
(N.M. and so. Colo. Sp. *alba*)

albayalde, *m.* [<Sp. *albayalde,* white lead] a kind of homemade face powder made with white clay.

albazo, *m.* [<Sp. *alba,* dawn] Col. N.M. Sp., surprise dawn attack against nomadic Indian camps.

albercoque, *m.* [<Sp. *albarcoque,* var. of *albaricoque*] apricot.

alberjón, *m.* See *alverjón.*

albolaria,*f.* [<N.M. Sp. *arbolaria*<Sp. *herbolaria*] woman herb healer.

alborucero, -ra, *adj.* [<Sp. *alborozo,* merriment] boisterous, noisy.

albularia, *f.* [<N.M. Sp. *albolaria* (var.)] herb healer.

alburucero, -ra,*adj.*[<N.M. Sp.*alborucero* (var.)] boisterous.

alcahuete, -ta, *m.* and *f.* [<Sp. *alcahuete*] pimp; rascal; *adj.,* permissive.

alcajol, *m.* [<Eng. alcohol] alcohol.

alcalde, *m.* [<Sp. *alcalde,* mayor] Indian pueblo officer assisting the *cacique* or chief. In old New Mexico the *alcalde* had powers of a judge.

alcanforina, *f.* [<Sp. *alcanfor,* camphor] mothball. See also *carbólico.*

alcanzado, -da, *adj.* [<Sp. *alcanzado,* hard up, broke] quick-witted; alert; financially well-off.

alcanzar, *vb.* [<Sp. *alcanzar*] to catch up; to succeed; *reflex.,* to make ends meet. (*Tiene buen trabajo pero no se alcanza.* He has a good job but he can't make ends meet.)

alegar, *vb.* [<Mex. Sp. *alegar*] to argue; to dispute. (*Han estado alegando toda la mañana.* They have been arguing all morning long.)

alegata, *f.* [<N.M. Sp. *alegar*] dispute; heated argument.

alegría, *f.* [<Mex. Sp. *alegría*] bot., Red

cockscomb; Lady bleeding; also, a kind of homemade rouge.

The belles of the ranchos and villages have a disgusting habit of besmearing their faces with the crimson juice of a plant or fruit called *alegría* . . . for the purpose of protecting the skin from the sun . . . by washing off the paint, the cheeks look as fresh and ruddy as the natural darkness of their skin will permit. (Josiah Gregg, *Commerce of the Prairies*)

alegrís, *m.* [<N.M. Sp. *alegría*] a kind of homemade rouge used by New Mexico women in the nineteenth century. See *alegría*.

alejo, -ja, *adj.* [<unknown origin] sloppy; ill-kempt.

alfalfilla, *f.* [<Sp. dim. of *alfalfa*] bot., Yellow sweet clover.

alfarfa, *f.* [<Sp. *alfalfa*] alfalfa (var.).

alfarfón, *m.* [<N.M. Sp. aug. of *alfarfa*] bot., Sweet clover.

alferecta, *f.* [<Sp. *alferecía*] epilepsy.

alfilería, *f.* [<Sp. *alfilerillo*, filaree] bot., Pinclover, a plant of the Cranesbill family. Also, *alfilerillo*.

algaraciento, -ta, *adj.* [<N.M. Sp. *algaraza*, noise] boisterous; noisy.

algaraza, *f.* [<Sp. *algazara*] hubbub, noise. Also, *algarazo*.

algodón, *m.* [<Sp. *algodón*] cotton; bot., Fremont cottonwood.

algodones, *m. pl.* [<N.M. Sp. *algodón*] cottonwood grove.

algotro, -tra, *pron.* [<Sp. *algún otro*] another; someone else.

alilañas, *f. pl.* [<Mex. Sp. *alilaya*] cunning, craftiness.

alimal, *m.* [<Sp. *animal*] animal; *adj.*, stupid.

alís, *m.* [<Sp. *alisar*, to smoothen] a plaster finish made with *tierra bayita*, a kind of yellow clay.

alivián, *m.* [<Sp. *aliviar*, to relieve] relief, aid; used in connection with marihuana and drugs (slang).

alivianado, -da, *adj.* [<N.M. Sp. *alivián*] said of a person under the influence of marihuana or drugs; stoned (slang).

alivianar, *vb.* [<N.M. Sp. *alivián*] to aid; to help.

alivioso, -sa, *adj.* [<Sp. *alivio*, relief] easy; done with ease.

alma, *f.* [<Sp. *alma*] soul. *¡Alma mía de tu alma!* You poor thing! *¡Mal haya tu alma!* Damn you!

almacén, *m.* [<Sp. *almacén*, store] a kind of shelf.

almena, *f.* [<Sp. *almena*, merlon of a battlement] Col. N.M., crenellated parapet around the roof of a building.

almendras, *f. pl.* [<Sp. *almendra*, almond] nuts in general, except peanuts. See *pinates*.

almetir, *vb.* [<Sp. *admitir*] to admit.

almirar, *vb.* [<Sp. *admirar*] to admire.

almitaño, *m.* [<Sp. *ermitaño*] hermit.

almorzar, *vb.* [<Sp. *almorzar*, to have lunch] to have breakfast.

almuada [*almwáda*], *f.* [<Sp. *almohada*] pillow; *pegársele las almuadas a uno*, to oversleep.

almuadilla [*almwadía*], *f.* [<Sp. dim. of *almohada*] one of the four perpendicular arms above the axle of a wagon; part of a horse's collar.

almuadita [*almwadíta*], *f.* [<Sp. dim. of *almohada*] cushion; pin cushion.

almuerzo, *m.* [<Sp. *almuerzo*, lunch] breakfast.

almur, *m.* [<Sp. *almud*] a measure of grain and dry fruit equivalent to half a bushel.

altamisa, *f.* [<Sp. *artemisa*] bot., Wormwood.

altanero, *adj.* [<Sp. *altanero*] haughty, bullying.

alto, *m.* [<Sp. *alto*, story, as of a building] attic; loft; gabled roof; *casa de alto*, two-story house.

alverjón, *m.* [<Sp. *arvejón*, aug. of *arvejo*, bastard chick-pea] pea; peas.

Toda esta tierra [seventeenth-century

New Mexico] *es fertilísima, que da con muy grande abundancia todo lo que en ella se siembra: maíz, trigo, frijoles, lentejas, habas, **alverjoes**, calabazas, sandías, melones, pepinos.*
All this land is exceedingly fertile; it produces in great abundance all that is planted therein: corn, wheat, beans, lentils, horse beans, peas, pumpkins, watermelons, cantaloupes, cucumbers. (Fray Alonso de Benavides, *Memorial*)

amacizar, *vb.* [<Sp. *macizo,* strong] to become stronger, harder. (*Ya está amacizando 'l agua.* The rain is getting stronger.)

amachado, -da, *adj.* [<Mex. Sp. *amacharse,* to balk] balking; insistent. Also, *amachón.*

amacharse, *vb.* [<Mex. Sp. *amacharse,* to become stubborn] to balk; to act stubborn; to refuse to move; to refuse to return a thing. (*Le presté un libro y se amachó con él.* I lent him a book and he has refused to return it.)

amadable, *adj.* [<Sp. *amable*] affable; amiable; a good mixer. Cf. Sp. *simpático.*

amargoso, -sa, *adj.* [<Sp. *amargo*] bitter, sour. (*Estas naranjas están murre amargosas.* These oranges are very bitter. *¡Qué amargoso este Rosenaldo!* What a sourpuss Rosenaldo is!)

amarre, *m.* [<Sp. *amarrar,* to tie] mock arrest during an old-fashioned dance. It was the custom, when anyone danced for the first time, to take the person and carry him in arms around the hall. This was called the **amarre.** Before he was allowed to go, someone close in friendship or relationship had to redeem him. This redemption was the *desempeño.* (Fabiola C. de Baca Gilbert, *We Fed Them Cactus*)

ambularia, *f.* [<Sp. *herbolaria*] a woman versed in the use of medicinal herbs. At one time people believed the *ambularia* was a witch.
The **ambularias** were graduates in witchcraft and held schools where beginners were taught how to bewitch and how to transform themselves into different things and animals. The **ambularias** that came into possession of the *piedra imán* were still more powerful; they knew everything and could transform themselves into any shape. The *piedra imán* was a fury stone which was fed needles and water, and if the stone was lost or stolen from its owner, the owner immediately lost her mind or dried up into a skeleton. (Cleofas M. Jaramillo, *Shadows of the Past*)

americano, -na, *m.* and *f.* [<Sp. *americano*] applied by older Indo-Hispanic Americans in New Mexico and southern Colorado to any non-Spanish-speaking whites. See also *anglo.*

amolado, -da, *adj.* [<Mex. Sp. *amolado*] broke; badly off financially.

amolar, *vb.* [<Mex. Sp. *amolar*] to bother, to annoy. (*No vengas a amolar.* Don't bother me.)

amole, *m.* [<Mex. Sp. *amole*<Náhuatl *amulli*] bot., Amole plant used in making soap.

amolillo, *m.* [<N.M. Sp. dim. of *amole*] bot., Wild licorice.

amuinado, -da, *adj.* [<Sp. *amohinado,* irritated] annoyed, irritated; restless; in ill humor; disgruntled, angry, grouchy.

amuinar, *vb.* [<Sp. *amohinar*] to annoy, to vex; *reflex.,* to become annoyed, restless; grouchy.

anancas, *prep.* [<Sp. *en ancas,* on the rump] *montar anancas,* to ride on the rump, i.e., behind the rider.

ananchar, *vb.* [<Mex. Sp. *anchar*] to widen.

ancón, *m.* [<Sp. *ancón*] cove. See *incón.*

ancho, *m.* [<Sp. *ancho,* wide] *no dar 'l ancho,* to fall short of expectations.

andabita, *f.* [<Sp. dim. of *aldaba*] latch.

andalón, -na, *adj.* [<Sp. *andar,* to walk] wandering; restless; of a roving disposition.

andar, *vb.* [<Sp. *andar*] *¡Ándale, pues!*

OK. *Andarle a uno,* to be in trouble; not to be able to stand a thing. (*Ya me anda.* I can't stand it anymore.)

anducio, -cia, *adj.* [<Sp. *andar*] wandering; roving.

angelito, *m.* [<Sp. *angelito,* little angel] a term of endearment; a representation of a cherub used as a decorative motif by New Mexico *santeros,* q.v. *Velorio de angelito,* wake for a dead child; *entierro de angelito,* burial of a dead child.

Children that have not been baptized are destined, according to the popular faith, to a kind of negative existence in the world of spirits, called Limbo, where they remain forever without either suffering punishment or enjoying happiness. Baptized infants, on the other hand, being considered without sin, are supposed to enter at once into the joys of heaven. The deceased child is then denominated an **angelito** (little angel), and is interred with joy and mirth instead of grief and wailing. It is gaudily bedecked with fanciful attire and ornaments of tinsel and flowers; and being placed upon a small bier, it is carried to the grave by four children as gaily dressed as their circumstances will allow; accompanied by musicians using the instruments and playing the tunes of the *fandangos;* and the little procession is nothing but glee and merriment. (Josiah Gregg, *Commerce of the Prairies*)

anglo, *adj., n.* [<Eng. Anglo, as in Anglo-Saxon] applied loosely in New Mexico and southern Colorado to any white European mixture, particularly an English-speaking white person coming into this area from the eastern and middle-western states. See also *bolillo, gavacho* and *tejano.*

angurriento, -ta, *adj.* [<Sp. *estrangurriento*] said of the person who voids urine with great difficulty.

anillo, *m.* [<Sp. *anillo*] ring; loop at the end of a rope; *anillo de ramal,* a special ring made up of two or more rings assembled into a single unit.

ánima, *f.* [<Sp. *ánima,* soul] *ser ánima una persona,* to be deceased. (*Y ¿quése mano Sarapio? Ya es ánima.* And where is old man Sarapio? He died.)

anisote, *m.* [<Sp. aug. of *anís,* anise] bot., Sagebrush; Wormwood.

anque, *conj.* [<Sp. *aunque*] even though.

ánsara, *f.* [<Sp. *ánsar*] gander; swan; wild goose. Also, *ánsera.*

ansí, *adv.* [<Col. N.M. Sp. *ansí*] thus; in that way. See also *ansina, asina.*

ansina, *adv.* [<Col. N.M. Sp. *ansina*] thus, in that manner.

anta, *f.* [<Sp. *anta,* elk] *anta blanca,* dressed buffalo skin, white elkskin; *anta gorda,* buckskin, deerskin; *pelar 'l anta,* to die.

antonce, *adv.* [<Sp. *entonces*] then, at that time. Also, *antonces.*

añidir, *vb.* [<Sp. *añadir*] to add; to add to.

áñil, *m.* [<Sp. *añil,* indigo] bot., Sunflower; *áñil del muerto,* bot., Goldweed; Crownbeard.

año, *m.* [<Sp. *año*] year; *del año 'e l' hebra,* old; *del año de upa,* old, old-fashioned; from the year one, antiquated.

apachangado, -da, *adj.* [<Mex. Sp. *pachanga,* noisy party] noisy, rowdy.

aparejo, *m.* [<Sp. *aparejo*] Terr. N.M., packsaddle.

The **aparejo** (or pack saddle, if it can be so styled), is a large pad consisting of a leathern case stuffed with hay, which covers the back of the mule and extends half way down on both sides. (Josiah Gregg, *Commerce of the Prairies*)

aparnado, -da, *adj.* [<N.M. Sp. *parna* <Eng. partner] chummy; close to someone; friendly, intimate.

apeñuscado, -da, *adj.* [<Am. Sp. *apeñuscado,* heaped up] jammed, crowded. (*Iba ese bos pero bien apeñuscado.* The bus was jam-packed.)

apeñuscar, *vb.* [<Am. Sp. *apeñuscar,* to

apergatado, -da, *adj.* [<Sp. *apercatado,* aware] impulsive.

apinchado, -da, *adj.* [<Sp. *pinchar,* to pinch] upset; angry.

apincharse, *vb.* [<Sp. *pinchar,* to pinch] to become upset or angry. See also *empincharse.*

aplastarse, *vb.* [<Sp. *aplastar,* to flatten] to sit down comfortably.

aplicación, *f.* [<Eng. application] application, as for a job. (*Ya puse mi aplicación.* I've put in my application.)

aplomarse, *vb.* [<Mex. Sp. *aplomarse*<Sp. *plomo,* lead] literally, to become heavy, like lead; to be slow in one's actions; to hesitate; to "miss the boat."

¡Apoco!, *interj.* [<Sp. *a poco,* soon after] I bet! Oh, yeah? You don't say! You're kidding!

apomarse, *vb.* [<N.M. Sp. *pomo,* spongy] to become spongy. (*Ya estos tanapes están apomados.* These turnips have become spongy.)

aprecio, *m.* [<Mex. Sp. *aprecio*] *hacer aprecio,* to mind, to pay attention to; *dar* or *tener aprecio,* to attend to. (*Esta plebe no hace aprecio.* These kids don't mind.)

aprevenir, *vb.* [<Sp. *prevenir,* to prepare] to get ready; to make plans. Also, *aprevinir.*

apriesa, *adv.* [<Col. N.M. Sp. *apriesa*] fast; in a hurry; quickly. (*No vayas tan apriesa.* Don't walk so fast.)

aprobar, *vb.* [<Sp. *probar*] to taste. (*Apruébelo está murre bueno.* Taste it; it's very good.)

aprontarse, *vb.* [<Sp. *aprontar,* to get ready quickly] to make an appearance; to turn up unexpectedly.

aprovechado, -da, *adj.* [<Sp. *aprovechado,* industrious, diligent] mean; said of someone who takes advantage of others, particularly the weak or unfortunate; bullying.

apuntarse, *vb.* [<Sp. *apuntar,* to stake, to put up] to join others, as in a game of chance.

heap up] to jam or pile up.

aquéllas (de aquéllas), *adj.* [<Sp. *aquéllas,* the former, those yonder] *de aquéllas,* out of sight, super (slang).

arabe [árabe] -ba, *m.* and *f.* [<Sp. *árabe,* Arab] Arab, Lebanese, Syrian.

araña, *f.* [<Sp. *araña*] spider; bot., Spider plant; *araña del sol,* deadly vinegaroon; *picarle la araña a una mujer,* to be pregnant. Also, a kind of chandelier (ceiling candle holder).

arañado, -da, *adj.* [<Mex. Sp. *arañado*] kiped; swiped, stolen (slang).

arañar, *vb.* [<Mex. Sp. *arañar*] to steal (slang).

arbolera, *f.* [<Sp. *arboleda*] grove; orchard.

arbolaria, *f.* [<Sp. *herbolaria*] herb healer. *Arbolarias* were formerly suspected of being witches. See *ambularia.*

arbularia, *f.* *Arbolaria* (var.).

arcina, *f.* See *harcina.*

arción, *m.* [<Mex. Sp. *arción*<Sp. *ación*] leather strap supporting the stirrup.

archivo, *m.* [<Sp. *archivo,* archive] folk poet or *pueta,* q.v.; scribe.

ardilla, *f.* [<Sp. *ardilla*] chipmunk; squirrel.

¡A redo vaya!, *interj.* [<Col. N.M. Sp. *a riedro vaya—riedro*<Lat. *retro,* behind] a kind of curse against the devil or an exclamation of surprise. Good heavens! Of all things!

arete, *m.* [<Sp. dim. of *aro,* hoop] eardrop; earring in general; a term applied to a child who always insists on tagging along with an older brother or sister.

arisco, -ca, *adj.* [<Mex. Sp. *arisco,* easily frightened] suspicious; distrustful.

armada, *f.* [<Eng. army] the armed forces, army; lucky break. *¡Qué armada!* What a lucky break! See also *armón.*

armarse, *vb.* [<Am. Sp. *armarse*] to get a lucky break. (*Te armates con ese carro.* You got a lucky break with that car.)

armas de pelo, *f. pl.* [<Mex. Sp. *armas de pelo*] Terr. N.M. Sp., chaps.
    Last but not least, there are the ***armas***

de pelo, being a pair of shaggy goat skins (richly trimmed across the top with embroidered leather) dangling from the pommel of the saddle for the purpose of being drawn over the legs in case of rain, or as a protection against brush and brambles. (Josiah Gregg, *Commerce of the Prairies*)

armitaño, *m.* [<Sp. *ermitaño*] hermit.

armón, *m.* [<Sp. aug. of *arma*] lucky break.

aroplano, *m.* [<Sp. *aeroplano*] airplane.

arpa, *f.* [<Sp. *arpa*] harp; *tirar 'l arpa*, to die (slang).

arranarse, *vb.* [<Sp. *arrellanarse*, to sit at ease] to squat; to become established; to settle down; to get married.

arrancado, -da, *adj.* [<Mex. Sp. *arrancado*] flat broke, destitute; *más arrancado que las mangas de un chaleco*, flat broke.

arranquera, *f.* [<Mex. Sp. *arrancado*] hard times; economic depression.

arrapar, *vb.* [<Sp. *rapar*] to crop; to shave the head.

arras, *f. pl.* [<Sp. *arras*, dowry] thirteen small coins which the groom gives to his bride as a pledge of his willingness to support her.

arrastrar, *vb.* [<Sp. *arrastrar*, to drag] *arrastrarle a uno*, to be good at or to excel at something.

arrastre, *m.* [<Mex. Sp. *arrastre*, stone mill] Terr. N.M. Sp., a kind of crude drag; min., a mortar and pestle method of crushing ore. The *arrastre* was also called a *molienda*.

arrastrón, *m.* [<N.M. Sp. *arrastrarle a uno*] lucky break. *¡Qué arrastrón!* What a lucky break!

arreador, *m.* [<N.M. Sp. *arrear*, to drive (cars)] driver; chauffeur.

arrear, *vb.* [<Sp. *arrear*, to drive (animals)] to drive a vehicle. Cf. Sp. *conducir* and Mex. Sp. *manejar*.

arrebosar, *vb.* [<Sp. *rebosar*] to overflow or run over, as a liquid from a container.

arrede, *adv.* [<Sp. *adrede*] on purpose; knowingly.

arrellenarse, *vb.* [<Sp. *arrellanarse*] to sit at ease; to be satisfied with one's situation. Cf. *arranarse*.

arremedar, *vb.* [<Mex. Sp. *arremedar*<Sp. *remedar*] to imitate; to mimic. Also, *aremellar*.

arrempujar, *vb.* [<Col. N.M. Sp. *arrempujar*<Sp. *empujar*] to push, to shove. *Arrempujón*, violent push.

arrendando, *pres. part.* [<unknown origin] *estar arrendando*, to be famished. (*Este muchito llegó arrendando*. This child was famished.)

arrentar, *vb.* [<Eng. to rent] to rent, to lease. (*Están arrentando*. They are renting.)

arreón, *m.* [<N.M. Sp. *arrear*] havoc; *hacer arreón*, to cause a great deal of havoc; to raise hell. (*El Maque hizo arreón con todos*. Mack raised hell with everyone.)

arrepentirse, *vb.* [<Sp. *arrepentirse*, to repent] to change one's mind; to repent; to be sorry. (*Siempre no vendió la yegua, se arrepintió*. He did not sell the mare after all; he had a change of mind.)

arresucismo, *m.* [<unknown origin] strong desire to do a thing; inspiration; rapture.

arribar, *vb.* [<Sp. *arribar*] to attain success; to prosper.

arribeño, -ña, *adj.* [<Sp. *arriba*] highlander; said of a person living along the Río Grande north of La Bajada in Santa Fe county.

arrimado, -da, *adj.* [<Mex. Sp. *arrimado*] moocher. (*El pescado y el arrimado a los tres días apestan*. Fish and moochers [unwelcome guests] stink after three days.)

arrimar, *vb.* [<Sp. *arrimar*, to place near] to shelter; to protect; to spank. (*Anoche le arrimaron al niño*. Last night they spanked the child.)

arrollar, *vb.* [<Col. N.M. Sp. *arrollar*] to lull to sleep.

arroz, *m.* [<Sp. *arroz*, rice] rice-sized peb-

bles on which Penitentes knelt as penance.

arrumbar, *vb.* [<Sp. *arrumbar,* to put a thing in a lumber room] to heap or pile up things in a careless manner.

arrumbe, *m.* [<N.M. Sp. *arrumbar*] snowbank. See also *tapanco.*

artes, *m. pl.* [<Sp. *artes,* arts] magic tricks; *hacer artes,* to perform magic tricks.

artesano, *m.* [<Sp. *artesano,* craftsman] wood-carver.

artista, *m.* [<Sp. *artista*] artist; magician.

arujos, *m. pl.* [<unknown origin] *hacer una cosa arujos* or *de arujos,* to lose a thing designedly or on purpose. In the San Luis Valley in southern Colorado an *arujo* is an outfit (dress).

arvejón, *m.* [<Col. N.M. Sp. *arvejón* (Benavides)] pea, peas.

ascenso, *m.* [<Sp. *ascenso,* raise] credit.

asegún, *prep.* [<Sp. *según*] according to. See also *asigún.*

aseguranza, *f.* [<Sp. *aseguranza,* security] insurance; insurance policy.

aserpiente, *f.* [<Sp. *serpiente,* serpent] crocodile; alligator.

aserrar, *vb.* [<Sp. *serrar* and var. *aserrar*] to saw.

aserrón, *m.* [<Sp. *aserrar*] large saw; two-handled saw.

aserronear, *vb.* [<N.M. Sp. *aserrón*] to saw with a large saw.

asignatura, *f.* [<Sp. *asignatura,* subject of study (biology, chemistry, etc.)] class assignment.

asigún, *prep. Asegún,* var.

asina, *adv.* [<Col. N.M. Sp. *asina*] in that manner; thus.

asolapado, -da, *adj.* [<Sp. *solapado,* cunning] antisocial; in a crouch, crouched; sneaky.

aspeta, *f.* [<Mex. Sp. *espeta,* hope] *estar a la aspeta,* to be waiting to be called to a job; to be on the alert or on the lookout.

astrónomo, *m.* [<Sp. *astrónomo,* astrono-

mer] meteorologist.

asusidiado, -da, *adj.* [<Sp. *susidio,* restlessness] restless, excited.

atacarse, *vb.* [<Sp. *atracarse,* to stuff oneself with food] to cram or glut oneself. *¡No te ataques!* Don't overdo it! *¡Atácate!* Now you have done it!

ataduras, *f. pl.* [<Sp. *atadura,* the act of tying together] garters.

atarantado, -da, *adj.* [<Sp. *atarantado,* bit by a tarantula] dizzy; groggy; half drunk; stupid; idiotic; absentminded.

atarantamiento, *m.* [<N.M. Sp. *atarantar,* to choke or strangle] dizzy spell; grogginess.

atarantar, *vb.* [<Sp. *atarantado*] to choke; to strangle; to knock out. (*A uno de los moqueteros me lo atarantaron.* One of the boxers was knocked out.)

atarantarse, *vb.* [<N.M. Sp. *atarantar*] to become dizzy; to faint.

atarque, *m.* [<Sp. *atracar,* to cram or glut] beaver-like river dam; backwater; pond. Cf. Sp. *remanso.*

atarrascazo, *m.* [<Sp. *atarazar,* to bite or wound with one's teeth] blow or hit on the head with the fingernails; akin to Sp. *coscorrón.*

atascado, -da, *adj.* [<Sp. *atascado,* bogged down] churlish; indecent; rude; stupid. (*¡Oh, suéltame, atascado!* Oh, let me go, stupid.)

atascar, *vb.* [<Sp. *atascarse,* to get bogged down] to penetrate; to stick one object into another.

atendencia, *f.* [<Eng. attendance] attendance. Cf. Sp. *asistencia.*

atender, *vb.* [<Sp. *atender,* to pay attention to] to attend a class, meeting, etc. Cf. Sp. *asistir.*

atengir, *vb.* [<Mex. Sp. *atingir,* to hit the mark] to understand, to comprehend.

atocar, *vb.* [<Sp. *tocar*] to feel; to touch.

atolate, *m.* [<Mex. Sp. *atole,* a kind of corn drink] mess; muddy mess; mudhole.

atole, *m.* [<Mex. Sp. *atole*] corn mush or

13

gruel; *dar atole con el dedo a alguno*, to deceive a person; *después de atole frío*, too late; *echar mocos en 'l atole*, to make a boo-boo or a faux pas; to say the wrong thing at the wrong time.

atomobil, *m.* [<Eng. automobile] auto, car. Words such as *atomobil, garache, gaselín, telefón*, came into New Mexico and southern Colorado from oral English before appearing in their standard Spanish form (*automóvil, garaje, gasolina, teléfono*). As a consequence of this, Hispanos in the area have retained the hispanicized English words in favor of the later correct Spanish forms.

atornillar, *vb.* [<Sp. *atornillar*, to screw on] to bring pressure to bear on someone; to put the screws on someone.

atorugar, *vb.* [<Sp. *atarugar*] to cram food, etc., into the mouth.

atrabancado, -da, *adj.* [<Mex. Sp. *atrabancado*, wild, blundering] impulsive; reckless, rash.

atrampado, -da, *adj.* [<N.M. Sp. *atrampar*, to block off, to trap] blocked off; trapped; run over, as by a vehicle.

atrampar, *vb.* [<Sp. *trampa*, trap] to trap; to snare; to run over. See also *trampar*.

atrancado, -da, *adj.* [<N.M. Sp. *atrancarse*] drunk; boorish, said especially of someone who will not listen to reason.

atrancar, *vb.* [<N.M. Sp. *tranca*, lock] to bar; to lock; to overfill a container with liquid; *haber* or *tener de algo hasta pa atrancar puertas*, to have an abundance of a thing; *reflex.*, to get drunk.

atranque, *m.* [<N.M. Sp. *atrancar*, to lock] an emotional blow or setback. *¡Qué atranque!* How disappointing!

atrás, *adv.* [<Sp. *atrás*] behind, toward the back; *dar pa atrás*, to return an object; *estar pa atrás*, to be backward; *venir* or *volver pa atrás*, to return or come back.

atrascender, *vb.* [<Sp. *trascender*] to give off a pleasant, agreeable aroma.

atraso, *m.* [<Sp. *atraso*, backwardness] frustration. *¡Qué atraso!* What a setback! How frustrating!

atravesado, -da, *adj.* [<Sp. *atravesado*, lying across] boring; contrary, disagreeable; *caerle atravesada una persona a otra*, to be disliked, repugnant. (*Esa me cae muy atravesada*. That woman bores me. [I can't stand that woman.] *Este niño es muy atravesado*. This child is very contrary.)

atrevido, -da, *adj.* [<Sp. *atrevido*, daring] mean, despicable; said of a person who takes advantage of others. Also, *aprovechado*.

atrijas, *f. pl.* [unknown origin] girl's or woman's panties.

atril, *m.* [<Sp. *atril*, lectern] bookshelf.

atrincar, *vb.* [<Sp. *trincar*, to bind securely] to press against; to chuck or wedge; to drink liquor; *atrincarse un hombre a una mujer*, to have sexual intercourse.

atrincón, *m.* [<N.M. Sp. *atrincar*] bump; collision; clash.

atrocidad, *f.* [<Sp. *atrocidad*, atrocity] destruction; *atrocidad y media*, quite a havoc.

atrociento, -ta, *adj.* [<N.M. Sp. *atroz*, destructive] careless; destructive; mischievous; playful, prankish; rude, unmannerly.

atropellar, *vb.* [<Sp. *atropellar*, to run over] to abuse. (*Tú vienes aquí nomás a atropellarnos*. You come here only to abuse us.)

atroteado, -da, *adj.* [<N.M. Sp. *atrotear*, to coax, to convince] brainwashed; convinced.

atrotear, *vb.* [<N.M. Sp. *trotear*<Sp. *trotar*, to trot] to get someone to move swiftly; to incite. (*La atrotearon que viniera a papearme*. They got her to come running and tell me off.)

atroz, *adj.* [<Sp. *atroz*, atrocious] careless; destructive, as a child with his clothes, shoes, etc.; mischievous; playful, prankish.

aturdido, -da, *adj.* [<Sp. *aturdido*, dazed] dazed; harebrained; stupid.

audencia, *f.* [<Eng. audience] audience.

audiencia, *f.* [<Sp. *audiencia*] Col. N.M. Sp., a judicial body possessing legislative, administrative, executive, and ecclesiastical functions.

auditorio, *m.* [<Eng. auditorium] hall; auditorium.

aumento, *m.* [<Sp. *aumento,* increase] Col. N.M. Sp., addendum; postscript; sideboard on a wagon.

auto, *m.* [<Col. N.M. Sp. *auto*] a religious folk play; proceedings of a case or lawsuit.

avareo, *m.* [<unknown origin, probably linked to Eng. average] average.

ávaro, -ra, *m.* and *f.* [<Sp. *avaro,* miser] miser; *adj.,* avaricious, selfish; tight, miserly.

aveno, *m.* [<Sp. *avena,* oats] oats; oatmeal. See also *otemil.*

aventada, *f.* [<Sp. *aventar,* to cast, to throw] lift; ride (in a vehicle). Also, *aventadita* and *aventón.*

aventarse, *vb.* [<Mex. Sp. *aventarse,* to let go; to let one's hair down] to let go; to do one's stuff or thing; to excel or be very good at something. (*Aviéntese, tía.* Let yourself go, auntie.)

aventón, *m.* [<Sp. *aventar,* to cast; to throw] push; lift, ride (in a vehicle).

averiguar, *vb.* [<Sp. *averiguar,* to investigate] to argue; to quarrel. (*No averigüen tanto.* Don't argue so much.)

averiguata, *f.* [<N.M. Sp. *averiguar,* to argue] heated argument; quarrel.

avispa, *f.* [<Sp. *avispa,* wasp] honeybee. See also *ovispa.*

avispero, *m.* [<Sp. *avispero,* wasp's nest] swarm of bees; *ponerse al avispero,* to be on the alert and ready to seize an opportunity.

avocado, *m.* [<Eng. avocado] avocado. Cf. Sp. *aguacate.*

ayacahuite, *m.* [<Mex. Sp. *ayacahuite* or *pino ayacahuite*] bot., Royal pine. Also called *pino real.*

ayate, *m.* [<Mex. Sp. *ayate*<Náhuatl *ayatl,* a kind of cloth made from agave fibers] a gunnysack-like cloth used by Indians of Mexico as a poncho; Col. N.M. Sp., a kind of poncho.

azonzado, -da, *adj.* [<Am. Sp. *azonzado,* silly, stupid] delirious.

azul, *m.* [<Sp. *azul,* blue] blue; an intense turquoise blue used on lower part of whitewashed walls and doors; *azul presado,* bluish purple; *azul viejo,* indigo blue.

Bueno es culantro pero no tanto.
Too much of a good thing is not good.

bable, *m.* [<Sp. *baúl* (*bable*<*baule*<*baul*<*baúl*)] cedar chest, footlocker, trunk.

baboso, -sa, *adj.* [<Mex. Sp. *baboso*] drooling idiot, simpleton; smart aleck.

bacha, *f.* [<Mex. Sp. *bacha*] cigar or cigarette butt.

bache, *m.* [<Sp. *bache,* pothole] deal; arrangement. (*Ahi estaban los dos y al fin se hizo el bache.* The two were there and finally the arrangement was made.)

bagre, *m.* [<Mex. Sp. *bagre*] catfish. Cf. Sp. *barbo.*

baica, *f.* [<Eng. bike] bicycle; motorcycle.

bailada, *f.* [<Sp. *bailar,* to dance] dance piece; dance; *echar una bailada,* to dance.

baile, *m.* [<Sp. *baile*] dance; *baile chango,* footwork; *baile de desquite* or *de desempeño,* a dance to fulfill some social obligation or promise; *baile de gusto,* "for fun" dance; *baile de prendorio,* engagement dance; *baile de San Vito,* St. Vitus dance.

baique, *m.* See baica.

bajito, *m.* [<Sp. dim. of *bajo,* low] chopped car or jalopy; a "low rider" (slang).

bal, *interj.* [<Col. N.M. Sp. *bah* and Lat. *aliud,* another thing] *¡Bal tú! Pero, ¿pa qué?* Oh, yeah? You don't say!

baleado, -da, *adj.* [<Mex. Sp. *baleado,* gunshot] wounded or killed by a shot from a firearm.

balear, *vb.* [<Mex. Sp. *balear,* to shoot at random] to wound or kill by a shot from a firearm.

balone, *m.* [<Eng. baloney sausage] bologna sausage; baloney; foolishness; nonsense.

balún, *m.* [<Eng. balloon] balloon.

bambalearse, *vb.* [<Sp. *bambolearse,* to stagger] to reel, to totter. (*El Elifaz andaba bambaleándose.* Eliphaz was tottering.)

bandeja, *f.* [<Sp. *bandeja,* tray] pan; *bandeja maqueada,* enamel pan.

bandera, *f.* [<Sp. *bandera*] flag; *manchar*

16

la bandera, to make a blunder.

bándido, *m.* [<Sp. *bandido*] bandit, robber; criminal, outlaw. See also *méndigo* for a change of accent.

banqueta, *f.* [<Mex. Sp. *banqueta*] sidewalk.

banquete, *m.* [<Sp. *banquete,* banquette] ledge or bench around the top of a house or kiva wall.

baquear, *vb.* [<Eng. to back] to back up. Cf. Sp. *retroceder.*

baquetón, *m.* See *vaquetón.*

baraña, *f.* [<Sp. *maraña,* place rendered impassable by brambles or briers] bramble patch, brier.

baratillo, *m.* [<Sp. *baratillo,* secondhand store] clearance sale.

barato, -ta, *adj.* [<Sp. *barato,* cheap (price wise)] cheap, stingy, tight.

barbacoa, *f.* [<Am. Sp. *barbacoa*] corn bin; loft for storing produce.

barcino, -na, *adj.* [<Sp. *barcino*] reddish with black.

bargueño, *m.* [<Sp. *bargueño,* gilt and painted desk] Col. N.M. Sp., traveling desk. Also, *vargueño,* q.v.

barropiedra, *m.* [<Sp. *barro,* clay, and *piedra,* stone] lit., clay stone; black colored clay or stone clay used in making pottery.

barullento, -ta, *adj.* [<Sp. *barullo,* confusion] noisy, rowdy.

basa, *f.* [<unknown origin] *hacer basa,* to cut up; to misbehave.

basas, *f. pl.* [<Col. N.M. Sp. *baxas*] casualties.

bastimento, *m.* [<Sp. *bastimento,* foodstuffs] lunch that is eaten out in the field.

basto, *m.* [<Sp. *basto,* pad] saddle skirt made of sole leather lined with undressed lambskin.

bastonero, *m.* [<Sp. *bastonero*] master of ceremonies at a dance, fiesta, banquet, etc.

A **bastonero** is responsible for supervising all arrangements down to the most minute detail, for banquets, fiestas, weddings, funerals, and other affairs requiring expert knowledge of technique and protocol. (William A. Keleher, *Memoirs*)

basudero, *m.* [<Sp. *basurero*<*basura*] rubbish dump; dung heap.

basura, *f.* [<Sp. *basura,* rubbish] *poner a uno de la basura,* to tell someone off.

batalla, *f.* [<Sp. *batalla,* battle] nuisance. *¡Qué batalla!* What a nuisance! What a hassle!

batán, *m.* [<Mex. Sp. *abatanado,* snarled] snarl, tangle, as in the hair; a knot in one's hair.

batarete, *m.* [<Mex. Sp. *batarete,* a mixed drink] mess; a kind of cereal made with roasted cornmeal; hodgepodge. Cf. Sp. *baturrillo.*

bate, *m.* [<Eng. bat] baseball bat.

bate, *m.* [<Sp. *batir,* to beat] mixture; mess; *hacer bates,* to make a mess, as with mud.

batea, *f.* [<Sp. *batea,* tray] prospector's pan; large wooden bowl.

batear, *vb.* [<N.M. Sp. *bate*<Eng. bat] to bat (baseball).

batería, *f.* [<Sp. *batería,* battery] flashlight; battery.

batir, *vb.* [<Sp. *batir,* to beat (cream, etc.)] *batirle el moco a alguno,* to give someone a beating.

bato, *m.* [<N.M. Sp. *Bato?,* name of a shepherd in the folk play, *Los pastores*] character, dude, fellow, guy. *¡Ese bato!* Hi, guy!

bau, *m.* [<Sp. *vaho?,* vapor] pleasure; *dar bau,* to give in to someone's whims; to please.

bau, *m.* [<Sp. *vado,* ford] level part of a river or stream.

baustizar, *vb.* [<Sp. *bautizar*] to baptize. (*Baustizaron al baby.* They baptized the baby.)

bayeta, *f.* [<Sp. *bayeta,* baize] woolen homespun.

bayetón, *m.* [<Sp. aug. of *bayeta*] baize

with nap.

bayo, -ya, *adj.* [<Sp. *bayo,* bay] dun-colored; *bayo coyote,* said of the dun-colored horse with a black stripe down its back.

bayoneta, *f.* [<Sp. *bayoneta,* bayonet] bot., a plant with stiff, upright leaves resembling bayonets.

becerrillo, *m.* [<Sp. dim. of *becerro,* calf] *cuero becerrillo,* calf rawhide used in the making of thongs and leather shoelaces. See also *crudillo.*

bejuco, *m.* [<Sp. *bejuquillo,* a kind of small gold chain] a round, braided choker-like gold chain with the figure of a goldfish attached in the form of a pendant. See also *cordón.*

bellota, *f.* [<Sp. *bellota*] acorn; *bellota de sabino,* juniper berry; mistletoe; a kind of bread made with flour from ground acorns; *dar bellota a alguno,* to bewitch someone.

beneficiar, *vb.* [<Sp. *beneficiar,* to cultivate] to weed, as a corn patch.

benerito, -ta, *adj.* [<Sp. *Benedicto*] blessed; person's name.

>*Cajita de Dios* **benerita,**
>*que se abre y se cierra*
>*y no se marchita.*
>Little box by God blessed
>It opens and closes but it
>never wilts.
>(*El ojo, The Eye,* N.M. Sp. riddle)

bequenpaura, *m.* [<Eng. baking powder] baking powder.

berrendo, *m.* [<Sp. *berrendo,* two-colored] antelope; *adj.,* mottled.

berrinche, *m.* [<Sp. *berrinche,* tantrum] temper tantrum; *hacerse uno de berrinche,* to want to be coaxed.

berruga, *f.* See *verruga.*

betabel, *m.* [<Mex. Sp. *betabel*] sugar beet. Also, *betabel de azúcar.* See also *raíces.*

betabelero, -ra, *adj.* [<Mex. Sp. *betabel*] sugar-beet worker.

bicoca, *f.* [<It. *bicocca?,* small stone] money (slang). See also *lana, manil, jando.*

bien, *adv.* [<Sp. *bien*] well; *bien a bien,* fair

and square. *¡Hace bien!* Good for him! *Ponerse uno bien,* to brag, to put oneself in an advantageous position; *no estar bien una persona,* to be mentally unbalanced.

bienhado, -da, *adj.* [<Sp. *bienhadado*] lucky; happy-go-lucky.

bigote, *m.* [<Sp. *bigote*] mustache; *mover el bigote,* to chat, to chew the rag..

bil, *m.* [<Eng. bill (statement)] bill; dollar bill.

bil, *m.* [<Eng. bale (hay)] bale.

bingo, *m.* [<Eng. bingo] game of bingo.

binguero, -ra, *adj.* [<Eng. bingo] said of a person who is very fond of playing bingo.

bironga, *f.* [<Eng. beer and Sp. *onga*] beer. Also, *birria.*

bísquete, *m.* [<Eng. biscuit] biscuit. See also *galleta.*

bizcochito, *m.* [<Sp. dim. of *bizcocho,* biscuit] a kind of sugar cookie.

bizcocho, *m.* [<Sp. *bizcocho,* biscuit] toast made in the oven; female organ (taboo); *hacerse bizcocho,* to refuse (taboo).

bizcochuelo, *m.* [<Sp. dim. of *bizcocho*] a kind of leavened bread. Once baked, the *bizcochuelo* is split open and put again in the oven to brown, hence the name *bizcochuelo* (baked on both sides).

blanco, *m.* [<Sp. *blanco,* target] *tirar blancos,* to shoot at targets (bottles, tin cans, etc.); *pl.,* blank spaces; blanks, as for a job application.

blandura, *f.* [<Sp. *blandura,* softness] looseness of bowels.

blanquear, *vb.* [<Sp. *blanquear*] to dawn; to whitewash (walls).

blanquillos, *m. pl.* [<Mex. Sp. *blanquillos*] eggs (rare).

blasón, *m.* [<Sp. *blasón,* honor] *solatar un blasón,* to start a rumor. See also *bolada, bulla.*

bloque, *m.* [<Eng. block] block; city block; the head.

boca (*boca de ángel*), *adj.* [<Sp. *boca,* mouth] *boca de ángel,* a term applied to

a shy person, particularly one who rarely complains about anything.

bocón, -na, *adj.* [<Sp. aug. of *boca,* mouth] said of the person with large, protruding lips; curser.

bofetazo, *m.* [<Sp. *bofetón*] a hard blow on the face.

bofo, -fa, *adj.* [<Sp. *fofo,* soft, spongy] physically weak; cowardly. See also *fatal.*

bogue, *m.* [<Eng. buggy] buggy.

boguecito, *m.* [<N.M. Sp. dim. of *bogue*] baby buggy.

boila, *f.* [<Eng. boiler] boiler.

bola, *f.* [<Sp. *bola,* ball] ball (general); doorknob; *no dar pie con bola,* to be disoriented or in a predicament, to run from pillar to post.

bola, *f.* [<Mex. Sp. *bola,* disorder, tumult] fight, riot; *dar bola,* to treat with indifference; to let something ride; *hacerse bola una persona,* to become confused out of nervousness; *de a bola,* many, a great number.

bola, *m.* [<unknown origin] Mexican silver one-peso coin (slang).

bolada, *f.* [<Mex. Sp. *bolada*<*bola,* occurrence] rumor; *soltar la bolada,* to start a rumor.

bole, *m.* [<Eng. baldy] said of a horse or cow with a white forehead.

boleta, *f.* [<Eng. ballot] ballot. Cf. Sp. *balota.*

bolillo, *m.* [<Mex. Sp. *bolillo,* a kind of breakfast roll] name applied to a non-Indo-Hispanic American white, an "Anglo"; roller, as on a washing machine; cylinder wax record; rolling pin. Cf. Sp. *rodillo.*

bolita, *f.* [<Sp. dim. of *bola,* ball] playing marble; *túnico de bolitas,* polka-dot dress; *pisar bolitas de oro,* to be on cloud nine; *frijol de bolita,* a kind of round-shaped bean.

bolito, *m.* [<Sp. dim. *m.* of *bola*] a brown, round-shaped variety of bean grown in mountain areas.

bolo, *m.* [<Mex. Sp. *bolo*<Lat. *volo,* I do (what a baby is supposed to answer when asked by the priest if he—the baby—is willing to take baptism)] a coin of small denomination given by the *padrino* to children at a wedding; shoeshine.

bolote, *m.* [<Mex. Sp. *borlote,* row, uproar] brawl, noisy dance or party; celebration.

bolsa, *f.* [<Sp. *bolsa,* purse] pocket; hot-water bottle.

bolsear, *vb.* [<N.M. Sp. *bolsa,* pocket] to pick someone's pocket.

bolso, *m.* [<Sp. *bolso,* money bag] a shell-trimmed band worn by Santo Domingo, New Mexico, Indian men. The *bolso* crosses a person's chest and back and is fastened at the belt.

bollito, *m.* [<Sp. dim. of *bollo,* small sugar roll] a kind of cookie.

bollo, *m.* [<Sp. *bollo,* small sugar roll] a kind of breakfast roll; female organ (taboo).

bombera, *f.* [<Mex. Sp. *bombo*] weak; weakling.

bombo, -ba, *adj.* [<Mex. Sp. *bombo,* weak] soft, weak.

bonche, *m.* [<Eng. bunch] bunch; bundle. (*Le costó un bonche.* It cost him a bundle [slang].)

bonete, *m.* [<Sp. *bonete,* bonnet] *arrojarse los bonetes.* To argue heatedly.

bonque, *m.* [<Eng. bunk] bunk bed; bed (slang).

boquera, *f.* [<Sp. *boquera,* eruption of the lips] cold sore.

boquinete, *m.* [<Mex. Sp. *boquinete,* said of a person with a harelip] sucker (fish); said of a person with a fish-like mouth.

boquisuelto, -ta, *adj.* [<Sp. *boca,* mouth, and *suelto,* loose] said of a person who cannot keep a secret.

borboración, *f.* [<Mex. Sp. *górgoro (gorgoración)*] gurgling sound.
　　Calabaza borboraza
　　llena de **borboración**

con el casco 'e la cabeza
y las patitas de león.
Pumpkin lunking,
Full of gurgling,
With its shell for a head
And legs like a lion.
(*La tortuga, The Turtle*, N.M. Sp. riddle)

boronía, *f.* [<Am. Sp. *boronía*, a dish made with eggplant and tomato] a small top. Cf. Sp. *perinola*.

borrega, *f.* [<Sp. *borrega*] sheep; ewe; *andar en la borrega*, to be working in a sheep camp; to tend sheep.

borrego, *m.* [<Sp. *borrego*] yearling lamb; cuckold.

borrego, *adj.* [<N.M. Sp. *borrego*] easygoing, ignorant.

borreguera, *adj.* [<Sp. *borrega*, sheep] of or pertaining to sheep; *f.*, sheepskin jacket.

borreguero, *adj.* [<Sp. *borrega*] of or pertaining to sheep (*campo borreguero*, sheep camp, etc.); *m.*, sheepherder.

boruca, *f.* [<Mex. Sp. *boruca*] *hacer una cosa de boruca*, to lose a thing designedly or on purpose; to change the subject.

bosque, *m.* [<Sp. *bosque*, woods] cottonwood grove; wooded area fringing a body of water, such as a lake, river, stream, etc.

bostecear, *vb.* [<Sp. *bostezar*] to yawn.

bota, *f.* [<Sp. *bota*] boot. (*Al que le venga la bota que la reciba* [or *que se la ponga*]. If the shoe fits, wear it.) *Dar la bota a alguno*, to give someone the boot; *botas*, leggings; soft leather flaps to cover the leg and foot; *andar en la bota*, to irrigate.

bote, *m.* [<Eng. bottle] jail; bottle. *Pásate el bote*, pass the bottle.

botija, *f.* [<Sp. *botija*, a kind of earthen jug] hot-water bottle.

bracero, *m.* [<Sp. *bracero*<*brazo*, arm] day laborer, Mexican farm worker.

bragado, -da, *adj.* [<Mex. Sp. *bragado*] striped, spotted.

brava, *adj.* [<Sp. *bravo*, brave, fierce] in heat, applied to cows, female dogs, etc.

breca, *f.* [<Eng. brake] brake, as in a car.

brel, *m.* [<Eng. bread?] a kind of coarse bread made by shepherds.

brincacharcos, *adj.* [<Sp. *brincar*, to jump, and *charcos*, puddles] hyperactive; jittery, unsettled; scatterbrained.

brincochar, *vb.* [<N.M. Sp. *brincacharcos*] to jump around.

brindarse, *vb.* [<Sp. *brindar*, to drink to another's health] to treat oneself to good food or good living.

broche, *m.* [<Sp. *broche*, brooch] safety pin; a snap, as on a harness. See also *fistol*.

broma, *f.* [<Sp. *broma*, joke, prank] delay; time-consuming difficulty; trouble; embarrassing difficulty; *meterse en bromas*, to get into difficulties. *¡Qué broma!* What a hassle!

bromoso, -sa, *adj.* [<N.M. Sp. *broma*, delay] delaying, slow; time-consuming.

brujo, *m.* [<Sp. *brujo*, sorcerer] sorcerer; Indian medicine man; *adj.*, psychic. (*Es muy brujo.* He is very psychic.)

buche, *m.* [<Sp. *buche*, craw, crop of birds] double chin; goiter; *echarse algo en el buche*, to grab something for keeps; to kipe.

bueyada, *f.* [<Sp. *buey*, ox] drove of oxen; group of ignorant men. Cf. Sp. *boyada*.

bueyero, -ra, *m.* and *f.* [<Sp. *buey*, ox] person in charge of caring for or driving oxen. Cf. Sp. *boyero*.

bulto, *m.* [<Sp. *bulto*, statue] image of a holy person carved in the round; ghost. (*Se nos aprontó un bulto.* A ghost appeared to us.) *Bulto de media talla*, a *bulto* with only the head and upper extremities carved in the round, the rest of the body consisting of a wooden frame covered with cloth.

bulla, *f.* [<Sp. *bulla*] noise; rumor. (*Aquí anda la bulla de que el rey quiere casar a la príncipa.* There is a rumor going around here that the king wants to marry off the princess.)

bulliciento, -ta, *adj.* [<Sp. *bulla,* noise] noisy; lively, merry, boisterous. Cf. Sp. *bullicioso.*

buñiga, *f.* [<Sp. *buñiga*] cow chip, cow dung. *¡Come buñigas!* Go to blazes!

buñuelo, *m.* [<Sp. *buñuelo,* fritter] Indian fried bread. The term *buñuelo* and *sopaipilla* (<Sp. dim. of *sopaipa*) are often used interchangeably to refer to the same kind of fritter. Also, *guñelo,* especially in southern Colorado.

buquipa, *m.* [<Eng. bookkeeper] bookkeeper; certified public accountant.

bura, *f.* [<Mex. Sp. *bura,* a kind of deer (*Odocoileus hemionus*)] mule deer; sorrel deer, desert mule deer.

The sorrel deer or "*bura*" . . . the figure of this animal is certainly gallant. Its body is like that of a mule, and its antlers astonish one's eyes, their branches rising from six to seven feet from base to tip. The flesh is said to be bad but the skins are very valuable. (Lansing B. Bloom, "Barreriro's Ojeada Sobre Nuevo Mexico," *New Mexico Historical Review*)

burriñates, *m. pl.* [<Mex. Sp. *burruñates*] a dish made with *cabrito* (goat) intestines fried in hot fat.

burrión, *m.* [<Sp. *gorrión*] sparrow. See also *gurrión.*

burro, -rra, *adj.* [<Sp. *burro,* ass] dumb, stupid; dunce.

burro, -rra, *m.* and *f.* [<Sp. *burro,* ass] donkey; *burro de carpintero,* sawhorse; *m.,* male mule deer; *burro manadero* (<Sp. *manada,* herd), seed donkey used among a herd of mares for the purpose of crossing with the mares to obtain mules.

busa, *f.* [<N.M. Sp. *abusado*<Sp. *aguzado*] sharp, smart; "on the ball." *¡A la busa!* Careful! Watch out! (slang).

buti, *adv.* [<Mex. Sp. slang *buti*] much; very (slang).

21

Con pacencia se gana el cielo.
Patience is its own reward.

cabaderiza, *f.* [<Sp. *caballeriza*] barn, shed for horses; stable. Also, *caballariza*.

caballerango, *m.* [<Mex. Sp. *caballerango,* head groom] bronco buster; cowboy. Eng. wrangler, one who tends and rounds up cattle and horses, is derived from *caverango<caballerango,* good horseman.

caballito, *m.* [<Sp. dim. of *caballo,* horse] small horse; pony; human ladder, as for scaling a wall; *los caballitos,* merry-go-round; *caballito del diablo,* a kind of dragonfly.

cabañuelas, *f.* [<Sp. dim. of *cabaña,* hut] name given to the first twelve days of the month of January. Each one of these days is supposed to show the kind of weather to be had during each of the twelve months of the new year.

cabeza, *f.* [<Sp. *cabeza,* head] Col. N.M. Sp., head or chief of a tribe; *cabeza de embarañada,* bot., a plant of the Aster family; *echarse por la cabeza,* to let the cat out of the bag, to spill the beans, to let out a secret.

cabildo, *m.* [<Sp. *cabildo,* corporation of a town] Col. N.M. Sp., municipal council headed by the *alcalde* or mayor.

cabo, *m.* [<Sp. *caber,* to fit] I fit. Normally a child's substitution for *quepo, cabo* is common in most northern New Mexico and southern Colorado villages, where the present indicative of *caber,* to fit, is conjugated as follows: *cabo, quepes, quepe, cabemos, ————, quepen.*

cabra, *f.* [<Sp. *cabra,* goat] goat, antelope; doe; *meterle las cabras a alguno,* to bring pressure to bear on someone; to take to court; *se le fueron las cabras,* he lost his marbles (slang).

cabrestear, *vb.* [<N.M. Sp. *cabresto,* rope] to lead stock by a rope.

cabresto, *m.* [<Mex. Sp. *cabresto,* horsehair rope] rope in general; guide or bell animal.

cabrilla, *f.* [<Sp. dim. of *cabra*] goat;

Las cabrillas, the Pleiades.

cabrón, *m.* [<Sp. aug. of *cabro,* billy goat] cuckold; pimp; S.O.B. (taboo).

cabronazo, *m.* [<Sp. aug. of *cabrón*] a hard blow.

cabús, *m.* [<Eng. caboose] caboose.

cacahuate, *m.* [<Mex. Sp. *cacahuate*<Náhuatl *cacahuatl*] peanut. *Don Cacahuate,* comic character in Southwest folklore. *Don Cacahuate* and his wife, *Doña Cebolla,* are usually the butt of a series of moron jokes.

cacaraquear, *vb.* [<Sp. *cacarear*] to cackle; to yak-yak; to chatter; to exaggerate one's own actions; to brag. Also, *caracaquear.*

cacarizo, -za, *adj.* [<Mex. Sp. *cacarizo*] pock-marked.

cacique, *m.* [<Am. Sp. *cacique,* political boss] Pueblo Indian chief and ceremonial leader.

cacombra, *f.* [<Eng. cucumber] cucumber. Cf. Sp. *pepinillo.*

cacomite, *m.* [<Mex. Sp. *cacomite*] bot., Wild onion. See also *cebollita.*

cacona, *f. pl.* [<Zuni *cacona*] a kind of turquoise ornament worn in colonial New Mexico by Zuni Indians.

All the people of this town [Zuni] wear turquoises hanging from their noses and ears; these ornaments are called ***cacona.*** (Percy M. Baldwin, "Fray Marcos' Relación," *New Mexico Historical Review*)

cacha, *f.* [<Sp. *cacha*] handle; *de mala cacha,* ill-disposed, mean; spiteful.

cachana, *f.* [<Mex. Sp. *cachane*] bot., a plant used medicinally. The root is used to ward off evil or witchcraft.

cachanilla, *f.* [<N.M. Sp. *cachana*] bot., a plant used medicinally.

cachar, *vb.* [<Eng. to catch] to catch; to kipe. (*Me cacharon.* They caught me [slang].)

cachetada, *f.* [<Mex. Sp. *cachetada*] a slap in the face. Cf. Sp. *cachete.*

cachetazo, *m.* [<Mex. Sp. *cachetazo*] a slap in the face.

cachina, *f.* [<N.M. Indian *kachina*] Indian ceremonial doll, supernatural symbol.

cachivaches, *m. pl.* [<Mex. Sp. *cachivaches*] trifles; odds and ends.

cacho, *m.* [<Mex. Sp. *cacho,* piece] piece (sexual connotation).

cachucha, *f.* [<Sp. *cachucha,* a kind of cap] canvas top of a covered wagon; top of a convertible; condom.

cachupín, *m.* [<Mex. Sp. *gachupín,* low-class, mean Spaniard] Spaniard (general). Also, *gachupín.*

cadajón, *m.* [<Sp. *cagajón,* horse dung] dung of donkeys, horses, mules, etc.

> *Mañana domingo*
> *se casa Benito*
> *con un borreguito.*
> *¿Quién es la madrina?*
> *Doña Catalina.*
> *¿Quién es el padrino?*
> *Don Juan Botijón.*
> *¿De qué hacen la fiesta?*
> *De un **cadajón.***
> *¿Quién se lo come?*
> *El perro pastor.*
> Tomorrow, Sunday,
> Benito is marrying
> A little lamb;
> Who's the maid of honor?
> Lady Catalina;
> Who's the best man?
> Sir John Botijón.
> What's for the reception?
> A large piece of dung;
> Who's going to eat it?
> The shepherd dog.
> (N.M. Sp. children's rhyme)

caer [*kái*], *vb.* [<Sp. *caer,* to fall] *caer agua,* to rain; *caer nieve,* to snow; *caerle bien una persona a otra,* to appeal to someone; *caerle un hombre a una mujer,* to court, to propose. (*El Frutoso le cayó a la Sofronia.* Frutoso proposed to Sofronia.) *Caerle tierra a una persona,* to have trouble, to meet one's equal.

café, *m.* [<Sp. *café,* coffee] cafe; restaurant; *no hacerle café una persona a otra,* to be socially unequal to someone. (*Malaquías no le hace café a la Rosenda.*

23

Malaquías is not Rosenda's equal.)

cafuso, -sa, *adj.* [<Port. *cafuso,* offspring of a Black and an Indian woman] black; ugly; very dark-complexioned. (*¡Cállate, negro cafuso!* Shut up, you dirty, ugly thing!)

cagalera, *f.* [<Mex. Sp. *cagalera*] the lower part of the colon.

Entre Melón y Melambes
mataron una ternera;
Melón se comió la carne
y Melambes, la cagalera.
Melón and Yulick
Butchered a calf;
Melón ate the meat
And Yulick my ass.
(N.M. and so. Colo. Sp. folk rhyme)

cagazón, *f.* [<Sp. aug. of *cagada,* excrement] scolding, dressing down.

caguillas, *adj.* [<Mex. Sp. *caguillas,* stingy] afraid.

caida [káiďa], *f.* [<Sp. *caída de agua*] waterfall.

caido [káiďo], *m.* [<Sp. *caída*] declivity; dip; landslip; *adj.,* madly in love (slang).

caja, *f.* [<Sp. *caja*] box; carved wooden chest; *caja del río,* river basin; *real caja,* safe, sub-treasury.

cajero, -ra, *m.* and *f.* [<Sp. *cajero*] cashier; clerk; *f.,* saleslady.

cajeta, *f.* [<Mex. Sp. *cajeta,* a kind of carmelized candy] applesauce, jelly. *Yela*(<Eng. jelly) is a more popular term for jelly.

No saben que soy el duce
la cajeta, la ensalada,
la azúcar, el piloncillo,
los anises y la gracia . . .
They don't know I am the candy
The jelly and the salad;
The white and brown sugar,
The aniseed in preserves,
And, above all, the grace.
(*Los Comanches,* N.M. Sp. folk drama)

cajete, *m.* [<Mex. Sp. *cajete*<Náhuatl *caxitl,* bowl] tub; tin tub, washtub.

cajetuda, *adj.* [<N.M. Sp. *cajete,* tub] said of a woman with large hips; a sexy female.

cajón, *m.* [<Sp. *cajón*] large box; box of a truck or wagon; coffin; wooden mold for adobes; letter box; drop box. Cf. Sp. *buzón.*

cajonería, *f.* [<N.M. Sp. *cajón,* coffin] funeral home or parlor, mortuary; coffin factory.

cajonero, *m.* [<N.M. Sp. *cajón,* coffin] coffin maker; funeral director; undertaker.

cajuetón, *m.* [<N.M Sp. aug. of *cajete*] large bowl.

calabacear, *vb.* [<Mex. Sp. *calabacear*] to turn down a proposal of marriage.

Ya no vivo en El Cerrito
donde usté me conoció;
'hora vivo más abajo,
donde me calabaceó.
I have moved from El Cerrito
Where we two first met;
Now I live down the hill
Where you said no to me.
(N.M. Sp. *verso popular*)

calabacilla, *f.* [<Sp. dim. of *calabaza,* gourd, pumpkin] a kind of wild gourd the approximate shape and size of a tennis ball.

calabacitas, *f. pl.* [<Sp. dim. of *calabaza*] squash; zucchini.

calabaza, *f.* [<Sp. *calabaza*] pumpkin; *calabaza mexicana,* garden pumpkin; *calabaza de pastel,* a specially prepared ripe pumpkin used for pumpkin pies; *dar calabazas una mujer a un hombre,* to reject or turn down a man's proposal of marriage.

calabozo, *m.* [<Sp. *calabozo,* dungeon] dungeon; jail.

calabrote, *m.* [<Sp. *calabrote,* stream cable] large, heavy rope.

caladas, *f. pl.* [<Col. N.M. Sp. *calada?,* craggy road] waves, as on one's hair.

calar, *vb.* [<Sp. *cala,* small piece cut out of a watermelon to try out its ripeness, color, flavor, etc.] to try, to sound out.

calave, *m.* [<Sp. *calavera,* skull] bones; skeleton. (*Ese chulo es puro calave.* That

dog is nothing but skin and bones.)

calcos, *m. pl.* [<Mex. Sp. slang, *calcos*] shoes (slang).

caldear, *vb.* [<N.M Sp. *caldo,* flattery] to compliment; to flatter; *caldearse una persona,* to brag. See also *caldo* (*echarse el caldo*).

caldera, *f.* [<Sp. *caldera,* boiler] volcanic valley.

caldero, -ra, *adj.* [<N.M Sp. *caldo,* flattery] said of a person who likes to flatter others; flirtatious.

caldito, *m.* [<N.M. Sp. dim. of *caldo,* flattery] thin soup; flattery; change of subject in a conversation to throw or put someone off.
> *Vide venir una indita*
> *bastante americanada,*
> *y a los pastores de Otero*
> *nomás **caldito** les daba.*
> I saw an Indian maiden coming,
> She acted like an Anglo;
> She gave Otero's shepherds
> Nothing more than flattery.
> (*Indita de Siete Lagunas,* N.M. Sp. folk song)

caldo, *m.* [<Mex. Sp. *caldo,* soup] broth, soup; flattery; *echarse uno el caldo,* to brag or to exaggerate one's achievements.

calentón, *m.* [<Sp. *calentar,* to heat] boiler; hot-water tank or reservoir in a wood stove.

calía, *f.* See *calilla.*

caliche, *m.* [<Sp. *caliche,* pebble in a brick, flake of lime] a crust of calcium carbonate ($CaCO_3$) formed on stony soil in arid regions.

caliente, *adj.* [<Sp. *caliente*] hot; *correrle caliente a uno,* to be in a predicament or in a fix; *estar caliente (el tiempo),* to be hot. (*¡Qué caliente está hoy!* How hot it is today.) Cf. Sp. *Hace calor.*

calilla, *f.* [<Sp. *calilla*] suppository.
> *Si esa chinche me picara*
> *y del piquete muriera,*
> *levantaría la nalga*
> *de **calía** me la metiera.*

If that bedbug were to bite me
And if I died from the bite,
I'd raise one of my buttocks
And use it as a suppository.
(*Trovos del Viejo Vilmas,* N.M. Sp. folk poetry)

calor, *f.* [<Sp. *calor* (*m.*)] heat; *mucha calor,* very hot.

calote, *m.* [<Sp. *cal,* lime] plaster cast; *adj.,* strong, muscular. Also, *colote.*

calquigüite, *m.* See *chalchigüite.*

calunia, *f.* [<Col. N.M. Sp. *calunia* (Molina)] calumny, libel, slander.

caluniador, -ra, *adj.* [<Col. N.M. Sp. *caluniador*] slanderer.

calvario, *m.* [<Sp. *calvario,* Calvary] site near a Penitente *morada* (chapter house). The *calvario* represents the hill of Calvary where Jesus is supposed to have been crucified.

calzonear, *vb.* [<N.M. Sp. *calzones,* pants] to defecate; to go through someone's pockets; to rob.

calzoncitos, *m. pl.* [<N.M. Sp. dim. of *calzones,* pants] basketball or track shorts.

calzones, *m. pl.* [<Sp. *calzones,* breeches] pants, trousers; *calzones rotos,* tramp; *meterse uno en sus calzones,* to wear the pants. (*Ella está metida en sus calzones.* She wears the pants.)

calzonudo, -da, *adj.* [<N.M. Sp. *calzones,* pants] brave; courageous; daring.

¡Calla!, *interj.* [<Sp. *callar,* to hush] You don't say! How strange!

callado, -da, *m.* and *f.* [<Sp. *callar,* to hush] Col. N.M. Sp., illegitimate child; in southern Colorado such a child is referred to as *"de los pajaritos del monte"* (from the birds of the forest).

calle, *f.* [<Sp. *calle,* street] street; space between rows in a sown field.

cama, *f.* [<Sp. *cama*] bed; felly of a wagon wheel.

camacho, *m.* [<Mex. Sp. *camacho,* a kind of duck?] lump on the forehead or head. See Mex. Sp. *chichón.*

25

camada, *f.* [<Sp. *camada,* litter] age; kind. (*Son de la misma camada.* They are of the same age.)

camaleón, *m.* [<Sp. *camaleón,* chameleon] horned toad.

camalta, *f.* [<Col. N.M. Sp. *cama alta*] bed. *El se echa en* **cama alta,** *en la esterica yo.* He lies down on a bed; I lie down on a mat. (*Romances de América,* Colección Austral)

camalteado, -da, *adj.* [<N.M. Sp. *camaltear,* to wear out someone in bed (sexually)] sexually worn out.

camaltear, *vb.* [<N.M. Sp. *camalta,* bed] to wear out somone in bed (sexually).

camaltita, *f.* [<N.M. Sp. dim. of *camalta*] crib; twin bed.

camandulero, -ra, *adj.* [<Sp. *camandulero,* full of tricks] experienced, especially in matters of sex.

camastrón, *adj.* [<Sp. *camastrón,* sly, cunning] old seed male; *viejo camastrón,* dirty old man.

cambiar, *vb.* [<Sp. *cambiar*] to change; to cash checks. *Cambiar* conjugates as follows: *cambeo, cambeas, cambea, cambiamos,———, cambean.*

cambullón, *m.* [<Sp. *cambullón,* swindle] *en cambullón,* in droves. *También algunas viejitas llegaron en* **cambullón** *y andaban como ratitas en la pisca del piñón.* Also some little old ladies Got there in droves; They went about like mice Picking up their piñon nuts. (N.M. Sp. folk song)

camellar, *vb.* [<Mex. Sp. *camellar*] to work (slang).

camello, *vb.* [<Mex. Sp. *camellar*] work (slang). See also *jale, chamba.*

camino, *m.* [<Sp. *camino*] road, way; *El camino,* the Milky Way.

camisa, *f.* [<Sp. *camisa*] shirt; canvas cover for a wagon. See also *cachucha.*

camote, *m.* [<Mex. Sp. *camote,* yam] sweet potato; yam; bulb (iris, lily, etc.); *adj.,* dunce, stupid.
Mira, sin hacer alarde, Chicoria, no seas **camote** *¡Cómo quieres desmentir a un padre y sacerdote!* Pay attention and don't brag, Chicoria, don't be a dunce. How can you say the father, A priest, is lying? (*Trovos del Viejo Vilmas, Chicoria y Otros Poetas,* N.M. Sp. folk poetry)

campamocha, *f.* [<Mex. Sp. *campamocha*] praying mantis. Cf. Sp. *rezadora.*

campanita, *f.* [<Sp. dim. of *campana,* bell] small bell; jingle bell.

campero, *m.* [<Sp. *campero,* friar who superintends a farm] said of the person who runs a sheep camp.

campito, *m.* [<Sp. dim. of *campo,* field] time. (*Dése un campito y vaya a vernos.* Give yourself a little time and come to visit us.)

composanto, *m.* [<Sp. *campo santo,* holy ground] burial plot in front of a church, cemetery.

canaigra, *m.* [<Mex. Sp. *canaigre*] bot., Dock root. Also, *canaigre.*

canal, *m.* [<Sp. *canal,* gutter] rain spout; roof gutter.

canaleja, *f.* [<Sp. dim. of *canal*] rain gutter.

canas, *f. pl.* [<Sp. *canas*] gray hair; *salirle canas a uno,* to get gray hair; *sacarle canas verdes a uno,* to drive one mad.

canasto, *m.* [<Sp. *canasto,* large basket] basket; bassinet; bushel.

candelaria, *f.* [<Sp. *Candelaria,* Candlemas] girl's name; Candlemas; bot., Torchweed.

candelilla, *f.* [<N.M. Sp. dim. of *candela*] frost particles in the air; name of a plant from which wax is extracted.

candil, *m.* [<Mex. Sp. *candil,* a kind of tin lamp] a kind of kitchen lamp using coal oil as fuel. (*Candil de la calle y escuridad de su casa.* Charity begins at home.)

canela, *f.* [<Sp. *canela*] cinnamon; *hasta*

los más de canela, even those from the best families.

canijo, -ja, *adj.* [<Mex. Sp. *canijo*] damned, wretched; *interj.,* Damn it!

canilla, *f.* [<Sp. *canilla,* shin bone] shin bone; *pl.,* extremely thin legs or wrists.

canillera, *f.* [<N.M. Sp. *canilla,* thin leg or wrist] leather strap used on the wrist.

canjilón, *m.* [<Sp. *cangilón*] ram's horn; *pl.,* antlers.

canoba, *f.* [<Am. Sp. *canoa*] trough; chute for conveying grain; rain gutter.

cantada, *f.* [<Sp. *cantada,* cantata] song; folk tune.

cantador, *m.* [<Sp. *cantador,* cantor] folk singer; singer.

cantaleta, *f.* [<Sp. *cantaleta,* confused noise, as of voices, instruments, etc.] the same old song; a repeated complaint. (*Aquí viene el Vitelio con la misma cantaleta de siempre.* Here comes Vitelio with his age-old complaint.)

cantina, *f.* [<Sp. *cantina,* canteen] bar, tavern; large wallet or leather box.

cantón, *m.* [<Sp. *cantón,* region] home; hometown (slang).

cantonear, *vb.* [<N.M. *cantón*] to live or to be staying at home (slang).

cañada, *f.* [<Sp. *cañada,* glen] a dry riverbed; a small canyon in the sierra.

cañaigra, *f.* [<Mex. Sp. *cañaigre*] bot., Wild pieplant; Sour dock root. Also, *cañaigre.*

cañatilla, *f.* [<N.M. Sp. *cañutillo*] bot., Mormon tea.

caño, *m.* [<Sp. *caño,* tube, iron pipe] *caño de camino,* culvert.

cañón, *m.* [<Sp. *cañón,* tube, pipe] stovepipe.

cañute, *m.* [<Sp. *cañuto,* iron pipe] metal pipe; a kind of flute; a baton used in the game of *cañute.* This game is played with four batons (*cañutes*), each with its respective markings and names: *el uno, el dos, el mulato,* and *el cinchado.*

cañutillo, *m.* [<Mex. Sp. *canutillo*] bot., a

plant used for its medicinal properties; *cañutillo del llano,* bot., Scouring rush.

caparejo, *m.* [<Sp. *aparejo*] Col. N.M., packsaddle.

The loads are carried on packsaddles of a peculiar shape, made for the purpose, and, in the language of the country, are called *caparejo.* They consist of a wide leather pad stuffed with hay or grass, which fits across the back of the animal, and extends some distance down the sides. They are secured with a wide bandage of sea-grass or leather, and are drawn as tight around the mule as can be borne. (W.W.H. Davis, *El Gringo*)

capaz, *adj.* [<Sp. *capaz*] capable; *hacerse capaz de algo,* to be cognizant of, to notice or take note of; *ser capaz de,* to be liable to. (*Es capaz de que te mate.* He is liable to kill you.)

capeada, *f.* [<Sp. N.M. *capearse,* to duck] act of ducking, as to avoid a blow.

capear, *vb.* [<Sp. *capa,* cape] to wave hello or good-bye from a distance; *reflex.,* to duck, as to avoid a blow.

capear, *vb.* [<Eng. slang to kipe] to help out; to hand over something on the sly (slang).

capero, *m.* [<Sp. *capa,* cape] caretaker of the costumes (capes) of the players in the *Matachines* dance.

capirotada, *f.* [<Mex. Sp. *capirotada*] bread pudding. The term *sopa,* q.v., is a more common word for this kind of pudding.

capirote, -ta, *adj.* [<Sp. *capirote,* said of the animal having the head of a different color than the body] said of an animal having eyes of different colors (one blue, one gray, for example); *cabra capirota,* black and white goat; *gallina capirota,* speckled hen.

caporal, *m.* [<Mex. Sp. *caporal*] overseer who works under a *mayordomo* (boss, manager).

capote, *m.* [<Sp. *capote,* raincoat] canvas cover or top of a wagon or converti-

ble; condom.

capulín, *m.* [<Mex. Sp. *capulín*<Náhuatl *capuli*] bot., Chokecherry; Wild cherry.

capusanto, *m.* [<Sp. *campo santo*] cemetery.

cara, *f.* [<Sp. *cara*] face; *darle a uno la cara al suelo,* to show a long face; *cara de papa,* ugly; *sacar la cara por alguien,* to stand up for someone.

caracaquear, *vb.* [<Sp. *cacarear*] to cackle. See also *cacaraquear.*

caracol, *m.* [<Mex. Sp. *caracol*] curl of hair; ringlet; Col. N.M., horse races among the Zuni Indians.

carajazo, *m.* [<Mex. Sp. *carajazo*<Sp. *carajo*] heavy blow.

carajo, -ja, *adj.* [<Sp. *carajo,* male organ] mischievous; impish; destructive. *¡Carajo!* Curses!

> *San Pedro tiró una piedra*
> *de una escalera pa abajo,*
> *y le respondió San Pablo,*
> *¡No tires, calvo carajo!*
> St. Peter hurled a stone
> From atop a ladder
> And St. Paul cried out:
> "Watch it, you impish baldpate."
> (N.M. Sp. *verso popular*)

carajón, *m.* [<Sp. *cagajón*] horse dung. See also *cadajón.*

carambada, *f.* [<Sp. *¡Caramba!,* Good heavens!] rash or inconsiderate act. *¡Qué carambada!* Oh, heck!

caramelo, *m.* [<Sp. *caramelo,* sugar candy] a homemade syrup used to sweeten *sopa* (bread pudding). This syrup is also called *azúcar quemada* (carmelized sugar). The *caramelo* is invariably diluted with water before pouring it on the *sopa.*

caravana, *f.* [<Sp. *caravana,* caravan] courtesy bow; a parade, as *Caravana de los paisanos* in Santa Fe.

carbólico, *m.* [<Sp. *carbólico,* carbolic] mothball.

carcaje, *m.* [<Mex. Sp. *carcaj*<Sp. *carcax,* quiver] thin, emaciated person. (*El Rutilio es un puro carcaje.* Rutilio is

nothing but skin and bones.)

carcamán, *m.* [<Mex. Sp. *carcamán*] a game of chance involving the use of dice in order to guess the lucky number in a raffle.

cárcula, *f.* [<Sp. *cárcola*] treadle, as in a loom.

carcular, *vb.* [<Sp. *calcular*] to calculate, to figure up, etc.

cárculas, *f. pl.* [<Sp. *cálculos*] calculations, computations.

cárculos, *m. pl.* [<Sp. *cálculos*] calculations, computations.

cardillo, *m.* [<Sp. dim. of *cardo*] thistle.

cardo santo, *m.* [<Mex. Sp. *cardosanto*] bot., a prickly, white-flowered poppy plant used medicinally to cure dysentery; also called *chicalote.*

carestolendas, *f. pl.* [<Sp. *carnestolendas*] the three carnival days before Ash Wednesday.

cargar, *vb.* [<Sp. *cargar*] to carry; to load; to wear. (*¡Qué buenos zapatos carga!* He wears some fancy shoes!) *Cargarle la viga a alguno,* to tell someone off; *cargar algo a la cuenta,* to charge to one's account.

carguero, *m.* [<Sp. *carga,* load] freight train.

carguitas, *f. pl.* [<Sp. dim. *pl.* of *carga,* load] *en carguitas,* piggyback. (*Se lastimó la Sofronia y tuvieron que llevarla en carguitas.* Sofronia got hurt and they had to carry her piggyback.)

caribe, *adj.* [<Am. Sp. *caribe,* Carib] a kind of chili sauce made with raw red chili peppers. See also *chile caribe.*

carichopo, -pa, *adj.* [<Sp. *cara,* face, and N.M. Sp. *chopo,* short] applied to the child whose feelings have been hurt; pouting.

caridad, *f.* [<Sp. *caridad*] charity; *pedir limosna para hacer caridad,* to rob Peter to pay Paul.

carmil, *m.* [<Sp. *carmín,* pale rose color] rouge.

carnal, -la, *m.* and *f.* [<Sp. *carnal,* carnal; flesh and blood] brother; *carnala,* sis-

ter (slang).

carnalismo, *m.* [<SW Sp. *carnal*, brother] brotherhood.

Carnalismo, a feeling or an allegiance that permeates the Chicano movement means a type of brotherhood within members of La Raza characterized by depth of feeling and allegiance to other *carnales.* It is the type of feeling and allegiance that many blood relatives have for one another. Once a Chicano is your *carnal,* he will stand by you through thick or thin. (Lydia R. Aguirre, "The Meaning of the Chicano Movement," *Social Case Worker*)

carne adobada, *f.* [<Sp. *carne*, meat, and *adobada*, pickled] meat pickled in hot chili sauce; chili pork.

carnerito, *m.* [<Sp. dim. of *carnero*, ram] name of a game in which two children take turns at hitting each other's knuckles until one of the two gives up.

carnero, *m.* [<Sp. *carnero*, ram] *carnero cimarrón,* Rocky Mountain bighorn; *carnero meso, carnero padre, carnero toro, carnero teretón,* seed ram.

carola, *f.* [<Sp. *escarola*?, plaited frill] a kind of saddle blanket used on donkeys and mules.

Al ensillar mi mulita
y al echarle la **carola**
me acordé de mi negrita,
esa mala pagadora.
As I saddled my mule
Saddle blanket and all,
I was thinking of my darling
And how she did me wrong.
(*La mulita,* N.M. Sp. folk song)

carpa, *f.* [<Am. Sp. *carpa*<Quechua *carppa,* canopy] tent; canvas top of a covered wagon. See also *camisa, cachucha.*

carpeta, *f.* [<Sp. *carpeta,* table cover] a kind of card game; gang.

carpolio, *m.* See *tarpolio.*

carramplón, *m.* [<Col. Sp. *carramplón*] flintlock musket.

carreta, *f.* [<Sp. *carreta*] ox cart, wheelbarrow; *carreta de la Muerte,* a small handmade wooden cart used by the Penitentes, q.v., and in which a figure of Death rides in processions; *pescar a uno de carreta,* to take advantage of someone.

carretela, *f.* [<Sp. dim. of *carreta*] buggy; *carretela de vidriera,* stagecoach.

carretil, *m.* [<Sp. dim. of *carrete*] bobbin.

carretilla, *f.* [<Sp. *carretilla,* pulley] spool (of thread).

carría, *f.* [<SW Sp. slang *carría,* static] *dar carría,* to bother, to harrass. (*Ese bato me da mucha carría.* That dude gives me a lot of static [slang].)

carrios, *m. pl.* [<unknown origin] time out; *pedir carrios,* to ask for time out (in the game of *chueco,* q.v.).

carrito, *m.* [<Sp. dim. of *carro,* carriage] toy car; street car. See also *carroza.*

carro, *m.* [<Sp. *carro*] car (auto); *carro 'e caballos,* wagon; *el carro,* astron., the Big Dipper in Ursa Major.

carroferril, *m.* [<Sp. *ferrocarril*] railroad; train (iron horse).

Ahí viene el **carroferril**
con dirección a Durango;
el que se embarca en él
Dios nomás sabe hasta cuándo.
Here comes the train
On its way to Durango;
Whoever gets aboard
Only God knows if he'll return.
(*El carroferril,* N.M. Sp. folk song)

carroza, *f.* [<Sp. *carroza,* large coach] streetcar; bus.

carrucha, *f.* [<SW Sp. slang *carrucha*] car (auto); jalopy.

cartera, *f.* [<Sp. *cartera,* wallet] envelope.

casa, *f.* [<Sp. *casa*] house; *cas' 'e corte,* courthouse; *cas' 'e segunda,* secondhand store.

cascaje, *m.* [<Sp. *cascajo,* gravel] parched earth; caked earth, especially when dry after a rain.

cáscara, *f.* [<Sp. *cáscara,* peel] a kind of homemade cosmetic; a cheap watch (slang); bark of a tree.

cascarear, *vb.* [<N.M. Sp. *cáscara,* bark

(of a tree)] to cut off the bark of a log, tree, etc.

cascarones, *m. pl.* [<Mex. Sp. *cascarones*] egg shells filled with confetti; *baile de cascarones,* a dance during which the dancers break confetti-filled eggshells over their partners' heads.

cascarria, *f.* [<Mex. Sp. *cascarria*] mud that adheres to one's shoes; an old worn-out car; jalopy.

cascarriento, -ta, *adj.* [<N.M. Sp. *cascarria*] covered with bits of dry mud; said also of animals with their fur or wool covered with cockleburs; shaggy.

cashira, *m.* and *f.* [<Pueblo Indian pronunciation of *Castilla,* Castile] Col. N.M., Spaniard; Spanish-speaking person.

casorio, *m.* [<Sp. *casorio,* hasty marriage; shotgun wedding] wedding. Cf. Sp. *casamiento.*

caspa, *f.* [<Sp. *caspa,* dandruff] grime; crust of filth on a person's body, and especially on some children's hands, elbows and feet.

caspudo, -da, *adj.* [<N.M. Sp. *caspa*] covered with crust of filth, especially on the hands.

castear, *vb.* [<Sp. *casta,* caste) to breed animals successfully.

Castilla, *f.* [<Sp. *Castilla,* Castile] Col. N.M., Spaniard; *de Castilla,* thoroughbred vs *del pais,* native; *rosa de Castilla,* a kind of wild rose.

castilleja, *f.* [<Sp. dim. of *Castilla*] bot., Bear tongue, a medicinal plant.

castira, *adj.* [<Sp. *Castilla,* Castile] Col. N.M., a term used by New Mexico Indians to refer to Spaniards. Also, *cashira.*

casto, -ta, *adj.* [<Sp. *casta*] half-breed; mixed-blood.

castrado, *m.* [<Sp. *castrar,* to castrate] a medium-sized billy goat that will be used eventually as a *chivato* or seed goat; a yearling lamb that will be used in time as a seed ram. See also *carnero.*

catacismo, *m.* [<Sp. *catecismo*] catechism.

catacizar, *vb.* [<Sp. *cauterizar,* to cauterize] to make up, as after a quarrel.

catágalo, *m.* [<Sp. *catálogo*] catalogue. Also, *catálago.*

cateado, -da, *adj.* [<N.M. Sp. *catos,* blows] beaten up; damaged.

cato, *m.* [<Mex. Sp. *catorrazo*] blow; *dar catos a uno,* to beat up. (*Hubo catos anoche.* There was a fistfight last night.)

catoche, *adj.* [<Mex. Sp. *catoche*] annoyed; angry (slang).

catrín, -na, *adj.* [<Mex. Sp. *catrín,* dandy] well-dressed, elegant.

cavador, *m.* [<Sp. *cavador,* digger] hoe. Cf. Sp. *azadón.*

cayús, *m.* [<Eng. cayuse, Cayuse Indians] mustang, horse.

cazuelón, *m.* [<Sp. aug. of *cazuela,* cooking pan] *cocer los cazuelones,* to prepare food in large amounts. See also *peroles.*

cebadilla, *f.* [<Sp. dim. of *cebada,* barley] bot., Deer's ears; Indian caustic barley.

cebolla, *f.* [<Sp. *cebolla*] onion; bulb of any bulbous root. See also *papa.*

cebollín, *m.* [<Sp. *cebollino,* young onion] bot., Wild onion; onion seeds; chives.

cebollita, *f.* [<Sp. dim. of *cebolla*] bot., Wild onion.

cedro, *m.* [<Sp. *cedro*] cedar; juniper bark used in dyeing; *cedro blanco,* bot., White cedar; *cedro colorado,* bot., Red cedar; *cedro chivo,* bot., Alligator juniper.

'ceitera, *f.* [<Sp. *aceitera*] oil can.

ceja, *f.* [<Sp. *ceja*] eyebrow; cliff.

celador, *m.* [<Sp. *celador,* watchman] warden in the sect of Penitentes.

celebro, *m.* [<Col. N.M. Sp. *celebro*] brain; cerebrum.

cemente, *m.* [<Sp. *cemento*] cement; concrete.

'cemita, *f.* [<Sp. *acemita,* bran flour] whole wheat flour; *harin' 'e cemita,* whole wheat or bran flour; a kind of sweet roll flavored with anise seeds. (*Cuando no hay pan, buenas son cemitas.* Half a loaf is better than none. [N.M. Sp. proverb.])

cencia, *f.* [<Sp. *ciencia*] science; memory; mental alertness.

30

cenicienta, *f.* [<Sp. *cenicienta*] Cinderella; *cenicienta golosa*, a girl who eats a great deal, is greedy, gluttonous.

ceniza, *f.* [<Sp. *ceniza*, ashes] *ceniza curada*, a specially prepared kind of ashes used in making an outdoor fire during rainy weather.

centro, *m.* [<Sp. *centro*, center] a kind of brooch with a clasp to catch or join the ends of a *bejuco* or *bejuquillo*, q.v.; a kind of board of directors of the Penitente sect; downtown. (*Voy al centro.* I am going downtown.)

'cequia, *f.* [<Sp. *acequia*, ditch] irrigation ditch. The term *acequia* is used in Santa Fe as the name of a street, *Acequia Madre* (main ditch).

cerezo, *m.* [<Sp. *cerezo*, cherry tree] cherry; cherry (sexual connotation); *árbol de cerezo*, cherry tree.

cerote, *m.* [<Sp. *cerón*, dregs of pressed wax formed into a cake] stool (excrement), turd.

Cíbola, *f.* [<Zuni *Shiwina*, tribal range] sixteenth-century Spanish name for Zuni and all the lands which later (in 1583) became known as *Nueba Mexico* (New Mexico).

cibolero, *adj.* [<N.M. Sp. *cíbolo*<*Cíbola*] buffalo hunter.

cíbolo, *m.* [<N.M. Sp. *Cíbola*<*Shiwina*, Zuni] buffalo; also called *vaca de Cíbola.*

Nuevo México insolente,
entre los **cíbolos** *criado,*
dime, ¿quién te ha hecho letrado
pa cantar entre la gente?
Insolent New Mexico
Brought up among the buffalo;
Tell me, who has taught you
To sing in front of people.
(*Trovos del Viejo Vilmas*, N.M. Sp. folk poetry)

cielo, *m.* [<Sp. *cielo* sky; *juntársele a uno el cielo con la tierra*, to become confused; to go to pieces.

ciénega, *f.* [<Am. Sp. *ciénega*<Sp. *ciénaga*] marsh, swampy land; small farm.

cienegoso, -sa, *adj.* [<N.M. Sp. *ciénega*] muddy, miry.

cientopiés, *m.* [<Col. N.M. Sp. *ciento pies* (Molina)] centipede.

cimarrón, *m.* [<Am. Sp. *cimarrón*, wild] stray animal living in the wilds. (*Un grito a tiempo saca un cimarrón del monte.* A stitch in time saves nine.) *Pl.*, boiling beans; *adj.*, shy, wild.

cimbra, *f.* [<Sp. *cimbrear*, to bend] bed spring; ridge.

ciminterio, *m.* [<Col. N.M. Sp. *ciminterio* (Molina)] cemetery.

cinchado, -da, *adj.* [<Mex. Sp. *cinchado*] striped; name of one of the batons used in the game of *cañute*, q.v.

cincho, *m.* [<Sp. *cincho*, cinch] *Está cincho.* (<Eng. It's a cinch.) It's a certainty.

cinta, *f.* [<Sp. *cinta*, ribbon] *cintas de los zapatos*, shoelaces. See also *cordones.*

cintillas, *f. pl.* [<Sp. dim. of *cinta*, ribbon] shoelaces.

cintopié, *m.* [<Mex. Sp. *cintopié*] centipede.

cisca, *f.* [<Mex. Sp. *cisca*, shame] fear; *tener cisca*, to be scared or afraid. Also, *cisco* (slang).

cizaña, *f.* [<Sp. *cizaña*, discord] tumbleweed; *meter cizaña*, to sow discord. Cf. Sp. *sembrar cizaña.*

cizañoso, -sa, *adj.* [<Sp. *cizaña*] a person who sows discord; instigator.

claco, *m.* [<Mex. Sp. *tlaco*, a three-centavo coin] Col. N.M. Sp., one eighth of a *real; pl.*, a few pennies.

clas, *f.* [<Eng. class] class; kind, sort. *¿De qué clas?* What kind?

clástico, *m.* [<Sp. *plástico*] poultice; *clástico de mostaza*, mustard plaster.

clavado, -da, *adj.* [<N.M. Sp. *clavarse*] rich, in the money (slang). (*La viuda se quedó clavada.* The widow was left well set financially.)

clavar, *vb.* [<Sp. *clavar*, to nail] to get, to grab. *¡Clávatela!* Grab it! Also, to spot. (*Le clavó el ojo.* He spotted her.)

clavarse, *vb.* [<Sp. *clavarse*, to nail] to get

a lucky break, to be fortunate (slang).

clavero, *m.* [<Sp. *clavero,* keeper of the keys] warp nailer in a loom.

clavo, *m.* [<Sp. *clavo*] nail; *pl.,* long sideburns in the shape of a nail; *poner el clavo y remacharlo,* to start a job and finish it.

clin, *f.* [<Sp. *crin*] mane (horse's, lion's, etc.).

clisarse, *vb.* [<Sp. *eclipsarse*] to become eclipsed; *ojos clisados,* dreamy, droopy eyes.

cloche, *m.* [<Eng. clutch] clutch. (*Este es un cloche de Ford.* This is a Ford clutch.)

cobija, *f.* [<Mex. Sp. *cobija*] blanket; shawl; homemade quilt; cover, as for a wagon. See also *cuilta.*

> Just as the blanket was the universal garment of the man, every village woman wore a *cobija,* or shawl. She folded a square of colored cloth into a triangle and tossed it over her head and shoulders as bonnet and cloak. (R.F. Dickey, *New Mexico Village Arts*)

cobijarse, *vb.* [<N.M. Sp. *cobija*] *cobijarse con la misma cobija,* to be in cahoots with someone; to be of the same ilk as someone.

cócano, *m.* [<Mex. Sp. *cócono,* young turkey] turkey. The terms *ganso* and *torque,* q.v., are far more common.

cocinear, *vb.* [<Sp. *cocinar*] to cook.

coco, *m.* [<Sp. *coco,* bogey man] bogey man; *meter el coco a alguno,* to frighten someone.

coco, *m.* [<Eng. cocoa] cocoa; pulverized chocolate; chocolate drink.

coconate, *m.* [<Eng. coconut] coconut.

coche, *m.* [<Sp. *coche,* coach] name of a game.

> *Coche* (coach), another game played, was similar to *El molino* [q.v.], except that each player was given the name of a town on the road from Bernalillo to Las Vegas. (Dudley Gordon, "Charles F. Lummis, 'Mr. South-

west'," *New Mexico Magazine*)

cochera, *f.* [<Mex. Sp. *cochera,* garage] storage shed.

cochi, *m.* [<Mex. Sp. *coche*<*cochino*] pig.

cochinada, *f.* [<Sp. *cochino,* pig] mess.

cochino, *m.* [<Sp. *cochino*] pig; *cochino barrilí,* glutton; *adj.,* dirty; nasty; obscene.

cochiteño, -ña, *adj.* [<N.M. Sp. *Cochití* <Keres *Ko-tyi-ti,* name of a Rio Grande Indian pueblo] a resident of Cochití.

cocho, *m.* [<Sp. *bizcocho,* biscuit] female organ (taboo).

codicil, *m.* [<Sp. *codicilo,* codicil] Col. N.M. Sp., a note, a sort of IOU.

> Coronado accepted the brown horse, not as a gift but as a loan, giving Oñate a note (*codicil*) which provided that the animal should be paid for or returned. (Herbert E. Bolton, *Coronado*)

codo, *m.* [<Sp. *codo*] elbow; *dar de codo,* to nudge, to give someone inside information.

cofre, *m.* [<Sp. *cofre,* chest] trunk. (The terms *petaca* and *petaquilla* are far more common.) Piggy bank.

coi, *m.* [<Tewa *coi*] Col. N.M. Sp., lower apartment of an Indian multifloor dwelling; underground shed. See *soterrano.*

cojinillo, *m.* [<Mex. Sp. *cojinillo*] net; pocket; a kind of pouch.

> The *corazas* of travelling saddles are also provided with several pockets called *coginillos,* a most excellent contrivance for carrying a lunch or bottle, or anything to which convenient access may be desired. (Josiah Gregg, *Commerce of the Prairies*)

col, *m.* [<Sp. *col* (*f.*)] cabbage. (*Curre a la era y tráete unos coles.* Run to the garden patch and bring a few heads of cabbage.)

cola, *f.* [<Sp. *cola*] tail; *cola larga,* the devil. The term *cola larga* is also applied to a person who enters or leaves a room and does not close the door behind

him. *Cola de pato*, Terr. N.M. Sp., a kind of leather housing to cover the entire haunches of a horse, mule, etc.; *no pescarle la cola a alguno*, said of a person who is hard to contact, or find at home.

colcha, *f.* [<Sp. *colcha*, coverlet] bedspread; a homemade embroidered coverlet often used as a tapestry. See *cuilta.*
In Spanish, *colcha* means quilt, but the embroideries on wool obviously were not quilts. (E. Boyd, *Popular Arts of Spanish New Mexico*)

colear, *vb.* [<Sp. *cola*, tail] Col. and Terr. N.M., the action of overturning a bull, cow or heifer by grabbing the animal's tail while on the run on horseback.

coleo, *m.* [<Mex. Sp. *coleo*] a sport in which a horseman takes an animal by the tail and, while on the run, overturns it.

colero, *m.* [<SW Sp. slang *colero*] a comb, especially one with a handle-like end. The *colero* is carried in a back pocket, and hence may be linked to the word *cola*, tail.

coliflor, *m.* [<Sp. *coliflor* (*f.*)] bot., cauliflower. (*A la Rufina no le gusta el coliflor.* Rufina doesn't like cauliflower.)

colita, *f.* [<Sp. dim. of *cola*, tail] bot., a plant of the Buckwheat family.

colmar, *vb.* [<Sp. *colmar*, to fill to the brim] *colmarle el jarro a alguno* (*El Melquiades ya me colmó el jarro con sus pendejadas.* I've had enough of Melquiades' foolishness. *A plato lleno lo colman.* Them that has, gits.)

coloquio, *m.* [<Sp. *coloquio*, colloquy] a religious folk play in dialogue form, written in poetry or in prose and with little or no plot.

color, *m.* [<Sp. *color*] *de medio color*, pink.

colorado, -da, *adj.* [<Col. N.M. Sp. *colorado*, vermilion (Molina)] red; redhead. Cf. Sp. *pelirrojo.* (*A m' papá lo llamaban el colorao.* People used to call Dad "Red.")

colorín, *m.* [<Mex. Sp. *colorín*, a kind of red seed] a kind of homemade rouge. Children are gay in white starched dresses and pink and blue stockings. The older little girls manage to steal enough *colorín* from their big sisters to imprint bright red spots on their cheeks. (Aurora Lucero White Lea, "Folkways and Fiestas," *New Mexico Magazine*)

coludo, -da, *adj.* [<Sp. aug. of *cola*, tail] *ratón coludo*, squirrel.

coluna, *f.* [<Col. Sp. *coluna* (Molina)] column.

collar, *m.* [<Sp. *collar*] *funda de collar*, sweat pad, as on a horse's collar.

comadre, *f.* [<Sp. *comadre*, ritual coparent] a term by which godparents address the mother of their godchild and by which the child's parents address the godmother. *La Comadre Sebastiana*, an image of Death in its skeleton form shown riding a cart (*carreta de la Muerte*) in Penitente processions. See *compadre.*

comal, *m.* [<Mex. Sp. *comal*<Náhuatl *comalli*] copper or iron griddle.
The stone or, later, copper griddle or *comal* and the iron trivet or *tinamaiste* were the principal hearth-side cooking devices. (E. Boyd, "Fireplaces and Stoves in Colonial New Mexico," *El Palacio*)

comancha, *f.* [<Plains Indian *Comanche*] Comanche squaw.

Comanche, *m.* [<Plains Indian *Comanche*] *Los comanches*, name of a Christmas skit in which the image of the Christ Child is kidnapped, supposedly by Comanche Indians (actually by villagers disguised as Indians). Also, a folk drama depicting the preparations for and the ensuing battle between Comanche Indians and Spanish soldiers in New Mexico (1870s).

comanchero, *m.* [<Plains Indian *Comanche*] Indian trader.

comelón, -na, *adj.* [<Sp. *comilón*] glutton.

comer, *vb.* [<Sp. *comer*] to eat; *comer con las dos manos*, to eat heartily, especially

at someone else's experise; *comerse a alguno por algo,* to pressure or bother a person for something. (*Ya me comen por su dinero.* They are pressuring me for their money.)

compa, *m.* [<Mex. Sp. *compa<compañero*] chum; friend.

compadre, *m.* [<Sp. *compadre,* ritual co-parent] a term by which godparents address the father of their godchild and by which the child's parents address the godfather. The terms *compadre* and *comadre* (plural *compadres*) are also used by parents-in-law when addressing one another.

companía, *f.* [<Eng. company] company. Cf. Sp. *compañía.*

complexión, *f.* [<Eng. complexion] complexion. Cf. Sp. *tez.*

complimentar, *vb.* [<Eng. to compliment] to compliment.

compostura, *f.* [<Sp. *compostura,* composition] carved cornice or crown decorating the top front of a *trastero* or cupboard; cosmetics, makeup.

comprender, *vb.* [<Sp. *comprender,* to comprehend] to hire; to engage, as by contract. (*El Celedonio está comprendido pa cuidar las borregas este mes.* Celedonio has been hired to herd the sheep this month.)

común, *m.* [<Mex. Sp. *común*] outhouse, toilet.

conciliario, *m.* [<Sp. *conciliar*] a kind of chairman of a Penitente council. It was the *conciliario* who opened a Penitente meeting; mediator.

concuño, -ña, *m.* and *f.* [<Sp. *concuñado,* a kind of brother-in-law] The term *concuño* explains the family relationship between two male in-laws married to sisters. Two women married to brothers are each others' *concuñas.*

concha, *f.* [<Sp. *concha*] shell; nickel or leather disc that forms a washer for saddle strings; silver or copper disc in the form of a shell used by Navajo Indians on belts; *hacerse a la concha,* to huddle up; to go to sleep; *trastes de* concha, chinaware.

conchabar, *vb.* [<Mex. Sp. *conchabar*] to come to an understanding; to talk someone into doing something; to get someone on your side; *reflex.,* to get married.

conchelle, *m.* [<Eng. conch shell?] dressed buffalo skin.

> **Conchelle** or **conchelli,** in New Mexican Spanish a masculine noun, meaning buffalo skin (dressed). (A.M. Espinosa, *Los Comanches*)

concho, *m.* [<Mex. Sp. *concho,* Indian] conch shell used in blowing to give signals; said of the person who walks in the heat of the sun without a hat; *maiz concho,* a kind of large grain corn used in commercial fried corn known as "crazy corn."

conchudo, -da, *adj.* [<Sp. *conchudo,* scaly] ill-bred person; shameless scoundrel; rogue (rare).

conducta, *f.* [<Sp. *conducta,* a number of mules or horses used to carry money from one place to another] Col. N.M. Sp., trade caravan; military expedition.

> **Conductas** were organized to go to Chihuahua, taking dressed deer, buffalo robes, sheep, tobacco, salt in exchange for luxuries of gold and silver, dress stuffs and confections, choice liquors and cheese. (Marie Dunn, "Thirty Families and a Priest," *New Mexico Magazine*)

conestipado, -da, *adj.* [<Sp. *constipado,* suffering from a common cold] constipated. See *constipado.*

congo, -ga, *adj.* [<Mex. Sp. *congo,* a kind of yellowish vegetable dye] *frezadas congas,* multicolored woolen blankets used as *subaderos,* or saddle blankets.

conocer, *vb.* [<Sp. *conocer,* to know] to know; to realize; to figure. (*Se estuvo dispierto hasta una hora que él conoció que la cabeza del borrego estaba ya asada.* He kept awake up to a time when he figured the lamb's head was already roasted.) To seek, as a wife. (*Este muchacho andaba conociendo mujer.* This

young man was seeking a wife.)

conquián, *m.* [<Mex. Sp. *conquián*] name of a card game.

conse, *m.* and *f.* [<Sp. *consentido,* pampered] a term of endearment used in reference to one's girl or boyfriend.

constipado, -da, *adj.* [<Eng. constipated] constipated. Cf. Sp. *estreñido.*

consuegros, *m. pl.* [<Sp. *consuegros*] a term used in reference to the in-law relationship among the parents of a married couple.

contado, *pt. part.* [<Sp. *contado,* enumerated] *echar de contado,* to tell someone off.

contesta, *f.* [<Eng. contest] contest; *contesta de belleza,* beauty contest.

contesta, *f.* [<Sp. *contestación*] answer, reply.

conti, *contr.* [<Sp. *con todo y*] together with.

contijoso, -sa, *adj.* [<Sp. *contagioso*] contagious. (*Es una enfermedad murre contijosa.* It's a very contagious disease.)

contimás, *contr.* [<Sp. *con todo y más*] let alone. (*Eso lo hacemos los probes, contimás los ricos.* We, the poor, do it, let alone the rich.)

contoy, *contr.* [<Sp. *con todo y*] together with.

> *Aunque tus padres me dieran*
> *los güeyes **contoy** carreta,*
> *no me casara contigo,*
> *ojos de borrega prieta.*
> Even if your parents gave me
> Oxen, cart and all,
> I wouldn't marry you
> With your eyes
> Like those of a black sheep.
> (N.M. Sp. *verso popular*)

contra, *f.* [<N.M. Sp. *contraria,* the opposite point of view or opinion] *dar contra,* to contradict. (*No le des contra porque se emperra.* Don't contradict him because he gets angry.) See also *contraria.*

contralanza, *f.* [<Sp. *contra,* against, and *lanza,* lance] a term applied to the extension of the pole under the box of a

wagon.

contralátigo, *m.* [<Mex. Sp. *contralátigo*] a kind of thong that holds the ring in the cinch of the saddle.

contrapecho, *m.* [<Sp. *contra,* against, and *pecho,* breast] breast roller in a loom.

contraria, *f.* [<Sp. *contraria,* contrary] opposite point of view.

contrarreata, *f.* [<Sp. *contra* and *reata,* lariat] a sort of rigging strap.

contrayerba, *f.* [<Mex. Sp. *contrayerba,* a medicinal plant] bot., Caltrop. *Arbolarias* have used the *contrayerba* as an antidote for almost any poison as well as to build up a person's blood.

convenencia, *f.* [<Sp. *conveniencia*] convenience; *pa su convenencia,* for his convenience.

convidado, -da, *adj.* [<Sp. *pt. part.* of *convidar*] to invite; *quedar convidado,* to have learned one's lesson. (*Vale más llegar a tiempo que ser convidado.* It's better to arrive in the nick of time than to be invited. [An expression said by a person who arrives at a place just as the table is being set for a meal.])

convite, *m.* [<Mex. Sp. *convite,* parade] invitation, in the form of a parade, to some public function (circus, dance, political rally, etc.). See also *gallo.*

A wagon was hitched, in which the **convite** for the *baile* started out. A fiddler, a guitarist, and a singer climbed into the wagon and rode around the three towns, playing and singing, finally coming back to the hall where the dance was to be held. This was the **convite**, the public invitation to the dance. (Cleofas M. Jaramillo, *Shadows of the Past*)

cónyugue, *m.* and *f.* [<Sp. *conyuge,* mate] consort, mate; *pl.,* married couple.

copa, *f.* [<Sp. *copa,* wineglass] drinking cup; *una copa de café,* a cup of coffee; *pl.,* drinks. (*Vamos a echarnos unas copas.* Let's have a few drinks.)

copete, *m.* [<Sp. *copete,* crest] *tener uno de algo hasta el copete,* to be fed up or dis-

gusted. (*Las tonteras del Celestino ya me tienen hasta el copete.* I've had enough of Celestino's foolishness.) See also *colmar el jarro.*

copetón, -na, *adj.* [<Mex. Sp. *copetón,* haughty] said of a hen or rooster with a large crest; conceited, haughty.

coqueta, *f.* [<Sp. *coqueta,* ferule] a kind of dangling earring adorned with jewels.

coralillo, *m.* [<Mex. Sp. *coralillo,* a shrub] bot., Red bearberry.

coraza, *f.* [<Sp. *coraza,* cuirass] a kind of saddle covering popular in Territorial New Mexico.

The *coraza* is a cover of embossed leather embroidered with fancy silk and tinsel, with ornaments of silver, and is thrown loose over the cushion and *fuste,* or saddle tree, the extremities of which protrude through appropriate apertures. (Josiah Gregg, *Commerce of the Prairies*)

cordillera, *f.* [<Sp. *corredera,* race strip] a street-like rural road with houses in a row along one or both of its sides. The term *cordillera* (*correllera* or *corrillera*) has been applied in the past to the row of houses along the *cordillera. Por cordillera,* by relays.

My grandfather, Don Vicente, bought part of the Arroyo Hondo grant and built for his family a big seventeen-room house, on the *cordillera* which connected the two main villages and ran along the edge of the lower ridge, flanked on the south side by the mansions of the *haciendados,* land and sheep owners. (Cleofas M. Jaramillo, *Shadows of the Past*)

cordón, *m.* [<Sp. *cordón,* cord] string, queue or line of people or animals; a round, braided gold chain, usually with the figure of a fish attached in the form of a pendant.

cormillo, *m.* [<Sp. *colmillo*] eyetooth; *enseñar el cormillo,* to bare one's fangs; *no dar ni cormillo,* to be exceedingly stingy. (*A burro dado no se le ve el cormillo.* Don't look a gift horse in the mouth.)

coronilla, *f.* [<Mex. Sp. *coronilla,* a flower of a climbing vine] bot., a plant of the Aster family (Blanket flower).

corregüela, *f.* [<Sp. *correhuela*] bot., Morning glory.

correr, *vb.* [<Sp. *correr,* to run] to dismiss, as from a job. (*Lo corrieron del trabajo.* They fired him.) To run, as for public office. (*Anda corriendo para alguacil mayor.* He is running for sheriff.) *Correrle caliente a alguno,* to be in a difficulty.

corretear, *vb.* [<Sp. *corretear,* to wander] to run someone ragged; to keep someone extremely busy. To correct school papers (<Eng. to correct). (*Se la pasó toda la noche correteando los tests.* She spent all night correcting tests.)

corrida, *f.* [<Col. Sp. *corrida,* flow, as of water] runoff; cattle ranch outfit; *corrida del gallo,* game of chicken pull; *corrida de argollas,* game on horseback in which a rider uses a lance to get iron rings (*argollas*) off a rack.

On San Juan day, July 25 [sic], the cowboys would stage some really exciting sport. The old Spanish game, *La Corrida del Gallo* (running the rooster), proved thrilling both to the cowboys taking part, and townspeople as well. A live rooster was buried in the sand up to its neck. Cowboys on their horses would choose sides, or teams, and each man in turn would lean low in his saddle as he raced past the poor rooster, seeking to pluck the fowl from its temporary grave. If the grab was successful, the fellow was off for a race, his team-mates protecting him from the onslaught of the opposing side, who sought a chance to get the rooster away from the rider and over their goal line. The winning team would later be treated to a dance by the losers. (Sadie L. George, "Frontier Town," *New Mexico Magazine*)

corrido, *m.* [<Sp. *corrido*] a popular ballad patterned after the Spanish *romance*

vulgar (popular ballad) of the eighteenth century.

corta, *f.* [<Sp. *corte,* cut] a small flock of sheep; a bunch of stray sheep.

cortada, *f.* [<Sp. *cortar,* to cut] a cut.

cortar, *vb.* [<Sp. *cortar,* to cut] *¡Córtale!* Cut it out! (<Eng. Cut it out.).

coruco, *m.* [<Mex. Sp. *curuco*] chicken louse. Also, *curucu, goruco* and *gorupo.*

cosa, *f.* [<Sp. *cosa*] thing; *cosa de,* about; *cosa nada,* hardly anything.

coser, *vb.* [<Sp. *coser,* to sew] *Cocer,* to boil, and *coser,* to sew, are confused in N.M. and so. Colo. Spanish. Both verbs change the stem vowel *o* to *ue* under the voice stress (*cueso, cueses, cuese, cosemos,* ———, *cuesen*). (*La Sirila cuese muy bien, pero yo cueso mejor con mi nueva Singer.* Sirila sews very well, but I sew better with my new Singer.)

cosijoso, -sa, *adj.* [<Sp. *cosijoso* and *cojijoso,* peevish, irritable] bothersome; having the qualities of a pest, a hanger-on.

costumbre, *m.* [<Sp. *costumbre (f.)*] custom. (*Tienen el costumbre de no contestar.* They have the bad habit of not answering.)

cotense, *m.* [<Mex. Sp. *cotense*] canvas; ticking. Also, *cotensio.*

cotilio, *m.* [<Eng. cotillion] See *cutilio.*

cotón, *m.* [<Sp. aug. of *cota,* doublet] jacket; *cotón de garra,* cotton jacket; *cotón de jerga,* heavy woolen sweater; *cotón de lona,* denim jacket; *cotón pinto,* Mackinaw; *cotones,* cotton goods; *no salir de cotón azul,* to be in the same rut.

cotonía, *f.* [<Sp. *cotonía,* a kind of cotton cloth] a cotton twill similar to cotton flannel.

coyaye, *m.* [<Tewa *coyaye*] bot., also known as *yerba de la víbora,* Rattlesnake weed.

coye, *m.* [<Tewa *coi*] lower apartment of an Indian multifloor dwelling. See also *soterrano.*

coyote, -ta, *m.* and *f.* [<Mex. Sp. *coyote*] said of the youngest child in a family; offspring of a mixed Anglo-American Indo-Hispanic marriage; native, of the country (*criollo*); *indios coyotes,* native Indians, i.e., from *Cíbola,* lands that eventually (after 1583) became the kingdom of New Mexico.

craqueado, -da, *adj.* [<N.M. Sp. *craquear* <Eng. to crack] chinked, cracked; crazy; silly.

craques, *f. pl.* [<Eng. crackers] soda crackers.

creido [kréido], -da, *adj.* [<Sp. *creído* <*creer,* to believe] candid; easily duped, naive; conceited.

cresta, *f.* [<Sp. *cresta,* crest] comb, as on a rooster; *picarle la cresta a alguno,* to irritate; to tease.

crestón, *m.* [<Sp. *cresta,* crest] hillock; summit.

criadillas, *f. pl.* [<Mex. Sp. *criadillas*] Rocky Mountain oysters.

criador, *m.* [<Sp. *criador,* breeder] breeder, rancher.

crimen, *m.* [<Sp. *crimen,* crime] false witness or accusation, slander, outrage. (*Es un crimen lo que están haciendo con la plebe hoy día.* It's an outrage what they are doing with our youth nowadays. *Le levantaron un crimen.* They accused him falsely.)

criminoso, -sa, *adj.* [<Col. N.M. Sp. *criminoso* (Molina)] libelous, slanderous.

criollo, *adj.* [<Am. Sp. *criollo,* born in the Americas] native, homegrown; thoroughbred.

crisanto, *m.* [<Sp. *crisantemo*] chrysanthemum.

crismes, *m. pl.* [<Eng. Christmas] Christmas season; Christmas gifts or presents. *¡Mis crismes!* A greeting used at Christmas time among friends (Merry Christmas). *Darle sus crismes a alguno,* to give someone his due or comeuppance.

cristiano, -na, *m.* and *f.* [<Sp. *cristiano,* Christian] said of a Spaniard as opposed to an Indian; name for the Spanish language; *hablar en cristiano,* to speak Spanish.

critiquear, *vb.* [<Sp. *criticar,* to criticize] to find fault with; to criticize. Also,

tritiquear.

crochar [krošár], *vb.* [<Eng. to crochet] to crochet. Cf. Sp. *tejido de gancho.*

croche [króše], *m.* [<Eng. crochet] crochet needle. Cf. Sp. *gancho.*

crucifico, *m.* [<Sp. *crucifijo*] crucifix.

crucita, *f.* [<Sp. dim. of *cruz (crucecita)*] small cross; girl's name.

cruda, *f.* [<Mex. Sp. *cruda*] hangover.

crudo, -da, *adj.* [<Mex. Sp. *cruda*] applied to a person suffering the aftereffects of overindulging in alcohol.

crudillo, *m.* [<Sp. dim. of *crudo,* raw] raw, as in *cuero crudillo;* calf rawhide used in making thongs and leather shoelaces. See also *becerrillo.*

cruque, *adj.* [<Eng. crook] crooked; *m.,* crook.

cruz, *f.* [<Sp. *cruz,* cross] *¡Póngote las cruces!* An expression used in conjunction with the sign of the cross to conjure or show amazement.

cuaco, -ca, *adj.* [<N.M. Sp. *chacuaco,* of little or no use] flimsy.

cuacha, *f.* [<unknown origin] sheep; sheep camp.

cuacho, -cha, *adj.* [<Mex. Sp. *cuachalote,* sloppy] short, uneven; said of a fowl when some of its feathers have been plucked out; *unas naguas cuachas,* uneven skirts.

cuajar, *vb.* [<Sp. *cuajar*] to jell or crystallize. *¡Eso no cuaja!* You are fibbing! I can't believe that!

¡Cuándo!, *interj.* [<Am. Sp. *¡Cuándo!,* Impossible! Never!] comment denoting skepticism; *m.,* a type of popular song with a refrain that ends with the *interj., ¡Cuándo!*

> . . . *éste sí no tiene fin* [*el chapulín*]
> *con todo viene acabando*
> *habrá otro animal sutil,*
> *pero ya como éste, ¡Cuándo!*
> This one [the grasshopper] knows no limits;
> It is eating everything;
> There might be insects more subtle,
> But like this one—Impossible!

(*Cuando de 1905,* N.M. Sp. folk poem)

cuanto, *adj.* [<Sp. *cuanto,* whatever] *de cuanto hay,* old-fashioned, old; *un túnico de cuanto hay,* an old-fashioned dress.

cuara, *m.* [<Eng. quarter] twenty-five cent coin; *caer cuara,* to be disagreeable or unpleasant. See also *peseta.*

cuaresmales, *m. pl.* [<Sp. *cuaresmal,* Lenten] Lenten dishes.

The Lenten days of penance become feast days of the palate. Housewives vie with each other in concocting *los cuaresmales,* Lenten dishes. On these days too, the true western hospitality is at its best. By eleven o'clock and until noon children go from house to house with a saucer of *sopa,* with a plate of *enchilada,* with a cup of *atole* that "mother made and hopes you enjoy it." (Margaret Abreu, "In the New Mexico Kitchen," *New Mexico Magazine*)

cuartear, *vb.* [<Sp. *cuartear,* to split into pieces] to remove the fat from pork.

cuartilla, *f.* [<Sp. *cuartilla,* fourth part of an *arroba*] Col. and Terr. N.M. Sp., a Mexican coin worth three *centavos* or one fourth of a *real.*

cuarto, *m.* [<Sp. *cuarto,* room] *cuarto de recibo,* living room; six-hour shift.

cuartón, *m.* [<Sp. *cuartón,* beam] log; sawlog.

cuartoneador, *m.* [<N.M. Sp. *cuartón,* log] logger. Also, *cuartonero.*

cuasi, *adv.* [<Col. N.M. Sp. *cuasi*] almost.

cuate, -ta, *m.* and *f.* [<Mex. Sp. *cuate*<Náhuatl *coatl,* snake] twin; chum, friend, pal.

cuatezón, *m.* [<Mex. Sp. *cuatezón*] chum, friend, pal.

cuatro, *adj.* [<Sp. *cuatro,* four] *pegar en cuatro,* to be hitting on all four (cylinders); in top shape.

cubo, *m.* [<Sp. *cubo,* bucket] *cubo de camino,* culvert; box in an irrigation ditch to form an outlet. (*Como los cubos de noria, unos suben y otros bajan,* an observation on the ups and downs of life.)

cucaracha, *f.* [<Mex. Sp. *cucaracha,* an old car] jalopy.

cucuy, *m.* [<Mex. Sp. *coco,* bogeyman, and *¡Uy!,* an expression denoting fright] bogeyman.

cucharita, *f.* [<Sp. dim. of *cuchara,* spoon] teaspoon; shoehorn.

cuchilla, *f.* [<Am. Sp. *cuchilla*] a strip of land or hill with one end narrower than the other; cliff.

cudicia, *f.* [<Col. N.M. Sp. *cudicia* (Molina)] covetousness, avarice; greed.

cuello, *m.* [<Sp. *cuello*] collar, as of a shirt; *bajarle el cuello a alguien,* to cut someone down to size; *pararse uno el cuello,* to put on airs; to think oneself superior to others; to show off.

cuenda, *f.* [<Sp. *cuenda,* end of a skein of silk or yarn] cord, string. (*Por la cuenda se devana la madeja,* an observation that a sample of a thing shows what the rest is like.) Cf. Sp. *Por el hilo se saca el ovillo.*

cuento, *m.* [<Sp. *cuento,* fairytale] folktale; *cuento de nunca acabar,* an endless story; the same old story (excuse).

cuera, *f.* [<Sp. *cuera,* a kind of leather jacket] a wide leather belt or sash placed around a donkey's rump in order to hold down the saddle; girl friend; *adj.,* good-looking.

cuerda, *f.* [<Sp. *cuerda,* cord] small whip used by Penitentes.

cueritos, *m. pl.* [<Sp. dim. of *cuero,* hide, skin] strips of pigskin after removal of the fat; bacon rinds, pork skins.

cuero, *m.* [<Sp. *cuero*] hide; *cuero congo,* leather strips (thongs) used for shoelaces; *cuero crudillo,* rawhide taken from the body of an animal dying of natural causes, i.e., not butchered. *Cuero crudillo* is soaked in water until softened and is used in the making of Indian-type moccasins called *teguas; adj.,* good-looking.

cuerpo, *m.* [<Sp. *cuerpo,* bodice] blouse (general). Cf. Sp. *blusa. Cuerpo de Educación,* Board of Education; *Cuerpo de Sanidad,* Board of Health; *en cuerpo,* uncovered.

cuerpoespín, *m.* [<Sp. *puerco espín*] porcupine. For other cases of metathesis see *carroferril (ferrocarril)* and *patarrabo (taparrabo).*

cuete, *m.* [<Mex. Sp. *cuete*<Sp. *cohete*] firecracker; pistol; fig., nothing. (*No le des ni cuete.* Don't give him anything.) *¡Come cuetes!* Go to blazes! The heck with you! *Andar* or *estar cuete,* to be drunk; *ponerse uno cuete,* to get drunk.

cuetear, *vb.* [<Mex. Sp. *cuetear*] to pistol whip; to shoot someone.

cuilta, *f.* [<Eng. quilt] homemade quilt; comforter, quilt. Cf. Sp. *colcha* and N.M. Sp. *colcha.*

cuipas, *f. pl.* [<Mex. Sp. *cuipó* or *cuipú,* a medicinal plant] shavings or thin slices of cedar or juniper bark.

New Mexican *médicas* are sometimes called upon to cure *hervor de sangre* (skin rash presumably caused by blood pressure). When this occasion arises, they boil two heaping handfuls of **cuipa** *de sabina* in a quart of water, strain the liquid when it has cooled, and add a teaspoonful of soda and a tablespoonful of salt. They sponge the entire body of the patient with this solution, and prescribe a complete rest until the itching, through this treatment, has disappeared. (Leonora S. M. Curtin, *Healing Herbs of the Upper Rio Grande*)

culantro, *m.* [<Col. N.M. Sp. *culantro* (Molina)] coriander. (Mod. Sp. *cilantro* is not a common term in New Mexico and southern Colorado.) Fig., anus, backside. (*Bueno es culantro pero no tanto,* a proverb recommending that one not do a thing to excess.)

culeco, -ca, *adj.* [<Sp. *clueco* (metathesis)] broody; *gallina culeca,* brooding hen.

> *La tuerta* **culeca**
> *pasó por aquí,*
> *convidando*
> *a todos sus amos,*
> *menos a mí.*
> The one-eyed brooding hen
> Just went by here;

She invited all her masters
All except me.
(N.M. and so. Colo. Sp. nursery rhyme)

culimpinado, -da, *adj.* [<Mex. Sp. *culimpinar*] on all fours.

culimpinarse, *vb.* [<Mex. Sp. *culimpinarse*] to get on all fours.

culo, *m.* [<Sp. *culo,* backside] anus (taboo); female organ (taboo); *ser culo una persona,* to be an ass. (*No seas culo.* Don't be an ass.)

culumpinado, -da, *adj.* See *culimpinado.*

cumanche, -cha, *m.* and *f. Comanche,* var.

cuna, *f.* [<Sp. *cuna*] cradle; name of a N.M. and so. Colo. folk dance featuring the holding of arms by two couples to simulate the rocking of a *cuna* or cradle.

cuncoso, -sa, *adj.* [<N.M. Sp. *cunques*] full of bran, crumbs or coffee grounds. (*¡Hi, qué café tan cuncoso!* This coffee is nothing but coffee grounds!)

cunques, *m. pl.* [<Zuni *cunques,* bits of corn (or cornmeal) used for ceremonial purposes] dregs; coffee grounds; crumbs; *cunques de la manteca,* bacon drippings; *tortillas cunques,* ground corn tortillas.

¿Qué andas buscando, gallina ciega?
Cunques *pa mis pollitos;*
¿Quése los pollitos?
Están debajo 'e la artesa.
What are you looking for,
Oh, blind hen?
Crumbs for my little chicks;
Where are your chicks?
They are under the wooden bowl.
(N.M. and so. Colo. Sp. children's rhyme)

cuña, *f.* [<Sp. *cuña*] wedge; *ser mala cuña,* to be a bad influence. (*No hay peor cuña que la del mismo palo,* a *dicho* or proverb pointing out that there is no worse enemy than a former friend [or relative] who has turned against a person.)

cuñado, -da, *adj.* [<Sp. *cuñado*] chum, friend, pal; protégé.

cuque, *m.* [<Eng. cookie] female organ (taboo).

cuques, *m. pl.* [<Eng. cookies] cookies.

curado, -da, *adj.* [<Sp. *curar,* to cure] "burnt," as in having learned one's lesson; *quedar curado,* to laugh exceedingly (slang).

curandero, -ra, *m.* and *f.* [<Sp. *curar,* to cure] healer; folk practitioner specializing in the use of home remedies and herbs.

Although folk medicine is in general known by all members of a cultural group, some persons, because of age, experience, or special interest, may have a more extensive knowledge than their neighbors and friends and thus acquire a somewhat specialized status. The *partera,* or midwife, is an example of such a person. In the field of general medicine, *médicas* and **curanderas,** whose knowledge of herbs and household remedies is somewhat greater than that of the general population, perform a similar function, being called upon for assistance when a medical problem gets beyond the competence of the patient or his relatives. None of them, of course, is a specialist in the Anglo sense of having a specialized kind of training and being given distinctive, formal recognition (licensure) for their skill. But they are specialists in the sense that they are considered to have greater knowledge of medical matters than other people in the population and perform a specialized function. (Lyle Saunders, *Cultural Difference and Medical Care*)

curco, -ca, *adj.* [<Am. Sp. *curco*] hunchbacked.

curcuspín, *m.* [<N.M. Sp. *cuerpoespín*] porcupine.

curia, *f.* [<Sp. *curia,* care, skill] ingenuity, skill; *ser de mucha curia,* to be fussy or fastidious, especially in the sense of being attentive to minute details; to be meticulous, industrious, painstaking.

curioso, -sa, *adj.* [<N.M. Sp. *curia*] ingenious, creative.

¡Curre!, *excl.* [<Col. N.M. Sp.<Galician Sp.?] Run! (*Curre, espanta ese chulo.* Run, chase away that dog.)

cursiento, -ta, *adj.* [<N.M. Sp. *cursio*] said of the person who is suffering from diarrhea.

cursio, *m.* [<Sp. *curso*] looseness of the bowels; diarrhea.

curuco, *m.* See *coruco*.

curvear, *vb.* [<Eng. to curve or throw a curve ball] to two-time a person; to cuckold.

curvia, *f.* [<Eng. curve] curve; shape. (*¡Qué curvias y yo sin brecas!* What curves and me without any brakes! [Admiring a female's curves.])

cusco, -ca, *adj.* [<Mex. Sp. *guzgo*] See *cuzco*.

cusquera, *f.* [<N.M. Sp. *cuzco*] See *cuzco, cuzquera*.

cute, *m.* [<Eng. coat (overcoat)] overcoat; *cute de agua,* raincoat; *cute de peluche,* fur coat.

cutilio, *m.* [<Eng. cotillion] an elaborate ballroom dance resembling a quadrille, with frequent changing of partners.

cuzco, -ca, *adj.* [<Mex. Sp. *guzgo*, gluttonous] greedy, hoggish; selfish, stingy; *m.* and *f., cuzquera,* stinginess.
> *Este se jalló un huevito,*
> *éste lo echó a frir,*
> *éste lo meneó;*
> *éste le echó sal*
> *y éste viejo* **cuzco**
> *se lo comió.*
> This one [one of the fingers] found a small egg,
> This one put it to fry;
> This one scrambled it,
> This one put salt on it,
> And this old stingy one
> Ate it all up.
> (N.M. and so. Colo. Sp. rhyme for a finger game)

Lo mismo es Chana que Juana.
(It doesn't make any difference.)

chacotear, *vb.* [<Sp. *chacotear,* to scoff] to tease; to flirt; to touch a person of the opposite sex. (*No se anden ahi chacoteando.* Don't be touching each other.)

chacotero, -ra, *adj.* [<Sp. *chacotero,* waggish] teaser, said of the person who flirts, touches or gets familiar with persons of the opposite sex; loud, noisy person.

chacuaco, -ca, *adj.* [<Mex. Sp. *chacuaco,* ugly, repugnant] flimsy; useless or of little use; unserviceable.

chacuaco, *m.* [<Mex. Sp. *chacuaco,* a species of elder] elderberry; the dark-bluish berry of this tree; cigar, cigarette (slang).

chacual, *m.* [<Mex. Sp. *chacual,* small leather basket] Col. N.M. Sp., gourd cup. *Chacuales* were lined with a vivid red color and decorated on the outside with flowers and foliage of different colors.

chacualear, *vb.* [<Mex. Sp. *chacualear,* to clatter] to make noise with the hands or feet while swimming or taking a bath.

cháchara, *f.* [<Sp. *cháchara,* chit-chat] idle talk; *hacer la cháchara,* to pretend, to make believe; *pl.,* junk, knickknacks.

chacho, *m.* [<Mex. Sp. *chocho,* a kind of locust] child-of-the-earth or Jerusalem cricket.

chaguaripa, *m.* [<Mex. Sp. *Sahuaripa,* a town in Sonora] a large straw hat.

chagüiste, *m.* [<Mex. Sp. *chagüistle*] a disease that affects certain grasses causing them to become yellowish brown.

chalán, -na, *adj.* [<Mex. Sp. *chalán,* garrulous, congenial] well dressed, elegant.

chalchigüite, *m.* [<Mex. Sp. *chalchihuite,* a kind of Mexican jade] turquoise.

¡Chale!, *interj.* [unknown origin, probably related to Eng. Charles, pronounced locally as *chales*] No! No way!

chalís, *m.* [<Sp. *chalís,* mohair] Col. N.M. Sp., a fabric made of goat's hair often

42

mixed with silk.

chalupa, *f.* [<Mex. Sp. *chalupa,* a canoe-like boat] jalopy; a kind of Mexican-style dish.

chamaco, -ca, *m.* and *f.* [<Mex. Sp. *chamaco,* child, kid] brat, child, kid; *los chamacos,* the kids.

chamba, *f.* [<Mex. Sp. *chamba,* odd job] job, work.

chambear, *vb.* [<Mex. Sp. *chamba*] to do odd jobs.

chamizal (*chamisal*), *m.* [<Mex. Sp. *chamizal*] sagebrush field.

chamizo (*chamiso*), *m.* [<Mex. Sp. *chamizo,* var. of *chamiza*] bot., Sagebrush; *chamizo jediondo, chamizo pardo,* vars. of Sagebrush; *chamizo blanco,* bot., Goldenrod.

champes, *m. pl.* [<unknown origin] the ripened fruit of a rose bush; rose hip; the yellow rose.

champión, *m.* [<Eng. champion] champion; *adj.,* outstanding.

champú, *m.* [<Eng. shampoo] shampoo.

chamuces, *m. pl.* [<Fr. *chamois*] women's moccasins; bedroom slippers.

chamuscar, *vb.* [<Sp. *chamuscar,* to scorch] to scorch on one side; to singe.

chamuscado, -da, *adj.* [<N.M. Sp. *chamuscar*] sun- or wind-burned; scorched; singed.

chamuz, *m.* [<Fr. *chamois*] bedroom slipper. See *chamuces.*

chamuza, *f.* [<N.M. Sp. *chamuz*<Fr. *chamois*] shammy skin or cloth; chamois. Cf. Sp. *gamuza.*

chan, *m.* [<Mex. Sp. *chan*<Náhuatl *chían*] bot., a plant of the Mint family used in the making of tea.

chanate, *m.* [<Mex. Sp. *chanate*<Náhuatl *zanatl,* ornith., a kind of black bird] black in color; a Black; black coffee (slang).

chancear, *vb.* [<Sp. *chancear,* to joke] to joke; to kid or to treat familiarly.

chancero, -ra, *adj.* [<N.M. Sp. *chancear,* to kid] said of the person who kids

around; congenial.

chancla, *f.* [<Sp. *chancla,* old worn-out shoe] an old shoe; any low-cut shoe; an oxford; *tirar chancla,* to dance.

chanclazo, *m.* [<N.M. Sp. *chancla*] blow with a shoe; *tirar chanclazo,* to dance.

chanclear, *vb.* [<N.M. Sp. *chancla*] to dance. Also, *chancletear.*

chango, -ga, *m.* and *f.* [<Mex. Sp. *chango*] monkey; name applied by northern New Mexicans to residents of the lower Rio Grande villages of New Mexico; *adj.,* clownish, foolish; *ponerse chango,* to take advantage of an opportunity.

changuito, -guita, *m.* and *f.* [<Mex. Sp. dim. of *chango*] small monkey; a term of endearment equivalent to English darling; boy or girl friend.

chante, *m.* [<Eng. shanty] home, house (slang); shack.

chanza, *f.* [<Eng. chance] break; chance; opportunity; a way out. (*Estos no dan chanza.* These guys don't give us a chance. *No hubo más chanza.* There was no other way out.) *Adv.,* perhaps. (*¿Van a ir ustedes? Chanza.* Are you going? Perhaps.)

chapa, *f.* [<Mex. Sp. *chapa*] lock (of a door); *darle a uno en la chapa,* to give someone a beating.

chapaneca, *adj.* [<Mex. Sp. *chapa,* heavy makeup, and *chapaneca,* short in stature] said of the woman who uses heavy makeup; *la chapaneca,* the bugbear. See also *máscara, pintureteada, payasa.*

chaparejos, *m. pl.* [<N.M. Sp. *chaparro,* shrub, and *aparejo,* gear] a kind of leggings made of leather; chaps.

chaparrito, -ta, *adj.* [<Mex. Sp. dim. of *chaparro*] short in stature; a term of endearment; shorty; boy or girl friend; sweetheart.

chaparro, -rra, *adj.* [<Mex. Sp. *chaparro*] short in stature.

chapeones, *m. pl.* [<unknown origin] name of persons in charge of the costumes of the Penitentes.

chaperito, *m.* [<N.M. Sp. dim. of *chapero*]

hat; a fancy hat; name of a New Mexico village.

chapero, *m.* [<Sp. *chapeo,* hat] palm-leaf or straw hat; worn-out hat; by extension, any hat. (*No salgas sin chapero.* Don't leave without your hat.)

chapete, *m.* [<Mex. Sp. *chapete,* a rosy spot on the cheek] smut growing on corn and wheat stalks; sexual intercourse (taboo).

chapetear, *vb.* [<Mex. Sp. *chapete*] to engage in sexual intercourse.

chapetonada, *f.* [<Mex. Sp. *chapete*] silver ornament on a saddle.

chapín, -na, *adj.* [<Sp. *chapín,* clog] pigeon-toed; crooked; said of the person who wears out his shoes on one side more than the other.

chapo, -pa, *adj.* [<Mex. Sp. *chapo*<Náhuatl *tzapa,* midget] short and squatty. Also, *chopo.*

chapolear, *vb.* [<Sp. *chapalear,* to clatter] to make a clattering noise with shoes that are too large for the wearer's feet.

chapucear, *vb.* [<Mex. Sp. *chapuza,* cheating] to cheat.

chapucero, -ra, *adj.* [<Mex. Sp. *chapucero*] cheat, cheater.

chapulín, *m.* [<Mex. Sp. dim. of *chapul*] grasshopper; insulting finger sign.

chapuza, *f.* [<Mex. Sp. *chapuza*] cheating; *hacer chapuza,* to cheat.

chaquegüe, *m.* [<Tewa] a mush or porridge made with blue cornmeal; the blue cornmeal itself.

chaqueta, *f.* [<Sp. *chaqueta*] jacket; *voltear la chaqueta,* to change sides in politics.

chaquetero, -ra, *adj.* [<Sp. *chaqueta*] said of the person who changes sides in politics.

chaquira, *f.* [<Mex. Sp. *chaquira*] beadwork; glass bead.

chara, *f.* [<Mex. Sp. *chara,* child?] ornith., meadowlark; male organ (taboo).

charchigüite, *m.* See *chalchigüite.*

charola, *f.* [<Am. Sp. *charola,* tray] baking pan; large bowl; serving dish; tray.

charolita, *f.* [<Am. Sp. dim. of *charola*] cereal bowl; *pl.,* Lenten dishes. See *cuaresmales.*

There was a great deal of exchanging done of *charolitas*—dishes—at noon both Holy Thursday and Good Friday. Neighbors and friends were seen carrying back and forth small bowls filled with *panocha, capirotada, torrejas,* or whatever other nice dish they had prepared. This exchange of special dishes went on in every small village during Holy Week. (Cleofas M. Jaramillo, *Shadows of the Past*)

charón, *adj.* [<N.M. Sp. aug. of *chara*] said of the man having a large organ; *m.,* large male organ (taboo).

charque, *m.* [<Eng. shark, a greedy person] hustler; *ser un charque,* to be sharp; to be "on the ball."

charquías, *f. pl.* [<Sp. dim. of *charcas*] Col. N.M. Sp., small pools of water.

*En veinte e siete del dicho, salimos de este parage e fuimos á dormir a la barranca, donde se volvió el caballo de Viruega, donde había unas **charquías** de agua honda.*

On the 27th of said month we left this camping site and went on to spend the night at the ravine, where Viruega's horse came back. There were some small pools of deep water here. (Gaspar Castaño de Sosa, *Memoria del descubrimiento*)

charro, -rra, *adj.* [<Mex. Sp. *charro,* picturesque] elegant, beautiful, as applied to clothes, dress, etc. (*¡Qué charro anda mi hijo!* How elegant my son looks!)

chas, *m.* [<Sp. *chas,* noise of wood cracking] *no dar de chas una cosa,* to turn sour, to go awry; to have an unexpected result; to fail.

chasco, *m.* [<Sp. *chasco,* disappointment] bad experience; mechanical failure; mishap; trouble; embarrassing difficulty; mess. *¡Qué chasco!* What a mess!

chascoso, -a, *adj.* [<N.M. Sp. *chasco*] trouble-ridden.

chatos, *m. pl.* [<Sp. *chato,* flat-nosed] pubic lice.

chaveta, *f.* [<Mex. Sp. *chaveta,* a kind of shoemaker's knife] *darle a alguno en la chaveta,* to beat up someone.

chavo, -va, *m.* and *f.* [<Sp. *ochavo,* a small coin] kid; boy or girl friend.

chavos, *m. pl.* [<Sp. *ochavos*] money in general.

chayote, -ta, *adj.* [<Mex. Sp. *chayote,* a kind of vegetable] sloppy, ill-kempt.

chayote, -ta, *adj.* [<Eng. shy] bashful, shy.

Chencha, *f.*[<Sp. *Hortensia*] *A lo que te truje, Chencha.* Let's get with it.

chequear, *vb.*[< Eng. to check] to check.

chequers, *m. pl.*[<Eng. checkers] checkers (game).

chere, *adj.* [<Eng. cherry] new; virginal; said of a girl who is a virgin. (*La Senaida está chere.* Senaida is a virgin.)

chical, *m.*[< N.M. Sp. *chico,*Chico bush] a thicket of Chico or Rabbit thorn bushes.

chicalote,*m.*[<Mex. Sp. *chicalote*<Náhuatl *chicalotl*] bot., a Prickly poppy plant with white flowers; also called *cardo santo.*

chicano, -na, *m.* and *f.*[<Col. N. M. Sp. *mexicano* [*mešikáno*], a resident of Mexico [*mešíko*], capital of the Aztecs] a Mexican American (loosely used term).

chiclano, *adj.* [<Mex. Sp. *chiclán*] said of the horse with only testicle or with only the epididymis. See also *pelilludo.*

chico, *m.* [<Sp. *chico*?] bot., Chico bush or Rabbit thorn, a shrub of the Nightshade family. See also *tomatillo.*

chicoria,*f.* [<Sp. *chicoria*] bot., Dandelion; Cankerwart.

chicos, *m. pl.* [<Mex. Sp. *chicales*?] specially prepared dehydrated corn used in flavoring beans, pork and other dishes.

chicharrones, *m. pl.* [<Mex. Sp. *chicharrones*] cracklings; the crisp meaty residue of hot fat. Cf. Sp. *fritada.*

chichero, *m.* [<N.M. Sp. *chiche,* breast]

brassiere.

chichi (*chiche*),*f.* [<Mex. Sp. *chiche,* mammary gland, breast] breast; teat; *dar chiche,* to breast-feed; *prendidos de la chiche* (or *de la teta*), feeding from the public trough.

chichigua, *f.* [<Mex. Sp. *chichigua*] wet nurse. The term *nodriza,* q.v., Sp. for wet nurse, is the common term used for an ordinary nurse.

chichigüite, *m.* [<Mex. Sp. *chalchihuite,* a kind of Mexican jade] turquoise.

chichincle,*m.*[<Mex. Sp.*achichincle*<Náhuatl *atl,* water, and *chichinqui,* sucker] fawner; flatterer; a hanger-on. Also, *chinchincle.*

chichón, *m.* [<Mex. Sp. *chichón*] lump growing or left after a blow (on the forehead, head, etc.). The term *camacho* is far more common in northern New Mexico and southern Colorado.

chichona, *adj.* [<Mex. Sp. *chiche,* teat] said of the woman having large breasts.

chiflado, -da, *adj.* [<Mex. Sp. *chiflado,* silly] angry, mad; childish.

chiflarse,*vb.* [<Mex. Sp. *chiflar*] to become upset or angry; to act silly, childish. (*No te chifles.* Don't act silly.)

chifleta, *f.* [<Mex. Sp. *chifleta,* innuendo] a hint; a sarcastic remark.

chiflón, *m.* [<Mex. Sp. *chiflón,* tube] flue; lamp chimney; stovepipe.

chifonete, *m.* [<Tewa?] Indian clown; said of an older woman who uses excessive makeup in order to give the impression that she is young. See also *achapanacada.* Cf. Sp. *carantoña.*

chiguata, *f.* [<Navajo *chiguata*] squaw; woman.

chihuil (*chigüil*), *m.* [<Navajo?] small valley.

chilar, *m.* [<Mex. Sp. *chile*] chili patch.

chile, *m.* [<Mex. Sp. *chile,* Náhuatl *chilli*] chili pepper; male organ; *chile caribe,* a kind of chili sauce made with raw chili peppers, garlic, salt, etc.; *chile 'e perro,* sty; *chile mango,* bell pepper; *chilepiquí,* a small, piquant red chili pepper; *chile*

puerco, bot., Pigweed.

chilero, -ra, *m.* and *f.* [<N.M. Sp. *chile*] chile vendor; tag applied by southern Coloradoans to Mexican-Americans from New Mexico.

chilorio, *m.* [<Mex. Sp. *chile*] a midnight supper at a *velorio* (wake), where the main course consists of a dish of red chile sauce with potatoes, pork, garlic, and salt.

chilote, *m.* [<Col. Sp. *xilote* [*šilóte*]] an ear of corn which is beginning to develop.

chillado, -da, *adj.* [<Mex. Sp. *a toda chilla*] fast; in a hurry; in a rush. (*Salió de aquí pero chillado*. He left here in a great hurry.) Angry, mad.

chimajá, *f.* [<Tewa?] bot., a medicinal plant of the Parsley family. Wild parsley. The *chimajá* has an edible root and a yellow flower.

chimal, *m.* [<Mex. Sp. *chimal*<Náhuatl *chimalli*, shield] Col. N.M., a homemade shield made of rawhide.

Chimayó, *m.* [<Tewa *tsimajó*, obsidian flake] N.M. place-name; Indian-type blanket; a detribalized Indian or *genízaro*, q.v.

chimayoso, -sa (*pl.* **chimayoses**), *adj.* [<Tewa *tsimajó*] rustic; countrified; a resident of the village of Chimayó.

chimolear, *vb.* [<Sp. *chisme*, gossip] to tattle.

chinadores, *m. pl.* [<Mex. Sp. *chinos,* curls] curling irons.

chincual, *m.* [<Mex. Sp. *chincual*<Náhuatl *tzinco,* in the anus, and *atl,* water] a kind of heat rash affecting babies; diaper rash.

chinchero, *m.* [<Sp. *chinche,* bedbug] place ridden with bedbugs; jail.

chinchicle, *m.* See *chichincle*.

chinchonte, *m.* [<Mex. Sp. *sinsonte*<*cenzontle*] ornith., mockingbird.

chinchorro, *m.* [<Mex. Sp. *chinchorro*] drove of animals; Terr. N.M. Sp., a small dragnet.

chinero, *m.* [<N.M. Sp. *chinos,* curls] curl-ing iron.

chinga, *f.* [<Mex. Sp. *chinga*] beating. *¡Qué chinga!* How disappointing! (taboo).

chingado, -da, *adj.* [<Mex. Sp. *chingado*] ruined; S.O.B. (taboo).

chingar, *vb.* [<Mex. Sp. *chingar*] to bother; to have sexual intercourse (taboo).

chingazo, *m.* [<Mex. Sp. *chingazo*] hard blow.

chingle, *m.* [<Eng. shingle] shingle; *techo de chingles,* shingle roof.

chingón, -na, *adj.* [<Mex. Sp. *chingón*] great; "out of sight"; spirited (taboo).

chinita, *adj.* [<N.M. Sp. *chino,* curl] rippling, applied to the surface of the water.

chinito, -ta, *m.* and *f.* [<Mex. Sp. *chinito*] an endearing term equivalent to English darling, honey, sweetheart.

chino, *adj.* [<Mex. Sp. *chino,* curl] curly, applied to the hair.

chino, *m.* [<Mex. Sp. *chino*] curl of hair; ringlet.

> *De los* **chinos** *de tu frente*
> *me darás para semilla,*
> *para acordarme de ti*
> *a todas horas del día.*
> Some of the curls on your forehead
> You will give me as a token,
> So that I will remember you
> At all hours of the day.
> (N.M. and so. Colo. Sp. *verso popular*)

chipe, *adj.* [<Eng. cheap] cheap, stingy. Also, *taite*.

chiple, *adj.* [<Mex. Sp. *chípil*<Náhuatl *tzipitl,* cry baby] said of the child who becomes sick upon being weaned, or due to the mother's becoming pregnant while still nursing the child; spoiled; *m.,* the next to the last or smallest child in a family. See also *coyote*.

chiquear, *vb.* [<Sp. *chico,* child] to treat somone like a child; to spoil or pamper; *reflex.,* to want to be begged or coaxed. (*Ya ella tiene con quien chiquearse.* She now has someone to spoil her.)

chiqueo, *m.* [<N.M. Sp. *chiquearse*] indul-

gence; caress.

chiqueón, -na, *adj.* [<N.M. Sp. *chiquearse*] spoiled; bothersome.

chiquero, *m.* [<Mex. Sp. *chiquero,* corral or stable] a small brush pen; pigpen; dirty place. (*El cuarto del Onofre parece un chiquero.* Onofre's room looks like a pigpen.)

chíquete, *m.* [<Col. N.M. Sp. *chíquete*<Náhuatl *chictli*] chewing gum; *chíquete de embarañada,* bot., a plant of the Aster family.

In May, small, yellow balls form on the plant **Chíquete de embarañada** (*Lygodemia juncla* Pursh) and the children gather them for gum. But, what is most surprising, these yellow balls turn bright blue when they are chewed and small boys can spit a nice long streamer at the family cat or sister's clean dress, or perhaps can scare mother a little into thinking they have been eating something perfectly horrible. . . . *chíquete de trementina,* chewing gum from the crystallized resin of the piñón tree; *chíquete güerito,* a kind of soft chewing gum made from the resin of the pine tree. (Leonora S.M. Curtin, *Healing Herbs of the Upper Rio Grande*)

chiquiao, *m.* [<N.M. Sp. *chiquearse,* to want to be begged or coaxed] a dance game during which poetic quatrains are exchanged by the participants.

chiquigüite (chiquihuite), *m.* [<Mex. Sp. *chiquihuite*<Náhuatl *chiqui-huitl*] bot., Osier willow rod; wicker basket.

Here, too, on All Soul's Day, gather the women of the pueblo, trim and comely in their festal best; each bearing upon her head a flaring rushen **chiquihuite** heaped with offerings, mostly grotesque-shaped little loaves of sweetened, well-shortened bread they have for days been baking in the outdoor *hornos.* (Charles F. Lummis, *Mesa, Canyon and Pueblo*)

chiquito, *m.* [<Sp. dim. of *chico,* child] baby. (*La vieja del Sarapio tuvo chiquito anoche.* Sarapio's wife had a baby last night.) *Hacerse el chiquito,* to act bashful or shy.

chiquitoso, -sa, *adj.* [<N.M. Sp. *chíquete,* chewing gum] sticky, applied especially to mud.

chiribí, *m.* [<Eng. shivaree] noise; noisy gathering or party; "where the action is"; excitement.

chirinola, *f.* [<Sp. *chirinola,* trifle] brawl; good time; excitement; binge, carousal; spree. (*El Maque anduvo en la chirinola toda la noche.* Mack was out all night on a binge.)

chirinolear, *vb.* [<N.M. Sp. *chirinola*] to go out for a good time.

chiripada, *f.* [<Mex. Sp. *chiripada,* chance] lucky break or stroke; *de chiripada,* by chance, by coincidence.

chirrión, *m.* [<Mex. Sp. *chirrión*] a kind of whip; *volteársele a uno el chirrión por el palito,* to get a taste of one's own medicine; said of something that backfires.

chirrionera, *f.* [<Mex. Sp. *chirrión,* bullwhip] a kind of snake.

chirrionero, *m.* [<Mex. Sp. *chirrión*] Col. N.M. Sp., mule driver.

chisguete, *m.* [<Sp. *chisguete,* spout] looseness of bowels; diarrhea. (*El Baldemar cayó aquí con chisguete.* Baldemar got here with diarrhea.)

chismolear, *vb.* [<Sp. *chisme,* gossip] to carry tales; to tattle.

chispa, *f.* [<Sp. *chispa,* spark] steel for striking fire with a flint; lighter; *ser uno muy chispas,* to be easy to upset or anger; *tener la chispa a la orilla,* to be very touchy or easy to anger.

Traditionally different, New Mexicans used the word **chispa** for the steel itself as well as for the sparks made by it or by a flame . . . The New Mexican **chispa** consistently was of iron, blacksmith-made and of elongated U shape, undecorated except for the incurved rat-tail ends. (E. Boyd, "The Use of Tobacco in Spanish New Mexico," *El Palacio*)

chispo, -pa, *adj.* [<Mex. Sp. *chispo,* elegant] dapper; elegant; well-dressed.

chisqueado, -da, *adj.* [<SW Sp. slang *chisquear,* to mess up] messed up; ruined; wrecked; badly off financially.

chisquear, *vb.* [<SW Sp. slang *chisquear*] to mess up, to ruin.

chiste, *m.* [<Sp. *chiste,* joke] joke, anecdote; folktale; trick. (*El chiste no es mear sino que el chorro haga espuma.* The trick is not to piss, but to get the piss to make foam.) *¡Oh, chiste!* You are kidding! *De chiste,* in fun, jokingly; *no tener chiste una cosa,* to be dull.

chistear, *vb.* [<Sp. *chiste,* joke] to kid; to joke.

¡Chite!, *interj.* [<Eng. shit] Heck! Shit!

chitear, *vb.* [<Eng. to cheat] to cheat (in school).

chiva, *f.* [<Mex. Sp. *chiva,* cocaine] cocaine; heroin; fink; *pl.,* belongings, baggage; *andar en la chiva,* to be working in a sheep camp; *meterle las chivas a alguno,* to pressure someone, as for payment of a bill, etc.; to sue; to make it hot for someone. (*El finance company le metió las chivas a la Dulcínea.* The finance company made it hot for Dulcínea.)

chivarrias, *f. pl.* [<Mex. Sp. *chivarrias*] kidskin chaps or leggings.

chivato, *m.* [<Am. Sp. *chivato*] seed goat; buck; rascal; S.O.B., villain.

chivito, -ta, *adj.* [<Sp. dim. of *chivo,* billy goat] mischievous; rascal.

chivo, *m.* [<Sp. *chivo,* male goat] male goat; S.O.B.; *adj.,* mean; mischievous; vengeful; *hacerle de chivo los tamales a alguno,* to deceive a person.

cho, *m.* [<Eng. show] movies, show. See also *mono, vistas.*

chococarse, *vb.* [<Col. N.M. Sp. *chocoque* [*šokóke*]<Náhuatl *xococ,* sour] to become sour.

chocolate, *m.* [<Eng. chocolate] chocolate candy; chocolate syrup.

chocolatero, *m.* [<Col. N.M. Sp. *chocolatera,* chocolate pot] a copper mug used for drinking cocoa.

chocoque [*šokóke*], *adj.* [<Col. N.M. Sp. *chocoque* [*šokóke*]] sour, spoiled. (*Esta leche está chocoque.* This milk is sour. *La güisa del Sammy le sirvió unos frijoles chocoques.* Sammy's girl friend served him some spoiled beans.)

chocoyle, *m.* [<Mex. Sp.?] bot., Violet wood sorrel.

chocoyol, *m.* [<Mex. Sp. *chocoyol*] bot., Watercress. Cf. Sp. *berro.*

chocroso, -sa, *adj.* [<Mex. Sp. *chocroso*] greasy, dirty, filthy.

chochita, *f.* [<Mex. Sp.?] bot., a kind of mountain grass.

chocho [*šóšo*], *adj.* [<Mex. Sp. *chocho,* pig] slow-moving; awkward; dirty, sloppy, unkempt.

chole, *excl.* [<Mex. Sp. *Chole*<*Soledad*] *¡Ya chole!* Cut it out! Enough!

cholejo, -ja, *adj.* [<unknown origin] carelessly dressed, ill-kempt, shabby.

cholla, *f.* [<Mex. Sp. *cholla*] bot., Buckhorn cactus; Cane cactus.

chombo, -ba, *adj.* [<Mex. Sp. *chombo,* buzzard?] *hacerse chombo,* to pretend ignorance for one's own convenience; to want to be coaxed or begged.

chones, *m. pl.* [<N.M. Sp. child's pronunciation of *calzones* [*kalčónes*], 'chones] panties.

chongo, *m.* [<Mex. Sp. *chongo,* chignon] queue-style hair worn by some Rio Grande Indians in New Mexico; *chongo* race, relay race held at Isleta Pueblo; *tabaco de chongo,* twist tobacco; *levantarse uno con el chongo atravesado,* to get up on the wrong side of the bed, to get up in ill humor.

chongudo, -da, *adj.* [<Mex. Sp. *chongo*] wearing the *chongo,* pigtails or braids.

chonguitos, *m. pl.* [<Mex. Sp. dim. of *chongo*] a dish consisting of goat (*cabrito*) intestines braided into a twist and fried in deep fat.

chonque, *m.* [<Eng. chunk] chunk, piece.

chonte, *m.* [<N.M. Sp. contraction of *chinchonte* (*sinsonte*), mockingbird] ornith., mockingbird; also applied to a

person who is always whistling.

chopo, *m.* [<Sp. *chopo,* poplar] bedroom slipper; rubber overshoe; *adj.,* short in stature.

choque, *m.* [<Eng. chalk] chalk. Cf. Sp. *tiza.*

choque, *m.* [<Eng. shock] shock; electric shock.

chora, *f.* [<Mex. Sp. *cachora,* a kind of iguana] male organ. See also *chara.*

choriz, *m.* [<Sp. *chorizo,* sausage] pork sausage; bologna sausage.

chorrera, *f.* [<Sp. *chorrera,* runlet] right of way or access space between two houses differently owned.

chorro, *m.* [<Sp. *chorro*] stream of things; *en chorro,* single file; in line.

chortes, *m. pl.* [<Eng. shorts] basketball or track shorts.

chota, *m.* and *f.* [<Mex. Sp. slang *chota,* fink, pig] cop, police officer; police force.

chote, *m.* [<Eng. schottische] a popular folk dance.

choteado, -da, *adj.* [<Eng. shot, ruined] shot; in a bad condition.

chotegón, *m.* [<Eng. shotgun] shotgun.

choza, *f.* [<Sp. *choza,* hut] house, hut; hogan; tepee.

¡Chu!, *interj.* [<Eng. Shoo!] used to scare away animals.

chuchear, *vb.* [<Mex. Sp. *chucho,* tattle-tale] to tattle; to fawn, to play up to; to cringe.

chucho, -cha, *adj.* [<Mex. Sp. *chucho*] affectionate; tattletale.

chuchulucos, *m. pl.* [<Mex. Sp. *chuchulucos,* knickknacks] knickknacks; small toys. Also, *chuculucos.*

chuchupate, *m.* [<Mex. Sp. *chuchupate,* a medicinal plant] bot., a kind of Wild celery; same as *oshá* in northern New Mexico, q.v.

chueco, *m.* [<Mex. Sp. *chueco,* crooked] name of a shinney-like game played with a ball and a curved club (*el chueco*). Cf. Sp. *chueca,* a cricket-like game. *Adj.,* twisted, crooked, bent.

chulo, -la, *m.* and *f.* [<Mex. Sp. *chucho?,* dog] cur, mongrel, mutt; dog.

chúmares [*súmares*], *m. pl.* [<unknown origin] underwear.

chupadero, *m.* [<Sp. *chupar,* to suck] a kind of cattle tick.

chupar, *vb.* [<Mex. Sp. *chupar*] to smoke. Cf. Sp. *fumar.*

churrete, *m.* [<Mex. Sp. *churrete*] smear (excrement).

churreteado, -da, *adj.* [<Mex. Sp. *churreteado,* spattered] dirty (with a dirty face); smeared with excrement.

churria, *f.* [<Mex. Sp. *churria,* looseness of bowels] prostitute; loose woman.

chutero, *m.* [<N.M. Sp. *chutear,* to shoot] troubleshooter; explosives expert.

chuzas, *f. pl.* [<Mex. Sp. *chuza,* move or stroke in a game of pool] Terr. N.M., a gambling game played with three billiard-like balls that were numbered. Also, a roulette-like game.

Communication was had with a large *sala* on which was to be found every kind of gambling game known in the West in those times, the principal games being *faro* and *monte,* and in the early days a game called **chusas,** the precursor of the roulette wheel of more recent times. (Ralph Emerson Twitchell, *Old Santa Fe*)

Dios da pero no acarrea.
God provides, but He has no special delivery
　service.
(God helps those who help themselves.)

daime, *m.* [<Eng. dime] ten-cent coin.
The names of American coins in cir-
culation are expressed in hispanicized
English: *cuara* (quarter), *daime* (dime),
dolar (dollar), *nicle* (nickel), etc. Occasionally *peseta* and *dos reales* are heard
for quarter, and *cuatro reales* for fifty
cents. *Tostón* (fifty cents) is common in
southern New Mexico.

dama, *f.* [<Sp. *dama,* lady] flower girl at
a *casorio* (wedding); maid of honor at
a dance.

danzada, *f.* [<Sp. *danza,* dance] a single
performance at a dance.

danzante, *m.* [<Sp. *danzante,* dancer] a
ceremonial dancer in the dance, *Los
Matachines.*

dañero, -ra, *adj.* [<Sp. *daño,* damage] destructive, as rats, coyotes, etc. Cf. Sp.
dañino.

dar, *vb.* [<Sp. *dar,* to give, produce] to
give; *a todo dar,* "cool," fine, splendid,
etc. *¡Dale!* Step on it. (Hurry.) *Darlas,*
to be all done in, exhausted; *darle al*
clavo, to hit the nail on the head; *dar
de chas una cosa,* to backfire; *dar en la
madre* or *en la torre,* to beat up someone; *darle a uno las doce,* to be unable
to stand a thing, to be in a bind; *no dar
pie con bola,* to be unable to find a solution to a problem; *dar calabazas una
mujer a un hombre,* to reject a man's
proposal for marriage.

dealtiro (*deatiro*), *adv.* [<Mex. Sp. *de
altiro*] extremely so. (*¿Se dañó mucho?
¡Dealtiro nada!* Is it damaged badly?
Extremely so!) *Deatiro,* terrible. (*¡Este
Roy sí es deatiro!* Roy certainly is terri-
ble!)

debasana, *f.* See *dobasana.*

decedido, -da, *adj.* [<Sp. *decidido*] bold,
daring, determined.

décima, *f.* [<Sp. *décima*] a ten or forty-
four line poem with various rhyme
patterns.

decir, *vb.* [<Sp. *decir*] to say; to match, to
harmonize, as an article of clothing
harmonizing with another. (*Ponte esa
corbata colorada para que le diga al vestido.*

50

Put on that red tie to match your suit.)

de cuanto hay, *adj.* [<Sp. *de cuanto hay,* of whatever there is on hand] old; old-fashioned. (*Un cute de cuanto hay,* an old-fashioned overcoat.)

de deveras, *adv.* [<Sp. *de veras*] really; truly; honestly.

dedo, *m.* [<Sp. *dedo*] finger; fink; squealer; *trabarle los dedos a alguno,* to turn someone down; to refuse (help, etc.).

dejar, *vb.* [<Sp. *dejar,* to leave] *dejar saber,* to let one know. (*Déjame saber.* Let me know.) Cf. Sp. *hacer saber. Por no dejar,* jokingly, in fun; not seriously.

delantar, *m.* [<Sp. *delantal*] apron; kitchen apron.

delicado, -da, *adj.* [<Sp. *delicado*] finicky, particular.

dende, *prep.* [<Col. N.M. Sp. *dende* (Molina)] since. (*Dende aquel día ya no ha vuelto.* He has not returned since that day.)

deoquis, *adj., adv.* [<Sp. *de oque,* gratis] free; gratis; unemployed. (*¿Qué razón me dan de la Colástica? Está deoquis la probe.* How about Colástica? She's unemployed, poor thing. *El Toribio me hizo el trabajito deoquis.* Toribio did the little job free of charge.) In vain, to no avail.

deputado, *m.* [<Sp. *diputado*] deputy; officer.

deputar, *vb.* [<Sp. *diputar*] to deputize.

derramadero, *m.* [<Sp. *derramar,* to spill] spillage; slope; sloping. Also, *redamadero.*

desafuciado, -da, *adj.* [<Col. N.M. Sp. *desafuciado*<Sp. *desahuciado,* despaired of] dejected, demoralized; frustrated, discouraged, sad.

desahijar, *vb.* [<Sp. *desahijar,* to wean] to wean (lambs); to weed.

desahije [*desáixe*], *m.* [<Sp. *desahijar,* to wean] act of weaning lambs; weaning time.

desaigre, *m.* [<Sp. *desaire*] slight.

desaigroso, -sa, *adj.* [<N.M. Sp. *desaigre*]

said of one who repeatedly slights others.

desapartar, *vb.* [<Sp. *des* and *apartar*] to separate. Cf. Sp. *apartar.*

desbarrumbado, -da, *adj.* [<Mex. Sp. *desbarrumbado*] dilapidated; in ruins; fallen or falling apart.

desborujado, -da, *adj.* [<N.M. Sp. *desborujar*] messed up, as a drawer, one's hair, etc.

desborujar, *vb.* [<Mex. Sp. *des* and *boruquear*] to search through a drawer leaving things in disarray; to mess up.

descalentar, *vb.* [<Sp. *escalentar,* to foment and preserve natural heat] to arouse sexually; *reflex.,* to become sexually aroused.

descalofriado, -da, *adj.* [<Sp. *escalofriado*] chilled; shivering.

descalzo, *m.* [<Sp. *descalzo,* barefooted] a kind of flatulence expelled without the usual accompanying noise. (*La Ursulita soltó un descalzo.* Ursulita dropped a silent rose.)

descansar, *vb.* [<Sp. *descansar,* to rest; to rest in peace] to rest; to recover from an illness. (*Y, ¿cómo está la Erminda? Ya descansó, ya anda andando.* And how is Erminda? She is well now and she's up and around.)

descanso, *m.* [<Sp. *descanso,* rest] shrine or rest usually marked by a heap of stones and a wooden cross.

The spot where Governor Pérez was killed is marked by a *descanso* or heap of stones surmounted by a cross, and may be seen a little to the right of the road as one drives from Santa Fe. (W.M. Berger, *Berger's Tourist Guide of New Mexico*)

descargado, -da, *adj.* [<N.M. Sp. *descargar*] discharged from the armed services.

descargar, *vb.* [<Sp. *descargar,* to unload] to discharge from the armed services.

descoger, *vb.* [<Sp. *descoger,* to expand] to choose, to select.

Una rosita de mayo

51

descollado

descogida entre millares;
entre más me estoy contigo,
más ganas me dan de estarme.
Loveliest of May roses
Chosen among thousands;
The more I am with you,
The more I feel like staying.
(N.M. and so. Colo. Sp. *verso popular*)

descollado, -da, *adj.* [<Sp. *descollar,* to excel] open; treeless, applied to a hilltop.

desconchinflado, -da, *adj.* [<Mex. Sp. *desconchinflado,* in disorder] unkempt, disorganized; silly.

descontarse, *vb.* [<Sp. *descontar,* to discount] to "split" or move away (slang).

descosido, -da, *adj.* [<Sp. *descosido,* ripped] said of a loose person who feels free and unattached.

descubrir, *vb.* [<Sp. *descubrir*] to discover; *descubrir el pastel,* to let the cat out of the bag; to spill the beans.

descuido, *m.* [<Sp. *descuido,* oversight] *en un descuido,* when you least expect it.

desdientado, -da, *adj.* [<Sp. *desdentado*] toothless or having a missing tooth.

desempeño, *m.* [<Sp. *desempeño*] act of redeeming a pledge.
It was the custom, when anyone danced for the first time, to take the person and carry him in arms around the hall. This was called the *amarre.* Before he was allowed to go, someone close in friendship or relationship had to redeem him. This redemption was the *desempeño.* The *desempeño* usually was a promise of a dance at a fixed date. (Fabiola C. de Baca Gilbert, *We Fed Them Cactus*)

desensartarse, *vb.* [<Sp. *desensartar*] to get out from under (fig.).

desfondingado, -da, *adj.* [<Sp. *desfondado,* with the bottom out or broken] said of a container (can, barrel, etc.) with its bottom out.

desgarratado, -da, *adj.* [<Sp. *desgarrado,* torn] raggedy, tattered.

desgotado, -da, *adj.* [<Sp. *escotado*] decolleté, low-cut (dress).

desgraciado, -da, *adj.* [<Sp. *desgraciado,* unfortunate] despicable; caddish; S.O.B. (taboo).

desguangüilado, -da, *adj.* [<Mex. Sp. *desguangüilado,* dressed in disarray] loose, as legs of a table; not firm.

desguanzado, -da, *adj.* [<Mex. Sp. *desguanzado*] faint, feeble, as a bedridden patient.

deshijadero, *m.* [<N.M. Sp. *deshijar*] lambing season; place where weaning of lambs takes place.

deshijar, *vb.* [<Sp. *desahijar*] to wean (lambs); to thin out (plants).

deshojar, *vb.* [<Sp. *deshojar,* to strip off the leaves] to husk, as corn. Cf. Sp. *deshollejar.*

deshoje, *m.* [<Sp. *deshoje,* the fall of leaves from plants] corn shucks (husks) used for *tamales,* "roll-your-own" cigarettes, etc.

desjaretado, -da, *adj.* [<Sp. *des,* to undo, and *jareta,* seam] tattered, ill-kempt; raggedy. (*No falta un roto para un desjaretado.* Every Jack has his Jill.)

desliz, *m.* [<Sp. *desliz,* slip or act of slipping] *desliz de nieve,* avalanche.

desmadrado, -da, *adj.* [<Mex. Sp. *desmadrado*] badly beaten (slang).

desmorecerse, *vb.* [<Mex. Sp. *desmorecerse*] *desmorecerse de risa,* to become blue in the face with laughter.

desmorecido, -da, *adj.* [<Mex. Sp. *desmorecerse*] blue in the face from excessive laughter or anger.

desocupado, -da, *adj.* [<Mex. Sp. *desocupar*] idle, unemployed, out of work.

desocupar, *vb.* [<Mex. Sp. *desocupar*] to dismiss or fire from a job. (*A la Solema la desocuparon del Mongomer.* Solema was fired from Montgomery Ward's.) See also *correr.*

desorillo, *m.* [<Sp. *des,* without, and N.M. Sp. *orillo*<*orilla,* edge] edging, as of a slab of wood.

despacioso, -sa, *adj.* [<Sp. *despacio*, slow] slow; slowpoke.

despadazar, *vb.* [<Sp. *despedazar*] to tear to pieces.

despanzurrado, -da, *adj.* [<Sp. *despanzurrado*] burst; torn, with the insides out.

desparachina, *adj.* [<Sp. *espadachín*, bully] said of the person who affects valor; garrulous. Also, *despadachina.*

desparecer, *vb.* [<Col. N.M. Sp. *desparecer*] to disappear. Cf. Mod. Sp. *desaparecer. Desparecer*, to send away, is used by Cervantes.

desparramar, *vb.* [<Sp. *desparramar*, to scatter] to spill (liquids). Cf. Sp. *derramar.*

despedida, *f.* [<Sp. *despedida*, farewell] a stanza in a ballad in which the composer takes leave of his listeners; name of a poetic composition in honor of a deceased person, or of someone leaving on a trip, going off to war, etc.

despedimento, *m.* See *despedida.*

despeletrear, *vb.* [<Eng. to spell] to spell. See also *espeletrear.*

desperficionado, -da, *adj.* [<N.M. Sp. *perfición*<Sp. *perfección*, beauty, grace] said of a person with a distorted face due to pain or anger; distorted; ugly in dress and physical appearance. (*La Sotelita está tan desperficionada que cuasi ni la conocía.* Sotelita is so changed [ugly] that I hardly recognized her.)

desperficionarse, *vb.* [<N.M. Sp. *perfición*] to make a mess of one's looks by trying to improve them, i.e., by putting on an excess of makeup or wearing something outlandish.

desplumado, -da, *adj.* [<Sp. *desplumar*, to deplume] *salir desplumado*, to come out or be defeated in a fight.

despostillado, -da, *adj.* [<Sp. *desportillado*] chinked, chipped, as glass, china, etc.

despostillar, *vb.* [<Sp. *desportillar*, to make nicks on a surface (paint, enamel, glass, china, etc.)] (*Este pichel está todo despostillado.* This pitcher is all chipped.)

desprender, *vb.* [<Sp. *desprender*] to unhitch (horses, mules); to detach.

desprovecido, *vb.* [<Sp. *desproveer*] lacking; deprived. Cf. Sp. *desprovisto.*

desquebrantar, *vb.* [<Sp. *des* and *quebrantar*] to break one's fast.

destapador, *m.* [<Sp. *des* and *tapador*, plug] plunger; corkscrew.

destartalado, -da, *adj.* [<Sp. *destartalado*, huddled] in disarray; topsy-turvy.

destemplamiento, *m.* [<Sp. *destemplar*, to distemper] *destemplamiento de cabeza*, headache.

destender, *vb.* [<Sp. *destender*, to fold] to spread, as a disease. This verb apparently has been confused with *extender*, to spread, to fan out.

destonado, -da, *adj.* [<Sp. *desentonado*] flat (music).

destornillado, -da, *adj.* [<Sp. *destornillar*, to unscrew] "nuts," silly.

destornudar, *vb.* [<Sp. *estornudar*] to sneeze.

destornudo, *m.* [<Sp. *estornudo*] sneeze.

destrabancado, -da, *adj.* [<Sp. *atrabancado*] careless, reckless.

destrampado, -da, *adj.* [<N.M. Sp. *destrampar*] free after being pinned down; shabbily dressed, in rags; drunken, drugged.

destrampar, *vb.* [<N.M. Sp. *des* and *trampar*] to free from an object that is pinning one down. See *trampar.*

destraviado, -da, *adj.* [<Sp. *extraviado*] stray; lost.

destripado, -da, *adj.* [<Sp. *destripar*, to disembowel] suffering from or having a hernia.

destriparse, *vb.* [<Sp. *destripar*] to rupture an intestine (*tripa*); to get a hernia.

desuciado (deshuciado), *adj.* [<Sp. *desahuciado*, given up] apathetic.

desvalerse, *vb.* [<Sp. *des* and *valerse*] to break a relationship with.

> *Carretita, carretón*
> *los que se valen al compadre*
> *y a la comadre y se desvalen,*
> *se les parte el corazón.*
> Little cart, large cart

Those who vow to be co-parents
And break the relationship
Will die of a broken heart.
(N.M. and so. Colo. *verso popular*)

desvelado, -da, *adj.* [<Sp. *desvelado*] deprived of sleep; having the qualities of a cad, wretch; euphemism for *desgraciado*, q.v.

desvestido, -da, *adj.* [<Sp. *desvestido*] undressed. Cf. Sp. *desnudo*.

desvestirse, *vb.* [<Sp. *desvestirse*] to shed one's clothes, to undress.

desviejar, *vb.* [<Sp. *des* and *viejo*] to get rid of old stock (cows, ewes, etc.).

detectivo, -va, *m.* and *f.* [<Sp. *detective*] detective.

devisar, *vb.* [<Sp. *divisar*] to descry at a distance.

devorado, -da, *adj.* [<Sp. *devorado*, devoured] in disarray, as a house; unkempt; mad, beside oneself with anger.

dexagerado, -da, *adj.* [<Sp. *exagerado*] given to extremes, said of one who overdoes things.

> *Mi marido es un hombre borracho*
> *y un hombre **dexagerado**,*
> *se mantiene en las cantinas*
> *sin penas y sin cuidado.*

My husband is a drunkard
And is given to extremes;
He is always in the saloon
Without worries or cares.
(N.M. and so. Colo. *verso popular*)

dexagerar, *vb.* [<Sp. *exagerar*] to overdo a thing; to overact.

día, *m.* [<Sp. *día*, day] *ir de mediodía pa abajo*, to be going down the drain, to be getting old. (*Ya la Toribia va de mediodía pa abajo.* Toribia is going down the drain [is getting old].) *Día de Acción de Gracias,* Thanksgiving; *dar los días,* to serenade those persons named Manuel or Manuela on New Year's morning.

> *Desde mi casa he venido*
> *con la nieve a la rodilla,*
> *a darle los buenos **días***
> *a Manuelita García.*

I've come from home

With the snow up to my knee
To say, "Good morning"
To Manuelita García.
(N.M. and so. Colo. Sp. quatrain from *Los días*)

diabla, *f.* [<Sp. *f.* of *diablo,* devil] she-devil; mischievous female. Cf. Sp. *diablesa.*

diablo, *m.* [<Sp. *diablo*] devil; *ser el mismo diablo,* to be as mean as hell, ruthless.

dialtiro, *adv.* [<Mex. Sp. *dialtiro*] extremely so; *adj.,* terrible, terribly mischievous.

diantre, *m.* [<Mex. Sp. *diantre*] imp, little devil; *adj.,* impish, devilish, evil, mean.

diasque, *m.* [<Mex. Sp. *diasque*<Náhuatl *diache*] excl. to express astonishment, surprise, etc.; *m.* and *f.,* devil, deuce.

diente, *m.* [<Sp. *diente*] tooth; *pegarle a alguno en el diente flojo,* to touch someone on a tender spot.

dientista, *m.* [<Sp. *dentista*] dentist.

dientón, -na, *adj.* [<Sp. *dentón*] having large, uneven teeth.

dieta, *f.* [<Sp. *dieta,* diet] postpartum period (40 days) in which the mother observes traditional ways of caring for her well-being (food, drink, sponge bathing, exposure, etc.).

diferenciarse, *vb.* [<Sp. *diferenciarse,* to differ] to disguise oneself; to appear different.

dijir, *vb.* [<Sp. *decir*] to say; to harmonize; to match. See *decir.*

dijunto, -ta, *m.* and *f.* [<Sp. *difunto*] deceased; apparition; ghost. (*Esa es la hermana de la dijunta Olivama Lasorda.* That woman is the sister of the late Olivama Lasorda.)

diluvio, *m.* [<Sp. *diluvio,* deluge] flash flood, freshet. See also *luvia.*

dioquis, *adv.* See *deoquis.*

dios, *m.* [<Sp. *Dios,* God; idol] *ser un dios,* to be very good at something; to excel. (*Este Palemón es un dios.* Palemón is certainly great.)

dipo, *m.* [<Eng. depot<Fr. *dépôt*] bus or

railroad station or terminal.

disconsuelo, *m.* [<Sp. *desconsuelo*] affliction, sorrow.

disflorear, *vb.* [<Sp. *des* and *florear,* to flower] to scan, as a road; to descry at a distance.

> *Me subí pa arriba 'el cerro*
> *a disflorear la ladera*
> *y alcancé a ver nítidos bultos*
> *y también la polvadera.*
> I went up to the hilltop
> To scan the hillside;
> I was able to make out
> Outlines of persons and dust clouds.
> (*Indita del Indio Victorio,* N.M. Sp. ballad)

disparar, *vb.* [<Sp. *disparar,* to fire (gun, rifle, etc.)] to pick up the tab; to pay for a round of drinks; to treat one's friends, relatives, etc. (*Esta vez le toca disparar a 'm primo Pantaleón.* This time it's cousin Pantaleón's turn to pay.)

disparate, *m.* [<Sp. *disparate,* absurdity] name of a folk poetic composition set to music. Other names for this type of composition are *mentiras* (tall tales) and *relaciones.*

> *Un ciego estaba escribiendo*
> *lo que un mudo decía*
> *y un sordo estaba escuchando*
> *pa platicarlo otro día.*
> A blind man was jotting down
> What a deaf-mute was saying,
> And a deaf man was listening
> In order to talk about it next day.
> (N.M. and so. Colo. Sp. *disparate*)

dispensa, *f.* [<Sp. *despensa,* pantry] storage shed; tool shed. See also *fuerte* and *fuertecito.*

dispensado, -da, *adj.* [<Sp. *dispensado,* excused] mentally retarded; idiotic, moronic. (*¿Quién se pone a decir eso? La Facundita lo dice. Sí, pero ella está dispensada.* Who has the temerity to say that? Facundita says it. Yes, but she's not all there.)

dispertar, *vb.* [<Col. N.M. Sp. *dispertar* (Calderón)] to awaken; to wake up.

dispierto, -ta, *adj.* [<Col. N.M. Sp. *dis-*

pierto] awake; knowledgeable; "on the ball."

diteria, *f.* [<Sp. *difteria*] diphtheria.

diversar, *vb.* [<Sp. *diversificar,* to diversify] to argue, as in a poetic joust; to converse in poetry.

divurcio, *m.* [<Sp. *divorcio*] divorce.

dobasana, *f.* [<Am. Sp. *damasana*] a kind of jug; a glass bottle enclosed in wickerwork.

doce, *f. pl.* [<Sp. *doce*] twelve; *darle las doce a una persona,* to be in a bind; not to be able to stand a thing; to get the urge. (*Anda más apriesa, Macedonia, ya me dan las doce.* Walk faster, Macedonia, I can't stand it.)

docena, *f.* [<Sp. *docena,* dozen] *representar catorce por docena,* to misrepresent; to represent more than one actually is or has. (*El Sabino siempre anda representando catorce por docena.* Sabino is always misrepresenting.)

dolar [*dolár*], *m.* [<Eng. dollar] dollar (*pl.,* dolares). The term *peso* (<Mex. *peso*) is much more common than *dolar.* (*Este cute me costó cien dolares.* This overcoat cost me a hundred dollars.) Cf. Sp. *dólares.*

dominita, *f.* [<Sp. *dominica?*] a tiny pillow-shaped sack worn by some persons together with their scapulary as a safeguard against evil.

dompe, *m.* [<Eng. dump] dump; dump heap. (*La Rafela y el Prudencio viven en un dompe.* Rafela and Prudencio live in a dump.)

dompear, *vb.* [<N.M. Sp. *dompe*] to dump; to break a relationship with. (*A la Nicolasa la dompió el Abedón.* Abedón broke up with Nicolasa.)

dona, *f.* [<Eng. doughnut] doughnut. (*Oye, Alfirio, anda tráete unas donas.* Say, Alfirio, go get some doughnuts.)

donado, *m.* [<Col. N.M. Sp. *donado*] a lay brother dedicated to a religious order without yet having taken the orders.

dormilones, *m. pl.* [<Sp. *dormilón,* sleepy head] bot., a plant of the Aster family.

dormirse

dormirse, *vb.* [<Sp. *dormirse*] to go to sleep; to solidify (cement, yeso, etc.). *Dormirse pidiendo,* to ask an exorbitant price for an item. (*Estos del flea market se duermen pidiendo.* These people at the flea market ask exorbitant prices.)

dos, *m.* [<Sp. *dos,* two] name of a playing card; name of one of the batons in the game of *cañute; dos por cuatro,* two-by-four (lumber); *en un dos por tres,* in a jiffy; right away.

drogas, *f. pl.* [<Sp. *droga,* artifice] *hacer drogas,* to cheat.

duce, *adj.* [<Sp. *dulce*] sweet; *papas duces,* sweet potatoes. (*Hicites esta sopa murre duce.* You made this pudding much too sweet.)

ducha, *f.* [<Sp. *ducha,* shower] douche. (*La Encarnación se dió una ducha durante su dieta.* Encarnación took a douche during her postpartum period.)

duende, *m.* [<Sp. *duende,* elf] dwarf; midget.

Dwarves (*los* **duendes**) are individuals of small stature, who frighten the lazy, the wicked, and in particular the filthy. The New Mexican idea about dwarfs is embraced in the above statement. The people express much uncertainty about the origin, whereabouts, and doings of dwarfs. (Aurelio Macedonio Espinosa, "New Mexican Folklore," *The Journal of American Folklore*)

durmilón, *m.* [<Sp. *dormilón,* sleepyhead] lazy person; a kind of nighthawk; also, a kind of stink beetle. Cf. N.M. Sp. *perrodo,* stinkbug.

durundún, *m.* [<N.M. Sp. *Juan Durundún,* onomatopoeic name] A children's game at Christmas time. Under the direction of an *agüelo,* a combination of bugbear and Santa Claus, children form in a circle and dance as they sing the song of *Juan Durundún.* Following is the chorus:

Baila, paloma
de Juan **Durundún;**
durundún, *dun, dun,*
durundún, *dun, dun.*
Dance, dove
Of John Durundún:
Durundún, dun, dun,
Durundún, dun, dun.
(*La paloma de Juan Durundún,* N.M. and so. Colo. Sp. children's game)

El que porfía mata venado.
He who perseveres goes far.

eclís, *m.* [<Eng. eclipse] eclipse.

echada, *f.* [<Sp. *echárselas,* to boast] boasting. (*Son más las echadas que las que están poniendo.* The brooding hens outnumber those that are laying [a familiar way of saying that a person is bragging].)

echar, *vb.* [<Sp. *echar*] to cast; to throw; to put out; *echar a alguno,* to kid, to make a person believe something being said (flattery, mostly). (*Al Aquino lo están echando.* They are kidding Aquino.) *Echar la plática,* to give a preaching to; *echar menos* <Sp. *echar de menos,* to miss; *echar por delante,* to get the best of. (*Los escueleros se echaron por delante a la mestra.* The pupils got the best of their teacher.) *Echar un chapulín,* to make an obscene gesture with a finger; *echarle a uno sus papas,* to give someone a piece of one's mind; *echarse un hombre a una mujer,* to have sexual intercourse; *echarse uno por la cabeza,* to let the cat out of the bag; *echar las cinco uñas,* to kipe, to steal.

echón, *m.* [<Sp. *echar,* to cast] the act of making someone believe something. (*¡Qué echón se dio Avaristo.* Avaristo certainly went for it hook, line and sinker.)

¡Echú!, *interj.* [<Eng. shoo!] expression used in getting a horse, mule, donkey, etc., to get going.

efectos, *m. pl.* [<Sp. *efectos,* goods] merchandise; *efectos secos,* dry goods. Cf. Sp. *telas.*

ejes, *m. pl.* [<Sp. *eje*] axle; *estar uno hasta los ejes,* to be up to one's neck.

elotes, *m. pl.* [<Mex. Sp. *elote*] tender ear of corn; *ciertos elotes,* you-know-who (when speaking of a person whose name one does not want to mention). (*Y, ¿cómo está ciertos elotes?* And how's you-know-who?)

embabucar, *vb.* [<Sp. *embaucar*] to deceive.

embanquetar, *vb.* [<Mex. Sp. *banqueta,*

57

embarañada, *f.* [<N.M. Sp. *embarañado* <Sp. *enmarañado,* entangled] bot., Cone flower, a plant whose leaves are chewed like chewing gum. See *chíquete de embarañada.*

embarañado, -da, *adj.* [<Sp. *enmarañado*] entangled, disheveled (hair).

embarañar, *vb.* [<Sp. *enmarañar*] to entangle.

embarrado, -da, *adj.* [<Sp. *embarrado,* plastered] soiled, dirty.

embarrar, *vb.* [<Sp. *embarrar,* to plaster] to smear; to get dirty.

embicionar, *vb.* See *imbicionar.*

embijado, -da, *adj.* [<Mex. Sp. *embijar*] soiled, dirty.

embijar, *vb.* [<Mex. Sp. *embijar*] to soil, as with excrement, mud, etc.

embocar, *vb.* [<Sp. *embocar,* to get into the mouth] to enter a place; to place a thing inside another; to hit. (*Embócale uno al Alfirio pa que se calle.* Hit Alfirio so he will shut up.)

embolado, -da, *adj.* [<Sp. *embolado,* with balls (*bolas*)] said of a bull with balls of cotton on the points of its horns. These balls are permeated with oil and set afire, causing a great deal of smoke, which makes the bull dizzy or drunk-like; drunk.

embolancia, *f.* [<Sp. *ambulancia*] ambulance; *ambolanza,* var.

embolarse, *vb.* [<Sp. *embolar,* to put balls of cotton on the tips of bulls' horns] to get drunk.

embone, *m.* [<Sp. *abono*] fertilizer. (*El Abedón le anda echando embone al zacatito.* Abedón is putting fertilizer on the lawn.)

emborucar, *vb.* [<Mex. Sp. *boruca,* noise] to confuse. (*Avarico emborucó a la Pancracia y le quitó dos suckers.* Avarico confused Pancracia and took two lollipops away from her.)

emborregado, *adj.* [<Sp. *borrego,* lamb] having the appearance of sheep in a flock; said of the sky with cirrus clouds; clouded.

> *Patio encharcado,*
> *cielo **emborregado**,*
> *sale un negrito*
> *culimpinado.*
> Patio full of puddles
> Sky full of clouds,
> A small Black comes out
> Walking on all fours.
> (*El perrodo, The Stinkbug,* N.M. and so. Colo. Sp. riddle)

embromado, -da, *adj.* [<N.M. Sp. *embromar,* to detain] detained. ('*M papá se quedó embromado en la plaza.* Father was detained in town.)

embromar, *vb.* [<Mex. Sp. *embromar,* to take someone's time with idle talk] to detain or delay; *reflex.,* to be detained. (*Rutiliano se embromó con el tractor y no pudo venir.* Rutiliano got tied up with the tractor and couldn't come.)

embromoso, -sa, *adj.* [<N.M. Sp. *embromar*] time-consuming; annoying, vexing. (*Este trabajo es muy embromoso.* This work is very annoying.)

embudo, *m.* [<Sp. *embudo,* funnel] funnel-shaped canyon.

After an hour had passed, an Indian, sent by the said don Luis, came to notify me that the inhabitants of this pueblo of Taos had been discovered and that they were in an *embudo* which is located in the center and at the entrance to the said mountains, on the peaks of which some of the said Taos rebels were stationed as sentinels. (J.M. Espinosa, *First Expedition of Vargas . . ., 1692*)

embutido, *m.* [<Sp. *embutido,* inlaid work] a kind of exquisite embroidery; *vb., embutir,* to embroider.

empacadora, *f.* [<N.M. Sp. *empacar,* to bale, to can] hay baler; canning machine.

empacar, *vb.* [<Sp. *empacar,* to pack in chests] to can (fruits, vegetables, etc.). Cf. Sp. *envasar.*

empadrinar, *vb.* [<Sp. *apadrinar*] to sponsor; to serve as godparents.

empalmar, *vb.* [<Sp. *empalmar,* to dovetail] to pile up.

empanaditas, *f. pl.* [<Sp. *empanaditas,* meat pies] small fruit or mincemeat turnovers.

empanturrado, -da, *adj.* [<Mex. Sp. *empanturrado*] satiated, glutted with food.

empanturrarse, *vb.* [<Mex. Sp. *empanturrarse*] to become glutted with food; to become satiated.

empanzarse, *vb.* [<Mex. Sp. *empanzarse*] to glut oneself with food; to become bloated.

empañar, *vb.* [<Sp. *apañar,* to pilfer] to catch, to apprehend.

empaque, *m.* [<Sp. *empaque,* packing] package; *parquete,* q.v., is a more common term.

emparejar, *vb.* [<Sp. *aparejar,* to get ready] to level, to smoothen, as a surface.

empatar, *vb.* [<Mex. Sp. *empatar,* to equal] to tie (a score). (*Los dos tiros están empatados.* The two teams are tied.)

empate, *m.* [<Sp. *empate,* equality] tie (as a score or game).

empavonado, -da, *adj.* [<N.M. Sp. *pavón,* pavement] paved. (*Ya la cordillera está empavonada.* The road is already paved.) See *cordillera.*

empavonar, *vb.* [<N.M. Sp. *pavón*] to pave (a street, driveway, highway, etc.).

empedido, -da, *adj.* [<Sp. *impedido*] crippled; bedridden; handicapped.

empegoso, -sa, *adj.* [<Sp. *empegar*] to cover with pitch (*pega*); applied to the child that insists on tagging along or "sticking" around when he is not wanted; hanger-on.

empelillado, -da, *adj.* [<N.M. Sp. *pelillo,* tender shoot of grass] said of the animal (donkey, horse, mule, etc.) that is weak and unable to perform due to having eaten nothing but *pelillo,* the tender shoots of grass.

empelotarse, *vb.* [<Col. N.M. Sp. *empelotarse* (Cervantes)] to undress.

empeloto, -ta, *adj.* [<Col. N.M. Sp. *empelotarse*] stark naked; undressed.

emperrado, -da, *adj.* [<Sp. *emperrado* <*perro,* dog] irritated, out of sorts; mad, angry. See also *enchulado.*

empinado, -da, *adj.* [<Sp. *empinado,* on tiptoes] bent; on all fours; slouched. (*Este baby le gusta estarse empinado.* This baby likes to get on all fours.)

empinar, *vb.* [<Sp. *empinar,* to raise] to knock down or out; to shoot down; *reflex.,* to get on all fours; *empinarse un hombre a una mujer,* to have sexual intercourse with a woman (taboo); *empinarse la botella,* to drink (liquor).

> *Tan, tan.*
> *¿Quién es?*
> *El Santiaguito de palo;*
> *¿Qué traes?*
> *Un preso.*
> *¿Qué delito cometió?*
> *Lo jallé comiendo queso*
> *y no me dio.*
> *Pues, la sentencia que le doy:*
> *Que se empine y le den una nalgada.*
> Knock, knock,
> Who's there?
> Little wooden St. James.
> What are you bringing?
> A prisoner.
> What crime did he commit?
> I caught him eating cheese
> And he didn't give me any.
> O.K. I sentence him
> To get on all fours and be spanked.
> (N.M. and so. Colo. Sp. children's game)
> *¿Qué está haciendo esa paloma*
> *sentada en esa 'zotea?*
> *Mirando los sinvergüenzas*
> ***empinarse** la botella.*
> What's that dove doing
> Seated on the rooftop?
> Watching the shameless rogues
> Drinking from their bottle.
> (N.M. and so. Colo. Sp. children's rhyme)

empinchado, -da, *adj.* [<Sp. *pinchar,* to

empincharse

prick or wound] annoyed; angry; upset.

empincharse, *vb.* [<Sp. *pinchar*] to become annoyed, angry or upset. (*No le piques la cresta al Fares porque lo haces empincharse.* Don't tease Fares, because you are going to get him mad.)

emplazado, *m.* [<Sp. *emplazar*, to cite before a judge] Col. N.M. Sp., fortified place; settlement; stronghold.

emponjado, -da, *adj.* [<Sp. *esponjado*] puffed up; inflated. (*Ahi va el Urbán emponjado como un torque.* There goes Urbán puffed up like a tom turkey.)

emponjarse, *vb.* [<Sp. *esponjarse*] to become puffed up or bloated.

emprendado, -da, *adj.* [<Sp. *prendado*, pledged] engaged to be married.

emprendimiento, *m.* [<Sp. *prender*, to seize] act of seizing the person representing Christ in an enactment of Christ's seizure by the Roman soldiers (N.M. Passion play).

empresario, *m.* [<Sp. *empresario*, agent] Col. N.M. Sp., a kind of land grant; grantee receiving the *empresario* or land grant.

emprestar, *vb.* [<Col. N.M. Sp. *emprestar*] to lend; to loan out.

empuercar, *vb.* [<Sp. *emporcar*] to soil. (*No vayas a empuercar tu túnico.* Don't go soil your dress. *Ya lo empuerqué, ya qué.* It's too late, I already did.) *Reflex.*, to get dirty. (*No te vayas a empuercar.* Don't go get dirty.)

empuyado, -da, *adj.* [<Sp. *puya*, goad] said of the person who gets a lucky break or improves his economic situation through a windfall.

enancas, *f. pl.* [<Sp. *en* and *anca*] butt, rump; *llevar a uno en las enancas*, to have one ride pillion.

enanchar, *vb.* [<Sp. *ensanchar*] to widen; to stretch. See also *estrechar* (<Eng. to stretch).

enantes, *adv.* [<Col. N.M. Sp. *enantes*] before.

enavegar, *vb.* [<Sp. *navegar*, to travel] to rove, to wander.

enca, *prep.* [<Sp. *en ca (sa de)*] at the home of. (*¿Ontá la Lisaida? Todos están enca mano Beno.* Where is Lisaida? They are all at old man Beno's.)

encaconado, -da, *adj.* [<Zuñi *cacona*] Col. N.M. Sp., wearing turquoise ornaments (*cacona*) on noses and ears. See *cacona.*

encajonado, *m.* [<Mex. Sp. *encajonado* <*cajón*, box] narrow passage or canyon; box canyon; *adj.*, boxed in.

encalada, *f.* [<Sp. *cal*, lime] job of whitewashing; *adj.*, whitewashed; said of females made up with a white homemade powder called *cáscara*, q.v. Cf. Sp. *encaladura.*

> *Al fin llegué a Santa Fe*
> *muy alegre y muy contento,*
> *sin nada de bastimento*
> *y todo el camino a pie;*
> *amigo, ¡qué fríos pasé!*
> *Y aquellas juertes nevadas,*
> *sufriendo güenas heladas*
> *viendo algunas cosas nuevas;*
> *De ahi pasé hasta Las Vegas*
> *a ver a las* **encaladas.**
> Finally I got to Santa Fe,
> Joyful and glad,
> Without any food
> And walking all the way.
> Friend, I sure was cold
> In those snowstorms
> And suffering from the cold,
> Seeing some new things.
> From there I went on to Las Vegas
> To see the white-faced women.
> (*La Severiana*, N.M. Sp. folk song)

encale, *m.* [<Sp. *encalar*, to whitewash] job of whitewashing.

encalmado, -da, *adj.* [<Sp. *encalmarse*, to be worn out with fatigue] parched with thirst. (*Probe muchito, llegó aquí encalmado.* Poor child, he got here parched with thirst.)

encalotado, -da, *adj.* [<N.M. Sp. *calote*, plaster of Paris cast] wearing a cast; *encolotado*, var.

encalotar, *vb.* [<N.M. Sp. *calote*] to put a plaster cast on.

encaminada, *f.* [<Sp. *encaminar,* to show the way] jaunt; pilgrimage.

Not only must they dance (the two oldest members of the village of Tortugas), they must take part in the **encaminada,** the pilgrimage to the summit of the mountain where an image of the Virgin lies hidden in a cave. (Margaret Page Hood, "The Day of the Virgin," *New Mexico Magazine*)

encaminar, *vb.* [<Sp. *encaminar,* to guide] to accompany someone a short distance; to show the way. (*La Apolonia ya se va; curre encamínala.* Apolonia is leaving; go with her a part of the way.)

encamorrado, -da, *adj.* [<Sp. *encamorrarse,* to embroil oneself in a dispute] drowsy; sleepy.

encanar, *vb.* [<Sp. *canas,* gray hair] to get gray hair; to grow old.

encandilado, -da, *adj.* [<Sp. *encandilado*] dazzled (with strong lights); crazy, "nuts"; dazed. (*Aquí estuvo la encandilada de la Maclovia.* Crazy Maclovia was here.)

encanicado, -da, *adj.* [<unknown origin] madly in love.

encanijado, -da, *adj.* [<Mex. Sp. *encanijado*] feeble, thin, weak. (*¿De quién es ese chulo tan encanijado?* Whose is that dog? He's nothing but skin and bones!)

encanillado, -da, *adj.* [<N.M. Sp. *canillas*] handcuffed; shackled. (*Al Meregildo lo llevaban encanillado.* They took Meregildo handcuffed.)

encarchado, -da, *adj.* [<Sp. *escarcha,* frost] covered with frost.

encargo, *m.* [<Sp. *encargo,* favor] *estar de ruego y encargo,* to be dependent on others, particularly with respect to transportation.

encarrujado, -da, *adj.* [<Mex. Sp. *encarrujado,* wrinkled] wavy or curly, applied to hair; bent down with age; stiff. Cf. Sp. *aterido.*

encartado, -da, *adj.* [<Sp. *encartar,* to outlaw] of mixed blood. (*Un chulito encar-*

tado de collie y German shepherd, a half-collie, half-German-shepherd puppy.)

encase, *prep.* [<Sp. *en casa de*] chez, at the home of. (*¿Onde va a ser el party? Encase Abundo.* Where is the party going to be? At Abundo's.)

encerado, *m.* [<Mex. Sp. *encerado,* waterproof canvas] a kind of window shade; an ointment made from tallow, candle wax, turpentine, *oshá* roots, and other ingredients.

encerrar, *vb.* [<Sp. *encerrar*] to enclose; to store away alfalfa, hay, straw, etc. (*¿Qués la plebe? Andan encerrando alfalfa.* Where are the kids? They are storing alfalfa.)

encimoso, -sa, *adj.* [<Sp. *encima,* above] with the qualities of a hanger-on, pest; bothersome, imposing.

encino, *m.* [<Sp. *encina,* bot., Evergreen oak] *encino roble,* bot., Live oak; Evergreen oak.

enciscado, -da, *adj.* [<Mex. Sp. *cisca,* shame] annoyed, angry; in ill humor; afraid. See also *cisca.*

encuentado, -da, *adj.* [<Sp. *cuentas,* accounts, bills] debt-ridden, said of the person who owes everyone.

encuentro, *m.* [<Sp. *encuentro,* encounter] *El encuentro,* a dramatization of the meeting of Christ and Mary during the Passion. *Llevarse de encuentro a uno,* to run over or drag someone along. (*Al Corpus se lo llevó de encuentro un caballo.* A horse dragged Corpus along.)

The Holy Friday processions are little different from those on Holy Thursday. At eleven in the morning a dramatization of the meeting of Our Lord and the Virgin during the Passion, *El encuentro,* is enacted. (Juan B. Rael, *The New Mexico Alabado*)

encuerado, -da, *adj.* [<Mex. Sp. *encuerado*] undressed; naked. Cf. Sp. *desnudo.*

encuerarse, *vb.* [<Mex. Sp. *encuerarse*] to denude; to shed one's clothes.

encuerdado, -da, *adj.* [<N.M. Sp. *encuerdar,* to overwind] overwound, as a

clock, watch, toy, etc.

encuerdar, *vb.* [<Sp. *en* and *cuerda,* winding] to overwind a clock, toy, watch, etc.

encuerdo, *m.* [<Sp. *encordar,* to tie with a cord] a cramp, as in a leg; a muscle twist; a charley horse.

enculado, *adj.* [<Mex. Sp. *enculado,* living in concubinage] said of the man having sexual intercourse with one particular female.

encumbrado, -da, *adj.* [<Sp. *encumbrado,* lofty (hill, mountain, etc.)] drunk, high in spirits.

enchagüistado, *adj.* [<Mex. Sp. *enchagüistado*] yellowish brown (grass).

enchagüistarse, *vb.* [<Mex. Sp. *chahuiste* or *chahuistle,* a disease affecting grasses] *enchagüistarse el zacate,* said of the grass that becomes yellowish brown with disease. See *chagüiste.*

enchancletado, -da, *adj.* [<Sp. *enchancletado,* wearing slippers] wearing slippers or shoes without socks or stockings; *enchancletarse,* to put on slippers (*chanclas*).

enchantado, -da, *adj.* [<N.M. Sp. slang *enchantarse,* to get married] married; living together without being married (slang).

enchantarse, *vb.* [<N.M. Sp. *chante*<Eng. shanty, shack] to get married or to live together without being married (slang).

enchilarse, *vb.* [<Mex. Sp. *chile*] to burn one's hands, lips, etc., when peeling hot chile peppers.

enchinado, -da, *adj.* [<N.M. Sp. *chinos,* curls, ringlets] said of the person wearing curlers.

enchinador, *m.* [<N.M. Sp. *chinos*] curling iron.

enchinar, *vb.* [<Mex. Sp. *enchinar*] to curl the hair; *reflex., enchinársele a uno el cuero,* to get goose pimples; *enchinarse uno el pelo,* to curl one's hair.

enchinchado, -da, *adj.* [<Sp. *chinche,* bedbug] angry, mad.

enchorrado, -da, *adj.* [<Mex. Sp. *chorro,*

line, file] in line; in a queue; in single file.

enchorrarse, *vb.* [<Mex. Sp. *chorro*] to get into single file.

enchulado, -da, *adj.* [<N.M. Sp. *chulo,* cur] angry, mad.

enchularse, *vb.* [<N.M. Sp. *chulo*] to become angry or mad.

endabita, *f.* [<Sp. dim. of *aldaba,* latch] latch. See also *andabita.*

endaime, *m.* [<Sp. *andamio*] platform, scaffold. See also *endamio.*

endame, *m.* [<Eng. dam] small dam to collect rain water for cattle; a *repres,* q.v.; a lining or casing in a well.

endamia, *f.* See *endamio, endaime.*

endamio, *m.* [<Sp. *andamio*] platform; scaffold.

ende, *prep.* [<Col. N.M. Sp. *ende* (Molina)] since. (*¿Ende cuándo están aquí? Ende ayer.* Since when have you been here? Since yesterday.) Cf. Sp. *desde,* since.

endeantes, *adv.* [<Col. N.M. Sp. *ende* and *antes,* long before] awhile ago.

endenantes, *adv.* [<Col. N.M. Sp. *ende* and *antes*] long before now; awhile ago; before; formerly.

endrogado, -da, *adj.* [<Sp. *en* and *droga*] drugged up; heavily in debt.

enferma, *adj.* [<Sp. *enferma,* ill, sick] *enferma de baby* or *de chiquito,* large with child, pregnant; *enferma de su tiempo,* menstruating.

enfermedad, *f.* [<Sp. *enfermedad,* illness] *enfermedad de los fríos,* malaria.

enfiestado, -da, *adj.* [<Sp. *fiesta*] enjoying a fiesta or celebration.

enfuriado, -da, *adj.* [<Sp. *furia,* fury] furious. Cf. Sp. *enfurecido.*

enganchado, -da, *adj.* [<Sp. *enganchar,* to hook] "hooked"; engaged.

engarruñado, -da, *adj.* [<Mex. Sp. *engarruñado,* shrunken] curled up, stiff, as with cold or from arthritis. (*La Albina tiene los dedos todos engarruñados.* Albina's fingers are completely curled up.)

*El día que salí de El Paso
no caminé muy contento,
pues no saqué bastimento
y de dinero iba escaso;
caminando muy despacio
por llegar a la Costilla,
al fin llegué a la Mesilla
después de pasar el río,
muy cansado y sin cuartilla
y **engarruñado** de frío.*
The day I left El Paso
I did not travel in joy
For I had no food
And was short of money.
I went on quite slowly
To get to La Costilla;
Finally I got to Mesilla
After crossing the river;
I was tired and penniless
And stiff from the cold.
(*La Severiana*, N.M. Sp. folk song)

engasado, -da, *adj.* [<Sp. *gas*] gassed up; very much in love.

engerido, -da, *adj.* [<Mex. Sp. *engerido*, cringing] stiff with cold or fear; shy, bashful, timid. (*¡Cómo es engerido este Epifanio!* Epifanio certainly is timid!) Sickly, sickly looking.

engrido, -da, *adj.* [<Mex. Sp. *engreído*, fond of<Sp. *engreído*, conceited] attached to (an object); fond of. (*La Zoila está muy engrida con su pony.* Zoila is very fond of her pony.)

engrirse, *vb.* [<Mex. Sp. *engreírse*] to become fond of or attached to a thing.

engrudado, -da, *adj.* [<Sp. *engrudo*, paste] dirty, soiled.

engrudar, *vb.* [<Sp. *engrudar*, to paste with *engrudo*] to get (a thing) dirty; to soil. See Sp. *engrudo.*

engualde, *adv.* [<Sp. *en igual de*] instead of. (*Engualde ir al venado deberías estarte aquí conmigo.* Instead of going hunting you should stay here with me.)

engüechar, *vb.* [<Sp. *en* and Eng. wedge] to wedge. (*Engüecha esa varilla para que puedas rajarla.* Put a wedge on that log so you can split it.)

engüerado, *adj.* [<N.M. Sp. *güero*<Sp.

huero, rotten, applied to an egg] said of the unhatched egg that becomes rotten. See also *agüerado.*

engüerarse, *vb.* [<N.M. Sp. *güero*, rotten] to become rotten (applied to eggs).

engüevarse, *vb.* [<N.M. Sp. *güevo* (Sp. *huevo* and related to *güevón*), lazy] to become lazy; to refuse to move. See also *amacharse.*

enguruñado, -da, *adj.* [<Sp. *engurriñado*, melancholy, applied to birds] curled up; stiff, as with arthritis. See also *engarruñado.*

enjarrado, -da, *adj.* [<N.M. Sp. *enjarrar*, to plaster] plastered.

enjarrador, -ra, *m.* and *f.* [<N.M. Sp. *enjarrar*, to plaster] plasterer; bricklayer; mason. (*La Colástica es buena enjarradora.* Colástica is a good plasterer.)

enjarrar, *vb.* [<N.M. Sp. *enjarre*, mud plaster] to plaster with a specially prepared mud or clay.

enjarre, *m.* [<unknown origin] mud or clay plaster; the act of plastering. (*¡Qué buen enjarre tiene esta pader!* This wall is very well plastered.)

enjengible, *m.* [<Sp. *jengibre*] ginger.
*El brandy es otro remedio
que llevando 'l interés
mézclenlo con **enjengible**
y échenle ahi tantita nuez,
pues yo me curé una vez,
se me jueron los dolores;
ni puetas ni cantadores
no dejen de conocer.*
Brandy is another cure
Which, if you're interested,
You can mix with ginger,
Adding a pinch of nutmeg.
Why, I cured myself once
And got rid of all pain.
Poets and singers
Know all this well.
(*La enfermedad de los frios*, N.M. Sp. folk song)

enjoscado, -da, *adj.* [<Sp. *enfoscado*, troubled] extremely out of sorts, infuriated, in ill humor.

enjoscarse, *vb.* [<Sp. *enfoscarse*, to become

63

uneasy, troubled] to become extremely infuriated.

enjotado, -da, *adj.* [<Col. N.M. Sp. *enxotado* [enšotaðo] put away in a corner] said of the person who stays home, away from school or work, and indoors, particularly in the kitchen; in the way. (*Y ¿quése el Franque? Ahi, 'stá enjotado en la cocina.* And what about Frank? He's there lazing around in the kitchen.)

enjote, *m.* [<Mex. Sp. *ejote,* string bean] *estar uno esperando que le traigan el enjote,* to expect others to wait on one hand and foot.

enlame, *m.* [<Mex. Sp. *enlame,* slime] scum; slime. (*Piedra movediza no cría enlame.* A rolling stone gathers no moss.) See also *lama.*

enlistado, -da, *adj.* [<Eng. enlisted] enlisted in the armed services. Cf. Sp. *alistado.*

enlistarse, *vb.* [<Eng. to enlist] to enlist. Cf. Sp. *alistarse.*

enmariguandado, -da, *adj.* [<Mex. Sp. *mariguana*] said of the person under the influence of marihuana; stupefied, dull.

enmojecer, *vb.* [<Sp. *enmohecer*] to rust. (*Ese cavador se va a enmojecer si lo dejas ahi juera.* That hoe is going to get rusty if you leave it outside.)

enmojecido, -da, *adj.* [<Sp. *enmohecido*] rusty. (*El Félique se ensartó un clavo enmojecido en un pie.* Félique stuck a rusty nail in one of his feet.) See also *mojoso.*

enmorecerse, *vb.* [<Sp. *esmorecerse* (Andalusia)] to become blue in the face from laughter or anger.

enmorecido, -da, *adj.* [<N.M. Sp. *enmorecerse*] blue in the face from laughter or anger.

enmugrar, *vb.* [<Mex. Sp. *enmugrar*] to soil; to get a thing dirty. (*No te vayas a enmugrar.* Don't go get dirty.)

enojada, *f.* [<Sp. *enojar,* to anger] fit of anger; quarrel. (*La Acasita y 'l Acorsinio se dieron una buena enojada.* Acasita and Acorsinio had quite a quarrel.) Cf. Sp. *enojo.*

enojón, -na, *adj.* [<Sp. *enojarse,* to become angry] peevish; easy to anger. ('*M primo Adonáis es murre enojón.* Cousin Adonáis is very peevish.) See also *nojón.*

enrabiatado, -da, *adj.* [<N.M. Sp. *enrabiatar,* to tow] towed; towed away.

enrabiatar, *vb.* [<Sp. *rabiatar,* to tie by the tail] to tow; to take in tow.

enraizar, *vb.* [<Mex. Sp. *enraizar*] to root; to take root.

enramada, *f.* [<Sp. *enramada,* bower] a kind of corral to trap wild horses; a fence made with tree branches. See also *ramieda.*

enranarse, *vb.* [<Mex. Sp. *arranarse*] to get married.

enredisto, -ta, *adj.* [<Sp. *enredar*] instigator, tattler.

enregistrar, *vb.* [<Sp. *registrar*] to register; to enroll; *carta enregistrada,* certified or registered letter.

enroña, *f.* [<Mex. Sp. *roña,* grudge] grudge; ill will, resentment. (*El Alarico y la Alcarita se tienen muncha enroña.* Alarico and Alcarita bear quite a grudge against each other.)

enroñar, *vb.* [<N.M. Sp. *roña,* grime] to dirty; to soil.

enroscado, -da, *adj.* [<Mex. Sp. *enroscado*] curled up, like a ram's horn or snake.

enroscarse, *vb.* [<Mex. Sp. *enroscarse*] to curl up like a ram's horn or snake.

ensartado, -da, *adj.* [<N.M. *ensartar,* to stick, to thread] stuck; threaded (needle). Cf. Sp. *clavar* and *enhebrar.*

ensartar, *vb.* [<Sp. *ensartar,* to string] to stick a thorn into; to thread a needle. (*Climaco se ensartó una espina en un pie.* Climaco stuck a thorn in one of his feet.)

ensarte, *m.* [<Sp. *ensartar,* to string] a line of things; a bunch; a series of things. (*Lo que dice el Amarante es un ensarte de mentiras.* What Amarante is saying is a bunch of lies.)

ensistido, -da, *adj.* [<N.M. Sp. *ensistir,* to

ensistir, *vb.* [<Sp. *insistir,* to insist] to insist; to tempt.

> *En el Río 'e Sapelló*
> *comenzó la suerte mía;*
> *¿Qué es lo que me sucedió,*
> *Virgen pura y madre mía,*
> *que el maldito me **ensistió***
> *a hacer tan grande avería?*
> In the River Sapelló
> My bad luck started.
> What happened to me,
> Oh, holy Virgin Mary,
> That the evil one tempted me
> To do such great harm.
> (*Indita de la Pablita,* N.M. Sp. ballad)

ensofiate, *m.* [<Mex. Sp. *estafiate*] bot., a medicinal plant. See also *estafiate.*

ensotado, -da, *adj.* [<Mex. Sp. *ensotado,* put away in a nook or corner] See *enjotado.*

entabicado, -da, *adj.* [<Mex. Sp. *tabique,* partition; jail] jailed; in jail; partitioned, as a room.

entabicar, *vb.* [<Mex. Sp. *entabicar*] to partition (a room); to jail (slang).

entarimado, -da, *adj.* [<Sp. *tarima,* movable platform] covered with a wooden floor. (*Un cuarto entarimado,* a room covered with a wooden floor.) *M.,* flooring.

entarimar, *vb.* [<Sp. *tarima*] to cover a floor with wood flooring.

entarime, *m.* [<Sp. *tarima*] flooring; wooden floor; platform.

entenga, *interr.* [<Sp. *tener,* to have] OK? Do you understand? Will you do it? (*Cuando venga el Secundino le dice que vaya a verme, ¿entenga?* When Secundino comes, will you tell him to go see me?) Also, *¿Tenga?, ¿Tengue?* and *¿Tengues?*

entengues, *interr.* [<Sp. *tener*] Do you hear? Do you understand? (*Dile a la Cleofas que vuelvo, ¿entengues?* Tell Cleofas that I'll be back. Do you hear?)

enterido, -da, *adj.* [<Sp. *aterido*] stiff with cold or fear.

enternecido, -da, *adj.* [<Sp. *enternecido* <*enternecer,* to move to compassion] stuck; in a rut.

enterrar, *vb.* [<Sp. *enterrar*] to bury; to sink (a post in the ground); *enterrarse uno una abuja, espina,* etc., to stick oneself with a needle, thorn, etc.

entibiar, *vb.* [<Sp. *entibiar,* to cool] to warm; to heat. (*Mira, Melquiades, entíbiame esta agua, está murre fría.* Look, Melquiades, warm this water for me; it's much too cold.)

entierro, *m.* [<Sp. *entierro*] burial; buried treasure.

entitulado, -da, *adj.* [<Sp. *intitulado*] entitled.

entitular, *vb.* [<Sp. *intitular*] to entitle; to give a title to.

entonación, *f.* [<Sp. *entonación,* intonation] air; melody, tune.

> Twenty-six of the hymns are sung to the accompaniment of an unnamed regional tune, merely described as *aire nacional* (national air), *canto nacional* (national hymn), *tonada del país* (a tune of the region), or *entonación mejicana* (a Mexican air). (J.B. Rael, *The New Mexican Alabado*)

entrada, *f.* [<Sp. *entrar,* to enter] Col. N.M. Sp., an exploring or reconnoitering military expedition.

éntrale, *imp.* [<Sp. *entrar*] start (eating, working, etc.); get started; go to it; begin; help yourself. (*Bueno, pos, éntrale.* OK, get started.)

entraña, *f.* [<Sp. *entraña,* entrail] bot., Buckhorn cactus; Cane cactus. See also *cholla, choya, velas de coyote.*

> The word cactus is taken from the Greek, *kaktos* meaning prickly plant, but the ***entraña*** is distinguished from the numerous varieties of prickly pear by its upstanding, erect stems, which, when completely dried, resemble a cylindrical piece of lattice work. These are sometimes gathered for canes, picture frames, or as

65

entriega

souvenirs and this probably accounts for its being called cane cactus. (Leonora S.M. Curtin, *Healing Herbs of the Upper Rio Grande*)

entriega, *f.* [<Sp. *entrega,* delivery] the act or ceremony of sponsors' (*padrinos'*) delivering a baptized child or a newly wedded couple to their respective parents; *entriega de bautismo,* baptismal *entriega; entriega de novios, entriega* of the newlyweds; *entriega de santo,* delivery of the village patron saint to the sponsors for the new year.

entrón, -na, *adj.* [<Mex. Sp. *entrón*] brave; courageous; determined. (*Este muchito sí es entrón.* This little kid is certainly determined.)

entrucharse, *vb.* [<Sp. *trucha,* trout] to get into a place (home, office, etc.), especially to meddle in someone else's business. (*El Abade se entruchó en mis negocios.* Abade meddled in my affairs.)

enyerbado, -da, *adj.* [<N.M. Sp. *enyerbar*<*yerba* (weed), to poison with a harmful herb] crazy, as a result of smoking marihuana or of having taken other drugs; also said of the horse that has eaten loco weed (*garbancillo*).

enyerbar, *vb.* [<N.M. Sp. *yerba,* weed] to poison with harmful herbs (*yerbas*) or poisonous powders. (*Al Crispiniano lo enyerbaron las güisas.* Crispiniano was poisoned by his girl friends.)

enzoquetado, -da, *adj.* [<N.M. Sp. *zoquete*] covered with mud; dirty or full of mud. Cf. Sp. *enlodado.*

enzoquetarse, *vb.* [<N.M. Sp. *zoquete*] to get dirty with mud. See *zoquete.*

¡Epa!, *interj.* [<Mex. Sp. *¡Epa!* and *¡Epale!*] Watch out! Look out! That's enough! Quit it!

epazote, *m.* [<Mex. Sp. *epazote*<Náhuatl *epatl,* skunk, and *tzotl,* filth] bot., a medicinal plant, Wormseed.

era, *f.* [<Sp. *era,* thrashing floor] vegetable garden or patch. (*Curre a la era y tráete unas raices.* Go to the garden patch and bring some red beets.)

¡Erre!, *interj.* [<Sp. *¡Arre!*] Get up! (Call to a donkey to start moving.)

escabroso, -sa, *adj.* [<Sp. *escabroso,* craggy, rough (terrain)] distrustful, suspicious; easily frightened. (*Al Erasto ya lo tienen escabroso los chotas.* Erasto is scared stiff of the police. *Suéltame. Ya me tienes escabroso.* Let go of me. You've conditioned me.)

escaldarse, *vb.* [<Sp. *escaldar,* to scald] to get burnt by the sun or a hot pavement to the point of getting blisters. (*La Frumencia tiene la espalda bien escaldada.* Frumencia's back is covered with blisters.)

escalereado, *m.* [<Sp. *escalera,* ladder, staircase] stairs, staircase.

escamado, -da, *adj.* [<Mex. Sp. *escamado,* wary] frightened, scared; astonished, surprised. (*Con tanta jumadera yo quedé bien escamado.* I was scared with all that smoke.)

escamarse, *vb.* [<Mex. Sp. *escamarse,* to become wary] to become frightened or scared.

escame, *m.* [<N.M. Sp. *escamarse*] fright; sudden terror.

escaparse, *vb.* [<Sp. *escaparse*] to have a narrow escape; *escaparse de,* almost, nearly. (*Nos escapamos de helar.* We almost froze [to death].)

escapatorio, *m.* [<Sp. *escapatoria*] escape; excuse. (*Tenemos que fregar los trastes, no hay escapatorio.* We have to wash the dishes; there's no way out.)

escarapelar, *vb.* [<Sp. *escarapelar,* to dispute, to quarrel] to strip off a surface of stucco, plaster, etc. (*Esta pader está toda escarapelada.* This wall is completely stripped off.)

escarbar, *vb.* [<Sp. *escarbar,* to scratch (a surface)] to dig (holes); to probe. (*La mierda, entre más le escarban, más jiede.* A shady affair becomes worse with the probing.)

escarfe, *m.* [<Eng. scarf] scarf. (*¡Qué escarfe tan colorado trae la Gertrudis.* What a red scarf Gertrude is wearing.)

escaso, -sa, *adj.* [<Sp. *escaso,* limited; small] lacking in common sense; resourceless. (*Este Atanasio sí no es nada escaso.* Atanasio is quite resourceful.)

escoba, *f.* [<Sp. *escoba*] broom; bot., a kind of grass used in the making of homemade brooms; *escoba de la víbora,* bot., Yellow weed; Rattlesnake weed. (*Al probe de Filogonio le zampó su vieja con una escoba.* Poor Filogonio; his wife hit him with a broom.)

escobetilla, *f.* [<Sp. dim. of *escoba,* broom] whisk broom. Cf. Sp. *escobilla.*

escobetín, *m.* Whisk broom, var.

escofaina, *f.* [<Sp. *escofina*] rasp.

escondijo, *m.* [<Sp. *escondrijo*] burrow; hiding place; hole.

escrachar, *vb.* [<Eng. to scratch] to reject; to scratch (a ballot), i.e., to reject some candidates on a ballot in favor of others.

escrache, *m.* [<Eng. scratch] fluke; *de escrache,* by chance or by coincidence. (*Los Tigers ganaron el juego de puro escrache.* The Tigers won the game by pure chance.)

escrebir, *vb.* [<Col. N.M. Sp. *escrebir* (Cervantes)] to write; to scribble. (*Voy a escrebirle a la Rafela a ver si me la traigo.* I am going to write to Rafela to see if I can get her to come and stay with me.)

escrepa, *f.* [<Eng. scraper] scraper. (*El Tranquilino va a tener que meterle la escrepa a esta tierra.* Tranquilino is going to have to use a scraper on this land.)

escudilla, *f.* [<Sp. *escudilla,* porringer] cereal or soup bowl. (*Esta escudilla está que no hay otra para los cornflakes.* This bowl is just right for the cornflakes.)

escuela, *f.* [<Sp. *escuela*] school; *escuela alta,* high school; *dar escuela,* to teach. See also *tichear.*

escueleros, *m. pl.* [<Mex. Sp. *escuelero,* elementary school teacher] elementary schoolchildren. (*Curre a ver si ya salieron los escueleros.* Go see if school has let out.)

esculcar, *vb.* [<Col. N.M. Sp. *esculcar,* to spy; to lurk] to search. (*Le esculcaron las bolsas pero no le jallaron el dinero.* They went through his pockets but did not find the money on him.)

escupión, *m.* [<Sp. *escorpión?*] a kind of yellow lizard found in sandy, rocky places.

escurana, *f.* [<Col. N.M. Sp. *escurana*] darkness. (*El otro día hubo una escurana en Nueva Yorka.* There was a blackout in New York the other day.)

escurecer, *vb.* [<Col. N.M. Sp. *escurecer*] to get dark. (*Salemos cuando ya esté escureciendo.* We will leave when it starts to get dark.)

escuridad, *f.* [<Col. N.M. Sp. *escuridad*] darkness.

escuro, -ra, *adj.* [<Col. N.M. Sp. *escuro*] dark; late. (*El bos llegó aquí ya escuro.* The bus got here when it was already dark.) Also, *de escuro,* late in the evening.

esfera, *f.* [<Sp. *esfera,* sphere] condition; mental state. (*No puedo alegar con ella cuando está en esa esfera.* I cannot argue with her when she is in that [mental] state.)

eslique, *m.* [<Eng. slicker] raincoat. (*Está cayendo muncha agua, pónte el eslique.* It's raining cats and dogs; put on your raincoat.)

esmorecerse, *vb.* [<Mex. Sp. *desmorecerse*] to become blue in the face with laughter or anger. See also *desmorecerse.* (*La Crescencia se esmoreció de risa con el chiste de Mano Cacahuate.* Crescencia became blue in the face with laughter with the joke about Mano Cacahuate.)

esmorecido, -da, *adj.* [<Mex. Sp. *desmorecido*] blue in the face from laughter or anger.

espabre, *m.* [<N.M. Sp. *espaura*] baking powder. See *espauda.*

espaldas mojadas, *f. pl.* [<Sp. *espaldas,* backs, and *mojadas,* wet] wetbacks, a name applied to undocumented Mexican laborers crossing the border into the United States.

espanto, *m.* [<Sp. *espanto,* fright] fright; ghost; *estar curado de espanto,* to be experienced. A kind of illness akin to shock which is produced by fright.

espantón, -na, *adj.* [<Sp. aug. of *espanto,* fright] easily frightened; given to exaggeration; harshly critical, censorious. (*¡Bal, Sebastiana, no seas tan espantona!* Oh, come on, Sebastiana, don't put on so! *Este burro es muy espantón.* This ass is easily frightened.)

espauda, *f.* [<Eng. yeast powder] yeast in powder form; baking powder. Also, *espaura, espabre.*

espavientoso, -sa, *adj.* [<Sp. *aspaviento,* fuss] excitable, emotional; given to exaggerated display of emotion.

especies, *f. pl.* [<Sp. *especie,* kind, sort] spices. Cf. Sp. *especias.*

espeitar, *vb.* [<Mex. Sp. *espeta,* the act of looking forward to a thing] to look forward to a thing; to prospect.

espeletrear, *vb.* [<Eng. to spell, and Sp. suffix *etrear*] to spell. Cf. Sp. *deletrear.*

espelma, *f.* [<Mex. Sp. *espelma*<Sp. *esperma,* stearin] paraffin; wax.

esperanza, *f.* [<Sp. *esperanza*] hope. (*La esperanza es la última que muere.* While there's life, there's hope.) *¡Qué esperanzas!* Impossible! That can never be!

esperanzado, -da, *adj.* [<Sp. *esperanza*] hopeful; said of one who hopes to be corresponded with in love or who hopes to achieve or receive a thing, favor, etc. (*El Emigidio está esperanzado que le escriba la Cornelia.* Emigidio has hopes that Cornelia will write to him.)

esperar, *vb.* [<Sp. *esperar,* to hope, and Eng. to expect (a baby)] (*La Eleuteria está esperando.* Eleuteria is expecting.)

esperma, *f.* See *espelma.*

espichadito, -ta, *adj.* [<Mex. Sp. *espichadito,* with its tail between its legs] abashed; confused; embarrassed. (*No sé qué jue lo que pasó pero el Severiano salió del meeting murre espichadito.* I don't know what happened, but Severiano left the meeting quite embarrassed.)

espichado, -da, *adj.* See *espichadito.*

espiche, *m.* [<Eng. speech] address, speech. (*¡Uh, qué espiche!* Gee, what a speech! *Díganle al Nicasio que eche él un buen espiche.* Tell Nicasio to make a real speech.)

espinacito, *m.* [<Sp. dim. of *espinazo,* spine, backbone] vertebra or segment composing the backbone.

"This is the first red chile this year," said Doña Paula. "It has **espinacito**— sections of the spinal column in it with plenty of garlic and orégano." (Fabiola C. de Baca Gilbert, *The Good Life*)

espinilla, *f.* [<Sp. *espinilla,* blackhead] pimple; *pl.,* acne. The Spanish word *espinilla* translates as both blackhead and pimple. In Southwest Spanish *espinillas* are pimples and the term blackhead is simply borrowed from English and used as such. (*La Atanasia se está sacando los blackheads.* Atanasia is squeezing her blackheads.)

espirina, *f.* [<Sp. *aspirina*] aspirin, bufferin, etc.

espuelear, *vb.* [<Sp. *espolear*] to spur on (an animal).

esque, *vb. exp.* [<Sp. *diz que*] they say that; that's what they say; that's what I hear, etc. (*¿Esque se mató el Eduvigen?—Esque.* Is it true that Eduvigen got killed? That's what I hear.)

esquina, *f.* [<Sp. *esquina*] corner; *sombrero de cuatro esquinas,* four-cornered hat. In colonial New Mexico three-cornered hats (*tricornios*) were worn by magistrates, and perhaps in fun someone might have shaped his hat into a four-cornered head covering.

Enamorado garriento
sombrero de cuatro esquinas,
anda, vete al gallinero
y enamora a mis gallinas.
You ragamuffin of a lover
With your four-cornered hat;
Go down to the chicken coop
And make love to my hens.
(N.M. and so. Colo. Sp. *verso popular*)

esquineado, -da, *adj.* [<Sp. *esquina,* corner] folded into a triangle.

esquinero, -ra, *adj.* [<Sp. *esquina,* street corner] loafer; said of one who whiles away his time standing on a street corner.

estación, *f.* [<Sp. *estación*] station; *estación de gasolina,* gas station. Cf. Sp. *surtidor.*

estachar, *vb.* [<Eng. to stash] to stash away.

estafeta, *f.* [<Sp. *estafeta,* rural post office] post office.

estafetero, -ra, *m.* and *f.* [<N.M. Sp. *estafeta,* post office] postmaster; postmistress.

estafiate, *m.* [<Mex. Sp. *estafiate*<Náhuatl *iztahuatl*] bot., a medicinal plant, Rocky Mountain sage.

estampa, *f.* [<Sp. *estampa,* print] postage stamp.

   Si fuera papel volara
   si fuera tinta escribiera;
   también si fuera una **estampa**
   en este sobre me fuera.
   If I were paper I would fly
   If I were ink I would write;
   Also, if I were a postage stamp
   I would go to you in this envelope.
   (N.M. and so. Colo. Sp. *verso popular*)

estancia, *f.* [<Am. Sp. *estancia,* farm] Col. N.M. Sp., a permanent homestead adjacent to a pastureland; landed property; small farm.

estanco, *m.* [<Sp. *estanco*] Col. and Terr. N.M. Sp., a government owned store.

estar, *vb.* [<Sp. *estar,* to be] *Está bien.* It's OK. *Usted está mal.* You are wrong. *Está caliente (el día).* It's hot (the day). *Hoy está murre frío.* It's very cold today. *Estar en todo menos en misa,* to be aware; to meddle. (*La Edicia en todo está, menos en misa.* Edicia is always into everything.) *¡Ahi 'stuvo!* There you are! That's it!

esteble, *m.* [<Eng. stable] barn; stable.

estenazas, *f. pl.* [<Sp. *tenazas,* pincers, foreceps] pliers.

estilar, *vb.* [<Col. N.M. Sp. *estilar*] to distill; to fall in drops (rain, snow).

estilla, *f.* [<Sp. *astilla*] chip; splinter. (*De tal palo, tal estilla,* a chip off the old block.)

estíquer, *m.* [<Eng. sticker] windshield inspection sticker. (*Con el winchil quebrado no te van a dar estíquer.* You are not going to get a sticker as long as you have a broken windshield.)

estógamo, *m.* [<Sp. *estómago*] stomach. The word *panza,* belly, is far more common. (*La yerbabuena es buena pal dolor de estógamo.* Mint is good for a stomachache.)

estrechar, *vb.* [<Eng. to stretch] to stretch. Sp. *estrechar* has the opposite meaning, to make narrow.

Favor referido, ni de Dios ni del diablo agradecido.
People do not appreciate being reminded of a
favor done them.

faceta, -to, *adj.* [<Mex. Sp. *faceto,* vain] conceited; dull; vain. (*¡Cómo es faceta esta Rumalda!* Rumalda is so conceited!)

faceteador, -ra, *adj.* [<N.M. Sp. *facetearse*] show-off; said of one who puts on airs. (*El Frumencio es murre faceteador.* Frumencio is quite a show-off.)

facetearse, *vb.* [<N.M. Sp. *faceta*] to show off; to put on airs.

fácil, *adv.* [<Sp. *fácil,* easy] maybe; possibly; could be. (*Oye, ¿Crees que vendrá la Rufina?—Fácil.* Say, do you think Rufina will come? Could be.)

factor, *m.* [<Col. N.M. Sp. *factor*] a royal official; a disbursing officer and supply agent.

factura, *f.* [<Sp. *manufactura?*] sawmill.

fachoso, -sa, *adj.* [<Sp. *fachoso,* having a ridiculous aspect] puffed up; arrogant.

falda, *f.* [<Mex. Sp. *falda*] brim of a hat.

faltar, *vb.* [<Sp. *faltar,* to be deficient] *adv., falta que,* perhaps; maybe; could be. (*Falta que no sea el Praxedes.* Perhaps it isn't Praxedes. *¿Crees que ganan el juego? Falta.* Do you think they will win the game? It could be.)

falteado, -da, *adj.* [<N.M. Sp. *faltear,* to spoil] spoiled; silly; foolish. (*Esta chamaca sí está bien falteada.* This girl is certainly spoiled.)

faltear, *vb.* [<Sp. *falta,* fault] to spoil. (*Por favor, no me faltee a los muchachos.* Please do not spoil my kids.)

faltearse, *vb.* [<N.M. Sp. *faltearse*] to act silly or spoiled to the point of being considered foolish or crazy; to want to be coaxed. (*Andale, no te faltees; canta la cantada de El piojo y la liendre.* Come on; don't act silly. Sing the song of "The Louse and the Nit.")

fandanguero, -ra, *adj.* [<Sp. *fandango*] said of the person who is fond of noisy dances, commotion and a good time. (*'M primo Irineo es más fandanguero que qué.* Cousin Irineo is quite fond of

commotion and a good time.)

fandango, *m*. [<Mex. Sp. *fandango,* row; commotion] dance; shindig.

farolazo, *m*. [<Mex. Sp. *farolazo,* a drink of brandy] a drink of liquor. (*Ven, vamos a echarnos un farolazo.* Come on, let's have a drink.)

farolito, *m*. [<Sp. dim. of *farol,* lantern] a kind of festive light, especially of the candle-in-a-paper-bag variety. *Farolitos* take their name from the word *farol,* lantern. See *luminarias.*

fashico, -ca, *m*. and *f*. [<N.M Sp. *fashico* (a child's pronunciation of Francisco)] a Black; *fashicos,* folk characters in N.M. and so. Colo. folklore. See *mano fashico.* *Adj.,* stupid, moron-like.

fatal, *adj*. [<Sp. *fatal,* unfortunate] brittle (things); delicate; feeble; fragile; physically weak. (*Aquí viene la Librada. No la atoques, es muy fatal.* Here comes Librada. Don't touch her, she is very feeble.)

fe, *f*. [<Sp. *fe,* faith] *ser uno de muy mala fe,* to be very unfriendly or distrustful; mean; *dar fe,* to nose around or pry into other people's affairs. (*Aquí viene mana Virginia a dar fe.* Here comes old lady Virginia just to nose around.)

fecha, *f*. [<Sp. *fecha,* calendar date, and Eng. social date] appointment; engagement; social date. (*Esta noche tengo fecha con mi güisa.* I have a date with my girl friend tonight.)

feria, *f*. [<Sp. *feria,* fair] state fair; small change; money ("bread"); *feriecita,* kids (small fry); *no volver ni por la feria,* to vanish.

feriar, *vb*. [<N.M. Sp. *feria*] to change; to exchange; to barter. In colonial times people who went to fairs to exchange animals, produce, etc., for commodities and other necessities spoke of *feriar unas cosas por otras* (exchange some things for others). The verb *feriar* is conjugated like N.M. Sp. *cambiar: fereo, fereas, ferea,* etc. See *cambiar.*

fiance, *m*. [<Sp. *fianza*] bond; bail.

fiebre, *f*. [<Sp. *fiebre*] fever; fever blister.

fiero, -ra, *adj*. [<Sp. *fiero,* fierce] ugly; homely; ungainly.

fierramienta, *f*. [<Sp. *fierro,* iron] hardware; tools. See Sp. *herramienta.*

fierro, *m*. [<Sp. *fierro,* iron] branding iron; brand; scrap iron; *pl.,* cents, pennies; tools.

Under Sp. law, the **fierro** was the brand of the original owner. When the animal was sold, a second brand, called the *venta* or buyer's brand, obliterated the first. (Roland F. Dickey, *New Mexico Village Arts*)

fierrocarril, *m*. [<Sp. *ferrocarril*] railroad. Also, *carroferril.*

fiestín, *m*. [<Sp. *festín*<*fiesta*] feast; banquet.

filo, *m*. [<Sp. *filo,* cutting edge] cutting edge; crease, as on pants or trousers.

finación, *f*. [<Sp. *fin,* end, close, termination, etc.] end; *la finación del mundo,* the end of the world.

físico, -ca, *adj*. [<Sp. *físico,* physical] finicky, particular, squeamish; foolish.

fistol, *m*. [<Am. Sp. *fistol,* scarf pin] safety pin.

flate, *m*. [<Eng. flat] flat, in the sense of wine or a tire being flat.

fletero, *m*. [<Sp. *flete,* freight] freight train; freighter; fruit and vegetable vendor.

flirtear, *vb*. [<Eng. to flirt] to flirt.

flor, *f*. [<Sp. *flor*] flower; *flor de ángel,* bot., Angel flower; *flor de San Juan,* bot., Tree primrose; *flor de Santa Rita,* bot., Painter's brush, Painted cup; *flor de sauz,* bot., Elderberry. See also *varas de San José.*

floreado, -da, *adj*. [<N.M. Sp. *florear,* to bloom] *salir floreado un asunto,* to backfire, to turn out badly. (*Les salió floreada su diligencia.* Their efforts were for naught.)

florear, *vb*. [<Sp. *flor,* flower] to bloom; to flower. Cf. Sp. *florecer.*

florería, *f*. [<Sp. *flor*] flower shop; green-

floresta

house.

floresta, *f.* [<Sp. *floresta*] forest; *La Floresta,* Forest Service.

florón, *m.* [<Sp. aug. of *flor,* flower] flower bouquet; name of a children's game similar to "Button, button, who has the button."

fogón, *m.* [<Sp. *fogón,* hearth] fireplace; furnace. See *jogón.*

foguera, *f.* [<Col. Sp. *foguera,* fire (Covarrubias)] blaze, bonfire; fire. See *joguera.*

fon, *m.* [<Eng. fun] fun; a good time.

fonazo, *m.* [<N.M. Sp. *fon*] a lot of fun; an exceptionally good time.

fonógrafo, *m.* [<Sp. *fonógrafo*<Eng. phonograph] *fonógrafo de bolillo* or *de vasito,* Edison-type cylinder phonograph; *fonógrafo de platillo,* Victrola-type phonograph.

forcha, *f.* [<unknown origin] mortarboard; mason's hawk.

forro, *m.* [<Mex. Sp. slang *forro*] an attractive, beautiful woman; sexpot (slang).

foturo, *m.* [<Sp. *futuro*] future.

fracasado, -da, *adj.* [<N.M. Sp. *fracasar,* to damage] damaged; dented, as a car's fender.

fracasar, *vb.* [<Sp. *fracasar,* to crumple] to dent; to fail; *m., fracaso,* fatal accident.

frastero, -ra, *m.* and *f.* [<Sp. *forastero*] outsider; stranger. (*La Petronila no es frastera, ella fue nacida aquí en El Cerrito.* Petronila is no outsider; she was born here in El Cerrito.)

fregada, *f.* [<Mex. Sp. *fregada*] bother, nuisance. *¡A la fregada!* What a mess! Now you (I, we) have done it!

fregadera, *f.* [<Mex. Sp. *fregadera*<*fregar*] nuisance; foolishness, tomfoolery, horseplay. *¡Qué fregadera!* What a mess! What a nuisance!

fregado, -da, *adj.* [<Mex. Sp. *fregar*] bothersome; cunning, sly; mean, mischievous; *m.,* imp; rascal. (*El Mauricio es un fregado; echó el gato en el común.*

Mauricio is a thoroughgoing rascal; he dropped the cat into the toilet.) *Estar uno fregado,* to be badly off financially or physically.

fregar, *vb.* [<Mex. Sp. *fregar,* to annoy, to bother; to wash dishes] to bother; to cheat (to rook). (*A la probe de la Librada la fregaron con su dinero.* They cheated poor Librada out of her money. *Ya el Gorgonio la fregó.* Gorgonio has had it.) *Fregarla de frío, de hambre, de sed, de sueño,* etc., to be unable to stand being cold, hungry, thirsty, sleepy, etc. (*Esta muchita ya la friega de hambre.* This child is famished.) *Fregar los trastes,* to wash the dishes; *fregar la pacencia,* to tax one's patience; *fregar pato,* to get a lucky break. (*¡Ya ni la friegan!* They are taking advantage of us!)

fregazo, *m.* [<Mex. Sp. *fregar*] hard blow; punch. (*El Sarapio y el Onésimo andaban a los fregazos.* Sarapio and Onésimo were punching each other.)

fregón, -na, *adj.* [<Mex. Sp. *fregar*] bothersome; strong, brave; splendid, wonderful. (*El baile de casorio estuvo fregón.* The wedding dance was wonderful.)

fresno, *m.* [<Sp. *fresno,* ash tree] homemade scraper consisting of a large log which is pulled over the land surface by a team of horses, mules, etc. By extension, an iron scraper dragged by a tractor. See also *escrepa.*

frezada, *f.* [<Sp. *frazada*] blanket; *frezada conga,* a multicolored blanket the size of a *subadero* or saddle blanket; *frezada tilma,* a kind of poncho worn by Indians. See also *cobija, tilma.*

friega, *f.* [<Mex. Sp. *friega*] annoyance, bother; beating. (*Al Aparicio le metieron una friega.* Aparicio was given quite a beating.) *¡Qué friega!* How annoying! What a nuisance!

frijol, *m.* [<Sp. *frijol,* kidney bean] beans, pinto beans; *pl.,* dish of beans. (*Pásame los frijoles, Justiniano.* Justiniano, pass me the beans.) *Frijoles refritos,* refried beans; *no ganar* or *no hacer ni pa los frijoles,* to earn very little. (*Ahi ontá el*

72

Severino no hace ni pa los frijoles. Severino makes very little in his present job.) *Frijoles de jarro,* canned beans; *frijol verde,* string beans.

frijolillo, *m.* [<Sp. dim. of *frijol,* kidney bean] bot., Locoweed.

frío, *m.* [<Sp. *frío,* cold] cold; *estar murre frío,* to be very cold. (*¡Qué frío está esta mañana!* How cold it is this morning!) *Los fríos* or *la enfermedad de los fríos,* malaria.

La enfermedad de los **fríos**
no hallo cómo puedan ser,
ellos traen mil disvaríos,
son de quitar y poner;
un puro agua nomás beber
sin quitarse la sequía,
y si beben todo un día
no hallo cómo puedan ser.
The chills
Just don't make any sense;
They make you delirious;
They come on and off;
It's a continuous drinking of water
And still the thirst persists,
And if they drink a whole day . . .
They just don't make any sense.
(*La enfermedad de los fríos,* N.M. and so. Colo. Sp. folk song)

frun frun, *m.* [<Mex. Sp. *fruncirse,* to act bashful] fear. (*El Silvestre no le entra a los catos porque tiene frun frun.* Silvestre doesn't join the fight because he is afraid.)

fuchi fuchi, *m.* [<Mex. Sp. *¡Fuchi!,* ugh!] fear. (*Al Frumencio se le hace fuchi fuchi.* Frumencio is afraid.)

fuella, *f.* [<Sp. *huella*] footprint; trace, track. (*Aquí se ven las fuellas del joso.* I can see the bear's tracks right here.)

fuerte, *m.* [<Sp. *fuerte,* fort] small storeroom for farm implements and fodder. Also, *fuertecito* and *dispensa. Adj.,* strong (coffee). (*Este café está murre fuerte.* This coffee is much too strong.) See also *juerte.*

fuertecito, *m.* [<Sp. dim. of *fuerte,* fort] small log cabin or adobe shack used as a granary or tool shed. See also *juertecito.*

fuerza, *f.* [<Sp. *fuerza,* strength] *¡De fuerza!* Naturally! Of course! To be sure! *¡A mí ni fuerza me hace!* It doesn't worry me at all!

funda, *f.* [<Sp. *funda,* case (pillowcase)] *funda de collar,* sweat pad on a horse's collar.

fundillo, *m.* [<Mex. Sp. *fundillo*] backside, anus; coward, said of someone lacking in guts; *pl.,* panties. (*Ya te rompites los fundillos.* You tore your panties.)

fundilludo, *adj.* [<N.M. Sp. *fundillo*] baggy, applied to pants or trousers.

Gusto con gusto siempre es gusto.
Pleasure with taste is always a pleasure.

gabacho, *m.* See *gavacho.*

gabazo, *m.* [<Sp. *gabazo,* bagasse] pulp, skin and seeds of grapes after pressing for juice.

gacho, -cha, *adj.* [<Sp. *gacho,* bent downward] bad; lousy. *¡Qué gacho!* What a bummer! (slang).

gachupín, *adv.* [<Am. Sp. *gachupín,* lowclass Spaniard] said of the person who speaks Spanish with a twang. (*La Blandina habla muy gachupín.* Blandina speaks Spanish with a twang.)

gaita, *f.* [<Mex. Sp. *gaita,* deceitful trick] trick, especially to escape pursuit or capture. (*El Ciriaco les hizo unas gaitas y se les juyó.* Ciriaco escaped from them with a few tricks of his.)

galán, *m.* [<Sp. *galán,* gallant] *"El galán,"* the devil. Also, *Pata Galán.*

galera, *f.* [<Mex. Sp. *galera,* long storage room] farm implement shed; long room of a house in which grain is stored.

galgo, -ga, *adj.* [<Mex. Sp. *galgo,* gluttonous] thin, emaciated; hungry-looking.

galopear, *vb.* [<Sp. *galopar*] to gallop.

gallero, -ra, *m.* and *f.* [<Sp. *gallo,* rooster] rider taking part in the game of *gallo* or *corrida del gallo.*

galleta, *f.* [<Sp. *galleta,* hardtack] biscuit. The term *bísquete* (<Eng. biscuit) is more common.

gallina, *f.* [<Sp. *gallina,* hen] chicken, hen; coward; *gallina frita,* fried chicken; *gallina de la tierra,* wild turkey; *gallina pininea,* bantam hen; *pata de gallina,* crow's feet; *gallina tecolota,* Plymouth Rock or speckled hen.

gallineta, *f.* [<Sp. dim. of *gallina*] Col. and Terr. N.M. Sp., roadrunner.

gallito, *m.* [<Sp. dim. of *gallo,* rooster] a stroll by musicians through a village to announce a dance, game or some other form of entertainment.

gallitos, *m. pl.* [<Sp. dim. of *gallo,* cock, rooster] a game in which two children

take turns at rubbing each other on the back of the hand until it bleeds, or until one of the contestants gives up.

gallo, *m.* [<Sp. *gallo*] cock, rooster; *"aquel gallo,"* the devil; *gallo gallina,* sissy ("chicken"); *gallo grande,* big shot; important person. Cf. Sp. *pez grande. Comer gallo,* to be looking for a fight. (*El Cesáreo comió gallo.* Cesáreo is looking for a fight.) *Corrida de gallo* or *correr el gallo,* game of the buried rooster in which riders vie with one another at picking up a rooster which has been buried in the sand up to its neck; *tocar gallo,* to advertise with music and much fanfare a coming event (dance, movies, game, etc.) and invite the public to attend.

gambusino, *m.* [<Mex. Sp. *gambusino*] petty miner; prospector; greedy person.

ganar, *vb.* [<Sp. *ganar,* to gain] to go in a certain direction. (*¿Par 'onde ganó el Cayetano?* Which way did Cayetano go?)

ganchete, *m.* [<Sp. dim. of *gancho,* hook] *mirar de ganchete,* to look askance; from the corner of one's eye. (*La Dominica se quedó mirando de ganchete al Librado y luego torció 'l hocico.* Dominica kept looking at Librado from the corner of her eye and then made a wry face.)

gandul, *m.* [<Sp. *gandul,* tramp] Col. and Terr. N.M. Sp., Indian warrior; brave; buck.

gansa, *f.* [<N.M. Sp. *ganso,* turkey] the hen of the turkey; girl or woman with a runny nose.

ganso, *m.* [<Sp. *ganso,* gander] tom turkey; stork. See also *torque.*

garache, *m.* [<Eng. garage] garage. Cf. Sp. *garaje.*

garambullo, *m.* [<Mex.Sp. *garambullo*] bot., Gooseberry; Gooseberry shrub.

garañón, -ña, *adj.* [<Mex. Sp. *garañón,* seed horse] seed horse; also said of the person who is much given to lust; *adj.,* lecherous.

garbancillo, *m.* [<Mex. Sp. *garbancillo de buey*] bot., Locoweed.

gargajear, *vb.* [<Sp. *gargajear,* to spit; to expectorate] to gargle. Cf. Sp. *gargarizar.*

gargantón, *m.* [<Sp. *garganta,* throat] a flat necklace with large brooch-like designs in floral effects. Also, *gargantilla.*

garifo, -fa, *adj.* [<Sp. *garifo* or *jarifo,* pompous, showy] skinny; physically weak. (*¡Qué garifo está el Maque!* How skinny Mack looks.)

garra, *f.* [<Mex. Sp. *garra*] rag; sanitary napkin; *traer la garra una mujer,* to be menstruating; *garra pa los trastes,* dish rag; *hecho (hecha) garras,* torn, raggedy, in rags; *garras,* rags, worn-out clothes, baggage. See also *garritas.*

garrancho, *m.* [<Mex. Sp. *garrancho,* rent or tear] a hole; a tear in one's clothes; a piece of cloth torn off; a rip. (*Ahi traes un garrancho en el túnico.* You have a tear in your dress.)

garrero, *m.* [<N.M. Sp. *garras*] junk; odds and ends; rags; worthless stuff.

garriento, -ta, *adj.* [<N.M. Sp. *garras*] raggedy, tattered, in rags. (*Garriento como mano Canuto.* In rags, like Canuto.)

garritas, *f. pl.* [<N.M. Sp. dim. of *garras,* rags] baggage; belongings; clothes.

garrocharse, *vb.* [<Sp. *garrochear,* to goad] to handle; to touch, said of children who touch and handle one another while playing. (*¡Cómo no me gusta que esta plebe se anden garrochando unos a otros!* How I hate for these kids to be handling one another!)

garrotero, *m.* [<Sp. *garrote,* cudgel] moocher, especially one who bums cigarettes or money; conductor (trains); *adj.,* stingy. (*¡Ah, cómo es garrotero este Quirino!* Quirino is so stingy!)

garruleta, *f.* [<Mex. Sp. *garraleta,* piece of an old rag] jalopy.

garruñal, *m.* [<Mex. Sp. *engarruñado,* curled up] field full of brambles and briers; thicket; *garuñal,* var.

gaselín, *m.* [<Eng. gasoline] gasoline; *se le acabó el gaselín* (fig.), he ran out of gas.

gasolinera, *f.* [<Eng. gasoline] gas station.

gato

Cf. Sp. *surtidor.*

gato, *m.* [<Sp. *gato,* cat] cat; trigger of a pistol or gun. Cf. Sp. *gatillo.*

gavacho, -cha, *m.* and *f.* [<Col. N.M. Sp. *gavacho*<Fr. *gavache,* southern Frenchman] foreigner; Anglo-American; gringo. Also, *gabacho.*

gavilla, *f.* [<Sp. *gavilla*] gang; political ring.

gazada, *f.* [<Sp. *gaza,* loop] noose; hangman's rope.

gaznate, *m.* [<Sp. *gaznate*] windpipe; throat.

gazuzo, -za, *adj.* [<Sp. *gazuza,* extreme hunger] said of the person who eats between meals, muncher; gluttonous.

genario, *m.* [<Sp. *geranio*] geranium.

generoso, *adj.* [<Sp. *generoso*] rich (wine); unsurpassed; excellent.

genio, *m.* [<Sp. *genio,* disposition] ill temper. (*Me hizo mal genio.* He received me coldly [scowlingly].)

genioso, -sa, *adj.* [<Mex. Sp. *genioso*] of a bad disposition.

genízaro, -ra, *m.* and *f.* [<Mex. Sp. *genízaro,* offspring of non-European parents of mixed blood] a non-Pueblo Indian captive rescued by the Spanish settlers from various nomadic tribes. See *jenízaro.*

gente, *f.* [<Sp. *gente,* people] visitors. (*Nos cayó gente.* We have company.) *Gente fina,* the elite; *gente de razón,* educated people; Col. N.M. Sp., non-Indians whose way of life followed Spanish rather than Indian customs; *adj.,* congenial, friendly.

gentiles, *m. pl.* [<Sp. *gentil,* gentile] Col. N.M. Sp., *gentiles,* non-Christianized Indians (Apaches, Comanches, Kiowas, Navajos, Pawnees, Utes, Wichitas, etc.) living in or roaming around the fringe areas of the Spanish settlements.

genuino, -na, *adj.* [<Sp. *genuino,* genuine] smashing, super. (*Un party pero genuino,* a really super party.)

gerga. See *jerga.*

gérmenes, *m. pl.* [<Sp. *germen,* seed] bacteria; germs. Cf. Sp. *microbios.*

gileño, -ña, *adj.* [<Col. N.M. Sp. *Xila* (Gila)<Apache *tsihl,* or *dzihl,* mountain; Mountain People] Gila Apache.

gimiriquear, *vb.* [<Mex. Sp. *girimiquear*] to whine, to whimper. Also, *gimiquear, girimiquear.*

gladiola, *f.* [<Eng. gladiola] gladiola. Cf. Sp. *gladiolo.*

gogote, *m.* [<Sp. *cogote*] nape of the neck.

golondrina, *f.* [<Mex. Sp. *golondrina*] a medicinal plant; bot., Spurge.

golondrino, -na, *adj.* [<Mex. Sp. *golondrino*] brownish yellow; tawny, the color of horses, mules, etc.

goloso, -sa, *adj.* [<Sp. *goloso,* fond of dainties] having a voracious appetite; gluttonous.

golpanazo, *m.* [<Sp. aug. of *golpe,* blow] heavy blow; thud.

gomitar, *vb.* [<Sp. *vomitar*] to vomit.

gorda, *adj.* [<Sp. *gorda,* fat; fat female] fat with child; pregnant.

gorgollones, *m. pl.* [<Sp. *borbollones*] *a gorgollones,* bubbling hot; *jirviendo a gorgollones,* bubbling hot. (*'L agua está jirviendo a gorgollones.* The water is bubbling hot.)

gorgorear, *vb.* [<Mex. Sp. *gorgorear,* to gargle; to warble] to bubble; to gobble, as a turkey.

gorgoritos, *m. pl.* [<Mex. Sp. dim. of *górgoros*] small bubbles.

górgoros, *m. pl.* [<Mex. Sp. *górgoros*] bubbles.

gorras blancas, *f. pl.* [<Sp. *gorras,* caps] white caps, a clandestine organization operating in San Miguel county, New Mexico, against Anglo-American expansion in that area (1880s).

gorrudo, -da, *adj.* [<Sp. *gorra* (*de gorra,* to sponge)] lazy; mooching; roguish.

goruco, *m.* [<Mex. Sp. *gorupo*] chicken louse.

gota, *f.* [<Sp. *gota,* drop] *ni gota,* not a

drop (of anything).

gotinado, -da, *adj.* [<Sp. *goteado,* speckled] spotted; sprinkled.

gracia, *f.* [<Sp. *gracia,* grace] name. *¿La gracia de su merced?* What is your name? *¿Su gracia?* Your name please? *Echar una cosa a la gracia,* to laugh off a thing. (*Le dije pero lo echó a la gracia.* I told him but he just laughed it off.) *¡Qué gracias!* or *¡Para esas gracias!* Big deal!

gradar, *vb.* [<Sp. *graduar*] to graduate. Cf. Sp. *graduarse.*

graje, *m.* [<Sp. *grajo*] crow (mostly in folktales).

grampa, *f.* [<Sp. *grapa*] staple.

grampa, *m.* [<Eng. grandpa] grandfather. Also, *grampo.*

grampear, *vb.* [<N.M. Sp. *grampa,* staple] to staple.

grande, *adj.* [<Sp. *grande,* large] old (in years); elderly; mature. (*Mana Faustina ya es mujer grande.* Old lady Faustina is an elderly woman.) *En sus grandes,* at its height or highest point.

grandulos, *m. pl.* [<N.M. Sp. *gandules*] Indian braves.

granear, *vb.* [<Eng. to grind] to grind (motor valves).

graniento, -ta, *adj.* [<Sp. *grano,* boil] covered with boils or acne.

granjeador, -ra, *adj.* [<Sp. *granjear*] said of the person who brings or works himself into another's favor. (*El Bernabe siempre ha sido muy granjeador.* Bernabe has always been very serviceable.)

granma, *f.* [<Eng. grandma] grandmother; granny.

grano, *m.* [<Sp. *grano*] grain (collective noun); Col. N.M. Sp., a copper coin equal to one twelfth part of a *real; grano enterrado,* pus-filled boil.

greira, *f.* [<Eng. grater] grater.

greña, *f.* [<Sp. *greña,* long, tangled hair] tangled or mussed up hair; *a toda greña,* in a hurry, at breakneck speed.

greñudo, -da, *m.* and *f.* [<N.M Sp. *greñas*]

a longhair.

gresco, -ca, *adj.* [<Sp. *gresca,* carousal] alert; lively; full of life. (*La Simonita es una niña muy gresca.* Simonita is a very lively child.)

greso, -sa, *adj.* [< Sp. *grueso*] corpulent; heavyset; thick.

gretas, *f. pl.* [<Sp. *grietas*] cracks. (*El Crisanto tiene las manos llenas de gretas.* Crisanto has chapped hands.)

gretudo, -da, *adj.* [<N.M. Sp. *gretas*] *cuero gretudo,* chapped skin.

greve, *m.* [<Eng. gravy] gravy.

gringada, *f.* [<Sp. *gringo,* foreigner] group of Anglo-Americans.

gringo, -ga, *m.* and *f.* [<Sp. *gringo,* foreigner] Terr. N.M. Sp., an English-speaking white person from the United States; a white foreigner; a Yankee; *gringo salado,* insipid gringo (an insult).
When the great influx of non-Spanish people occurred after 1848, the New Mexicans referred to them generally as "*gringos.*" In origin, this term was not one of opprobrium, but simply meant any foreigner (not Spanish or Indian) who spoke the Spanish language without a good accent—unintelligibly. A Spanish dictionary published in 1787 shows that *gringo* (perversion of *griego,* Greek) was used in Spain long before Mexicans of the Southwest applied the term. (*New Mexico. A Guide to the Colorful State*)

gripa, *f.* [<Mex. Sp. *gripa,* grippe] flu, influenza; common cold.

grique, *adj.* [<Eng. Greek] Greek.

grisma, *f.* [<Sp. *brizna,* bit, fragment] bit; speck; *ni grisma,* not a bit, nothing.

griso, -sa, *m.* and *f.* [<Eng. greaser] low-class Mexican national.

gritos, *m. pl.* [<Sp. *gritos,* shouts] *a gritos y sombrerazos,* by the skin of one's teeth; barely.

groga, *f.* [<Mex. Sp. *drogas,* debts] *hacer grogas,* to delay; to cheat.

77

grojellas, *f. pl.* [<Sp. *grosellas*] currants.

grulla, *f.* [<Sp. *grulla,* crane] sandhill crane. (*A tu tierra grulla, que ésta no es tuya.* Go home, crane; this is not your land. Said to someone who is not welcome.)

grullo, -lla, *adj.* [<Mex. Sp. *grullo*] dark gray; mouse-colored, applied to horses, mules, etc.

guacamole, *m.* [<Mex. Sp. *guacamole*<Náhuatl *ahuacamulli*] guacamole dip.

guaco, *m.* [<Mex. Sp. *guaco,* a medicinal plant] bot., Stinkweed; Rocky Mountain bee plant, whose roots are used to obtain a black paint.

guacha, *f.* [<Eng. washer, flat metal ring] washer; wristwatch (slang); *pl.,* exaggerations, lies.

guache, *m.* [<Eng. watchman] watchman; guard. Also, *guacho.*

guachita, *f.* [<N.M. Sp. *guacha,* metal washer] small, round, flat washer-like stone that children throw over the surface of the water in a lake, river, etc. Cf. Sp. *laja.*

guadaña, *f.* [<Sp. *guadaña,* scythe] load of hay; hayrack; hay wagon. Also, *guadaña de paja,* load of hay.

guaino, -na, *m.* and *f.* [<Eng. wino] wino; alcoholic.

guajalote, *m.* [<Mex. Sp. *ajolote*<Náhuatl *axolotl*] a kind of salamander.

guaje, *m.* [<Mex. Sp. *guaje*] gourd; *hacer guaje a alguno,* to deceive or fool someone.

guajito, *m.* [<Mex. Sp. *guaje,* gourd] small gourd; Col. and Terr. N.M., tobacco flask.

guajolote, *m.* [<Mex. Sp. *guajolote,* turkey] turkey (so. N.M.); tiger salamander. See *guajalote.*

gualde, *adv.* [<N.M. Sp. *engualde*] instead of.

guamanil, *m.* [<Sp. *aguamanil*] washstand.

guamazo, *m.* [<Mex. Sp. *guamazo*] a blow on the face with the hand. Cf. Sp. *bofetada.*

guango, -ga, *adj.* [<Mex. Sp. *guango* <*guangoche,* burlap] loose, slack; flabby; loose fitting; baggy.

guangoche, *m.* [<Mex. Sp. *guangoche*] burlap; gunnysack.

guangochudo, -da, *adj.* [<Mex. Sp. *guangoche*] loose; loose fitting; baggy.

guapo, -pa, *adj.* [<Sp. *guapo,* bold] energetic; applied to a person who goes out on a cold day without too much clothing; handsome.

guarache, *m.* [<Mex. Sp. *guarache*] a kind of sandal with tire-casing sole.

guardapolvo, *m.* [<Sp. *guardapolvo*] a kind of border, usually made of oilcloth, which was attached to kitchen walls to keep the whitewash from getting on one's clothes.

guardia, *m.* and *f.* [<Sp. *guardia,* guard] *ángel de la guardia,* guardian angel. Cf. Sp. *ángel de la guarda.*

guardián, *m.* [<Sp. *guardián*] Col. N.M. Sp., the superior of a convent of the order of St. Francis.

guarefol, *m.* [<Mex. Sp. *garibol?*] decoration, ornament (dress).

guargüero, *m.* [<Sp. *gargüero*] gullet; windpipe; throat.

guasa, *f.* [<Mex. Sp. *guasanga,* noisy mirth; racket] noise; hearsay; rumor; by extension, the memory (reminder).

Sandovalito,
toda tu gente
ya se acabó,
ya se acabó,
y acá la **guasa**
nomás quedó.
Sandovalito,
All your people are dead;
All are dead!
Their memory
Is all that remains.
(*Indita de Sandovalito,* N.M. Sp. folk song)

guato, *m.* [<Eng. wad] wad; bundle of money (slang).

guayabe, *m.* [<Tewa *buwayabe,* paper

bread] a kind of wafer-like bread made with blue cornmeal. The Hopi Indians call this same bread *piki;* the Zuni Indian name for the *guayabe* is *hewe.*

They [the Pueblo Indians] make another quality of bread from maize different from the *tortilla,* the use of which is principally confined to the Indians, which is called **guayabe.** The corn is first ground in the metate, and then mixed with water into a thin paste when it is baked before the fire in flat stones heated for that purpose. The paste is laid on in exceedingly thin layers, and is almost immediately baked and peeled off, when a new supply is placed upon the stone. (W.W.H. Davis, *El Gringo*)

Guayuma, *f.* [<Eng. Wyoming] the state of Wyoming. (*El Venancio anda en la borrega en Guayuma.* Venancio is working in a sheep camp in Wyoming.)

guayumero, *m.* [<N.M. Sp. *Guayuma*] sheepherder working in Wyoming. (*Aquí van llegando los guayumeros.* The Wyoming sheepherders are just arriving.)

güeja, *f.* [<Mex. Sp. *güeja*<*cahita bueha,* a bowl made from a gourd shell] baldhead, baldplate; head. Also, a smoking pipe bowl or any vessel made out of a gourd or pumpkin shell. *¡Cuidado con la güeja!* Watch your head! (Said or indicated by a sign at the entrance of a low cave, room or any other low entrance.)

güelada, *f.* [<N.M. Sp. *güelo*<Sp. *vuelo,* flight] *de güelada,* fast, quickly (slang).

güelta, *f.* [<Sp. *vuelta*] turn; stroll; *jugarle una güelta a alguno,* to play a trick on someone; *darle sus güeltas a alguno,* to give someone a good thrashing; *tirar la güelta,* to die.

güerinche, *adj.* [<Mex. Sp. *güerinche*] blondish; light-complexioned. Also, *güeruncho.*

güero, -ra, *adj.* [<Mex. Sp. *güero*] light-complexioned; blond; foreign; *m.* and *f.,* darling.

guerra, *f.* [< Sp. *guerra*] war; annoyance; trouble. (*¡Hi', cómo da guerra esta plebe!* Damn, these kids give one a lot of trouble!)

guerrista, *adj.* [<N.M. Sp. *guerra,* trouble] annoying; bothersome; troublesome.

güevo, *m.* [<Sp. *huevo,* egg] egg; testicle; *a güevo,* forcefully, by force; *andar uno que no le cabe un güevo,* to be exceedingly elated and proud. (*Anda el Maque que no le cabe un güevo.* Mack is overcome with joy and pride.) *Tener un hombre los güevos mero a medio,* to be a real macho; *costar una cosa un güevo y parte del otro,* said of a thing that is exceedingly expensive.

güevón, -na, *adj.* [<N.M. Sp. aug. of *güevo*] large testicle; indolent, lazy; shiftless. (*Elías era más güevón que el pastor Bartolo.* Elias was lazier than Bart the shepherd.)

güey, *m.* [<Sp. *buey*] ox; cuckold; *adj.,* stupid.

guía, *f.* [<Sp. *guía,* guide] Col. and Terr. N.M. Sp., guideline; bill of lading; invoice; shoot or sucker of a vine; bell or lead animal; ensign or banner; opening in an irrigation ditch ('*cequia*); *La guía,* the North Star.

guiangue, *m.* [<Eng. gang] gang. (*Por aquí pasó el Prudencio con su guiangue.* Prudencio and his gang just went by here.)

güíjalo, *m.* [<Mex. Sp. *güíjalo,* turkey] tom turkey (so. N.M.).

güila, *f.* [<Mex. Sp. *güila*] loose woman; prostitute.

güilanchar, *vb.* [<Mex. Sp. *güilanche*<*güilana,* to crawl] to pamper a crawling infant; to spoil (children).

güilo, -la, *adj.* [<Mex. Sp. *güilo,* crippled; disabled] dizzy; doped up; half-witted; reeling, staggering.

güinche, *m.* [<Eng. winch] winch.

güinchil, *m.* [<Eng. windshield] windshield (car). Also, *vidrio* and *virdio.*

güini, *m.* [<Eng. wienie] wiener, frankfurter; vienna sausage.

güique, *adj.* [<Eng. weak] physically weak; weakened.

güirigüiri, *m.* [<onomatopoeic term] chatter; yak-yak.

güisa, *f.* [<Eng. sweetheart (*güisa*<*juisa* <*suijá*)] sweetheart, girl friend; *adj.*, beautiful, good-looking.

güisero, -ra, *adj.* [<N.M. Sp. *güisa*] said of the person who goes after individuals of the opposite sex.

güiso, *m.* [<N.M. Sp. *güisa*] boyfriend, sweetheart; *adj.*, handsome, good-looking.

güisque, *m.* [<Eng. whiskey] whiskey; hard liquor.

guñelo, *m.* See *buñuelo.*

gurrión, *m.* [<Sp. *gorrión*] sparrow. Also, *burrión.*

gusano, *m.* [<Sp. *gusano*] worm. (*La Feliciana se levantó con el gusano salido.* Feliciana got up on the wrong side of the bed.)

Hacerle bien al ingrato es lo mismo que ofenderlo.
Not everyone appreciates kindness.

ha, *vb.* [<Sp. *haber,* to have] I have, he has. New Mexicans and southern Coloradoans use the third person singular of *haber* for both the first and third person forms. (*Yo no ha visto nada.* I haven't seen anything.)

habas, *f. pl.* [<Sp. *habas,* beans] horse beans.

habitito, *m.* [<Sp. dim. of *hábito,* habit, dress] a garment in the form of a nightshirt that is put on a sick child in the hope that he will get well.

hábito, *m.* See *habitito.*
When their children were ill, the mothers made votive promises. If the child were cured through the intercession of a certain saint, the mother would have *el hábito* (the habit of the saint) put on the child. An intimate *comadre* was invited as godmother (*madrina*). She sewed the red habit of el Santo Niño or the blue or brown ones of St. Anthony or St. Joseph, had them blessed, and with a prayer, holding a lighted candle, she slipped the *hábito* on the child. He wore it under his clothes until the habit wore out. (Cleofas M. Jaramillo, *Shadows of the Past*)

hablador, -ra, *adj.* [<Sp. *hablador,* talkative] gossipmonger; liar.

hacer, *vb.* [<Sp. *hacer*] to do, to make; *hacer diligencia,* to try; *hacer guaje a alguno,* to deceive, to fool. *¡Qué le hace!* It doesn't matter. *Hacer que* and verb, to pretend. (*Hacía que lloraba.* He was pretending that he was crying. *El Rosebaldo está haciendo que hace.* Rosebaldo is pretending to be doing something.) *Hacer raya,* to make a hit; *hacerse,* to refuse. (*Andale, Pilar, no te hagas.* Come on, Pilar, don't say no.) *¡Qué se me hace!* Oh, yeah? (I don't believe it!) *Hacerse uno viejo, gordo, feo,* etc., to begin to get old; to become fat, ugly, etc. (*¡Qué vieja se está haciendo la Figenia!* Figenia is getting so old!) *Hacerse uno de mil colores,* to become embarrassed; *hacérsele a uno,* to seem to one. (*¡Vi a la Frumencia y se me hizo tan fea!* I saw Frumencia and she

seemed so ugly to me! *Al Edumenio ya se le hace que no se casa con la Atanasia.* Edumenio seems to think that he will never marry Atanasia.)

haciendado, *m.* [<Sp. *hacendado*] rich hacienda owner; land or sheep owner.

hacha, *f.* [<Sp. *hacha*] ax; torch; *pasársele a uno 'l hacha,* to go to extremes, to overdo a thing.

hachazo, *m.* [<Sp. *hachazo*] blow with an ax. *¡Qué hachazo!* What a boo-boo (faux pas). See also *manchón.*

hachazuela, *f.* [<Sp. dim. of *hacha*] hatchet; small ax.

hachón, *m.* [<Sp. aug. of *hacha*] large ax; homemade torch used in processions at Christmas in Taos Pueblo.

hallar, *vb.* [<Sp. *hallar*] to find; to discover; to realize; *hallársela una persona,* to fall into a habit. (*Ya la Cipriana se la halló venir a echarme mis papas.* Cipriana has gotten into the habit of coming over to tell me off.) Sp. *hallar* is invariably pronounced [*xayár*] in N.M. and so. Colo. Spanish. See *jallar.*

hambre, *m.* [<Sp. *hambre* (*f.*)] hunger. *Tener mucho hambre,* to be very hungry; *ser una persona 'l hambre del mundo,* to be very stingy.

hambriento, -ta, *adj.* [<Sp. *hambriento*] hungry; stingy; selfish.

harcina, *f.* [<Sp. *hacina*] haystack; hayloft.

harina, *f.* [<Sp. *harina*] flour; *harina 'e 'cemita,* a kind of whole wheat flour used in the making of *cemitas* (coffee cakes); *harina pa chaegüe,* ground blue cornmeal used in the making of a porridge (also called *chaegüe*); *harina 'e maiz,* cornmeal; *harinilla 'e maiz,* a finely ground corn flour made from roasted blue corn.

hatajo, *m.* [<Sp. dim. of *hato,* flock] small flock; bunch; lots. Col. and Terr. N.M. Sp., a string of mules (mule train); *un hatajo de mentiras,* a bunch of lies; *un hatajo de veces,* many times.

hay, *vb.* [<Sp. *hay* < *haber*] *de cuanto hay,* old-fashioned; old. (*La Rafela trae un túnico de cuanto hay.* Rafela is wearing an old-fashioned dress.)

hechizo, -za, *adj.* [<Sp. *hechizo,* artificial] homemade, rather than store-bought.

helarse, *vb.* [<Sp. *helarse*] *¡Ya me helo!* I'm freezing! Cf. Sp. *¡Ya me hielo!*

helera, *f.* [<Sp. *helar,* to freeze] icebox; refrigerator. Also, *hielera.*

hermano, -na, *m.* and *f.* [<Sp. *hermano*] brother; *hermano carnal,* blood brother; *hermano de disciplina,* flagellant; *hermano de leche,* foster brother; *hermano mayor,* older brother; presiding officer of a Penitente brotherhood; *hermano salido a luz,* said of a Penitente who no longer has to wear a hood in Penitente Easter rites.

hético, -ca, *adj.* [<Sp. *hético,* consumptive] marasmic, emaciated, especially as applied to a child suffering from malnutrition and showing an enlarged stomach and an emaciated body.

hicotea, *f.* [<Am. Sp. *hicotea,* a kind of water turtle] a small turtle. (*La Odosia está como la hicotea; se le va en puro pujar.* Odosia is like the turtle; she's nothing but groans.) Also, *jicotea.*

hielera, *f.* [<Sp. *helar,* to freeze] icebox; refrigerator; a very cold room. (*Este cuarto es una hielera.* This room is as cold as an icebox.)

hierba, *f.* [<Sp. *hierba,* grass] weed, weeds. (*Esta yarda es una pura hierba.* This yard is nothing but weeds.) Also spelled *yerba.*

hierbajes, *m. pl.* [<Sp. *herbajes,* herbage] herbs (general); a collection of herbs. (*Aquí viene mano Beno con sus hierbajes.* Here comes old man Beno with his herbs.)

hierbero, -ra, *m.* and *f.* [<Sp. *hierbas,* herbs] herbalist; herb doctor; seller of medicinal herbs; weeds or pile of weeds. *¡Qué hierbero!* What an awful lot of weeds!

higuita, *f.* [<Sp. *higa,* amulet] a charm or amulet in the form of a closed fist with the thumb sticking out between the index finger and the third or middle finger. An *higuita* is usually worn by a

child around his neck to ward off the evil eye (*mal ojo*).

hijadero, *m.* [<Sp. *ahijadero*] lambing season; lambing site.

hijado, -da, *m.* and *f.* [<Sp. *ahijado*] godchild; *hijado de pila,* baptismal godchild.

¡Hi[jo]!, *interj.* [<Sp. *hijo*] Damn! (*¡Hi . . . qué fiera está la güisa del Alanís.* Damn, Alanis' girl friend is ugly!)

¡Hijo!, *interj.* [<Sp. *hijo*] Damn! Good gosh! (*¡Hijo 'e la qué viejota!* Damn, what a sexpot! *¡Hij' 'e Nea, qué vieja tan fiera!* Damn, what an ugly old woman!)

hilachas, *f. pl.* [<Mex. Sp. *hilacha*] rags, tatters; *ser uno puras hilachas,* to be nothing but rags. (*Mana Irinea es puras hilachas.* Old lady Irinea is nothing but rags.)

hilachento, -ta, *adj.* [<Mex. Sp. *hilachento*] in rags, raggedy, tattered.

hilo, *m.* [<Sp. *hilo*] thread; grain; *contra 'l hilo,* against the grain; *jallarle 'l hilo a una cosa o a una persona,* to follow the grain; to find a way; to get along with someone. Clothesline. See also *percha.*

hispano, -na, *adj., m.* and *f.* [<Sp. *hispano*] Hispanic; a person of Spanish or Indo-Hispanic descent native to the American Southwest.

hocico, *m.* [<Sp. *hocico,* snout] snout; mouth. (*Al Adelmo le dieron en 'l hocico.* Adelmo got a good beating.) *¡Cállate 'l hocico!* Shut your mouth! Shut up!

hogarse, *vb.* [<Sp. *ahogarse*] to choke; to drown. (*El muchito de la Criselda se hogó en la 'cequia.* Criselda's child drowned in the ditch.)

hoguera, *f.* [<Sp. *hoguera*] bonfire; bonfire used as a *luminaria,* q. v. The term *joguera* may be more common.

hojas, *f. pl.* [<Sp. *hoja,* leaf] inner leaves of corn husks used as paper for hand-rolled cigarettes.

The constant making and lighting of *cigarritos* entailed carrying about a small kit of "makings"—*punche,* **hojas** ("papers"—actually inner leaves of corn husks, cut into convenient squares), tinder, flint, and steel. (E.

Boyd, "The Use of Tobacco in Spanish New Mexico," *El Palacio*)

hojelata, *f.* [<Sp. *hoja de lata, hojalata*] tin, as in tin can (*un jarrito de hojelata*); pl., homemade tin hair rollers. (*La Anselma anda toda la plaza con sus hojelatas.* Anselma goes all over town with her homemade tin hair rollers.)

hojero, *m.* [<N.M. Sp. *hojas*] Terr. N.M. Sp., a kind of beaded wallet in which society ladies carried *hojas* (cigarette papers) for hand-rolled cigarettes.

The *hojas* were most likely to be carried in a buckskin wallet rather than one of leather or velvet, although some ladies had them of embroidered silk, or, after 1840, of bead-work. (E. Boyd, "The Use of Tobacco in Spanish New Mexico," *El Palacio*)

hombrada, *adj.* [<Sp. *hombre,* man] said of the woman with a man's characteristics. (*La Wenceslada es medio hombrada, ¿no te parece?* Wenceslada is somewhat mannish, don't you think?)

hombrecito, *m.* [<Sp. dim. of *hombre*] male child; baby. (*¿Qué tuvo la Seferina, hombrecito o mujercita? Hombrecito.* Is Seferina's baby a boy or a girl? A boy.)

hombrera, *adj.* [<Sp. *hombre*] man crazy; said of the woman who likes to go out with many men. (*Las hijas de la Praxedis son más hombreras que qué.* Praxedis' daughters are very man crazy.)

hombrote, *adj.* [<Sp. aug. of *hombre*] applied to a *macho,* a he-man; said of the boy or young man who does chores with enthusiasm and zest. (*¡Mi hijo Marcelino es muy hombrote!* My son, Marcelino, is quite a man.)

horita, *adv.* [<Mex. Sp. *horita* <dim. of Sp. *ahora*] just now; immediately; right away. (*¿Qués el Cleofes? Horita se va iyendo.* Where is Cleofes? He left just a moment ago.)

hormiga, *f.* [<Sp. *hormiga*] ant; *hormiga colorada,* red ant; *hormiga mielera,* honey ant; *hormiga mochilera,* a kind of pouched ant; *hormiga perroda,* a small,

stinking red ant; *hormiga voladora,* flying ant; termite.

The honey ants [**hormigas** *mieleras*] or pouched ants, are known for storage of honey in their abdomens, collected as it oozes from live galls on scrub oak branches growing near their nests. The insects' bodies are so elastic they often become greatly swollen with their amber liquid and children enjoy pinching them and sucking the sweet. This they do with impunity since these ants cannot bite. (Leonora S. M. Curtin, *Healing Herbs of the Upper Rio Grande*)

hornacina, *f.* [<Sp. *hornacina,* vaulted niche] a kind of glass niche.

Since the church to the Spanish Colonial was first consideration in his daily living, it is safe to say that the first tin articles fashioned were those destined for the church or private chapel. This is evidenced by the numerous articles found today that formerly were in church use: *arañas,* ceiling candle holders, *pantallas,* wall candle holders, *candeleros,* candlesticks, *nichos,* niches, and **hornacinas**, niches entirely of glass. (Carmen Espinosa, "Color for Mi Casa," *New Mexico Magazine*)

horno, *m.* [<Sp. *horno*] oven; large beehive-shaped outdoor oven; large iron frying pan.

On Monday and Tuesday of Holy Week the conical adobe ovens were seen smoking throughout the three villages, while the week's supply of bread and *panocha* was being baked. The mud ovens must be blessed before using them, or they won't bake the bread right; it will come out soggy. To bless the oven, salt is sprinkled on the cross and prayers recited. (Cleofas M. Jaramillo, *Shadows of the Past*)

horrores, *m. pl.* [<Sp. *horror*] havoc, destruction.

hueja, *f.* See *güeja.*

huero, *m.* See *güero.*

huesito, *m.* [<Sp. dim. of *hueso,* bone] small bone; *huesito sabroso,* anklebone. (*La Nicasia anda cojeando porque se dio un golpe en el huesito sabroso.* Nicasia is limping because she hit herself on the anklebone.)

hueso, *m.* [<Sp. *hueso*] bone; *pl.,* dice (<Eng. bones). (*Lo mejor de los huesos es tirarlos.* The best thing about "bones" is to throw them.) *Ser una persona puros huesos,* to be very thin, emaciated. (*El probe de mano Labriano es puros huesos.* Poor old man Labriano; he's nothing but skin and bones.)

huevo, *m.* See *güevo.*

huevón, huevona, *adj.* See *güevón.*

huevonera, *f.* [<Sp. *huevo,* egg] the act of being or feeling lazy. (*La huevona de la Ramona todavía no se levanta. ¡Qué huevonera!* Lazy Ramona is not up yet. How lazy can you get!)

huevudo, *adj.* [<Mex. Sp. *güevo* (*huevo*)] a he-man (*macho*).

huiso, -sa, *m.* and *f.* See *güisa.*

hule, *m.* [<Sp. *hule*] rubber; inner tube; linoleum; oilcloth; rubber band; *pl.,* condoms; rubber shoes (galoshes). (*Las llantas de hoy en día ya no tienen el hule que tenían las de antes, 'hora cuasi todas son tubeless.* Today's tires no longer have inner tubes like yesterday's tires; now almost all are tubeless. *Esta mañana le trajieron el hule de la cocina a mana Sinforosa.* Old lady Sinforosa got her kitchen linoleum this morning.)

húmido, -da, *adj.* [<Col. N.M. Sp. *húmido* (Villagrá)] humid, damp.

> *Resollando vertía y derramaua*
> *sobre la enjuta arena guijarrosa*
> *del **húmido** licor una gran copia.*
> Breathing audibly he shed and
>   spilled
> On the dry and pebbly sandy ground
> An abundance of the humid essence
>   of life.

(Gasper Pérez de Villagrá, *Historia de la Nueba Mexico*)

húngaro, -ra, *m.* and *f.* [<Sp. *húngaro,* Hungarian] gypsy; fortune-teller.

Ir por lana y volver trasquilado.
To come out on the short end of a deal.

íchite, *m.* [<Mex. Sp. *istle* <Náhuatl *ixtli,* vegetable fiber] fiber cord; curled shavings of wood used for stuffing or packing.

idea, *f.* [<Sp. *idea*] *tenerle mala idea a alguno,* to have it in for someone; to bear ill will toward someone. See also (*mala*) *pica.*

ideático, -ca, *adj.* [<Sp. *ideático,* "nuts"] finicky, fussy; stubborn.

ideoso, -sa, *adj.* See *ideático.*

idomia, *f.* [<Sp. *idioma* (*m.*), language] Spanish language. (*Estos americanos, nomás aprender 'l idomia les falta.* All these gringos need is to learn the Spanish language.)

igualado, -da, *adj.* [<Mex. Sp. *igualado*] lacking in respect toward superiors, especially by treating them familiarly.

igualarse, *vb.* [<Mex. Sp. *igualarse*] to feel equal to a superior.

ijadero, *m.* See *'hijadero.*

ijotes, *m. pl.* [<Mex. Sp. *ejotes,* string beans] vines of the green-bean plants.

imágines, *f. pl.* [<Sp. *imágenes*] images; reflections.

imbicionar, *vb.* [<Sp. *ambicionar,* to covet] to get someone, especially a child, to covet a thing or to form a bad habit; to tempt, to tantalize; to corrupt. (*No imbiciones a ese muchito con ese chocolate.* Don't tempt that child with that chocolate candy.)

impitoso, -sa, *adj.* [<Sp. *impetuoso*] impetuous; impulsive; violent. (*Ese Tercio sí es impitoso, pa que vea.* Tercio really is impetuous, to give you an example.)

imponerse, *vb.* [<Sp. *imponerse,* to impose oneself] to become accustomed or used to. (*Yo no estoy impuesto a tanto ruido.* I am not used to so much noise.)

impuesto, -ta, *adj.* [<N.M. Sp. *imponerse,* to become accustomed to] accustomed, used to; *mal impuesto,* overindulged, spoiled. (*¡Ah, cómo tienen mal impuesto a este chamaco!* Gosh, you really have

85

this kid spoiled.)

incenso, *m.* [<Sp. *incienso*] incense.

incón, *m.* [<Col. N.M. Sp. *encón,* cove] a bay or beach in the middle of a wide stream or river; bend of a river, sheltered cove.

El trece del dicho, salimos deste parage e fuimos a dormir tres leguas de allí; en un encón, estaba el pueblo último donde habíamos salido, una legua de nosotros.
On the thirteenth of the aforesaid we left this camping site and went on to spend the night three leagues from there; at a bend of a river was situated the last pueblo from which we had departed, a league from us. (Gaspar Castaño de Sosa, "Memoria del Descubrimiento," *Documentos ineditos*)

inconar, *vb.* [<Sp. *enconar*] to infect or cause infection.

incono, *m.* [<Sp. *encono,* ill will] inflammation, infection; infected sore area supposedly brought about by a person who is believed to have the power to infect another's sore or inflamed spot.

inconoso, -sa, *adj.* [<Sp. *enconoso*] apt to cause or produce inflammation; said of the person who is believed to have the power to infect another's sore or inflamed spot.

If a person had a cut or sore he must stay away from outsiders. If the sore became inflamed after he had attended some gathering of people, or someone had come into the room where the sick person was, the person was blamed for having affected the sore.

The sick must be especially careful of a woman carrying a baby for a woman in this condition was believed to be most *inconosa.* The woman was perfectly innocent of having caused any harm; it was just some unconscious, uncontrollable, malignant power in her, as in the ones who caused the evil eye [*mal ojo*]. (Cleofas M. Jaramillo, *Shadows of the Past*)

incuentro, *m.* [<Sp. *encuentro,* encounter] meeting; *El incuentro* (Penitente rite), an enactment of the meeting of Christ and the Virgin Mary during the Passion.

indiada, *f. pl.* [<Sp. *indio,* Indian] a large group of Indians; *adj.,* Indian-like, or following the ways of life of the Indians.

indiana, *f.* [<Mex. Sp. *indianilla*] printed calico. Also, *indianilla.*

*Ahí viene el carroferril
viene cargado de indianas;
viene quebrando los precios
de las tiendas mejicanas.*
There comes the train,
It is loaded with calico;
It is breaking the prices
Of the Mexican stores.
(*El carroferril,* N.M. Sp. folk song)
Womenfolk of the ruling class varied the plain chemise with *indianilla,* a cotton print made in Mexico in imitation of East India block-prints. (Roland F. Dickey, *New Mexico Village Arts*)

indino, -na, *adj.* [<Sp. *indigno*] unworthy.

indita, *f.* [<Mex. Sp. *indita,* a song in praise of an Indian maiden] Indian maiden; a New Mexico ballad with an imitative Indian melody and a refrain in which the word "Indita" stands out. In the ballads the term *indita* refers to the Virgin of Guadalupe, Mexico's dark-complexioned patron saint.

*Adiós, Rumaldo Gallegos,
padre desafortunado,
se te murió 'l único hijo
que tenías a tu lado,
'biéndose muerto el otro
Trinidad, allá en Colorado.
¡Ay, indita, pídele al cielo
que les dé consolación
a los padres de Gallegos.*
Farewell, Rumaldo Gallegos,
Most unfortunate parent;
The only son you had with you
Has now passed away;
Your other son having died
In Trinidad, Colorado.
Alas, Indita, pray to God

To bring comfort
To the parents of Gallegos.
(*Indita de Rumaldo Gallegos*, N.M. Sp. ballad)

infante, *m.* [<Eng. infant] infant, baby.

infeitarse, *vb.* [<Sp. *infectarse*] to become infected.

infierno, *m.* [<Sp. *infierno*] hell; *en el quinto infierno,* an expression to indicate a great distance.

influencia, *f.* [<Sp. *influenza*] the flu.

ingenio, *m.* [<Sp. *ingenio,* talent] car engine. (*Este carro tiene un ingenio de trescientos caballos.* This car has a three-hundred horsepower engine.)

Inglatierra, *f.* [<Sp. *Inglaterra*] England.

ingüente, *m.* [<Sp. *ungüento*] ointment, salve.

inmortal, *f.* [<Mex. Sp. *inmortal,* a medicinal plant of the Milkweed family] bot., Antelope horns, Spider milkweed.

inocente, *m., f.* [<Sp. *inocente*] child; *adj.,* simpleminded, mentally retarded person; idiot. *¡Inocente para siempre!* April fool!

inorante, *adj.* [<Col. N.M. Sp. *ynorante*] ignorant.

instanciar, *vb.* [<Sp. *instar*] to press or urge a request or petition.

íntico, -ca, *adj.* [<Sp. *idéntico*] identical; the "spitting image."

introducido, -da, *adj.* [<Sp. *introducir,* to introduce or to bring into notice] active; expressive; gregarious, outgoing, applied especially to one who easily wins the goodwill of those around him.

introdución, *f.* [<Sp. *introducción*] introduction, in the sense of introducing a speaker to an audience or introducing one person to another. Cf. Sp. *presentación.* Col. and Terr. N.M. Sp., a kind of introduction duty on commodities.

introducir, *vb.* [<Sp. *introducir,* to introduce] to introduce, in the sense of making persons acquainted with each other. Cf. Sp. *presentar.*

intuato, -ta, *adj.* [<Sp. *intacto*] intact; *adv.,* exactly. (*El refrigerador está intuato como lo dejamos.* The refrigerator is exactly as we left it.)

inventorio, *m.* [<Eng. inventory] *venta de inventorio,* inventory sale.

inverniz, -za, *adj.* [<Sp. *invernizo,* hibernal] said of the lamb or heifer born in winter.

invicionar, *vb.* See *imbicionar.*

ipazote, *m.* See *epazote.*

ir, *vb.* [<Sp. *ir,* to go] *ir chillado* (*a todo chile, a todo güelo,* or *a sesenta*), to be in a hurry; to go full speed; *ir a pie y tierra,* to go on foot; *ir de medio día pa abajo,* to show one's age; *ir (salir) pa juera,* to go to the bathroom; *ir pa atrás,* to go back, to return.

iriaza, *f.* [<Sp. *eriaza*] uncultivated field; stubble field.

ispiado, -da, *adj.* [<Sp. *espiar,* to warp] said of the mount with sore or split hooves as a result of traveling over hard or rocky surfaces.

isque, *vb. exp.* [<Sp. *diz que*] Did you know that . . . ? They say that . . . , etc. Also, *esque.*

ivel, *m.* [<Sp. *nivel*] level; spirit level.

iyendo, *vb.* [<Col. N.M. Sp. *y yendo,* lit., going there] going. (*Óyeme, Core, no quiero que te me andes iyendo de noche.* Listen, Core, I don't want you to be going out at night.)

izque, *vb. ex.* [<Sp. *diz que*] they say that; rumor has it that. That's what they say. (*¿Izque te casates? Izque.* Is it true that you got married? That's what they say.)

Jugando, jugando, nace un niño llorando.
In play and in fun a squealing baby can be born.

jabla, *f.* [<Sp. *jaula*] cage; wire enclosure.

jablarse, *vb.* [<N.M. Sp. *jabla*] to get into a car; to climb aboard. (*Apúrate, Rubel, jáblate.* Hurry, Rubel, climb aboard [slang].)

jabón, *m.* [<Sp. *jabón*, soap] *jabón de lejía*, homemade laundry soap made with lye and pork lard. When pine oil is added to this soap it is called *jabón de trementina.*

jaboncillo, *m.* [<Sp. dim. of *jabón*] a specially prepared face soap made from the *jabón de lejía.*

Home-made hard soap was cooled, the top skimmed off into another pot and boiled with water until no lye was left. The soap was cooled, cut up into shavings and put into a bag; the bag was put into a pail of water covered with corn husks and left to soak for three days, the water being changed every day. Then the bag was drained out of the water, the soap mixed with melon seeds, *rome-ro*, wild rose leaves, and home-made bran starch; the whole mixture was ground into a paste and formed into little cakes which were set out in the sun to dry. These *jaboncillos* were used as a face soap only and were kept as something very precious. (Cleofas M. Jaramillo, *Shadows of the Past*)

jacal, *m.* [<Mex. Sp. *jacal*<Náhuatl *xacalli*] a small hut with walls consisting of rows of vertical poles (*varillas*) filled in between with mud.

jacalear, *vb.* [<Mex. Sp. *jacal*] to go visiting with neighbors; to gossip; to tattle. (*La Senaida se la pasa jacaleando con las vecinas.* Senaida spends her time gossiping with the neighbors.)

jacalero, -ra, *adj.* [<Mex. Sp. *jacal*] said of the person that spends his or her time gossiping with neighbors.

jaiguaras, *adj.* [<Eng. high waters] said of trousers that are so short they hardly go down to one's ankles.

jaina, *f.* [<Eng. honey] girl friend; girl (slang). (*El Colás anda en la chirinola con su jaina.* Colás is out having a good time with his girl friend.)

jainear, *vb.* [<N.M. Sp. *jaina*] to look for or go out with girls (slang).

jaira, *f.* [<Eng. harrow] harrow, a farm implement for leveling the soil and preparing it for planting.

jaitón, -na, *adj.* [<Eng. high-toned] affectedly stylish; well-groomed.

jaitunato, -ta, *adj.* [<Eng. high-toned] See *jaitón.*

jajar, *vb.* [<Mex. Sp. *jajar*<Sp. *jadear*, to pant] to pant with anticipation or expectation. (*Las botijonas de las cuatas están jajando porque te caigas.* The fat twins are panting with expectation to see you fall down.)

jalado, -da, *adj.* [<Mex. Sp. *jalarse*, to get drunk] drunk; tipsy.

jalador, -ra, *adj.* [<Mex. Sp. *jalar*, to work] said of a good worker or one who is not afraid to work.

jalar, *vb.* [<Mex. Sp. *jalar*<Sp. *halar*, to pull] to haul or tow; to pull; to work (slang).

jale, *m.* [<Mex. Sp. slang *jale*] job; work. (*El Gualberto está deoquis, no tiene jale.* Gualberto is staying home; he doesn't have a job.)

jalón, *m.* [<Mex. Sp. *jalón*] pull; *de un jalón*, all at once; *estar algo de un jalón*, to be just right, perfect or wonderful. (*¿Cómo estuvo el party? Estuvo de un jalón.* How was the party? It was wonderful.)

jamachar, *vb.* [<Eng. how much?] to haggle; to "talk turkey." (*¿Quése 'm primo Pantaleón? Ahi 'stá jamachando con el gabacho.* Where is cousin Pantaleón? There he is haggling with the gringo.)

jamache, *m.* [<Eng. how much?] how much?; *estar a jamache*, to haggle.

jambado, -da, *adj.* [<Mex. Sp. *jambado*] gluttonous. (*Un chulito encartado de cuzco y jambado.* A small dog, half-greedy and half-gluttonous.)

jambar, *vb.* [<Mex. Sp. *jambar*, to take something greedily] to pilfer; to steal. Also, *jambear.*

jambo, -ba, *adj.* [<N.M. Sp. *jambar* or *jambear*] thievish; given to stealing.

jamón, *m.* [<Sp. *jamón*] ham; bacon; *jamón blanco* (or *salado*), salt pork; *jamón de almuerzo*, bacon.

janchar, *vb.* [<Eng. honcho, leader] to grab; to kipe (slang).

janche (janchi), *adj.* [<N.M. Sp. *janchar*] avaricious; grabby.

jando, *m.* [<Eng. handout] money; "bread" (slang).

jaque, *m.* [<Eng. hack] a kind of carriage; buggy.

jara, *f.* [<Sp. *jara*, a kind of shrub] bot., Sandbar willow; *jara de la hoja redonda*, bot., Round-leaf sandbar willow; rod, a slender twig used for whipping mischievous children.

jaral, *m.* [<Sp. *jaral*] Sandbar willow thicket.

jarazo, *m.* [<N.M. Sp. *jara*] blow with a *jara* or willow rod.

jare, *vb. exp.* [<Eng. howdy] hello, hi, howdy.

jaresa, *f.* [<Sp. *cresa*] maggot. See also *queresa.*

jarirusa, *vb. ex.* [<Eng. How-d'-ye-do, sir] how do you do? *Hablar jarirusa*, to speak English.

jariusa, *vb. ex.* [<Eng. How-d'-ye-do, sir] how are you? (*Jariusa, Mrs. Martínez, como 'sta, güena?* How are you, Mrs. Martínez, are you well?)

jarrería, *f.* [<N.M. Sp. *jarro*, tin can] a great number of tin cans; pile of discarded tin cans.

jarrito, *m.* [<N.M. Sp. dim. of *jarro*] tin can. (*Curre a la tienda y tráeme un jarrito de leche Pete.* Run to the store and bring me a can of Pet milk.)

jarro, *m.* [<Sp. *jarro*, clay jar] tin can; *colmarle el jarro a alguno*, to be the limit, to have had enough. (*Ya el Rosebaldo me colmó el jarro con su güiri-güiri.* I've had enough of Rosebaldo's yakety-yak.)

jarrumbre, *f.* [<Sp. *herrumbre*] rust of iron; iron-like taste. Also, *jerrumbre.*

jaspe, *m.* [<Col. N.M. Sp. *jaspe,* gypsum (Molina)] chalk; gypsum; homemade whitewash; *adj.,* off-white.

jatancioso, -sa, *adj.* [<Sp. *jactancioso*] arrogant; boastful.

jatearse, *vb.* [<Sp. *jactarse*] to boast; to brag.

jato, *m.* [<Col. N.M. Sp. *hato* [*xáto*], part of a flock] flock of sheep.

> *Te doy el perro y el gato*
> *el jato y el almirez*
> *tan sólo porque te quedes*
> *esta noche y otras tres.*
> I will give you the dog and the cat
> The flock and the mortar,
> If only you will stay
> This night and three more.
> (*El pastor tonto,* N.M. and so. Colo. Sp. ballad)

Jauja, *f.* [<Col. N.M. Sp. *Jauja*] a land of plenty mentioned in sixteenth- and seventeenth-century Spanish songs still sung in New Mexico.

> *Desde la tierra de Jauja*
> *me mandan solecitar,*
> *que me vaya, que me vaya*
> *de un tesoro a disfrutar.*
> From the land of Jauja
> They have sent for me,
> Asking me to go
> Some treasure to enjoy.
> (*La tierra de Jauja,* N.M. Sp. folk song)

jedentina, *f.* [<Mex. Sp. *jedentina*] foul smell, stench.

jeder, *vb.* [<Sp. *heder*] to stink. (*Se le hace que a él no le jiede.* He thinks he's so great!)

jediondilla, *f.* [<Mex. Sp. *jediondilla*] bot., Creosote.

> Here is some *mariola,* rubber bush, which is so good for bringing down a fever. And this is **hediondilla,** creosote, to use for baths when there is high fever. (Fabiola C. de Baca Gilbert, *The Good Life*)

jefe, *m.* [<Sp. *jefe,* chief] chief; boss; *jefe político,* political boss. *Jefe, jefa, jefito, jefita* are terms used in Southwest Spanish for father, mother (the old man, the old woman). (*Tengo que ir a ayudarle a mi jefito.* I have to go and help my old man.)

jején, *m.* [<Am. Sp. *jején,* gnat] mosquito, gnat.

jemiquear, *vb.* [<Mex. Sp. *jemiquear* and *jeremiquear*<*Jeremías* (Jeremiah)] to be crying or sobbing constantly.

jenízaro (genízaro), -ra, *m.* and *f.* [<Sp. *jenízaro*] a person of mixed blood; an Indian captive ransomed by the Spanish authorities from his Apache, Comanche, Navajo, or Ute masters and used by his rescuers as a domestic or soldier; also, a descendant of these ransomed Indians; *adj.,* dark-skinned.

> The term "**genízaro**" has been derived from the Turkish *yeni,* new, and *cheri,* troops; hence the English "Janizary," a member of a body of Turkish infantry made up of slaves, conscripts, and subject Christians. In Spanish the word came to be applied specifically in different periods and situations to various non-typical groups or blood mixtures. In New Mexico it was used to designate non-Pueblo Indians living in more or less Spanish fashion. Some of them were captives ransomed from the nomadic tribes, and their mixed New Mexico-born descendants inherited the designation. Church and civil records reveal such varied derivations as Apache, Comanche, Navajo, Ute, Kiowa, Wichita, and Pawnee. Many had Spanish blood, clandestinely or otherwise. They all bore Christian names from baptism and Spanish surnames from their former masters; belonging no longer to any particular Indian tribe, they spoke the broken Spanish observed by Domínguez [Fray Francisco Atanasio Domínguez]. (Eleanor B. Adams and Fray Angélico Chávez, *The Missions*

of New Mexico, 1776)

jeremiquear, *vb.* [<Mex. Sp. *jeremiquear*] to sob; to whimper. See *jemiquear.*

jeresas, *f. pl.* [<Sp. *cresas*] maggots. Also, *queresas* and *jaresas.*

jerga, *f.* [<Col. N.M. Sp. *xerga* [*šérga*] (Molina), a kind of sackcloth] Col. and Terr. N.M. Sp., a coarse twilled woolen stuff used for floor coverings; rug; carpet.

For this purpose [rugs] coarser yarn was spun . . . The *jerga* (also spelled *gerga* or *xerga*) was woven in lengths about two feet wide and sewn together so that the floor was covered wall to wall with this carpet, usually a diagonal twill but sometimes herringbone or diamond weave. The common kind was of light and dark natural wool colors. (E. Boyd, *Popular Arts of Spanish New Mexico*)

The fabric most used by the common people was called *jerga*, a coarse woolen cloth resembling rough serge. Depending upon the fineness of the yarn and the tightness of the weave, *jerga* was employed variously for skirts and trousers, carrying cloths, and saddle blankets. For suitings, the material was dyed red, dark blue, or cocoa brown, and worn pieces were pieced together in checkers for carpeting. (Roland F. Dickey, *New Mexico Village Arts*)

jerrar, *vb.* [<Sp. *errar*, to commit errors] to miss (a mark or bull's eye, a blow, etc.). (*Le tiré al jarro pero le jerré.* I shot at the tin can but I missed it.) See also *mistear.*

jerrumbre, *f.* [<Sp. *herrumbre*] rust of iron; taste of iron. Also, *jarrumbre.*

jervir, *vb.* [<Sp. *hervir*] to boil (liquids). (*Antes de beber agua del río la Rafela siempre la jierve. A mí no me gusta 'l agua jervida.* Rafela always boils river water before drinking it. I don't like boiled water.)

Jesús, *m.* [<Sp. *Jesús*] Jesus (Jesse). *¡Jesús!* God bless you (upon sneezing)! *Gritarle a Jesús,* to call out the name of Jesus, as a person is breathing his last; *Jesús Nazareno,* the Man of Sorrows.

When a sick person was in his last agony, the *rezador,* whose profession it was to recite prayers at religious gatherings, was called in to **gritarle a Jesús,** call out the name of Jesus three times as the person was expiring. (Cleofas M. Jaramillo, *Shadows of the Past*)

¡Jesús y cruz!, interj., said by people in old New Mexico before going into a body of water to swim.

The waters of lakes and rivers are said to sting (*pican*) during the month of May; and those who bathe therein always say before entering into the water, to cure it, "*¡Jesús y cruz!*" (Aurelio Macedonio Espinosa, "New Mexican Spanish Folklore," *The Journal of American Folklore*)

jeta, *f.* [<Sp. *jeta*] thick, heavy lips; *darle a alguno en la jeta,* to give someone a good beating; *colgar jeta,* to be upset, annoyed or angry. (*El Faustino traía una jeta que le colgaba.* Faustino had a long face [seemed upset]. *El Amarante también traiba una jeta que se la pisaba.* Amarante also seemed very upset.)

jetón, -na, *adj.* [<Sp. *jeta*] said of a person having thick, protruding lips.

jícara, *f.* [<Mex. Sp. *jícara*<Náhuatl *xicalli*, a kind of gourd] a drinking vessel made from a gourd shell cut in half; a chocolate mug. Also, the head. *¡Usen la jícara!* Use your head!

jicarilla, *f.* [<Mex. Sp. dim. of *jícara*] a drinking cup made from a gourd shell cut in half; a gourd cup; a bowl-shaped wicker basket.

jicote, *m.* [<Mex. Sp. *jicote*<Náhuatl *xicote*] wasp.

jicotea, *f.* [<Mex. Sp. *hicotea*] a small turtle. (*Está como la jicotea: se le va en puro pujar.* He is like the turtle; he is nothing but groans.)

jicotera, *f.* [<Mex. Sp. *jicote*] wasps' nest; swarm of wasps.

91

jiel, *f.* [<Sp. *hiel*] bile; gall; gallbladder; *echar la hiel,* to work very hard.

¡Jijo!, *interj.* [<Mex. Sp. *¡Jijo!*<Sp. *hijo*] Damn! Good gosh!

jilote, *m.* [<Mex. Sp. *jilote*<Náhuatl *xilotl*] roasting ear of corn; name of a folk dance (*El jilote*).

jimeriquear, *vb.* [<Mex. Sp. *jirimiquear*] to sob; to whimper. See also *jemiquear, jeremiquear.*

jito, -ta, *m.* and *f.* [<Sp. dim. of *hijo,* son] a term of endearment for *hijo, hija* (son, daughter). Northern New Mexico and southern Colorado Spanish-speakers are very fond of nouns in their diminutive form.

joca, *f.* [<Eng. hawk] plasterer's hawk.

joda, *f.* [<Mex. Sp. *joder,* to annoy, to bother] a beating. (*Le metieron una joda al Tercio.* Tercio got a good beating. *Juimos a la papa y nos metieron una buena joda.* We went to work in the potato fields and they really worked us hard.) The words *joda, joder, jodido,* etc., are considered taboo terms.

jodal, *m.* [<N.M. Sp. *joda*] a lot of; a great number of anything. (*Tengo un jodal de cosas que hacer.* I have a great many things to do [taboo].)

jodazo, *m.* [<N.M. Sp. *joda*] a hard blow (taboo). Cf. Sp. *golpazo* (<*golpe*).

joder, *vb.* [<Mex. Sp. *joder*] to annoy, to bother; to have sexual intercourse (taboo).

jodido, -da, *adj.* [<N.M. Sp. *joder*] badly off (financially or physically). (*Está bien jodido; perdió todo lo que tenía.* He is really badly off; he lost everything he had [taboo].)

jodón, -na, *adj.* [<N.M. Sp. *joda*] first-rate; great; super; strong. (*Hicieron un baile pero jodón.* They made a first-rate dance [taboo].) Cf. Am. Sp. *macanudo.*

joganza, *f.* [<Col. N.M. Sp. *holgança* [*xolgántsa*]] pleasure. (*El muerto a la barranca y el vivo a la joganza.* The dead to the hillside and the survivors to their fun.)

jogata, *f.* [<Col. N.M. Sp. *hogata*<*huego* [*xwégo*] fire] blaze; bonfire.

jogón, *m.* [<Col. N.M. Sp. aug. of *huego* [*xwégo*], fire] fireplace; room heater; *jogón de campana,* kitchen fireplace with a hood; *jogón de pader* or *padercita,* a kind of corner fireplace.

joguera, *f.* [<Col. N.M. Sp. *hoguera* [*xogéra*], fire flames] bonfire; bonfire-type *luminaria,* q.v.

¡Jojolas!, *interj.* Keen! Swell! (slang).

jola, *f.* [<Col. and Terr. N.M. Sp. *jola,* one-eighth part of a *real*] small change; penny (slang).

jolgorio, *m.* [<Sp. *holgorio*] mirth, noisy merriment, carousal.

jolino, -na, *adj.* [<Mex. Sp. *jolino*] having little or no tail (said mostly of barnyard fowl).

jololote, *m.* [<N.M. Sp. *jolote*] corncob. Also, *jolote.*

jolote, *m.* [<Mex. Sp. *olote*] corncob.

joncho, -cha, *adj.* [<unknown origin] spongy; rotten; barren, as a cow, woman, etc. See also *orra.*

jonda, *f.* [<Col. N.M. Sp. *honda* [*xónda*]] sling; an eye or ring at one end of a lariat through which the other end is slipped in order to form a noose.

jondable, *m.* [<Col. N.M. Sp. *hondable* [*xondáble*] sunken] the sunken part in a river or stream, especially one forming a whirlpool; a whirlpool.

No mas que seys pozuelos se mostraban sobre la superficie de la tierra, como rodelas todos, y de hondo una quarta el que mas **hondable** *estaba.*

Only six small holes could be seen on the surface of the land, all like shields, and the most sunken one was no more than eight inches deep. (Gaspar Pérez de Villagrá, *Historia de la Nueba Mexico*)

jondear, *vb.* [<N.M. Sp. *jonda*<Sp. *honda*] to discard; to throw out. (*Ella le jondeó con la puerta.* She slammed the door on him. *La Prudencia jondeó hoy al Frutoso.* Prudencia threw Frutoso out of

the house today.)

jondo, -da, *adj.* [<Col. N.M. Sp. *hondo* [*xóndo*]] deep.

jongo, *m.* [<Col. N.M. Sp. *hongo* [*xóngo*]] mushroom; *mandar a uno a frir jongos,* to tell someone to go to the devil; to ruin someone.

jonuco, *m.* [<Mex. Sp. *jonuco,* cubbyhole] said of a homemade, unprofessional looking room added on to a house.

jornada, *f.* [<Sp. *jornada,* a one-day's journey] *Jornada del muerto,* Journey of Death, name of a desert area in south-central New Mexico; *jornada de recua,* day's journey of a pack drove.

The day's travel is made without a nooning respite; for the consequent unloading and reloading would consume too much time: and as a heavily-packed *hatajo* should rarely continue en route more than five or six hours, the ***jornada de recua*** (day's journey of a pack-drove) is usually but twelve or fifteen miles. (Josiah Gregg, *Commerce of the Prairies*)

jorongo, *m.* [<Mex. Sp. *jorongo,* a kind of poncho] a knot or coil of hair worn at the top of a woman's head.

jorunda, *f.* [unknown origin] bugbear; witch.

josco, -ca, *adj.* [<Col. N.M. Sp. *hosco* [*xósco*] *baço en color* (ochre?)] grayish brown; faded or colorless.

Una vaca josca
pasó por el mar,
pegando bramidos
sin ser animal.
A grayish brown cow
Crossed the ocean,
Bellowing away
Without being an animal.
(*La nube, The Cloud,* N.M. and so. Colo. Sp. riddle)

joseado, -da, *adj.* [<N.M. Sp. *joso,* bear] mussed up; in disarray. (*Alguno anduvo en mi cajón y me lo dejó todo joseado.* Someone got into my drawer and left it all mussed up.)

josear, *vb.* [<N.M. Sp. *joso,* bear] to search or go through clothes, a drawer, etc., and leave things in disarray.

josijoso, -sa, *adj.* See *cosijoso.*

joso, -sa, *m.* and *f.* [<Sp. *oso*] bear. (*Juimos al venado y nos salió un joso tamañote.* We went hunting and met up with a huge bear.)

josquere, *m.* [<Navajo *hoskere* (taboo word)] *andar en el josquere,* to be sowing one's wild oats.

joto, -ta, *adj.* [<Mex. Sp. *joto,* effeminate] *m.* and *f.,* homosexual (derog.).

joyo, *m.* [<Sp. *hoyo*] hole; pothole; name of a game in which round, flat stones (*tejas*) are thrown into a small hole in the ground (*el joyo*). See *teja.*

Juan Moco, a term applied to a very untidy, dirty person.

juato, *m.* [unknown origin] fuss; ado. (*¡Bal, qué juato! Ni que juera el rey.* What fuss! You'd think he was the king!)

judío, -ía, *m.* and *f.* [<Sp. *judío*] Jew; said of an infant not yet baptized; *adj.,* stingy, tight.

juego, *m.* [<Col. N.M. Sp. *huego* [*xwégo*] (Molina)] fire; fever blister; *juego manso,* slow fire; game (in general), as *juego de football, de basketball,* etc.; gambling. (*Al Fabián le gusta muncho el juego.* Fabián likes gambling a great deal.)

juerte, *adj.* [<Sp. *fuerte*] strong; brave. (*Este niño no llora, es muy juerte.* This child doesn't cry; he's very brave.)

juerte, *m.* [<Sp. *fuerte,* fort] hut, shed or small outbuilding for storing hay. Also, *juertecito.*

juerza, *f.* [<Sp. *fuerza*] strength; *a juerza,* by force; *de juerza,* naturally; of course.

juez, *m.* [<Sp. *juez,* judge] *juez receptor,* Col. N.M. Sp., a judge delegated to conduct judicial proceedings on behalf of a superior.

jugar, *vb.* [<Sp. *jugar*] to play; to gamble; *de por jugar,* in jest; jokingly.

juir, *vb.* [<Col. N.M. Sp. *huir* [*xwír*]] to flee (*juigo, juyes, juye, juyemos,*———,

juyen).

juisque, *m.* [<Eng. whiskey] whiskey; brandy; hard liquor in general.

julano, -na, *m.* and *f.* [<Sp. *fulano*] a term used in reference to a person whose name one does not wish to divulge.

julio, *m.* [<Sp. *julio*] *julio de hilo,* warp roller in a loom; *julio de tela,* cloth roller.

jumadera, *f.* [<Sp. *humareda*] a great deal of smoke.

jumate, *m.* [<Mex. Sp. *jumate*<Náhuatl *xumatl,* a ladle made from a gourd shell] a dipper made from a gourd shell; dipper.

In the kitchen, Teodora set a pot of the strained milk to boil in the roomy hearth of the *fogón de campana,* its wide hood extending out over the posts set on *tinamastes* on the coals. She took from the coals the pot of blue *atole* gruel, set it on the door sill and sat by it, cooling it by letting the hot gruel drop in the air from a gourd *jumate,* which she dipped and raised with a quick, deft twist of her hand. (Cleofas M. Jaramillo, *Shadows of the Past*)

jumazo, *m.* [<Sp. *humazo,* smoke] fumigation; *dar jumazos a un cuarto,* to fumigate a room.

jumear, *vb.* [<Sp. *humear*] to emit smoke.

jumitos, *adj.* [<N.M. Sp. dim. of *jumo*] said of a person with a very short (fum-

ing) temper; touchy.

jumo, *m.* [<Sp. *humo*] smoke. (*Los jogones de campana no hacen muncho jumo.* Fireplaces with a hood keep smoke at a minimum.)

jura, *f.* [<SW Sp. *jura*<Sp. *jurar*] the police; the law; policeman, policewoman; patrol wagon.

¡Jura!, *interj.* [<Sp. *jurar,* to swear] You don't say! Swear (to it)!

jurundio, *m.* [<unknown origin] bugbear.

jurundún, *m.* [<unknown origin (probably onomatopoeic)] a kind of buzzing insect.

jurupián, *m.* [<unknown origin] bugbear.

juzgar, *vb.* [<Sp. *juzgar,* to judge] to judge; to find fault; to estimate. (*Yo juzgo que habrá como unas diez millas de aquí a Santa Fe.* I estimate that it must be some ten miles from here to Santa Fe.)

juzgón, -na, *adj.* [<Mex. Sp. *juzgón*] accuser, faultfinder; said especially of one who pries into other people's affairs or one who accuses others impulsively without actually having all the facts. (*No hagas cosas buenas que parezcan malas porque la gente es muy juzgona.* Don't do good deeds that may appear suspect, because people often misjudge.)

La mentira es como el maíz: sola sale.
Lies are like corn, they crop up by themselves.

labioso, -sa, *adj.* [<Mex. Sp. *labioso*] insincere, given to the use of lip service; crafty, cunning.

labor, *f.* [<Mex. Sp. *labor,* cornfield] Col. and Terr. N.M. Sp., mine pit.
Some municipal provisions have been established in pursuance of which any person may open a *labor,* or pit on occupied ground not nearer than ten paces to another. (Josiah Gregg, *Commerce of the Prairies*)

lacena, *f.* [<Sp. *alacena*] shelf; *lacena del jogón,* mantelpiece.

lacre, *m.* [<Mex. Sp. *lacre,* a kind of red color] a thinly woven cotton material used in lining and to cover *cajones de muerto* (coffins); a kind of black velvet.

ladeado, -da, *adj.* [<Sp. *ladeado* <*lado,* side] inclined to one side; crooked; said of a swindler. (*El Policarpo y 'l Eduviges son muy ladeados.* Policarpo and Eduviges are a pair of swindlers.)

ladino, -na, *adj.* [<Am. Sp. *ladino*] sharp, smart; intelligent; said of the child who starts speaking at a very early age (3–4 years).

ladino, -na, *m.* and *f.* [<Am. Sp. *ladino*] Col. N.M. Sp., half-breed; said of the Indian who spoke his native tongue and Spanish.
No one is to make battle, including the friendly Indian warriors, who are to be told this by interpreters, although most of them and their captains are *ladinos* and understand and speak our language. (José Manuel Espinosa, *First Expedition of Vargas into New Mexico, 1692*)

lado, *m.* [<Sp. *lado*] side; *por el lado,* with the grain; *dar a alguno por el lado,* to treat someone with kid gloves.

ladrón, *m.* [<Sp. *ladrón*] thief; *ladrón fino,* ringleader of thieves; the smartest thief.

lagañas, *f. pl.* [<Col. N.M. Sp. *lagañas* (Molina)] bleariness of the eyes.

lagañoso, -sa, *adj.* [<N.M. Sp. *lagañas*]

bleary; with one's eyes emitting a slimy humor; bleary-eyed.

lagartijo, *m.* [<Sp. dim. of *lagarto*] lizard. The term *lagarto* (as in standard Spanish) is more common.

lagarto, *m.* [<Sp. *lagarto*] swindler; thief; lizard; alligator.

lágrimas, *f. pl.* [<Sp. *lágrimas*, tears] *lágrimas de Cristo,* staurolite crystals in the form of a cross; fairy crosses.

> Many of us have seen these perfect little stone crosses known to Anglos as Fairy Crosses, to Spanish-Americans as *Lágrimas de Cristo* (Tears of Christ), and to Indians as Stones of the Gods. (Merlin Wendland, "Staurolite, Starbright," *New Mexico Magazine*)

lagrimilla, *f.* [<Sp. dim. of *lágrima,* tear] bird shot; buckshot.

laguna, *f.* [<Col. N.M. Sp. *laguna, lagunajo* (Molina)] lake. The Spanish term *laguna* for lagoon is virtually unknown in New Mexico.

lama, *f.* [<Mex. Sp. *lama*] moss. (*Piedra movediza no cría lama.* A rolling stone gathers no moss.) See also *enlame.*

lambe, *adj.* [<N.M. Sp. *lamber* <Sp. *lamer,* to lick] flatterer; apple polisher; *m.,* bootlick; bootlicker.

lamber, *vb.* [<Sp. *lamer*] to lick; to play up to someone; to cater to; to polish the apple.

> *Un viejito y una viejita*
> *hicieron una escalerita;*
> *subió el viejito y no se quebró,*
> *subió la viejita y no se quebró,*
> *subió el becerro y no se quebró,*
> *subió la vaca y se quebró.*
> *¿Acuál pesaba más?*
> *La vaca.*
> *Álzale la cola y **lámbele** la caca.*
> A little old man and a little old woman
> Made a small ladder.
> The little old man climbed it
> And it did not break;
> The little old woman climbed it
> And it did not break;
> The calf climbed it
> And it did not break;
> The cow climbed it
> And it broke!
> Which weighed more?
> The cow.
> Raise her tail and lick it.
> (N.M. Sp. children's *chiste*)

lambeta, *adj.* [<N.M. Sp. *lamber*] said of one who is always polishing the apple; bootlicker.

lambido, -da, *adj.* [<N.M. Sp. *lamber*] smooth and pressed down, as hair à la Rudolph Valentino.

lambión, -na, *adj.* [<N.M. Sp. *lamber*] applied to an apple polisher.

lambiscón, -na, *adj.* [<Mex. Sp. *lambiscón*] flatterer; bootlicker.

lambisconear, *vb.* [<Mex. Sp. *lambisconear*] to flatter; to play up to someone.

lambrijo, -ja, *adj.* [<Mex. Sp. *lambrijo*] hungry-looking; starving; skinny.

lambusco, -ca, *adj.* [<Mex. Sp. *lambusco*] fond of sweets; gluttonous; hungry (rare).

lámpara, *f.* [<Sp. *lámpara,* lamp] clever, witty; crooked, cunning, sharp.

lamparazo, *m.* [<Mex. Sp. *lamparazo*] a drink of whiskey or any hard liquor.

lana, *f.* [<Sp. *lana,* wool] money (slang); *lana verdín,* greenbacks; *ir por lana y volver trasquilado,* to set out to accomplish some task and fail; to get the short end of a deal.

lángaro, -ra, *adj.* [<Mex. Sp. *lángaro*] hungry, hungry-looking; petty thief; kleptomaniac; rascal, rogue.

langosta, *f.* [<Sp. *langosta*] *La langosta,* a plague of grasshoppers.

lanita, *f.* [<Sp. dim. of *lana,* wool] lint, fuzz; nap.

largucho, -cha, *adj.* [<Sp. dim. of *largo*] tall and lanky.

Las posadas, *f. pl.* See *posadas* (*Las posadas*).

lástico, *m.* [<Sp. *elástico,* elastic] rubber

band.

lastimada, *f.* [<Sp. *lastimar,* to hurt] hurt, injury.

latía, *f.* [<Sp. *latilla,* dim. of *lata,* log] wood lath; small peeled poles used as lath in beamed ceilings.

The master bedroom is distinctive for its well-proportioned corner fireplace and its beamed ceiling, with *latías,* or saplings, laid in herringbone design above the beams. (Amy P. Hurt, "Houses with a Past," *New Mexico Magazine*)

latón, *m.* [<Sp. *latón,* latten brass] galvanized corrugated iron; sheet metal; tin roofing.

The galvanized iron [*latón*], or "tin" roof was widely adopted by native villagers, since it eliminated constant repairs to the earthen roof, and if properly constructed, the overhanging eaves protected adobe walls. (Roland F. Dickey, *New Mexico Village Arts*)

lavada, *f.* [<Sp. *lavar,* to wash] washing. (*Todo saldrá en la lavada.* It all comes out in the wash.)

lavadero, *m.* [<Sp. *lavar*] washboard; scrubboard. The term is also applied to a road that resembles a washboard.

lavandija, *f.* [<Sp. *sabandija,* an insect] a kind of water bug.

lavastín, *m.* [<N.M. Sp. *lavar,* to wash] whitewash; calcimine.

leche, *f.* [<Sp. *leche,* milk] milk; *leche agria,* buttermilk; *leche clan,* custard; *leche cuajada,* buttermilk; *leche de jarro,* canned milk; *leche nevada,* ice milk, ice cream.

Tecolote, ¿d"ónde vienes?
De la Sierra Colorada,
voy a vender cacahuates
pa' comprar leche nevada.
Owl, where are you coming from?
From the red-colored sierra;
I am going to sell peanuts
In order to buy some ice cream.
(*El tecolote,* N.M. and so. Colo. Sp. folk song)

lecheros, *m. pl.* [<Sp. *leche,* milk] bot., Milkweed. Also, *lechones* and *lechugas.*

lechuda, *adj.* [<Sp. *leche,* milk] said of a cow with a large udder.

lechuguilla, *f.* [<Mex. Sp. *lechuguilla*] a small species of the Agave or Century plant] bot., Sand verbena; Indian hemp; Dogbane.

lechuza, *f.* [<Sp. *lechuza,* screech owl] Coquimbo owl; a small owl-like bird that hovers over prairie-dog mounds; also called *lechuza tucera* (<*tuza,* prairie dog), prairie-dog owl.

This owl has been called the *Coquimbo* owl. Its note, whether natural or imitative, much resembles that of the prairie dog. (Josiah Gregg, *Commerce of the Prairies*)

lelo, -la, *adj.* [<Sp. *lelo,* stupid] staring; stupefied; shocked. (*Faustina se quedó lela cuando realizó que el matador era su hijo, el Odosio.* Faustina remained speechless when she realized that the murderer was her own son, Odosio.)

lemita, *f.* [<unknown origin] bot., Squawbush; *pl.,* the berries of this bush; *jugar a las lemitas,* to play with a baby's feet as the child lies in his crib. The mother repeats the following rhyme with the baby's feet:

Estas dos patitas
jueron a cortar lemitas;
corre 'l una,
corre 'l otra,
corren las dos juntitas.
These two little feet
Went to gather berries;
This one runs,
The other one runs;
They both run together.
(N.M. Sp. children's rhyme)
The tall, green *Lemitas* bushes formed a hedge along the lower ridge. The green berries furnished an acid drink, and the hard gum boiled in water made a nice flavored chewing gum. (Cleofas M. Jaramillo, *Shadows of the Past*)

lemitar, *m.* [<N.M. Sp. *lemitas,* Squawbush

lengón

berries] Squawbush field. Name of a New Mexico village.

lengón, -na, *adj.* [<Mex. Sp. *lengón* <Sp. *lengua,* tongue] gossipmonger; tattletale; "loud mouth."

lengonear, *vb.* [<N.M. Sp. *lengón*] to gossip, to carry tales; to engage in idle talk.

lengua, *f.* [<Sp. *lengua,* tongue] *lengua de vaca,* bot., Yellow dock; Sour dock.

lengua larga, *f.* [<Sp. *lengua,* tongue] gossipmonger, tattletale.

lépero, -ra, *adj.* [<Mex. Sp. *lépero*] shameless; tricky; *m.* and *f.,* rogue, scoundrel; petty thief.

The arrival of the wagons produced a great deal of bustle and excitement among the natives. *"Los americanos"*— *"Los carros"*—*"La entrada de la caravana"* were to be heard in every direction; and crowds of women and boys flocked around to see the newcomers; while crowds of **léperos** hung about as usual to see what they could pilfer. (Josiah Gregg, *Commerce of the Prairies*)

lepra, *f.* [<Sp. *lepra,* leprosy] eczema.

letra, *f.* [<Sp. *letra,* a kind of song whose first lines are amplified (*glosadas*)] As used in N.M. folk plays, a *letra* is a strophe that is sung rather than spoken, and serves as a refrain or as an introduction to some subsequent action or event.

leva, *f.* [<Mex. Sp. *leva,* frock coat (slang)] dress coat; *leva de hule,* raincoat; *leva borreguera,* sheepskin coat.

levantado, -da, *adj.* [<Sp. *levantarse,* to arise from bed] up; out of bed; up and around. (*¿Ya está levantado el Tercio?* Is Tercio up and around?)

libertoso, -sa, *adj.* [<Sp. *libertad,* liberty] free; enjoying freedom.

librería, *f.* [<Sp. *librería,* bookstore] library. Cf. Sp. *biblioteca.*

libro, *m.* [<Sp. *libro,* book] book; grade in school. (*El Mabricio nomás hasta 'l libro tres jue pero 'stá muy bien puesto.* Maurice did not go beyond the third grade in school, but he is well established.)

liebro, *m.* [<Sp. *liebre,* hare] a drunk; a wino.

liga, *f.* [<Sp. *liga*] garter; rubber band. See also *lástico.*

limpiada, *f.* [<Sp. *limpiar,* to clean] cleaning; house cleaning; act of cleaning one's clothes, etc. Cf. Sp. *limpiadura.*

limpiamocos, *m. pl.* [<Sp. *limpiar,* to clean, and *mocos,* discharge from the mucous membranes of the nose] handkerchief.

líncere, *m.* [<Sp. *lince,* lynx] weasel; *adj.,* acute, cunning; sharp, smart.

lindero, *m.* [<Sp. *linde,* boundary] small irrigation ditch between two parcels of land or between two properties. (*Está seco el lindero. Yo creo que nos cortaron 'l agua.* The ditch is dry. I believe they've cut off our water.)

línea, *f.* [<Sp. *línea,* line] persuasive speech. (*¡Hi . . . qué línea la del Gerardo!* What a line Gerardo has!)

lío, *m.* [<Sp. *lío,* entanglement] *echar lío,* to court; the act of courting a young woman.

lion, *m.* [<Eng. lion] mountain lion; puma; cougar.

lírico, *adv.* [<Sp. *lírico*] by ear, i.e., without formal training, especially in music or vocal art. (*La Gorgonia sabe tocar la guitarra pero sólo lírico.* Gorgonia knows how to play the guitar, but only by ear.)

lirio, *m.* [<Sp. *lirio*] iris; lily.

The Spanish New Mexicans assert that the iris roots are poisonous. Through what evidently is a quirk of terminology, they refer to the plant as **lirio,** whereas the strict Spanish translation of the word is lily and not iris. (Leonora S.M. Curtin, *Healing Herbs of the Upper Rio Grande*)

lisa, *f.* [<Sp. *liso,* plain] shirt (slang).

lisón, *m.* [<Sp. *alisar,* to make smooth] a final combing of one's hair before going out; the act of fixing up (slang).

98

lisos, *m. pl.* [<Sp. *liso,* smooth] harness frame in a loom.

liviano, -na, *adj.* [<Sp. *liviano,* light; of little weight] fast (in speed). (*¡Cómo es liviano este Gregorio!* Gregorio is certainly fast!)

lo, *adv.* [<Sp. *luego*] immediately; *lo lo,* immediately; right then and there.

lobo, *m.* [<Mex. Sp. *lobo*] said of the person who has a quarter blood relationship with a person of another race; a person with one "Anglo" grandparent; monkey wrench; wolf (<Eng. wolf), said of the man who is fond of women; *lobo de cañute,* pipe wrench; *adj.,* of mixed blood.

logros, *m. pl.* [<Sp. *logro,* gain] *apostar hasta logros,* to bet anything.

lombral, *m.* [<Sp. *umbral* ('l umbral)] timber for a threshold (lintel).

lomo, *m.* [<Sp. *lomo,* the back of an animal] back. Cf. Sp. *espaldas. Sobarle el lomo a alguno,* to play up to someone. (*Cuando no hay lomo de todo como.* When I cannot get sirloin, I'll eat any meat. [Beggars can't be choosers.])

lona, *f.* [<Sp. *lona,* canvas; blue denim; *pl.,* levis; overalls.

lonche, *m.* [<Eng. lunch] lunch; *cara de lonche,* said of a person considered to be a pushover. (*Le vieron cara de lonche.* They saw him coming [considered him an easy victim].)

lonchear, *vb.* [<N.M. Sp. *lonche*] to have lunch (*loncheo, loncheas, lonchea, loncheamos, ——, lonchean*).

lonchera, *f.* [<N.M. Sp. *lonche*] lunch pail.

longdistans, *m. pl.* [<Eng. long distance] a kind of union suit or heavy winter underwear.

lonja, *f.* [<Mex. Sp. *lonja,* slice of fat] fat; *pl.,* blubber. *Echar lonja,* to lounge, to take it easy; to get fat.

lucas, *adj.* [<Mex. Sp. *lucas,* "nuts"] crazy; "nuts."

lucha, *f.* [<Sp. *lucha,* struggle] *hacer la lucha,* to try.

luego, luego, *adv.* [<Col. N.M. Sp. *luego luego*] forthwith, right away; on the spot.

lugar, *m.* [<Sp. *lugar,* place] *tomar lugar un suceso,* to take place (as an event). Cf. Sp. *tener lugar.*

lumbre, *adj.* [<Mex. Sp. *lumbre*] hard, as a child's being hard on clothing, shoes, etc. (*El muchito de la Sofronia es muy lumbre con sus calzones.* Sofronia's boy is very hard on his pants.)

lumbrera, *f.* [<Sp. *lumbrera,* skylight] opening or breather on top or on the side of an adobe oven (*horno*). (*Lumbrera de la calle y escuridad de su casa.* Charity begins at home.)

lumbrero, *m.* [<Sp. *lumbre,* fire] fireman, fire fighter.

lumbricias, *f. pl.* [<Mex. Sp. *lumbrices,* earthworms] earthworms, tapeworms; also, *lumbrices; adj.,* *lumbriciento, -ta,* suffering from worms.

luminaria, *f.* [<Sp. *luminaria,* festive light] any of several festive lights (bonfires, candle-in-sack lights, votive lights, etc.), which are displayed as a sign of festivity and rejoicing, especially at Christmas time.

lurio, -ria, *adj.* [<Mex. Sp. *lurio*] crazy; goofy; "nuts."

luvia, *f.* [<Col. N.M. Sp. *lluvia* [*lúbia*], heavy rain] flash flood; squall. See also *diluvio.*

No lloro pero me acuerdo.
(How things have changed!)

llaneros, *m. pl.* [<Sp. *llaneros,* plainsmen] the Plains clan of the Jicarilla Apaches. See also *olleros.*

The Jicarillas are divided into two bands, the *Olleros,* or Mountain clan, and the **Llaneros**, or Plains clan. Each spring in by-gone years the two clans would separate, the Mountain people going to the country around Taos and Española and along the Chama river, where they did a little farming and hunting and a little raiding of the Pueblos. The Plains clan went east into the New Mexico plains and into the Texas Panhandle, where they hunted buffalo. In the fall the tribe united and a general thanksgiving celebration was held. (Betty Woods, "Jicarilla Fiesta," *New Mexico Magazine*)

llano, *m.* [<Sp. *llano,* plain] *Llano estacado* (Stockaded Plain), the Staked Plains in eastern New Mexico and western Texas.

The [Coronado] expedition [1541] skirted Cerro Cuervo, and probably entered the basin of Pajarito Creek in the vicinity of present Newkirk. Toward the east they could see the imposing line of rampart-like cliffs which gave the vast level expanse ahead of them the name of **Llano Estacado** (Stockaded or Palisaded Plain), later mis-translated by Anglo Americans into "Staked Plains," which completely misses the point of the Spanish designation. They were called Stockaded Plains from the rimrock which at a distance looks like a stone fortification. The usual explanation about driving stakes to avoid getting lost is an engaging folk tale. (Herbert E. Bolton, *Coronado, Knight of the Pueblos*)

llegar, *vb.* [<Sp. *llegar*] to arrive; to stop by. *¡Lleguen, lleguen!* Stop by, come on over (visit with us).

llena, *f.* [<Sp. *llenar,* to fill; to glut] fill-

ing. (*Este muchito no tiene llena.* This kid doesn't know when to stop eating.)

llorona (*La llorona,* the wailing woman), *f.* [<Sp. *llorar,* to cry, to wail] a ghost. People believe *La llorona* to be: 1. the ghost of a woman seeking her children who died at birth. The ghost wails in the night as a sign of danger or impending death; 2. a soul from Purgatory atoning for its sins; 3. the spirit of an Aztec goddess to whom babies were sacrificed, and who is heard during the night looking for children to carry off; 4. the ghost of *La malinche,* the "tongue" or interpreter and mistress of Cortés, conqueror of Mexico, who betrayed her people for her lover; 5. the ghost of an unmarried young woman who, to spite her paramour and father of her two children, drowns them when she discovers that he is making plans to leave her in order to marry a wealthy society lady whom his mother has chosen for him. The latter version of this legend appeared in book form in the 1920s.

Más sabe el diablo por viejo que por diablo.
The devil knows more because he is old than because he is the devil.
(Experience is the best teacher.)

macana, *f.* [<Mex. Sp. *macana,* war club] cudgel; male organ (taboo).

maceta, *f.* [<Mex. Sp. *maceta,* flowerpot] crap. *¡Come maceta!* Go to blazes!

macucho, -cha, *adj.* [<Mex. Sp. *macucho*] cunning, sly; experienced.

machín, *m.* [<Mex. Sp. *machín,* monkey] a kind of marmot or woodchuck.

macho, *adj.* [<Sp. *macho,* male] strong, virile and brave; *pararle el macho a alguno,* to put a stop to, or keep someone from doing a thing.

machona, *adj.* [<Sp. *f.* of *macho,* potent] barren female; tomboy.

machorra, *f.* [<Mex. Sp. *machorra*] barren female; tomboy. See also *orra.*

madera, *f.* [<Sp. *madera,* wood] fib, lie; flattery. *Dar madera,* to flatter. *¡Madera!* You are kidding. (That's a lie.) *¡No madera!* I am serious. (It's no lie.)

madereado, -da, *m.* and *f.* [<N.M. Sp. *madera*] conceited person; boaster; show-off.

maderear, *vb.* [<N.M. Sp. *madera*] to flatter; to compliment; *reflex.,* to boast; to show off.

maderista, *adj.* [<N.M. Sp. *madera*] fibber; flatterer; liar. Also, *maderisto.*

madero, *m.* [<Sp. *madero,* wooden beam] heavy wooden cross used by N.M. and so. Colo. Penitentes during their religious ceremonies at Easter time.

madre, *f.* [<Sp. *madre,* mother] Col. and Terr. N.M. Sp., female cook for a company of muleteers; *a toda madre (ATM),* great, wonderful; "far-out." *Mentarle la madre a alguno,* to insult or taunt someone, esp. by mentioning the word *"madre"* in a derogatory way. *¡Ni madre!* No way! *No tener uno ni madre,* to be destitute, penniless. *¡Qué madre!* How gorgeous! (Applied to a woman.)

madrecita, *f.* [<Sp. dim. of *madre*] an endearing term used to refer to one's grandmother.

madrina, *f.* [<Sp. *madrina*] bell mare;

bridesmaid; godmother.

madurarse, *vb.* [<Sp. *madurarse,* to ripen (fruit)] to mature. (*Ya se maduró mi aseguranza.* My insurance policy has matured.)

máfrico, *m.* [<Eng. maverick] an unbranded animal, especially a calf or steer; a stray.

magacín, *m.* [<Eng. magazine] magazine, review.

maiste, *m.* [<Mex. Sp. *mástil*<Náhuatl *maxtlatl*] flat of the thigh in beasts from the flank to the hock.

maiz [*máis*], *m.* [<Sp. *maíz*<West Indies *mahís*] *maiz azul,* blue corn; *maiz cahuilense,* a kind of multi-colored corn used mostly for chicken feed; *maiz concho* (<Quechua *kumcho*), a large, white corn used in the making of roasted corn referred to commercially as "crazy corn"; *maiz duce,* sweet corn; *darle su maiz a alguno,* to give someone a beating.

majada, *f.* [<Sp. *majada,* shepherds' camp for the night] shelter for sheep; dung of goats, sheep, etc.; excrement in a child's diaper or pants.

maje, *adj.* [<Mex. Sp. *maje*] dunce; stupid.

majote, *m.* [<N.M. Sp. *majada,* excrement] stool (fecal matter).

mal, *m.* [<Sp. *mal,* evil] evil; harm; *hacer mal,* to cause harm or damage; *hacer un mal,* to hurt or harm. *¡Mal ajo!* Confound it! *Mal hablado,* curser, swearer. *¡Mal haya quien!* Well, of all things! Can you beat that? What do you know?, etc. *Mal hijo,* bad son, a local legend of a young man who raised his hand against his father and how heaven punished him.

I was a very young child when the *mal hijo* passed through our village, but he impressed me for life. Mounted on a burro, he went from town to town preaching to the young, showing them his clenched hand and the scar on his wrist where the knife turned and stuck when he raised it to strike his father. The earth had opened beneath him and swallowed him up to his waist. His mother ran for the priest; the priest came, and after many prayers and sprinkling with holy water, the earth released him. Repentant of his sin, he promised to travel over the world, advising the young to respect and obey their parents. (Cleofas M. Jaramillo, *Shadows of the Past*)

mala, *adj.* [<Sp. *mala,* bad] *mala cacha,* cantankerous, ill-tempered; *mala mujer* or *mala suegra,* tumbleweed; *a la mala,* treacherously.

malacariento, -ta, *adj.* [<Mex. Sp. *malacariento*] with a wry face; said of someone who is always scowling or who shows a long face to those whom he contacts. (*El Acorsinio me cae muy atravesado. Es muy malacariento y siempre trae una jeta que se la pisa.* I can't stand Acorsinio. He is always scowling and always has a long face.)

malacate, *m.* [<Mex. Sp. *malacate*] spindle, whirligig spindle; the pin by which the thread is formed and on which it is wound.

Much of the spinning is done with the *huso* or ***malacate*** (the whirligig spindle), which is kept whirling while the thread is drawn. The dexterity with which the females spin with this simple apparatus is truly astonishing. (Josiah Gregg, *Commerce of the Prairies*)

maldiciento, -ta, *adj.* [<Sp. *maldiciente*] said of the person who swears a great deal and who uses profane or obscene language at every turn. (*Yo no conozco a nadien tan maldiciento como el Jim.* I know of no one who swears as much as Jim.)

maldito, -ta, *adj.* [<Sp. *maldito,* wicked] cursed; damned; *m.* (*El maldito*), Satan, the devil.

En el Río 'e Sapelló
comenzó la suerte mía;
¿Qué es lo que me sucedió,
Virgen pura y madre mía,

maleado

que el **maldito** me ensistió
a hacer tan grande avería?
In the River Sapelló
My bad luck started.
What happened to me,
Oh, holy Virgin Mary,
That the devil tempted me
To do such great harm.
(*Indita de la Pablita*, N.M. Sp. ballad)

maleado, -da, *adj.* [<Sp. *pt. part.* of *malear*, to corrupt] ill-advised; brainwashed.

maleficiado, -da, *adj.* [<Sp. *pt. part.* of *maleficiar*] bewitched or made ill through witchcraft.

maleficio, *m.* [<Sp. *maleficio*] enchantment; spell.
The general name for any evil or harm caused by a witch is, in New Mexico, *maleficio.* (Aurelio M. Espinosa, "New Mexican Spanish Folklore," *The Journal of American Folklore*)

maleta, *f.* [<Sp. *maleta*, valise] ladies' handbag; saddlebag; wallet.
One burro with pack saddle carries two kegs of water; another, the bedding and tent, while on the last one are the *maletas*—saddlebags containing cooking utensils and food. (N. Howard Thorp, "Following the Flock," *New Mexico Magazine*)

malhecho, *m.* [<Sp. *malhecho*, evil deed] enchantment; spell. Also, *maleficio.*

maliciada, *f.* [<N.M. Sp. *maliciar*] gossip; hint; innuendo.

maliciar, *vb.* [<Sp. *maliciar*, to suspect maliciously] to realize; to suspect.

mal impuesto, -ta, *adj.* [<Sp. *impuesto*, imposed] spoiled.

malinche, *f.* [<Mex. Sp. *malinche*, the "tongue" or interpreter of Hernán Cortés] name of the female character (a small girl) in the dance of *Los Matachines*, q.v. Also, a ghost.

malino, *m.* [<Sp. *maligno*, malignant] *El malino*, the evil one, the devil.

malo, *m.* [<Sp. *malo*, evil, bad] *El malo*, the devil.

mal ojo, *m.* [<Sp. *mal*, evil, and *ojo*, eye]

evil eye. Also, *mal de ojo.*

malora (malogra), *f.* [<Mex. Sp. *malora*, mischievous] an evil spirit said to appear in the form of a rolling ball of cotton; *adj.*, mischievous, bullish.
La malora is an evil spirit which wanders about in the darkness of the night at the crossroads and other places. It terrorizes the unfortunate ones who wander alone at night, and has usually the form of a large lock of wool or the whole fleece of wool of a sheep (*un vellón de lana*). Sometimes it takes a human form, but this is rare; and the New Mexicans say that when it has been seen in human form, it presages ill fate, death, or the like. When it appears on dark nights in the shape of a fleece of wool, it diminishes and increases in size in the very presence of the unfortunate one who sees it. It is also generally believed that a person who sees *la malora*, like one who sees a ghost (*un difunto*), forever remains senseless. When asked for detailed information about this myth, the New Mexicans give the general reply, "It is an evil thing" (*es cosa mala*). (Aurelio M. Espinosa, "New Mexican Spanish Folklore," *The Journal of American Folklore*)

maloso, -sa, *adj.* [<Sp. *malo*, mean, and suffix *-oso*] evil, mean, wicked. (*Esta Cleofes sí que es maloso, para dale una idea.* Cleofes is really mean, just to give you an example.)

malpais, *m.* [<Sp. *mal país*, bad terrain] lava beds; badlands.

mallugar, *vb.* [<Sp. *magullar*] to bruise (fruits, vegetables).

mamantar, *vb.* [<Sp. *amamantar*] to breastfeed.

mamasola, *f.* [<unknown origin] a sure move in the game of *pitarrila*, q. v.

manadero, *adj.* [<Mex. Sp. *manadero*] *burro manadero*, seed donkey set apart to mate with mares.

mancornadora, *f.* [<Mex. Sp. *mancorna-*

dora] hooker, prostitute; two-timing female.

mancornar, *vb.* [<Sp. *mancornar,* to tie two head of cattle by the horns so both can work as a team] to hook, as a hooker. See *mancornadora.*

mancuerna, *f.* [<Sp. *mancuerna,* a pair of animals or things] a kind of yoke made with a double rosary which is placed around the necks of a couple about to be married in church and while they are still kneeling before the priest. The *mancuerna,* put on by the priest or by one of the mothers of the couple, symbolizes the joining of the pair in holy matrimony. After taking holy communion, the young people may take off the *mancuerna* and store it away as a memento.

mancuernillas, *f. pl.* [<Mex. Sp. *mancuernillas*] cuff links.

manchón, *m.* [<Sp. aug. of *mancha,* stain] large stain. *¡Qué manchón!* What a disgrace! How embarrassing! *Hacer un manchón,* to blunder; to make a boo-boo.

mandón, *m.* [<Sp. *mandar,* to command] Col. N.M. Sp., head or chief of an Indian tribe; *adj., bossy.*

*A los **mandones** y cabezas se les requirió que se sosegasen y volviesen al estado de antes.*

The heads and chiefs were given notice to calm down and to return to their former state.

(Gaspar Pérez de Villagrá, *Historia de la Nueba Mexico*)

manejador, *m.* [<Sp. *manejar,* to handle] manager. Cf. Sp. *gerente.*

mangana, *f.* [<Sp. *mangana*] a fancy throw of a lasso; a type of loop used in lassoing.

All sorts of loops were invented in order to make personal contact between man and beast. Along the Mexican border the vaqueros brought the ***mangana*** into being. It is a neat way of "forefooting," the ***mangana*** *de pie* being a loop open on the ground and the catch made when an animal

steps into it with its forefeet, and the ***mangana*** *de cabra,* popular in goat roping, where the roper manages to get the loop into a figure 8 and catches its quarry around the neck and forefeet at the same time. (John L. Sinclair, "Spinning Them Fancy," *New Mexico Magazine*)

manganilla, *f.* [<Sp. dim. of *mangana*] a small figure-8 loop. See *mangana.*

mangos, *m. pl.* [<Sp. *mangos,* mangoes] bell peppers. See *chile* (*chile mango*).

manía, *f.* [<Sp. *manía,* mania] bad habit.

manil, *m.* [<Eng. money [män'ē] money; bread (slang).

manito, -ta, *m.* and *f.* [<Mex. Sp. dim. of *mano<hermano*] friend; neighbor; dear. (*¡No, manita, ni lo pienses!* No, dear, don't even think about it!) *Los manitos,* the New Mexicans, a term applied by Mexican immigrants to northern New Mexicans of Indo-Hispanic descent.

mano, *f.* [<Sp. *mano*] hand; small oblong pumice stone which is rubbed back and forth on a *metate* or grinding stone; *a mano* (or *a la mano*), down, down payment; *dar una mano,* to help; to give a helping hand; *de segunda mano,* second hand, used; *mano de obra,* handiwork; *meter mano,* the act of the male touching or handling the female's parts; *pedir la mano de una señorita,* to ask for a young woman's hand in marriage; *tener buena mano,* to have a green thumb; to have a natural aptitude or knack for doing things; *tener mala mano,* to have negative results when undertaking a project. *La mano negra,* the Black Hand, name of an activist organization operating in northern New Mexico in the 1920s. *Pararse de manos,* to anticipate, to jump to conclusions.

mano, -na, *m.* and *f.* [<Mex. Sp. *mano<hermano,* brother] friend, old man. (*Mano Francisco,* brother Francis. *Aquí nos cayo mano Labre.* Old man Labre dropped in on us.)

manofashico, *m.* [<N.M. Sp. *mano Fashico*

105

<*Francisco*] a character in N.M. and so. Colo. Spanish folklore. *Manofashicos,* or simply *fashicos,* are described as being morons or retarded individuals and are the object or butt of moron jokes; *adj.,* dark-complexioned; unkempt, untidy.

manorroto, -ta, *adj.* [<Sp. *manirroto*] extravagant, spendthrift; wasteful.

manque, *conj.* [<Sp. *mas aunque*] even if, even though.

mansito, *m.* [<Sp. dim. of *manso,* tame] cuckold; *adj.,* tame; pusillanimous.

manta, *f.* [<Sp. *manta,* bleached cotton] Col. and Terr. N.M. Sp., coarse cotton cloth used in the making of skirts, petticoats, shawls, kerchiefs, bed sheets, bed hangings, etc. *Manta de techo,* muslin ceiling cloth; min., a streak of pay gravel.

mantelina, *f.* [<Sp. *mantellina* [*mantelína*]] a short cloak worn by women.

mantelito, *m.* [<Sp. dim. of *mantel,* tablecloth] napkin. Cf. Sp. *servilleta.*

mantención, *f.* [<Sp. *manutención*] support; livelihood.

mantenido, *m.* [<Sp. *pt. part.* of *mantener,* to support] bum; moocher; pimp; especially the man who is kept by a woman.

mantilla, *f.* [<Sp. *mantilla,* veil] diaper. Also, a kind of saddle blanket for winter use.

mantona, *f.* [<Sp. *mantón,* a kind of shawl] a kind of cloak or cape.

Mother brought out her black taffeta silk **mantona** to wear for the funeral. This silk cape was made with three lace flounces trimming the circular bottom, and the black lace veil fastened at the collar dropped over her head ... The **mantonas** were worn in mourning and at the church services during Lent and Holy Week. (Cleofas M. Jaramillo, *Shadows of the Past*)

Manueles, *m. pl.* [<Sp. *Manuel*<*Emanuel*] New Year's Day serenade given to persons named Manuel or Manuela.

New Year's day is the day of *los **Manueles**,* and the women and men called by this name were serenaded on this day ... We awakened with the sound of music and singing at our front door; my husband in bathrobe and bedroom slippers opened the door and was greated by the usual verse:

Por aquí caigo,
por aquí levanto,
a darle los buenos días,
pues hoy es día de su santo.
This way I stumble,
This way I rise
To wish you happiness
On your saint's day.
(Cleofas M. Jaramillo, *Shadows of the Past*)

manzana, *f.* [<Sp. *manzana*] apple; *manzana americana,* bot., Delicious apple; *manzana de Adán,* Adam's apple; *manzana* (or *manzanita*) *de San Juan,* a kind of local apple that ripens early (by St. John's day, June 24); *manzana del pais,* local or homegrown apple; *manzana molida,* apple butter, applesauce.

manzanita, *f.* [<Sp. dim. of *manzana*] *la manzanita de Adán,* Adam's apple; *manzanita de San Miguel,* crab apple; min., a lode of gold-bearing quartz; bot., Pointleaf manzanita.

maña, *f.* [<Sp. *maña,* cleverness] bad habit; *darse mañas,* to find a way or solution; to manage.

mañana, *f.* [<Sp. *mañana,* morning] *hacer la mañana,* to take a drink of liquor (brandy, whiskey, etc.) in the early part of the morning.

mañaneador, -ra, *adj.* [<Sp. *mañanear,* to rise very early] early riser.

mañanitas, *f. pl.* [<Sp. dim. of *mañana*] a kind of morning serenade adopted from Mexican folklore.

*Estas son las **mañanitas***
que cantaba el Rey David
a las muchachas bonitas
se las cantamos aquí.
This is the song

King David used to sing;
We are singing it here
To all the pretty girls.
(Mexican folk song)
Also, one of several names for the Mexican *corrido* or ballad.

mañoso, -sa, *adj.* [<Sp. *maña,* cunning] cunning; knavish.

mapa, *f.* [<Sp. *mapa* (*m.*)] map. (*Tráeme la mapa.* Bring me the map.)

maque, *m.* [<Mex. Sp. *maque,* a kind of lacquer] house paint; *dar maque,* to paint (houses, barns, etc.).

maquear, *vb.* [<N.M. Sp. *maque*] to paint (houses, fences, barns, etc.).

máquina, *f.* [<Sp. *máquina,* machine] automobile; motor; *máquina de rajar,* sawmill; *a toda máquina,* full speed; fast, in a hurry; very nice, super, far out (slang).

maravilla, *f.* [<Sp. *maravilla,* common marigold] bot., Wild four-o'clock.

marbolina, *f.* [<Eng. marble?] a kind of glazed marble.

marcado, -da, *adj.* [<Eng. marked] marked; stolen (slang).

marcial, *m.* [<Sp. *marcial,* martial] fort, fortification, stronghold.

Capitán Chía,
Capitán Chía,
rinda su marcial;
jeya, jeya, jeya,
jeya, jeya, jeya.
Captain Chia
Captain Chia
Surrender your fort;
Jeya, jeya, jeya,
Jeya, jeya, jeya.
(N.M. Sp. folk song)

marchante, -ta, *m.* and *f.* [<Mex. Sp. *marchante*] customer. Also used in so. Spain (Andalusia).

Marías, *f. pl.* [<Sp. *María,* Mary] *Las tres Marías,* astron., the three stars forming the belt of Orion.

mariguana, *f.* [<Mex. Sp. *mariguana*] bot., Marihuana, a plant of the Hemp family.

mariguano, -na, *adj.* [<Mex. Sp. *mari-* *guana*] marihuana addict. Also, a person under the influence of dope, drugs.

mariola, *f.* [<Mex. Sp. *mariola*] bot., Rubber bush.

mariquilla, *f.* [<Sp. dim. of *María,* Mary] bot., Goldenrod.

maroma, *f.* [<Mex. Sp. *maroma*] somersault; *echar maromas,* to perform acrobatic stunts; *las maromas,* the circus.

maromear, *vb.* [<N.M. Sp. *maromas*] to perform gymnastic or acrobatic feats.

maromero, -ra, *m.* and *f.* [<Mex. Sp. *maro-* *mero*] acrobat; *pl.,* circus people; pinto beans; Mexican jumping beans; *pl.,* sperm (slang).

marquesote, *m.* [<Mex. Sp. *marquesote,* a kind of caramel] a kind of light sponge cake.

Then and there I made up my mind that ***marquesotes*** were the last word in pastry de luxe . . . However, the forty eggs as the chief ingredient for ***marquesotes*** were nothing as compared to the problems of the early settlers' wives when they wanted to bake light bread or cake. There was no baking powder nor soda. (Margaret Abreu, "In the New Mexico Kitchen," *New Mexico Magazine*)

marranada, *f.* [<Sp. *marrano,* pig] mess.

martigón, *m.* [<Sp. *almartigón*<*almártiga*] a kind of homemade halter.

maruca, *f.* [<Sp. *Maruca* (Mary)] Col. and Terr. N.M. Sp., a name applied to an Indian girl or woman taken from the Indians and reared by a Spanish-speaking family. See *jenízaro.*

máscara, *f.* [<Sp. *máscara,* mask] name applied to a middle-aged woman who uses an excess of cosmetics to hide her wrinkles; homely or ugly female. Cf. Sp. *carantoña.*

mashi, *m.* [<Mex. Sp. *machiche*] the devil. Also, *mashishi; adj.,* impish.

In New Mexican Spanish the Devil is known by various names, el ***ma-*** ***shishi,*** el diablo, el malo. There is little difference in the meaning of these names. All three are epithets of the Devil . . . the Devil is not an important factor in New Mexican Spanish folklore and he is not even feared. (Aurelio M. Espinosa, "New Mexican Spanish Folklore," *The Journal of American Folklore*)

mastranzo, *m.* [<Sp. *mastranzo*] bot., Apple mint. N.M. and so. Colo. *arbolarias* (female herbalists) recommend *mastranzo* to induce menstruation.

masudo, -da, *adj.* [<Sp. *masa,* dough] doughy; pasty; applied mostly to breads.

mata, *f.* [<Sp. *mata,* shrub] plant; herb.

matachín, *m.* [<Sp. *matachín*<It. *matassino*] a dancer in the *Matachines* ritual dance; said of a person ridiculously dressed and wearing a mask; a kind of clown. *Los Matachines,* an old Spanish ritual dance with traditional European overtones. The *Matachines* dance was introduced in New Spain (Mexico) by the early settlers and was later modified by the clergy to include aspects of Aztec rituals and the clash of Spanish and Mexican Indian cultures. Moctezuma (Emperor Moctezuma II of the Aztecs) and Malinche (interpreter and mistress of the conqueror of Mexico, Hernán Cortés) figure among the various characters of this dance, which is performed in some Spanish settlements and Indian pueblos on August 10.

matada, *f.* [<Sp. *matar,* to make a horse's back sore by the rubbing of the harness] sore on a horse's back. Cf. Sp. *matadura.*

matalote, *m.* [<Col. Sp. *matalote* (Cervantes)] a horse in poor condition, a nag (rare).

matarique, *m.* [<Mex. Sp. *matarique*] bot., a medicinal plant.

mataseca, *f.* [<Sp. *mata,* plant, sprig, and *seca,* withered] an indoor game designed to keep children quiet in the evening. Children are sat around the kitchen table and told that the first of them to utter a sound or speak out will have to eat the *mataseca,* previously specified as being a carcass covered with maggots, excrement, etc.

mateo, -a, *m.* and *f.* [<N.M. Sp. *mato* <*surumato*] euphemism for *surumato,* a derogatory term applied to Mexican immigrants at the end of the nineteenth century; the term is still in use today.

mato, *m.*<*surumato,* var. See *surumato.*

matraca, *f.* [<Sp. *matraca,* rattle] a rattle or homemade clacker used by N.M. and so. Colo. Penitentes in their religious ceremonies on Good Friday.

matralladora, *f.* [<Sp. *ametralladora*] machine gun.

matraquero, *m.* [<Sp. *matraca*] Penitente brother in charge of making rattling noise with the *matraca.*

maverico, *m.* [<Eng. maverick] a stray animal, especially an unbranded calf. The term *máfrico* is more common, q.v.

mayate, *m.* [<Mex. Sp. *mayate*<Náhuatl *mayatl,* a multicolored beetle] black beetle; a Black. The term is also applied to a dark-complexioned person.

mayor, *m.* [<Eng. mayor] city mayor. Cf. Sp. *alcalde.*

mayorcito, -ta, *adj.* [<Sp. *mayor,* older] young boy or girl in his or her late teens; *m.* and *f.,* teenager.

mayordomo, *m.* [<Sp. *mayordomo,* steward] patron or sponsor of the annual church fiesta in a village; foreman or manager; overseer; a subordinate officer in a Penitente brotherhood; ditch boss.

mazmorro, *m.* [<Sp. *mazmorra?*] nose bag for feeding grain to horses, mules, etc. Cf. Sp. *morral.*

mecapal, *m.* [<Mex. Sp. *mecapal*<Náhuatl *mecapalli*] a wide belt or sash for carrying objects.

mecate, *m.* [<Mex. Sp. *mecate,* fiber rope] cord; rope; string; *pl.,* shoestrings.

mecatear, *vb.* [<Mex. Sp. *mecatear,* to tie

with ropes] to beat someone with a rope; *mecatearlas,* to die.

meco, -ca, *m.* and *f.* [<Mex. Sp. *chichimeca,* Apache-like Indian in the Valley of Mexico at the time of the occupation of the valley by the Aztecs] Indian in general; a left-handed person; *pl.,* sperm (taboo).

mecha, *f.* [<Eng. match] match; light, as for a cigarette. Also, wick<Sp. *mecha.* The word *fósforo* (as in standard Spanish) is more common in northern New Mexico and southern Colorado.

mechas, *f. pl.* [<Mex. Sp. *mechas*] disheveled hair.

mechero, *m.* [<Mex. Sp. *mechero*] disheveled hair.

mechón, *m.* [<Sp. aug. of *mecha,* wick] a kind of homemade torch consisting of oil-soaked sticks bound together about a long pole.

mechudo, -da, *adj.* [<Mex. Sp. *mechudo*] applied to a person with disheveled hair. See also *greñudo.*

medecina, *f.* [<Sp. *medicina*] medicine; *medecina pa las moscas,* insecticide.

media luna, *f.* [<Sp. *media luna,* half moon] the white part of a fingernail.

medias, *f. pl.* [<Col. N.M. Sp. *medias*<Sp. *medias piernas*] socks; stockings; *medias caidas, adj.,* a term applied to a disorganized person who is always late for his appointments; *medias de hilo,* cotton stockings.

médica, *f.* [<Sp. *médica,* female physician] female folk practitioner who invariably combines the functions of an *arbolaria,* a *curandera,* a general practitioner, an herbalist, a midwife, and a practical nurse.

Although folk medicine is in general known by all members of a cultural group, some persons, because of age, experience, or special interest, may have a more extensive knowledge than their neighbors and friends and thus acquire a somewhat specialized status. The *partera,* or midwife,

is an example of such a person. In the field of general medicine, *médicas* and *curanderas,* whose knowledge of herbs and household remedies is somewhat greater than that of the general population, perform a similar function, being called upon for assistance when a medical problem gets beyond the competence of the patient or his relatives. None of them, of course, is a specialist in the Anglo sense of having a specialized formal recognition (licensure) for their skill. But they are specialists in the sense that they are considered to have a greater knowledge of medical matters than other people in the population and perform a specialized function. (Lyle Saunders, *Cultural Difference and Medical Care*)

médico, *m.* [<Sp. *médico,* an M.D.] an herb healer. Invariably the *médico* performs more or less the same functions as an *arbolaria.* In addition to this, he is often a *sobrador* (a combination of masseur and chiropractor) and is sought after by the male who might find it embarrassing to call upon a *médica* or a woman healer.

medio, *m.* [<Sp. *medio,* one half] Col. and Terr. N.M. Sp., half a *real,* a silver coin equivalent to 6¼ *centavos* or half a *real; medio a medio (tenerlos medio a medio),* to be macho; to be strong and resolute.

mejicano, -na, *adj.* [<Sp. *mexicano,* Mexican] Col. and Terr. N.M. Sp., a New Mexican of Indo-Hispanic descent; a Mexican national; the Indian language of the Valley of Mexico (Aztec or Náhuatl); the Spanish language in New Mexico and southern Colorado; *hablar en mejicano,* to speak Spanish.

melacera, *f.* [<N.M. Sp. *melaz,* syrup] place or shed where syrup is made. Also, *mielero, mielera* and *melacero.*

melado, *m.* [<Sp. *melado*<*miel,* honey; covered with honey] a kind of thick, homemade syrup used in sweetening *sopa,* or bread pudding; *adj.,* honey-colored.

melárchico, -ca, *adj.* [<Mex. Sp. *melárchico*] depressed; homesick; listless; melancholy, sad.

> Children and even pet animals, having become greatly attached to a person who went away and left them, became *melárchicos* (melancholy) and refused to eat. Babies became sick, and a red ribbon was tied on their wrist as a cure. Birds also refused to eat or sing, and died, when they became *melárchicos*. (Cleofas M. Jaramillo, *Shadows of the Past*)

melaz, *m.* [<Sp. *melaza*] Karo syrup; molasses; pancake syrup; corn or cane syrup.

mema, *adj.* [<Mex. Sp. *mema*] a term applied to a baby girl born with a partially closed vulva. Also, a flat-chested woman.

memoria, *f.* [<Sp. *memoria*] memory; a kind of ring made up of two or more rings which fit together into a single unit. The term *anillo de ramal* is also used for this type of ring. An "In memoriam" poem appearing in Spanish language newspapers.

memorioso, -sa, *adj.* [<Sp. *memoria*, memory] said of the person who has a good memory. (*Al mentiroso le conviene ser memorioso.* Liars must have good memories.)

memorizar, *vb.* [<Eng. to memorize] to commit to memory, to memorize. Cf. Sp. *aprender de memoria.*

méndigo, -ga, *m.* and *f.* [<Sp. *mendigo*] beggar; pauper; *adj.*, despicable; treacherous; S.O.B.

menear, *vb.* [<Sp. *menear*] to stir; *menear la cabeza,* to nod.

menjamín, *m.* [<Sp. *Benjamín*] favorite son; teacher's pet.

menoleño, -ña, *adj.* [<Eng. Menaul, a Presbyterian school in northeast Albuquerque] a student at Menaul School; a Menaul graduate or alumnus.

menos de, *adv.* [<Sp. *nada menos que*] only.

(*Menos de ayer estuvieron aquí.* They were here only yesterday.)

menso, -sa, *adj.* [<Mex. Sp. *menso*] dumb, stupid.

mente, *m.* and *f.* [<Sp. *mente*] mind; *cambiar de mente,* to change one's mind; *hacer la mente,* to make up one's mind. (*Todavía no hago mi mente.* I haven't made up my mind yet.) *Usar el mente* (or *la mente*), to think; to use one's mind; *perder la mente,* to go crazy; to lose one's mind.

mentira, *f.* [<Sp. *mentira*] lie; a kind of poetic composition exalting the characteristics of animals or insects. *¡No mentira!* It's no lie!

mentolate (mentolato), *m.* [<Eng. mentholatum] mentholatum.

menudo, *m.* [<Mex. Sp. *menudo*] Mexican-style tripe.

meramente, *adv.* [<Mex. Sp. *mero*] almost. (*Hija, meramente que oigo a San Antonio.* Daughter, I can almost hear St. Anthony.)

meras, *f. pl.* [<Mex. Sp. *f.* of *mero*] acme, height. (*El baile estaba en sus meras.* The dance was in full swing. *El Maque andaba en sus meras.* Mack was at the height of his celebrating.)

mero, *adv.* [<Mex. Sp. *mero*, almost] almost, exactly. (*Ya mero llegan.* They are almost here. *Aquí mero cayó.* It fell right here.) *Adj.*, true, real. (*El es el mero diablo.* He is a real devil. *El es su mero mero* [*amante*]. He is her one and only [lover].)

mesalina, *f.* [<Sp. *mesa*, table] waitress; girl who waits on tables in saloons.

mescal, *m.* [<Mex. Sp. *mezcal*] an intoxicating drink made from the stalk and leaf base of the maguey or agave plant.

mescalero, *adj.* [<N.M. Sp. *mescal*] maker of *mescal*; *m.* and *f.*, Mescalero Apache Indian.

> This [*mescal*], like other larger plants of the genus, was used by the Indians in making *mescal.* The thick leaves were cooked in large pits

made in the ground and lined with stones, which were first fired, then filled with the plant. It is from their preparation of this article of food that the **Mescalero** Apaches receive their name. (E.O. Wooton and Paul C. Standley, *Flora of New Mexico*)

mesilla, *f.* [<Sp. dim. of *mesa*, table] small tableland or plateau; a narrow, semicircular cliff over the bed of a stream.

mesmo, -ma, *adj.* [<Col. N.M. Sp. *mesmo,* Mod. Sp. *mismo*] same; similar; self. (*Yo mesmo lo digo.* I myself say it.)

meso, *adj.* [<unknown origin] seed ram (*carnero meso*).

mestela, *f.* [<Sp. *mistela*, a spiced wine drink] an aromatized and sweetened liquor used as a beverage. Also, *mistela*.
In olden days, every bar in the region was graced by a bottle of whiskey containing *chimajá*, and at Los Lunas, its flowers, with sugar, were added to a jug of whiskey, and allowed to stand for two years. This made an excellent cordial called **mestela**, which was served in tiny glasses at fiestas and other celebrations. (Leonora S.M. Curtin, *Healing Herbs of the Upper Rio Grande*)

mesteño, -ña, *adj.* [<Sp. *mesteño*<*Mesta,* stockman's corporation] a stray; wild, unbranded horse.

mestenero, *adj.* [<Sp. *mesteño*, wild horse] mustang hunters.
Another sport that took these men to the plains was walking down wild horses. **Mesteñeros**, the takers of mustangs, using many mounts and never pushing them beyond a walk, could keep a stallion and his band of mares moving until they wearied utterly, and could be roped and thrown. (Erna Fergusson, *Our Southwest*)

mestro, -tra, *m.* and *f.* [<Sp. *maestro*] teacher.

meter, *vb.* [<Sp. *meter*, to put away] *¡Métele!* Hurry up! *Meterse uno en sus calzones,*

to wear the pants; *meterse el sol,* for the sun to set; *metida del sol,* sunset.

metiche, *adj.* [<Mex. Sp. *metiche*] busybody; gossip; meddler.

metlacahuitl, *m.* [<Náhuatl *metlacahuitl*] Col. N.M. Sp., pole used for hanging skins (pelts, hides, etc.) to dry.

mexicano, -na, *adj.* [<Sp. *mexicano*] Terr. N.M. Sp., a Mexican national; a New Mexican of Mexican descent; the Spanish language as spoken in New Mexico and southern Colorado. Also, *mejicano.*

mezcal, *m.* See *mescal.*

mezquino, *m.* [<Mex. Sp. *mezquino*] wart. Cf. Sp. *verruga.*

mezquitama, *m.* [<Mex. Sp. *mezquitama*] Col. N.M. Sp., a kind of bread or sweet roll made by N.M. Indians.
And these people, who must have numbered more than a thousand Indian men and women, who were settled in their *rancherías* and grass huts, came out to meet us, among them men, women and children, and each one brought his present of **mezquitama**, which is made (*hecho*) of a fruit like the carob bean. (Espejo Expedition into New Mexico, *Colección de documentos inéditos*, Vol. XV)

miel, *f.* [<Sp. *miel*] honey; *miel virgen,* virgin honey; *miel mexicana,* Karo-type syrup.

mielero, *m.* [<Sp. *melero*, place where honey is kept] shed or place where syrup (*melaz*) is made; cane mill.
A great attraction for the village children in the fall of the year was the **mielero**. This mud stove was built against the outside wall of a house in the same style as the *braseros* in the old Mexico kitchens. It was made of plastered adobes in the shape of a narrow, long table with six holes on the top, where earthen pots were set to boil . . . The women poured the liquid [the juice from the pulp] with a gourd dipper into the *ollas,*

strained it, and boiled it until the juice was clear red. (Cleofas M. Jaramillo, *Shadows of the Past*)

miembra, *f.* [<Sp. *f.* of *miembro,* member] female member of a club, organization, etc.

miembresía, *f.* [<Sp. *miembro,* member] membership.

mierda, *f.* [<Sp. *mierda,* excrement] *traer la mierda prendida,* to be guilty; to be implicated in some wrongdoing.

mil, *m.* [<Sp. *mil,* one thousand] *estar uno en sus mil y mil,* to be on cloud nine.

milagro, *m.* [<Sp. *milagro,* miracle] *¡Qué milagro!* What a pleasant surprise! (said upon receiving a visitor—friend, relative, neighbor, etc.—whom one has not seen for some time); name of a poetic composition exalting the exploits of a saint, *Los milagros de San Antonio,* for instance.

mimbreño, -ña, *m.* and *f.* [<Sp. *mimbre,* willow] name of one of the Apache Indian tribes.

mirruña, *f.* [<Mex. Sp. *mirruña*] a small bit of anything; a crumb. *¡Qué mirruña!* How stingy can you get! What stinginess!

misa, *f.* [<Sp. *misa,* church mass] *venir a misa y quedarse al rosario,* to overstay one's visit; *misa de aguinaldo,* Col. and Terr. N.M. Sp., an evening mass on Christmas Eve, at the conclusion of which gifts were given to household servants.

misionario, -ria, *m.* and *f.* [<Eng. missionary] missionary. Cf. Sp. *misionero.*

mistear, *vb.* [<Eng. to miss] to miss a mark, target, etc. (*La Macedonia le tiró a los blancos pero les misteó a todos.* Macedonia shot at the targets but missed every one of them.)

mistela, *f.* See *mestela.*

mitimita, *adv.* [<Sp. *mitad y mitad*] by halves; halfers; in equal amounts or portions.

mitote, *m.* [<Mex. Sp. *mitote,* disturbance] Col. N.M. Sp., a dance with drinking and a great deal of noise; noise, disturbance; gossip.

And day and night, during the three days that we stayed there, they always made *mitotes* and balls, and dances. (Espejo Expedition into New Mexico, *Colección de documentos inéditos,* Vol. XV)

moco (mocos), *m.* [<Sp. *mocos*] discharge from the mucous membranes of the nose; *colgarle el moco a uno,* to be annoyed or angry; *echar mocos en 'l atole,* to say something out of place, to commit a faux pas; *sacarle el moco a alguno,* to give someone a bloody nose; to make someone get a runny nose from a strenuous workout. (*Esos ejercicios te sacan el moco.* That kind of exercise will give you a runny nose.)

mocoso, -sa, *adj.* [<Sp. *mocos,* snivel] snively, snotty; young upstart, brat; *la mocosa,* sheep camp; sheep work. (*El Canuto anda en la mocosa.* Canuto is out tending sheep.)

mocha, *f.* [<Mex. Sp. *mochar,* to chop; to cut] shunt engine in a railroad yard (rare).

moche, *m.* [<Eng. mush] cooked cereal, especially oatmeal (*otemil*).

mocho, -cha, *m.* and *f.* [<Mex. Sp. *mocho*] said of the person who has lost an arm or a leg; cf. Sp. *manco.* The term *mocho* is also applied to a bull, cow, steer, etc., with only one horn. *El mocho,* Spanglish, a mixture of Spanish and English in one's language; *adj.,* hypocrite.

modito, *m.* [<Sp. dim. of *modo,* manner] sarcastic tone of voice. (*Me lo dijo con modito.* He said it to me sarcastically.)

mofoso, -sa, *adj.* [<Sp. *mofarse,* to sneer] sneering.

mogote, *m.* [<Mex. Sp. *mogote*] isolated grove; clump of trees or scrub brush standing isolated in a plain or prairie; name of a so. Colo. village.

mojado, -da, *m.* and *f.* [<Sp. *mojar,* to wet] wet; wetback; undocumented Mexican

immigrant.

mojino, -na, *adj.* [<Mex. Sp. *mojino*<Sp. *mohíno,* black] said of a chocolate-colored animal, especially a cow or bull, with a black snout.

mojo, *m.* [<Col. N.M. Sp. *moho [móxo]*] mildew; rust.

mojoso, -sa, *adj.* [<Col. N.M. Sp. *moho*] moldy; covered with mildew; rusty.

molacho, -cha, *adj.* [<Mex. Sp. *molacho*] toothless or missing some teeth.

molcas, *m.* [<Mex. Sp. *molcas*] a term used to refer to someone one does not want to mention by name, you-know-who (rare).

molendero, *m.* [<Sp. *molendero,* miller] horned toad (mentioned in riddles and folk poetry).

molesta, *f.* [<Sp. *molestia*] annoyance, bother, trouble, inconvenience. (*No vale la molesta.* It is not worth the trouble.)

molienda, *f.* [<Mex. Sp. *molienda*] a crushing mill. Also, an *arrastre* for minerals, q.v.

molino, *m.* [<Sp. *molino,* mill] mill; *El molino,* a N.M. children's game.

molón, -na, *adj.* [<Mex. Sp. *molón*] annoying; bothersome.

molote, *m.* [<Mex. Sp. *molote*] braid worn by some N.M. Pueblo Indians.

mollera, *f.* [<Sp. *mollera,* top of the head] fontanel.

La **mollera** (the fontanel or soft spot on a baby's head) which is believed to cave in and cause illness, is treated as follows: the midwife boils a pinch of *manzanilla* in a little water. When it is still lukewarm, she takes a small quantity in her mouth and then, putting her lips to the child's head, sucks until the **mollera** has resumed the correct position. After the sucking, salt may be put on the spot, or, better, a piece of linen is spread with the thoroughly beaten white of an egg, placed on the head, and allowed to dry there. Another method of bringing up the fontanel is to fill a pail half-full of warm water, then, taking the baby by the feet, to dip the top of his head in the water. The suction, as his head is pulled out, raises the fontanel. Then the white of an egg is applied as before. All sorts of ailments are attributed to the falling of the soft spot, but these methods will surely cure it. (Leonora S. M. Curtin, *Healing Herbs of the Upper Rio Grande*)

mollete, *m.* [<Mex. Sp. *mollete*] a kind of sweet roll.

mompes, *m. pl.* [<Eng. mumps] mumps.

mona, *f.* [<Sp. *mona,* drunk] annoyance, bother; beating; mark, target. See also *friega.*

monarca, *m.* [<Sp. *monarca,* monarch] *Monarca,* the player representing Aztec emperor Moctezuma II in the dance of *Los Matachines.*

monda, *f.* [<Mex. Sp. *monda,* beating] the male organ.

monito, *m.* [<Mex. Sp. dim. of *mono,* doll] witches' doll; figurine; *pl.,* comics.

A New Mexican fell ill and went to see a *médica* in Santa Fe. She told him he was *embrujado* [bewitched] and that he should go home and look for a **monito** (a doll in his image) behind the toilet. He followed instructions and found one buried a few feet behind the privy. He destroyed the **monito** and was cured. (Lyle Saunders, *Cultural Difference and Medical Care*)

mono, *m.* [<Mex. Sp. *mono,* doll (*muñeco*)] effigy or doll made by a witch; movies; show; *adj.,* clownish.

montecito, *m.* [<Sp. dim. of *monte,* woods] outer edge of a forest.

montera, *f.* [<Sp. *montera,* a kind of cap] cloth sunbonnet.

> *Montera sobre montera*
> *montera de rico paño,*
> *el que no me la adevine,*
> *ni en todo el año.*
> Bonnet upon bonnet

113

Bonnet of fine cloth;
He who fails to guess
Will not guess in a year.
(*El col, The Cabbage*, N.M. riddle)

Montezuma, *m.* [<Mex. Sp. *Montezuma*] *esperar a Montezuma*, to wait in vain for a thing.

montoso, -sa, *adj.* [<Sp. *montuoso*, hilly] wooded land.

moño, *m.* [<Sp. *moño*, knot of hair] *levantarse uno con el moño atravesado*, to get up on the wrong side of the bed.

mope, *m.* [<Eng. mop] mop.

mopear, *vb.* [<Eng. to mop] to mop.

moqueño, -ña, *m.* and *f.* [*Moqui* (Indian)] Moqui Indian.

moquetazo, *m.* [<Sp. aug. of *moquete*, blow on the face] hard blow on the face or nose; hard blow in general.

moquetero, *m.* [<Sp. *moquete*] boxer, prizefighter. Also, someone fond of fighting.

moquis, *m. pl.* [*Moqui* (Indian)] Moqui Indians.

mora, *f.* [<Sp. *mora*, mulberry] berry; strawberry. Cf. Sp. *fresas* (strawberries). *Pescar a alguno en las moras*, to catch someone in the act (with his hands in the cookie jar).

morada, *f.* [<Sp. *morada*, dwelling] Penitente chapel and chapter house of the organization.

moradilla, *f.* [<Sp. dim. of *mora*, mulberry] bot., Verbena.

morcilla, *f.* [<Sp. *morcilla*, blood pudding] blood sausage.

morcillo, -lla, *adj.* [<Mex. Sp. *morcillo*] The term *morcillo* is applied to reddish-colored cattle having white legs.

mordaz (mordaces), *m.* [<Sp. *mordaza*, nippers] clothespin. See also *palitos de la ropa*, *trampas* and *trampitas*.

morete, *m.* [<Mex. Sp. *morete*, bruise] bruise from a blow; black-and-blue mark. The term *moretón* (<standard Sp. *moretón*) is more common.

moreteado, -da, *adj.* [<N.M. Sp. *morete*] bruised up; black-and-blue from blows.

morillo, *m.* [<Mex. Sp. *morillo*, crossbeam] jamb post. Also, a fat person.

morirse, *vb.* [<Sp. *morirse*] to die; to solidify, as cement or plaster. (*Ten cuidado que no se te muera el cemente.* Be careful; don't let the cement die [harden].)

mormado, -da, *adj.* [<Mex. Sp. *mormado*] said of the person suffering from nasal congestion.

mormarse, *vb.* [<Mex. Sp. *mormarse*] to get a stuffed up nose.

mormurar, *vb.* [<Sp. *murmurar*] to backbite; to detract or talk behind a person's back.

moro, -ra, *adj.* [<Mex. Sp. *moro*] applied to horses having a bluish white color with dark brown spots.

Moros y Cristianos. A traditional Spanish dramatic presentation on horseback of a skirmish between *moros* (Moors) and *cristianos* (Spaniards) for the possession of the Holy Cross.

*Septiembre 8, Día de Nuestra Señora, fue la gran fiesta de la dedicación de la dicha Yglessia de Sant Joan Baptista, bendixola nuestro Padre Comissario, y consagró las aras y cálices; predicó el Padre Salazar, y á la tarde hizo todo el real, fiesta, con una buena escaramuza de **moros y cristianos**, éstos á pie y con arcabuzes, y aquellos á caballo con lanzas y adargas.*

On September 8, the day of Our Lady, was celebrated the great feast of the dedication of the aforesaid church of St. John the Baptist. Our commissary father blessed it and consecrated the altars and the chalices. Father Salazar delivered the sermon and that evening the whole camp celebrated with a good skirmish between Moors and Christians, the former on horseback, using lances and shields, and the latter on foot and bearing harquebuses.
(Ytinerario, *Documentos inéditos*, Vol. XVI)

morrodo, -da, *adj.* [<Sp. *modorro*] drowsy, sleepy; dull, slow at learning.

mortorio, *m.* [<Sp. *mortuorio*] mortuary, funeral home.

mosca, *f.* [<Sp. *moscatel* (wine)] wine in general.

mosco, *m.* [<Sp. *mosco,* mosquito] housefly. Cf. Sp. *mosca.*

mosquita, *f.* [<Sp. dim. of *mosca*] small fly; *mosquita muerta,* a female who feigns meekness.

mostacilla, *f.* [<Sp. dim. of *mostaza,* mustard] bot., Peppergrass, a plant of the Mustard family.

mostrarse, *vb.* [<Sp. *mostrar,* to show] to go back on one's word.

mostro, *m.* [<Col. Sp. *mostruo* (Cervantes)] monster; hydrocephalic child.

mota, *f.* [<Sp. *mota,* mote] cotton ball; powder puff; white spot on a cow's forehead; bot., marihuana (slang); *levantarse uno con su mota,* to get up on the wrong side of the bed; to be in ill humor.

moto, *m.* [<Sp. *moto*<*motocicleta*] motorcycle; *adj.,* doped up, as with *mota* (marihuana).

moverse, *vb.* [<Sp. *moverse*] to move. *¿Qué se mueve?* What's new? What's up? (slang).

movida, *f.* [<Sp. *mover,* to move] mode of operation, procedure; plans; date or social engagement; "the ropes" (slang).

movido, -da, *adj.* [<Mex. Sp. *movido,* noisy] aggressive; active; said of a person with a lot of drive.

moyote, *m.* [<Mex. Sp. *moyote,* a kind of flying beetle] mosquito.

muchachada, *f.* [<Mex. Sp. *muchachada*] "the boys"; a group of boys and girls; a gang.

muchito, -ta, *m.* and *f.* [<Sp. dim. of *muchacho*] little boy; kid, child. (*El muchito de la Feliza se levantó con su mota.* Feliza's little boy got up on the wrong side of the bed.)

mudos, *m. pl.* [<Sp. *mudo,* mute] bogey-men at Christmastime.

Dec. 24th. Young men and boys in disguise (wolves, bears) some wear paper sacks over their faces; many put on women's dresses. Come into homes and execute grotesque dances and cut all sorts of silly capers all without uttering a single word, to the delight of the adults and the terror of the children. (Herminia B. Chacón, "The Christ Child Comes to New Mexico," *New Mexico Magazine*)

muela, *f.* [<Sp. *muela,* molar] molar; chewing tobacco; *hacerse uno muelas de gallo,* to pretend not to understand what is being said; to act conceited.

muerto, *m.* [<Sp. *muerto*] corpse; floor joist; railroad tie; *pl.,* timbers.

mugrero, *m.* [<Sp. *mugre,* grime] junk; worthless things.

mugroso, -sa, *adj.* [<Sp. *mugre,* filth] dirty, filthy; greasy. Cf. Sp. *mugriento.*

muina, *f.* [<Sp. *mohína,* animosity] displeasure; ill humor.

muino, -na, *adj.* [<Sp. *mohíno*] fretful; grouchy, peevish; restless.

mujer, *f.* [<Sp. *mujer*] woman; wife; *buena mujer,* bot., a plant of the Loasa family. See also *pegapega. Mujer de la calle,* prostitute.

mujercita, *f.* [<Sp. dim. of *mujer,* woman] baby girl. (*La Soveida tuvo una mujercita.* Soveida gave birth to a baby girl.)

mujerero, *adj.* [<Mex. Sp. *mujerero*] fond of women or given to spending his time gossiping in the kitchen with the women.

mujerota, *adj.* [<Sp. aug. of *mujer*] hardworking or brave female ("a lot of woman").

mula, *f.* [<Sp. *mula,* mule] mule; stubborn or hard to handle female; homemade corn liquor; whiskey. Col. and Terr. N.M. Sp., (*mulas*) unsalable goods; *mula blanca* (<Eng. white mule), cheap liquor.

mulato, *m.* [<Sp. *mulato,* mulatto] name of a baton used in the game of *cañ-*

ute, q. v.

One of the four *cañutes* was striped all over by narrow lines, running from the center, which was marked by a line all around the middle of the wooden cylinder, to the two ends like the bars on a barber's pole. These lines were burnt into the *cañute's* surface and produced a fascinating brown. At the closed end it had four straight lines burned into it. By name this *cañute* was called *"El mulato."* (Reginaldo Espinosa, "Cañute," *New Mexico Magazine*)

mulera, *f.* [<Sp. *mula,* mule] Col. and Terr. N.M. Sp., bell mule.

mulero, -ra, *m.* and *f.* [<N.M. Sp. *mula* <Eng. mule, corn whiskey] bootlegger; *adj.,* said of the person who likes or is fond of homemade liquor.

muncho, -cha, *adj.* [<Sp. *mucho*] much; a great deal.

mundo, *m.* [<Sp. *mundo*] world; *pedir este mundo y el otro por una cosa,* to ask an exorbitant price for an article. Also, *dormirse* (*se duermen pidiendo*).

muñeco, *m.* [<Sp. *muñeca,* a small bundle of medicinal ingredients] a cord or cloth band worn by a pregnant woman. About the time that the first movements of the baby are felt, the mother begins wearing a *muñeco,* a cord or cloth band which is wrapped tightly around the waist to keep the foetus in place and prevent damaging the upper organs of the mother. (Lyle Saunders, *Cultural Difference and Medical Care*)

muñiga, *f.* [<Sp. *boñiga*] cow dung or cow chip.

murciégalo, *m.* [<Col. N.M. Sp. *murciégalo,* Mod. Sp. *murciélago*] bat. The term *ratón volador* is a more common term in New Mexico.

murimundo, -da, *adj.* [<Sp. *moribundo,* near death] goofy; applied to a simpleton.

murir, *vb.* [<Sp. *morir*] to die. *Morir* and *murir* are alternate forms in N.M. and so. Colo. Spanish.

murre, *adv.* [<Sp. *muy,* very, and prefix *re*] very. (*Esta muchita es murre gente.* This child is very friendly.)

musarañas, *f. pl.* [<Mex. Sp. *musarañas*] grimaces; gestures; *hacer musarañas,* to make wry faces.

mushas, *f. pl.* [<Col. N.M. Sp. *muxas* [*mûśas*]<Lat. *musso, mussas.* Cf. It. *muso,* snout] the front part of the face. (*¡Cállate o te doy en las mushas!* Shut up or I'll hit you in the mouth!)

musho, -sha, *adj.* [<N.M. Sp. *mushas,* the front part of the face] pug-nosed; stuck-up.

música, *f.* [Sp. *música,* music] music. (*Música pagada mal sonada.* Music paid for in advance has a sour sound. I.e., a job paid for in advance is not always done right.) *Música de boca,* harmonica; fig., the mouth. (*Le dieron en la música.* They hit him in the mouth. I.e., they gave him a beating.) The term *música* is also applied to a small bright red insect that emits a musical sound.

muslos, *m. pl.* [<Sp. *muslo,* thigh] muscles. See also *ñervos.*

Noche alegre, mañanita triste.
A night of revelry, a morn of grief.

nacer, *vb.* [<Sp. *nacer,* to be born] *nacerle a uno,* to feel like. (*Lo hago porque me nace.* I am doing it because I feel like it.)

nacimiento, *m.* [<Mex. Sp. *nacimiento*] crèche or manger scene; source of a stream.

    The visit of Joseph and Mary at Bethlehem is enacted at a number of homes in the village [*Las posadas*]. Lucifer conceals himself in each home and rejects the wayfarers; then he finally welcomes them at one house where a *nacimiento* or crèche has been prepared for the Christ Child. (T.M. Pearce, "The New Mexican Shepherds' Play," *Western Folklore*)

nación, *f.* [<Sp. *nación,* nation] Indian tribe.

nacho, *adv.* [<Eng. Naturally!] naturally, of course.

nadien, indef. *pron.* [<Sp. *nadie*] nobody, no one. The addition of an extra consonant at the end of a word, such as *nadie,* is rare.

nagüelita, *f.* [<Mex. Sp. *nana agüelita*] granny, grandma, grandmother.

nagüilla, *f.* [<Sp. dim. of *naguas*] breeching (on a harness).

nagüitas, *f. pl.* [<Sp. dim. of *naguas,* underpetticoat] small slips; *adj.,* sissified; said of someone who is afraid.

nalgazo, *m.* [<Sp. aug. of *nalga,* buttock] blow or push with the buttocks.

nalgón, -na, *adj.* [<Sp. aug. of *nalga,* buttock] having large buttocks; *pájaro nalgón,* a nobody; an unimportant person in political circles.

nana, *f.* [<Mex. Sp. *nana* <Náhuatl *nantli*] mother, mom, mommy; nanny (as in nanny goat).

nanero, -ra, *adj.* [<N.M. Sp. *nana,* mother] said of the child who does not want to be separated from his mother; spoiled.

narco, *m.* [<Eng. narcotics] narcotics agent (slang).

naretón, -na, *adj.* [<Sp. *nariz,* nose] said

117

of the person with a large or protruding nose. Cf. Sp. *narigón*.

natilla, *f.* [<Sp. *natillas,* custard] butterfat; custard.

navajó (navajoses), *m.* [<Tewa *Naɵa,* cultivated field] a member of the Navajo community; Navajo Indian. Cf. Sp. *nava,* plain surrounded by mountains.

necho, -cha, *adj.* [<Col N.M. Sp. *nexa* [*néša*] <Náhuatl *nexectic,* ashen-colored] yellowish, said especially of wheat tortillas when they have an excess of baking powder or when they are made with bicarbonate of soda instead of baking powder. Mexican corn tortillas are said to be *nejas* (<Náhuatl *nexectic*) or ashen-colored when an excess of lime powder is used in boiling the corn.

nel, *adv.* [<Mex. Sp. *nel* <Nelson, a diplomat in Woodrow Wilson's time] The euphemism *Nel* (No) is a remnant of the original negative expression, *"Nelson le dijo a Wilson,"* heard throughout Mexico during World War I. The adverb *nel* is now usually followed by the word *mano* (<*hermano,* chum). *¡Nel, mano!* No, chum! No, no way! See also *¡Chale!*

Nicanor, *m.* [<Sp. *Nicanor,* a man's name] *No estés como Nicanor, terco.* Don't be insistent (stubborn).

nicle, *m.* [<Eng. nickel] nickel, a five-cent coin. See *cuara.*

nievada, *f.* [<Sp. *nevada*] snowfall; snowstorm.

nina, *f.* [<Sp. *madrina*] godmother.

nito, -ta, *m.* and *f.* [<Mex. Sp. *nito* <Sp. *hermanito*] dear, friend. (*¡Bal, nita! ¿pero pa qué?* Heavens, dear, what for?)

nixtamal, *m.* [<Mex. Sp. *nixtamal*] corn boiled in lime water from which a paste (*masa*) is made for tamales or tortillas; the unground *nixtamal* (hominy) is used for *posole.*

Some of the white corn was made into **nixtamal**, boiled in lime water until the skin peeled off, then washed and dried for *posole;* the remainder

was ground on the *metate* (a long, black pumice stone). This dough was used for making *tamales.* (Cleofas M. Jaramillo, *Shadows of the Past*)

nochecita, *f.* [<Sp. dim. of *noche,* night] nightfall; dusk.

nodriza, *f.* [<Sp. *nodriza,* wet nurse] nurse. Cf. Sp. *enfermera.*

nodrizo, *m.* [<N.M. Sp. *nodriza,* nurse] male nurse; male nurse's aide; orderly in a hospital.

nojao, -da, *adj.* [<Sp. *enojado*] annoyed; angry.

nojarse, *vb.* [<Sp. *enojarse*] to become annoyed or angry.

nojón, -na, *adj.* [<N.M. Sp. *nojarse*] easily annoyed or angered; peevish, touchy.

noquear, *vb.* [<Eng. to knock out] to knock out. (*Al Willie lo noquearon con uno que le dieron en 'l hocico.* Willie was knocked out with a blow on the mouth.)

norte, *m.* [<Sp. *norte,* north] guide; inspiration; north; north wind.

norteado, -da, *adj.* [<Mex. Sp. *norteado,* dull-brained] silly; ignorant; stupid; bewildered; lost. (*Andamos norteados, Maque.* We've lost our way, Mack.)

nosca, *f.* [<Sp. *rosca* (euphemism)] backside; the buttocks. (*Le dieron una patada en la nosca.* They kicked his butt.)

novedoso, -sa, *adj.* [<Sp. *novedoso,* novel, original] curious; fond of the latest gossip or news.

novilear, *vb.* [<N.M. Sp. *novilero*] to pry; to nose around or pry into other people's business.

novilero, -ra, *adj.* [<Sp. *novelero,* fond of hearing and telling the latest news] curious, as a cat, goat, etc.; gossip monger.

nuevas, *f. pl.* [<Sp. *nuevas,* news] news; *hacerse uno de nuevas,* to act surprised.

nuevecientos, *adj.* [<Sp. *novecientos*] nine hundred.

nuevecito, -ta, *adj.* [<Mex. Sp. *nuevecito*] new; brand new; in mint condition.

nuez, *f.* [<Sp. *nuez,* walnut] nutmeg. Cf.

Sp. *nuez moscada.*
 El brandy es otro remedio
 que llevando 'l interés,
 mézclenlo con enjengible
 *y échenle ahi tantita **nuez***
 pues yo me curé una vez . . .
 Brandy is another cure
 Which, if you're interested,
 You can mix with ginger,

Adding a pinch of nutmeg,
Why, I cured myself once.
(*La enfermedad de los fríos,* N.M. Sp.
folk song)

nunca, *adv.* [<Sp. *nunca,* never] *¡Mas que
 nunca!* Never!

nutria, *f.* [<Sp. *nutria,* otter] beaver (Sp.
 castor).

Más vale maña que juerza.
(Brain over brawn.)

ña, *f.* [<Sp. *ña* <*señá* <*señora,* a title of address equivalent to English Mrs.] The title *ña* is rare, the more common form being Mrs. (Eng. Mrs.) (*¿Cómo está la Mrs. Martínez?* How is Mrs. Martínez?)

ñervos, *m. pl.* [<Col. N.M. Sp. *niervos*] muscles; nerves. (*¡Cómo me duelen los ñervos!* My muscles ache so much!)
    *Rollizos **niervos,** cuerdas y costales*
    qual si fueran dos muros poderosos
    assí parados se quedaron.
    Strong muscles, of the ribs and legs as if they were two powerful walls. Thus they remained standing.
    (Gaspar Pérez de Villagrá, *Historia de la Nueba Mexico*)

ñervoso, -sa, *adj.* [<N.M. Sp. *ñervos*] nervous; tendinous, applied to meats.

ñervudo, -da, *adj.* [<N.M. Sp. *ñervos,* muscles] tough, tendinous, applied to meats.

ñublado, -da, *adj.* [<Col. N.M. Sp. *ñublado* (Molina)] cloudy.

ñublarse, *vb.* [<Col. N.M. Sp. *ñublarse*] to become cloudy.

ñublina, *f.* [<Sp. *neblina*] mist, fog.

ñudo, *m.* [<Col. N.M. Sp. *ñudo,* knot (Molina)] knot. (*Este orillo no sirve pa nada, tiene munchos ñudos.* This slab is worthless; it is full of knots.)

ñudoso, -sa, *adj.* [<Col. N.M. Sp. *ñudoso,* knotty (Molina)] knotty, as wood. See also *abatanado* for knots in hair, string, etc. *Madera ñudosa,* knotty pine boards.

Ojos que no ven, corazón que no siente.
Eyes that do not see, heart that does not feel.
(Out of sight, out of mind.)

obispa, *f.* [<Sp. *avispa,* wasp] See *ovispa.*

obispón, *m.* [<N.M. Sp. aug. of *ovispa*] See *ovispón.*

ocote, *m.* [<Mex. Sp. *ocote* <Náhautl *ocotl,* pitch pine] bot., Ocote pine; Pitch or Torch pine.

ocotillo, *m.* [<Mex. Sp. dim. of *ocote*] bot., a thorny desert shrub variously known as Candlewood, Coachwhip cactus, Devil's walking stick, Jacob's staff, Monkeytail cactus, etc.

ocotoso, -sa, *adj.* [<N.M. Sp. *ocote*] having a high pitch content (applied to woods).

ocupar, *vb.* [<Sp. *ocupar,* to occupy] to need; to occupy. (*Vamos a ocupar tres huevos pal queque.* We are going to need three eggs to make the cake.)

ochá, *f.* See *oshá.*

oficio, *m.* [<Col. N.M. Sp. *oficio*] official government communication.

ofrecimiento, *m.* [<Sp. *ofrecimiento,* offering] offering; the portion of the Shepherds' Play (*Los pastores*) where shepherds go up to the manger and present their individual gifts to the Christ Child.

'ogadero ('hogadero), *m.* [<Sp. *ahogadero,* a kind of throatband] throatband or latch, a part of the headstall of a bridle or halter.

'ogar ('hogar), *vb.* [<Sp. *ahogar*] to drown; to choke; to smother.

oido [óiđo], *m.* [<Col. N.M. Sp. *oydo* (Molina)] ear, inner ear; sense of hearing. Cf. Mod. Sp. *oído.*

ójala, *interj.* [<Mex. Sp. *ójala* <Sp. *ojalá,* God grant] I (we, they, etc.) hope to God. Like fun! That's what you think! Also, *ójale.*

ojelata, *f.* See *hojelata.*

ojero, *m.* See *hojero.*

ojetar, *vb.* [<Sp. *objetar*] to object; to oppose.

ojo, *m.* [<Sp. *ojo,* eye] *¡Ojo!* Heads up! Watch out! *Ojo caliente,* hot spring; *ojo*

121

oler

de agua, (water) spring; *ojo de buey,* a kind of rainbow; *ojo de perdiz,* partridge eye, a kind of diamond twill used in weaving *jerga; hacer ojo* (or *mal de ojo*), to cast a spell. *¿Con qué ojos, divina tuerta?* How?, with what money? *Ser uno puros ojos,* to be emaciated, very thin.

oler, *vb.* [<Sp. *oler,* to smell] The verb *oler* differs from standard Spanish *oler* in its conjugation in the present indicative and present subjunctive (*olgo, oles, ole, olemos*—as in standard Spanish, and *olen*). There is no second personal plural form in any of the tenses. The present subjunctive follows the first person singular of the present indicative: *olga, olgas,* etc.

ololote, *m.* [<Mex. Sp. *olote* <Náhuatl *olotl,* core] corncob. Also, *olote.*

olla, *f.* [<Sp. *olla,* pot] pot; chamber pot; jug; pail; slop jar, etc.; *olla del carbón,* coal bucket; *olla de empacar,* pressure cooker; *pl.,* clay pots; pots and pans; pottery.

olleros, *m. pl.* [<Sp. *olla,* pot] pot makers; the mountain clan of the Jicarilla Apaches. See *llaneros.*

onda, *f.* [<Sp. *onda*] wave; *agarrar la onda,* to catch on; to get it (to understand); to become aware. *¡Qué buena onda!* What good luck! What a good trip! (slang).

onza, *f.* [<Sp. *onza*] Col. and Terr. N.M. Sp., a gold coin worth sixteen dollars.

opas, *f. pl.* [<Quechua *upa,* mute] trifles (rare).

ora, *adv.* [<Sp. *ahora*] now; shortly. (*Ora venemos.* We'll be right back.)

oración, *f.* [<Sp. *oración*] prayer; *pl.,* the Angelus; evening prayers.

órale, *adv.* [<SW Sp. *ora* and *le*] alright; OK, fine; *excl.,* Hi! Listen!

oreja, *f.* [<Sp. *oreja*] ear; *agachar las orejas,* to act meek; *parar oreja,* to perk up one's ears; *trampar oreja,* to go to bed; *orejas de burro,* a kind of bugbear; *orejas de venado,* bot., Deer's ears. See *cebadilla.*

orejón, *m.* [<Sp. *orejón*] slice of dry fruit (apple, apricot, peach, etc.); cuckold; *adj.,* having large ears; a kind of bumblebee.

oremos, *m. pl.* [<Sp. *oremos,* let us pray] Christmas treats (candy, fruit, nuts, etc.) given to children on Christmas Eve and Christmas morning; *los oremos,* children and youngsters who go from house to house asking for *oremos* and threatening to break down doors and windows if they do not get them.

> *Oremos, oremos,*
> *angelitos semos,*
> *del cielo venemos*
> *a pidir oremos,*
> *y si no nos dan,*
> *puertas y ventanas*
> *nos la pagarán.*
> Let us pray, let us pray,
> We are little angels;
> We are coming from heaven
> To ask for treats,
> And if you don't give us any
> Your windows and doors
> Will pay for it.
> (N.M. Sp. strophe recited by the *oremos*)

orero, -ra, *m.* and *f.* [<Sp. *oro,* gold] goldsmith. Cf. Sp. *orfebre.*

organza, *f.* [<Sp. *holganza,* entertainment] amusement; diversion. (*El muerto al pozo y el vivo a l'organza.* The dead to the grave and the living to their fun.)

orillo, *m.* [<Sp. *orillo,* edge] rough pine slab.

orita, *adv.* [<Mex. Sp. *ahorita*] just now; a little while ago; in a little while.

oro, *m.* [<Sp. *oro*] gold; *oro colador,* gold leaf; *adj.,* American currency, vs. *plata,* Mexican currency; *cien pesos oro,* a hundred dollars.

oropel, *m.* [<Sp. *oropel*] tinsel; tinfoil; *hilo de oropel,* gold-studded thread.

oroplano, *m.* [<Sp. *aeroplano*] airplane.

or'ora, *adv.* [<Sp. *ahora, ahora*] presently, just now. (*Or'ora se van iyendo.* They

just now left.)

orra, *adj.* [<Mex. Sp. *machorra*] said of the female animal that is barren or sterile. Also, the female animal not touched by the male.

ortero, *m.* [<Sp. *hortera,* a kind of wooden bowl] Col. N.M. Sp., basin; dip.

ortiguilla, *f.* [<Sp. dim. of *ortiga*] nettle, thistle.

orutar, *vb.* [<Sp. *eructar*] to belch.

oscurana, *f.* [<Mex. Sp. *oscurana*] dark; darkness; blackout. See *escurana.*

oshá, *f.* [<Indian?] bot., medicinal plant, Wild celery; a plant of the Parsley family.

ovispa, *f.* [<Sp. *avispa,* wasp] honeybee, wasp.

ovispón, *m.* [<N.M. Sp. aug. of *ovispa*] bumblebee, drone, hornet. (*Le picó un ovispón a la Mónica.* Monica was stung by a hornet.)

oyodín, *m.* [<Eng. iodine] iodine; Mercurochrome.

Pa pendejo no se necesita mestro.
To be a fool one needs no school.

pa, *prep.* [<Col. N.M. Sp. *pa,* for (Molina)] for; in order to; *pa adelante,* pregnant (taboo). (*La Grabiela está pa adelante.* Grabriela is pregnant.)

pacencia, *f.* [<Sp. *paciencia*] patience.

pachuco, -ca, *m.* and *f.* [<SW Sp. *pachuco*] Chicano zoot-suiter, originally from El Paso, Texas.

pader, *f.* [<Sp. *pared*] wall.

paderón, *m.* [<Sp. *paredón*] standing wall.

padrastro, *m.* [<Sp. *padrastro,* stepfather] hangnail; stepfather.

padre, *adj.* [<Mex. Sp. *padre,* large, colossal] wonderful. (*¡Qué padre estuvo el party!* The party was wonderful! *¡Qué padre es la vida!* How sweet life is!)

pagar, *vb.* [<Sp. *pagar,* to pay] to get even. (*Me la pagas.* I'll get even with you.) To pay. (*No paga hacer favores.* It doesn't pay to do favors.)

pagué, *m.* [<Tewa?] bot., Fetid marigold, a medicinal plant.

pais [páis], *m.* [<Sp. *país*] country; home-town; region; village; *del pais,* home-grown, local.

Each region has its own crafts, its special local products, its exclusive fiestas, its plays, dances, and folk ways. In speaking of *"mi pais"* a native does not refer to the state, but rather to his own region, more often to his special village. (Aurora Lucero White, "Folkways," *New Mexico Magazine*)

paisano, *m.* [<Mex. Sp. *paisano*] roadrunner; pheasant. See also *gallineta.*

The roadrunner has many names. It is called *paisano, correcamino, chaparral* cock, lizard bird, snake killer, *churca,* cock of the desert, etc. (Illon Chase, "Roadrunner," *New Mexico Magazine*)

paiser, *m.* [<N.M. Sp. *pais*] countryman; said of the person from one's home-town or village.

pajarito, *m.* [<Sp. dim. of *pájaro*] small bird; name given to a male child's or-

gan; *adj., de los pajaritos del monte,* illegitimate, gift of God (baby).

pájaro, *m.* [<Sp. *pájaro*] bird; *pájaro nalgón,* a Mr. Nobody; a windbag; *pájaro piñonero,* bluejay; *pájaro de siete colores,* said of a person wearing articles of clothing of various (non-matching) colors.

pajecita, *f.* [<Sp. dim. *f.* of *paje,* page, valet] flower girl attending a bride.

pajue, *m.* [<unknown origin] idle talk; gossip; mischievous lie.

pajuela, *f.* [<Mex. Sp. *pajuela,* sulphur match] a tomboy; a female who is always on the go; a liberated female.

pajuelazo, *m.* [<Mex. Sp. *pajuela,* sulphur match] a drink of whiskey; sound of a falling body; thud; blow with a whip.

pajuelear, *vb.* [<Mex. Sp. *pajuela*] to flap, as a flag; *pajuelearle a alguno,* to excel, to be very good at something. (*Al Prudencio le pajuela pa correr.* Prudencio is good at running.) See also *arrastrarle.*

pala, *f.* [<Sp. *pala*] shovel; crane; *hacerle la pala a alguno,* to be in cahoots with someone; to back someone who is lying or exaggerating.

palagar, *m.* [<Sp. *paladar*] palate.

palero, -ra, *adj.* [<N.M. Sp. *pala (hacer la pala)*] conniving; said of someone who backs another person in telling a lie or exaggerating.

paleta, *f.* [<Sp. *paleta,* blade or bone of the shoulder] leg of lamb.

palito, *m.* [<Sp. dim. of *palo*] small stick; *El palito,* name of a children's game; *palito de los dientes,* toothpick; *palitos de la ropa,* clothespins.

palma, *f.* [<Sp. *palma,* palm tree] three-pronged wand used by the *Matachines* in their dance (*Los Matachines*); bot., Soapweed; Yucca (*palmilla*).

palmilla, *f.* [<Mex. Sp. *palmilla*] Sp. dim. of *palma,* bot., Soapweed; Yucca.

palo, *m.* [<Sp. *palo,* stick] *palo amarillo,* bot., Fremont's barberry, a shrub of the Barberry family; *palo blanco,* bot., Aspen; also, pimp, procurer; *palo de Brasil,* bot., Logwood; *palo duro,* bot., Mountain mahogany; *palo ensebado,* greased pole. Cf. Sp. *cucaña.* ¡*Palo!, interj.,* a sound in imitation of a hard blow.

palomilla, *f.* [<Mex. Sp. *palomilla,* gang] butterfly; children (small fry); gang.

palomillo, *m.* [<Sp. dim. of *palomo,* palomino] Col. N.M. Sp., a kind of mottled pony; a pinto.

Ponies were bred for it [buffalo hunting], often of the creamy stock Queen Isabella sent to Mexico, *palomillos* . . . "paint horses." (Erna Fergusson, *Our Southwest*)

palomita, *f.* [<Sp. dim. of *paloma,* dove] small dove; turtledove; butterfly; moth; *m.,* pigeon.

palomo, -ma, *adj.* [<Am. Sp. *palomo*] beige or cream-colored. Cf. *palomino.*

pan, *m.* [<Sp. *pan*] bread; *pan de cemita,* a kind of whole wheat bread; *pan del sábado,* a gift, usually in the form of groceries, which schoolchildren took on Saturdays to the village teacher in exchange for teaching them Christian doctrine. *Pan duce,* pastries, sweet rolls; *de pan llevar, prep.,* fit or prepared for planting, applied to land.

pandearse, *vb.* [<Sp. *pandear,* to bend] to cringe, as with pain; to get one's feelings hurt; to complain; to be concerned. (¿*Qué estás pandeándote?* Why are you so concerned?)

panderete, *m.* [<Sp. *pandereta,* tambourine] an uneven haircut; a chunk of hair or a furrow in a haircut.

pandito, -ta, *adj.* [<Mex. Sp. *pando,* swaybacked] vain or conceited; self-satisfied.

pando, -da, *adj.* [<Mex. Sp. *pando*] swaybacked; excessively drunk.

panear, *vb.* [<Mex. Sp. *pan,* a name for the female organ] a male's sexual overture toward a woman (derog.). See also *mano (meter mano).*

paniles, *m. pl.* [<unknown origin] sideboard on a truck or wagon. Also, *pañiles.*

panilla, *f.* [<Sp. dim. of *pana,* velveteen] velvet, velveteen.

panjoto, -ta, *adj.* [<Mex. Sp. *panjotudo*] fat; sloppy.

panjotudo, -da, *adj.* [<Mex. Sp. *panjotudo*] fat; sloppy.

panocha, *f.* [<Mex. Sp. *panocha*, a kind of raw brown sugar] a pudding, conserve or dessert made from ground wheat grain which has been sprouted. Also, female organ (taboo).

panqueque, *m.* [<Eng. pancake] pancake; waffle.

pantalones, *m. pl.* [<Sp. *pantalones*, pants] *pantalones rabones,* knee breeches. The word *calzones* (pants, trousers, slacks, etc.) is a more common term for pants.

pantalla, *f.* [<Sp. *pantalla*, lampshade] Col. and Terr. N.M. Sp., wall candle holder. Since the church to the Spanish colonial was first consideration in his daily living, it is safe to say that the first tin articles fashioned were those destined for the church or private chapel. This is evidenced by the numerous articles found today that formerly were in church use: *arañas,* ceiling candle holders; *pantallas,* wall candle holders; *candeleros,* candlesticks; *nichos,* niches, and *hornacinas,* niches entirely glassed. (Carmen Espinosa, "Color for Mi Casa," *New Mexico Magazine*)

pantera, *adj.* [<Mex. Sp. *pantera*, brave] said of a person who is smartly dressed; dapper. (*¡Qué pantera anda el Acorsinio esta mañana!* How dapper Acorsinio looks this morning!)

pantura, *f.* [<unknown origin] a kind of hinge (rare).

panza, *f.* [<Sp. *panza*, belly] a dish made with tripe, hominy and chili; belly, stomach. (*Dice la Rosenda que le duele la panza.* Rosenda says she has a stomachache.)

panzón, -na, *adj.* [<Sp. *panzón,* largebellied man] fat; *estar panzona una mujer,* to be pregnant.

pañiles, *m. pl.* [<unknown origin] sideboard on a truck or wagon. Also, *paniles.*

paño, *m.* [<Sp. *paño,* cloth] handkerchief; *valse del paño,* lit., waltz of the handkerchief, a folk dance in which a handkerchief is used by the dancers. Pregnancy mask or darkening of a woman's facial area during pregnancy.

pañoleta, *f.* [<Mex. Sp. *pañoleta*] a kind of mantilla.

papa, *f.* [<Mex. Sp. *papa*] potato; *la papa,* a political plum. (*Ahi 'stá la papa.* It's yours for the asking.) *Papas duces,* sweet potatoes; *papas tostadas,* potato chips; *no tener uno ni pa la papa,* to be short on grocery money; *echarle sus papas a alguno,* to scold or tell someone off; bulb (iris, lily, etc.).

papá, *m.* [<Sp. *papá,* dad] daddy, papa; *papá grande,* grandfather.

papada, *f.* [<Sp. *papada,* double chin] chance; opportunity.

papalina, *f.* [<Sp. *papalina,* a kind of cap with flaps] sunbonnet; beating; thrashing; *ponerle una papalina a alguno,* to give someone a good thrashing.

papalote, *m.* [<Mex. Sp. *papalota* <Náhuatl *papalotl,* butterfly] kite; windmill.

papalotear, *vb.* [<N.M. Sp. *papalote,* windmill] to flap in the wind; *papalotearle a alguno,* to excel or be extremely good at something. (*Al Frutoso le papalotea para cantar.* Frutoso is good at singing.)

papalotitos, *m. pl.* [<Mex. Sp. *papalota,* butterfly] sweetpeas.

papear, *vb.* [<N.M. Sp. *papas,* scolding] to scold or tell someone off. See *papa,* above.

papel, *m.* [<Sp. *papel,* paper] newspaper; paper in general; *papel del común* (or *del privao*), toilet tissue.

papelito, *m.* [<N.M. Sp. *papel,* paper] *leerle a alguno su papelito,* to get to know someone's behavior; to get someone's number. (*Ya le leyeron su papelito.* They are on to his tricks.)

papera, *f.* [<Sp. *papera,* mumps] goiter; mumps.

papero, *m.* [<N.M. Sp. *papas,* scolding] a great number or pile of potatoes; a scolding. (*¡Qué papero le pusieron!* What

a scolding he got!) *Adj.*, sarcastic; said of the person who is always scolding others. Also, *papiento* and *papión*.

papitas, *f. pl.* [<N.M. Sp. dim. of *papas*, potatoes] small potatoes; *papitas de tordo*, a kind of small, round potatoes.

papos, *m. pl.* [<Sp. *zapatos* (child's pronunciation)] shoes.

paquete, *m.* [<Mex. Sp. *paquete*] elegant carriage or bearing.

parada, *f.* [<Mex. Sp. *parada*] *mala parada*, ill turn or wicked trick. (*Le hicieron una mala parada.* They played a dirty trick on him.)

parado, -da, *adj.* [<Sp. *parado*] stopped; standing; protruding; *en parado*, standing with legs apart, a position assumed by the man at the bottom of a *caballito* or human ladder formed to scale walls, fort enclosures, etc. *Piedra Parada* (Standing Rock), N.M. Sp. name of Shiprock; *caer parado*, to be lucky everywhere one goes; to fall among friends.

paragua, *m.* [<Sp. *paraguas*] umbrella; parasol. Also, *paragüe* and *pariagüe*.

paraiso [paráiso], *m.* [<Sp. *paraíso*] paradise; the Garden of Eden; heaven.

paraje, *m.* [<Sp. *paraje* <*parar*, to stop] camping ground or encampment; location; stop.

paralís, *m.* [<Sp. *parálisis*] paralysis.

parar, *vb.* [<Sp. *parar*] to stop; *pararle 'l agua a alguno*, to put a stop to someone's actions or activities; *pararse el cuello*, to put on airs.

pardear, *vb.* [<N.M. Sp. *pardo*, gray] to become dusky or shadowy. (*Ya está pardeando.* It is getting dark.)

pardito, -ta, *adj.* [<N.M. Sp. *pardo*] grayish.

pardo, -da, *adj.* [<Col. N.M. Sp. *pardo* <Lat. *pardus*] gray. Cf. Sp. *pardo*.

pardusco, -ca, *adj.* [<N.M. Sp. *pardo*, gray] grayish.

parejo, -ja, *adj.* [<Sp. *parejo*, equal, similar] even; smooth, as a surface. (*¿Pa qué*

es tanto brinco estando el suelo tan parejo? An expression meaning, You're making a mountain out of a molehill.)

pares, *m. pl.* [<Sp. *par*, pair] *¿Pares o nones?*, Odd or Even, a children's game. The early New Mexican women used the gourds as darning balls. And their children play a well-known game with the wild squash seeds. One holds a few of them in his closed fist and another tries to guess their number. The command, *¡Adivina, buen adivinador!* "Guess, good guesser," often is varied by the question, *¿Pares o nones?* Odd or even? (Leonora S. M. Curtin, *Healing Herbs of the Upper Rio Grande*)

pariagüe, *m.* [<Sp. *paraguas*] umbrella.

parientes, *m. pl.* [<Eng. parents] parents; relatives.

parna, *m.* and *f.* [<Eng. partner] pal; partner; friend.

parparear, *vb.* [<N.M. Sp. *párparo*, eyelid] to blink; to wink.

párparo, *m.* [<Sp. *párpado*] eyelid.

parque, *m.* [<Sp. *parque*] park; ammunition. Also, a card issued to schoolchildren in territorial days. Schoolteachers issued the *parques* for good behavior, perfect attendance, exceptional class work, or for some heroic deed and exempted the bearer of such a card from a *pela*, or thrashing, a total of ten times. Each time a pupil was about to be punished, he would show his *parque* to the school master, who then would merely reprimand the child and cut or punch out one of the ten exceptions (much like a restaurant meal ticket) until eventually all the exceptions were used up. *Parques* could be voided for serious offenses. (Amador Abeyta, Sabinal, N.M.)

parquear, *vb.* [<Eng. to park] to park a vehicle.

parquero, -ra, *m.* and *f.* [<N.M. Sp. *parque nacional*, national park or forest] forest ranger.

parquete

parquete, *m.* [<Sp. *paquete,* package] package; paper sack, paper bag.

párraco, *m.* [<Sp. *párroco,* parson] curate; parish priest.

parranda, *f.* [<Mex. Sp. *parranda*] drinking spree; noisy party.

parrandear, *vb.* [<Mex. Sp. *parrandear*] to go on a drinking spree in the company of friends and women.

parrandero, -ra, *adj.* [<Mex. Sp. *parrandero*] said of a person who is fond of drinking sprees and merriment.

partida, *f.* [<Sp. *partida,* crew; gang] flock of sheep usually numbering a thousand head.

> The *caporal* . . . furnished the sheep camps with provisions, and it was his duty to make sure that water was available for the **partidas** under the care of each shepherd. A **partida** usually consisted of a thousand head of sheep. (Fabiola C. de Baca Gilbert, *We Fed Them Cactus*)

partidario, *m.* [<Sp. *partidario,* partisan] sharecropper; tenant farmer; an independent stockbreeder.

partido, *m.* [<Sp. *partido,* profit] Col. N.M. Sp., political district into which a province was divided; political party; flock of goats, sheep, etc.; *tener partido con todos,* to get along well with everyone; a system of shares.

partirse, *vb.* [<Sp. *partirse*] to get excited; to become upset or riled (used mostly in folktales).

parva, *f.* [<Sp. *parva*] large group; flock of birds. Also, *parvada* and *parvón.*

pasatiempo, *m.* [<Sp. *pasatiempo,* pastime] hysterical parade during the Santa Fe fiesta.

pasearse, *vb.* [<Sp. *pasearse*] to go for a stroll. *Vayan a pasearse.* Come on over for a visit. (This expression is used by a person inviting another to pay him or her a visit.)

pasión, *f.* [<Sp. *pasión,* passion] a kind of prayer.

pasmado, -da, *adj.* [<Mex. Sp. *pasmado*] soggy or wet, applied to wood; pithy or spongy.

pastel, *m.* [<N.M. Sp. *pastel,* pie] *descubrir el pastel,* to let the cat out of the bag; to spill the beans.

pasteo, *m.* [<Sp. *pasto*] pasture.

pastilla, *f.* [<Sp. *pastilla,* lozenge] coin of small denomination (usually a dime) given by the *padrino* (godfather) to children attending a baptismal ceremony.

> Refreshments were served to the godparents and intimate friends invited to the feast. La **pastilla** was asked of the *padrinos* in fun by the grownups, but the children received nickels and dimes, and the baby was given a five or ten-dollar gold piece, according to the means of the godparents. (Cleofas M. Jaramillo, *Shadows of the Past*)

pastorela, *f.* [<Mex. Sp. *pastorela*] shepherds' play also known as *Los pastores,* a dramatic presentation in which shepherds go to Bethlehem to offer gifts to the Christ Child.

pastores (Los pastores). See *pastorela.*

pata, *f.* [<Sp. *pata,* foot or leg of beasts] *pata de gallina,* crow's foot (wrinkles at the outer corners of the eyes); *pata de gallo,* pattern in a game played with string and the ten fingers of the hands; *Pata Galán,* euphemism for the devil; *ir a pata,* to walk (to hoof it); *salir con una pata más corta que la otra,* to miscalculate; to figure wrong.

patada, *f.* [<Sp. *patada* and Eng. kick (fig.)] kick of liquor or a firearm; *darle patadas al mundo,* to go out into the world; *estar una cosa de la patada,* to be bad (applied to a situation). *¡Hijo 'e la patada!* Damn!

patarrabo, *m.* [<Sp. *taparrabo*] breechcloth; loincloth.

patatús, *m.* [<Sp. *patatús,* fainting spell] epileptic fit.

patita, *f.* [<Sp. dim. of *pata*] small foot; *patita 'e la paloma,* bot., Quaker bonnet

(flower); *patita 'e lion,* bot., Wild geranium; *mujeres de la patita,* prostitutes; streetwalkers.

patito, *m.* [<Sp. dim. of *pato,* duck] small duck, duckling; bot., Buffalo pea; Wild sweet pea; *echar patitos,* to throw stones obliquely on the surface of the water (duck and drake).

pato, *m.* [<Sp. *pato,* duck] duck; teapot. *¡Al agua, patos de la laguna!* Let's get started! *Cola de pato,* a leather housing attached to the cantle of a saddle; *creerse uno tan pato,* to think oneself better than others; *fregar pato,* to get a lucky break or have unexpected good luck.

pautado, -da, *adj.* [<Sp. *pactado*] in agreement with the devil, said of a person who supposedly has made a pact with the devil.

pavón, *m.* [<prob. related to Eng. pavement] pavement; paved road.

payasa, *f.* [<Sp. *f.* of *payaso,* clown] said of an older woman who uses excessive makeup.

pazote, *m.* See *epazote.*

pazotillo, *m.* [<N.M. Sp. dim. of *pazote*] bot., Horseweed.

peaje, *m.* [<Col. N.M. Sp. *peaje*] toll, tribute.

peco, -ca, *m.* and *f.* [<Col. and Terr. N.M. Sp. *peco*] an inhabitant of the Indian pueblo of Pecos.

pecheras, *f. pl.* [<Sp. *pechera,* bosom of a shirt] bib, overalls.

peda, *f.* [<N.M. Sp. *pedo, peda*] drunk; drunken spree. Cf. Sp. *borrachera. (Andan en la peda.* They are out on a drunken spree.) *Adj.,* drunk. *(La Gertrudis anda peda.* Gertrude is drunk.)

pedernal, *m.* [<Sp. *pedernal,* flint] flintstone knife; any hard stone that can produce a spark.

The "flint" was not true flint, as that material is not locally available. New Mexicans used the term *pedernal* for obsidian and other hard stone harder than limestone and sandstone, as well as for the volcanic peak which produced so much prehistoric artifact material—the *Cerro de Pedernal.* (E. Boyd, "The Use of Tobacco in Spanish New Mexico," *El Palacio*)

pedista, *adj.* [<N.M. Sp. *pedo,* disturbance] boisterous; said of someone fond of disturbances or commotion.

pedo, *m.* [<Mex. Sp. *pedo*] commotion; disturbance; *hacer una cosa de pedo,* to laugh off a thing or turn it into ridicule; *hacerle pedo un hombre a una mujer,* to flirt with a woman. *(El Elifás le anda haciendo pedo a la Figenia.* Elifás is flirting with Figenia.) *Adj.,* drunk *(m.* and *f.*).

pedorrera, *f.* [<Sp. *pedorrera,* flatulence] commotion; disturbance; noise.

pedrero, *m.* [<Sp. *pedrero,* swivel gun] Col. N.M. Sp., a small homemade howitzer using balls of stone, spikes, etc.

The first capital building was built in Pueblo style, three stories high, around a square. In the plaza were planted the *pedreros,* or small howitzers, using balls of stone. (Clara D. True, "Forgotten Capital," *New Mexico Magazine*)

pega, *f.* [<Sp. *pegar,* to stick or adhere] glue; paste. Also, *pegapega.*

pegajoso, -sa, *adj.* [<Sp. *pegajoso,* sticky] sticky; bothersome; pesky, as a child that wants to go everywhere with an older brother or sister; hanger-on.

pegapega, *f.* [<Mex. Sp. *pegapega,* a kind of thistle] bot., a thistle of the Loasa family; the term is also applied loosely to any mucilage or glue. See also *mujer (buena mujer).*

pegar, *vb.* [<Sp. *pegar*] to strike; to make a hit with someone; to date someone. *(El Cleofes está pegando con la güerita.* Cleofes is making a hit with the blonde.)

pela, *f.* [<Mex. Sp. *pela*] whipping, beating, thrashing.

pelada, *f.* [<Mex. Sp. *pelada (la mera pelada)*] the naked truth; the spot. *(Esa canción me dio en la mera pelada.* That

129

song hit me where it hurts.)

peladera, *f.* [<Mex. Sp. *peladera*] rip off; highway robbery.

pelado, -da, *adj.* [<Mex. Sp. *pelado,* tramp] broke; penniless.

pelagartear, *vb.* [<Mex. Sp. *pelagartear*] to swindle; to pull the wool over someone's eyes.

pelagartero, -ra, *adj.* [<Mex. Sp. *pelagartero*] swindler; petty thief.

pelarse, *vb.* [<Mex. Sp. *pelarse*] to leave; "to split"; *pelárselas,* to be anxious, eager. (*Están que se las pelan por que te caigas.* They are eagerly waiting for you to fall.)

pelegrino, -na, *adj.* [<Sp. *peregrino*] pilgrim; *adj.,* strange, rare.

> *Dios con artificio fino*
> *pintó al divino portento*
> *y a María en su entendimiento*
> *como que es pintor divino*
> *con amor muy **pelegrino***
> *para madre la eligió.*
> God with His fine workmanship
> Painted the divine wonder
> And in his judgment,
> Being a divine painter,
> With a very strange love
> Chose Mary for a mother.
> (A.M. Espinosa, "Romancero Nuevomejicano," *Revue Hispanique*)

pelenqueador, -ra, *m.* and *f.* [<N.M. Sp. *pelenquear*] scavenger, beachcomber.

pelenquear, *vb.* [<unknown origin] to gather; to pick up on the run; to scavenge.

peleonero, -ra, *adj.* [<Sp. *pelear,* to fight] said of the youth who is always fighting or looking for a fight; quarrelsome.

pelerina, *f.* [<Mex. Sp. *pelerina* <Fr. *pelerine,* a kind of cape] raincoat; topcoat.

pelillo, *m.* [<Mex. Sp. *pelillo,* a kind of grasslike plant] tender grass; fuzz.

pelilludo, *adj.* [<N.M. Sp. *pelillo*] said of the horse or male donkey not completely castrated, i.e., still with the use

of one testicle.

pelito, *m.* [<Sp. dim. of *pelo*] a tiny bit; a small portion or a fraction of anything. (*Todavía le falta un pelito para la libra.* It is not quite a pound; it needs a tiny bit more.)

pelizcar, *vb.* [<Sp. *pellizcar* <*peḷiӨkár*] to pinch.

pelizco, *m.* [<Sp. *pellizco* <*peḷiӨko*] pinch; pricking sensation.

pelo, *m.* [<Sp. *pelo*] hair; fur wrap; *de pelo en pecho,* brave; daring; macho; *pelo y rostro,* the very image. (*La Angela es el pelo y rostro de papá.* Angela is the very image of my father.) *No tener pelos en la lengua,* to be outspoken; *quedar algo al puro pelo,* to fit just right.

pelón, -na, *adj.* [<Mex. Sp. *pelón*] baldheaded; hairless or having very short hair; difficult; risky; said also of the animal (cow, goat, ram) with only one horn. *La pelona,* Death.

pelorina, *f.* See *pelerina.*

pelota, *f.* [<Col. N.M. Sp. *en pelota,* in one's underclothes] stark naked.

pelotero, -ra, *m.* and *f.* [<Sp. *pelotero,* ball maker] baseball player.

peluche, *m.* [<Mex. Sp. *peluche,* plush] fur; *cute de peluche,* fur coat.

pelusa, *f.* [<Mex. Sp. *pelusa*] gang; riffraff.

pelusero, *m.* [<Sp. *pelo,* hair] excessive body hair.

pellas, *f. pl.* [<Sp. *pella,* roll of raw lard] flab; rolls of fat on a person; *echar pellas,* to grow fat; to lie around idle.

pellejo, *m.* [<Sp. *pellejo*] skin; *ser una persona el puro pellejo,* to be nothing but skin and bones; to be emaciated, skinny.

pena, *f.* [<Sp. *pena,* sorrow] bashfulness; shyness; embarrassment.

penco, *m.* [<Mex. Sp. *penco,* horse] motherless animal, especially a lamb; said of the man who is accepted and favored by another man's wife; *adj.,* applied to a runt.

pendejada, *f.* [<Mex. Sp. *pendejada,* stupid act] blunder; boo-boo; foolishness; stupidity.

pendejo, -ja, *adj.* [<Mex. Sp. *pendejo,* cowardly; stupid] awkward; dull, slow; stupid.

pene, *m.* [<Eng. penny] one-cent coin; penny.

penitensaria, *f.* [<Eng. penitentiary] penitentiary, "the pen." See also *la pinta.*

penitente, *adj.* [<N.M. Sp. euph. of *pendejo*] silly; crazy; foolish; stupid. (*No hagas eso, no seas penitente.* Don't do that; don't be foolish. *¡Qué hombre tan penitente!* What a stupid man!)

penitente, *m.* [<Sp. *penitente,* penitent] said of one who does penance; *los penitentes* (or *los hermanos penitentes*), a Roman Catholic brotherhood of Indo-Hispanic origin that observes certain rites related to the Passion of Christ. These rites include fasting, flagellation, the enactment of the Last Supper, scenes from the Passion, and the singing of *alabados* or religious songs (hymns of praise).

penquero, -ra, *adj.* [<N.M. Sp. *penco,* orphaned lamb] said of the person who raises orphaned lambs; *m.,* large number of *pencos.*

pepenar, *vb.* [<Mex. Sp. *pepenar* <Náhautl *pepena,* to pick up what has been scattered on the ground] to pick up; to stop by for someone. (*Te pepeno a las ocho.* I'll pick you up at eight.)

pepitoria, *f.* [<Mex. Sp. *pepitoria*] a kind of candy made with brown sugar and pumpkin seeds.

peras, *f. pl.* [<Sp. *pera,* pear] pears; *ponerle a uno las peras a dos reales,* to give someone his comeuppance; to give someone a good thrashing.

percíngula, *f.* [<Sp. *porciúncula*] a religious feast formerly observed in northern New Mexico and southern Colorado. Also, *precíngula.*

percha, *f.* [<Sp. *percha,* clothes rack] chicken roost; clothesline; ornith., robin.

perdido, *adj.* [<Sp. *perdido,* lost] *de perdido,* at least; at a minimum. (*De perdido se tardaron quince minutos pa llegar a donde estaba el carro.* They took at least [a minimum of] fifteen minutes to get to where the car was.)

perejundia, *f.* name of one of the dancers in *Los Matachines* (a man dressed as a woman).

perfición, *f.* [<Col. N.M. Sp. *perfición*] likeness, resemblance. (*No le jallo perfición a esta muchacha.* I cannot place this girl [although she does look familiar].)

perfil, *m.* [<Sp. *perfil,* profile] drawnwork or lacework.

perfilar, *vb.* [<N.M. Sp. *perfil*] to make lacework.

pergamino, *m.* [<Sp. *pergamino,* parchment] applied to a sheepskin that has lost all its wool and remains in an extremely dry condition.

pergate, *m.* [<Indian?] nipple of a woman's breast.

pericos, *m. pl.* [<Mex. Sp. *perico,* a plant] bot., a kind of Canna plant.

periquear, *vb.* [<Sp. *perico,* parrot] to chatter; to gossip.

periquera, *f.* [<Sp. *perico,* parrot] peanut gallery in a theatre.

perjurio, -ria, *m.* and *f.* [<Sp. *perjuro*] perjurer.

perol, *m.* [<Sp. *perol*] kettle; *cocer los peroles,* to prepare large amounts of food; *comerse una persona los peroles,* to be famished, to eat heartily. (*El Maque se comió los peroles.* Mack was famished.)

perra, *f.* [<Sp. *perra,* bitch] female dog. *Hacer la perra* (or *la perrita*), to goldbrick; to pretend to be working.

perrada, *f.* [<Sp. *perrada*] pack of dogs; *andar a la perrada,* to be at each other's throat. (*La Perfilia y su viejo andaban a la perrada en el baile.* Perfilia and her husband were at each other's throats at the dance.)

perrera, *f.* [<Sp. *perro,* dog] gang in a

free-for-all fight.

perrilla, *f.* [<Mex. Sp. *perrilla*] sty (rare). See *chile* (*chile 'e perro*).

perrito, *m.* [<Sp. dim. of *perro*] small dog; puppy; *perrito de agua,* a kind of river rat.

perro, -rra, *adj.* [<Sp. *perro*] mean; *perro viejo,* experienced; *m., perro chato,* bulldog.

perrodo, -da, *adj.* [<Sp. *pedorro*<*pedo,* flatulence] flatulent; *m.,* a kind of black beetle; a stinkbug; *hormigas perrodas,* a kind of stinky red ants.

persecutar, *vb.* [<Eng. persecute] to persecute. Cf. Sp. *perseguir.*

persogar, *vb.* [<Sp. *aspersogar*] to tether; to tie with a tether or rope.

pesa, *f.* [<Sp. *pesa,* weight] weighing scale.

pésame, *m.* [<Sp. *pésame* (*Me pesa.*)] an expression of sorrow at someone's death. The normal expression in New Mexico and southern Colorado, addressed individually to each member of a bereaved family, is *"Siento mucho su pesar."* (I am so sorry for your grief [or for your loss].) Condolences. (*Vamos a dale el pésame a mano Beno.* Let's give old man Beno our condolences.)

pescuezudo, -da, *adj.* [<Sp. *pescozudo*] having a large neck.

peseta, *f.* [<Sp. *peseta,* euph. of *pesado,* dull] boring; disagreeable; unpleasant; unbearable. (*El Sarapio me cae pesado.* I can't stand Sarapio.) Quarter; Col. and Terr. N.M. Sp., a silver coin worth two *reales* or twenty-five *centavos.*

pespuntear, *vb.* [<Sp. *pespuntar,* to backstitch] to sew with a back seam; to dance on tiptoe.

pesudo, -da, *adj.* [<Sp. *peso*] rich; in the money; "loaded" (slang).

pesuña, *f.* [<Sp. *pesuña,* hoof] hoof; *ir a pesuña,* to "hoof it" (slang).

petaca, *f.* [<Mex. Sp. *petaca*<Náhuatl *petacalli*] chest; a hamper made of rawhide; trunk (general); *pl.,* hips; buttocks.

petaquilla, *f.* [<Mex. Sp. dim. of *petaca*] small trunk; footlocker.

petate, *m.* [<Mex. Sp. *petate*] mat; *enrollar el petate,* to roll the mat (to die) (rare).

petencia, *f.* [<Sp. *apetencia*] appetite; hunger.

petón, *m.* [<Sp. aug. of *peto,* false blouse front] a kind of blouse.

petrol, *m.* [<Eng. patrol] highway patrol. Also, *petrolino.*

petunia, *f.* [<Eng. petunia] petunia.

peyote, *m.* [<Mex. Sp. *peyote*] bot., Peyote, a kind of cactus with button-like tops which are chewed, especially by some Indians, for their hallucinogenic effects.

pial, *m.* [<Mex. Sp. *pial*] a kind of lasso with which a steer or calf is roped or lassoed by a hind foot.

pica, *f.* [<Sp. *pica,* pike] ill will; *tenerle mala pica una persona a otra,* to have it in for someone; to bear ill will toward someone.

> De Chimayó para arriba
> nuestra gente está muy rica;
> al que no tiene dinero
> le tienen muy mala **pica**.
> North from Chimayó
> Our people are very rich;
> They bear ill will
> Toward him who has no money.
> (N.M. Sp. *verso popular*)

picada, *f.* [<Sp. *picar,* to sting] bite (insect, snake, etc.); dim., *picadita,* a kind of marble game.

picado, -da, *adj.* [<Sp. *picado,* pitted] pockmarked; left with a strong desire; *quedarse uno picado,* to be left licking one's chops; annoyed; angry; shocked.

picapica, *f.* [<Mex. Sp. *picapica,* any of several plants that irritate upon contact] bot., a kind of poison ivy.

picar, *vb.* [<Sp. *picar,* to prick] to bite, as an insect; to harm. (*Le picó el frío.* He caught cold.) To goad, to spur on. *¡Pícale!* Hurry up! Step on it! *Picarle la araña a una mujer,* to become pregnant; *picarle la cresta a alguno,* to tease, to

provoke someone to anger. *¿Qué te pica?* What's wrong with you?

picardía, *f.* [<Sp. *picardía,* knavery] bad or blasphemous word.

picarse, *vb.* [<Sp. *picarse,* to be vexed] to develop a taste or desire for something; to become addicted.

pico, *m.* [<Sp. *pico*] pickax; *de pico y pala,* pick and shovel; the mouth; a kiss (especially *piquito*). (*La que da el pico, da el nico.* The girl that kisses does not stop at kissing.) Male organ (euph.).

picolargo, *m.* [<Mex. Sp. *pico largo*] ornith., snipe.

picón, *m.* [<N.M. Sp. *picado,* left with a strong desire] a whetting, a taste. (*Lo hago nomás pa dales un picón.* I do this just to give them a taste.)

picha, *f.* [<Col. Sp. *pixa* [*píša*]] male organ. Cf. Sp. *pija.*

pichel, *m.* [<Mex. Sp. *pichel*] a kind of pitcher.

pichete, *m.* [<unknown origin] large mole or birthmark.

pichicuate, -ta, *m.* and *f.* [<Mex. Sp. *pichicuate* <Náhuatl *pitza huac,* a poisonous snake] said of the child who is born after the mother has given birth to twins. Also, a small snake; the male organ.

pichón, *m.* [<Sp. *pichón*] pigeon; sexual intercourse.

pichonear, *vb.* [<N.M. Sp. *pichón*] to engage in sexual intercourse.

pichudo, *adj.* [<N.M. Sp. *picha*] having a large *picha* (male organ).

pidiche, *adj.* [<Mex. Sp. *pidiche,* moocher] said of the person who is always asking for things; a moocher, a parasite.

pidigüeño, -ña, *adj.* [<Sp. *pedigüeño*] said of the person who is continuously asking for things.

pie, *m.* [<Sp. *pie*] foot; *a pie fijo,* without letup, without stopping, incessantly; *piecito,* small foot; sprig or shoot off a plant; *un piecito de genario,* a shoot of geranium.

piedra, *f.* [<Sp. *piedra,* stone] pebble; rock; stone; tombstone; *piedra infernal,* silver nitrate; *piedra lipe,* lime powder; *piedra lumbre,* flint; *piedra de moler,* grindstone; *estar una cosa tres piedras,* to be excellent, fine. *Piedra imán* or *imana,* lodestone (used by some people to attract love or wealth).

piedroso, -sa, *adj.* [<Sp. *piedra*] rocky, stony. Cf. Sp. *pedregoso.*

piensos, *m. pl.* [<Sp. *pienso,* thought] thoughts. (*Esos son sus piensos.* Those are his thoughts. That is his opinion.)

pierda, *f.* [<Sp. *piedra*] pebble; rock; stone.

pierde, *m.* [<Sp. *perder,* to lose] loss. (*No tiene pierde.* You can't go wrong. You can't lose.)

pierna, *f.* [<Sp. *pierna,* leg] Col. and Terr. N.M. Sp., a width used in measuring the *manta* or cloth.

The **pierna** was not a specific measurement and was varied according to the demands of the *encomendero.* (E. Boyd, *Popular Arts of Spanish New Mexico*)

pieza, *f.* [<Sp. *pieza,* piece] dance piece; phonograph record. Also, *platillo.*

pilateño, -ña, *adj.* [<Sp. *Pilato,* Pilate] dictatorial; ruthless; *órdenes pilateñas,* ruthless orders.

pilguanejo, -ja, *m.* and *f.* [<Mex. Sp. *pilguanejo* <Náhuatl *pilhuan,* son, and suffix *-ejo;* child reared in a convent to serve the clergy] nickname of a colonial poet known as *El Viejo Vilmas; adj.,* ignorant; stupid.

En el pueblo de Oposura
repicaron las campanas;
cuando yo bajé de allá,
*ya era muerto El **Pilguanejo**.*
In the town of Oposura
The church bells tolled;
When I left that place
Old man Vilmas was dead.
(*Trovos del Viejo Vilmas,* N.M. Sp. folk poetry)

pilinguito, -ta, *adj.* [<Mex. Sp. *pilinguito*] small, tiny.

pilmama, *f.* [<Mex. Sp. *pilmama* <Náhuatl *pilli*, son, and *mama*, one who carries] wet nurse; baby-sitter.

pilón, *m.* [<Mex. Sp. *pilón*, something given into the bargain] bonus, extra; lagniappe; *de pilón*, extra, gratis.
Las viejitas a cuartilla,
las muchachas a tostón,
las nueras a diez centavos
*y las suegras de **pilón**.*
Our ladies for pennies,
Girls for fifty cents;
Daughters-in-law for a dime
And mothers-in-law as a bonus.
(N.M. Sp. *verso popular*)

piloncillo, *m.* [<Mex. Sp. *piloncillo*] brown sugar in small pylon-shaped cakes.
Therefore these poor miners [*gambusinos*] lead a miserable life after all. When short of means they often support themselves upon only a *real* each per day, their usual food consisting of bread and a kind of coarse cake-sugar called ***piloncillo***, to which is sometimes added a little crude ranchero cheese. (Josiah Gregg, *Commerce of the Prairies*)

pinabete, *m.* [<Sp. *pino abeto*, a kind of pine] pine tree in general.

pinacate, *m.* [<Mex. Sp. *pinacate*, a kind of black beetle] stinkbug; a Black; *adj.*, moronic, slow, stupid.
Les daré el ¿Cómo les va?
que el trovar es mi deseo;
*estos cuatro **pinacates***
de a quince me los tanteo.
I will say, "How are you?"
For I felt like versifying;
Stinkbugs like these
I beat fifteen at a time.
(*Trovos del Viejo Vilmas*, N.M. Sp. folk poetry)

pinates, *m. pl.* [<Eng. peanuts] peanuts.

pinche, *adj.* [<Mex. Sp. *pinche*, worthless] crummy; damned; stingy; vile, wretched. (*No traigo ni un pinche daime pal teléfon*. I haven't got a crummy dime for a phone call.)

píndora, *f.* [<Sp. *píldora*] medicinal pill.

pinganillas, *f. pl.* [<Mex. Sp. *en pinganillas*, on tiptoe] in a squatting position. Cf. Sp. *en cuclillas*.

pingo, -ga, *adj.* [<Mex. Sp. *pingo*, the devil] out of balance; with one leg shorter than the other, as a chair, table, etc.; drugged or high on drugs (slang); horse.

pingorongo, -ga, *adj.* [<Mex. Sp. *pingorongo*, beak] restless.

pingorotear, *vb.* [<N.M. Sp. *pingorongo*] to be restless or jumping around, as children. (*No anden ahi pingoroteando en esa camalta*. Quit jumping on that bed.)

pinineo, -a, *adj.* [<unknown origin] dwarfed; small. *Gallinas pinineas*, bantam chickens.

pininos, *m. pl.* [<Sp. *pinitos*, first steps taken by a child] *hacer pininos*, to take one's first steps.

pinsel (*a pinsel*), *adv.* [<Sp. *pinrel*, foot] *a pinsel*, on foot. (*Vamos a pinsel*. We are going to "hoof" it [slang].)

pinta, *f.* [<Sp. *pinta*, spot] resemblance; *la pinta*, the "pen" (penitentiary); *adj.*, speckled.

pintarse, *vb.* [<Mex. Sp. *pintar* (*hacer pinta*, to play hooky)] to go away, to leave, to split (slang); *pintarse el pelo*, to dye one's hair. Cf. Sp. *teñir*.

pinto, *m.* [<Sp. *pinto*, painted] pinto (horse); inmate in a penitentiary; *pl.*, pinto beans; name of one of the batons in the game of *cañute*, q.v.; *adj.*, pinto, mottled; *poner pinto a alguno*, to tell someone off.

pintureteada, *adj.* [<Sp. *pintura*, paint] said of the woman who uses facial makeup to excess. See also *máscara* and *payasa*.

piñón, *m.* [<Sp. *piñón*, scrub pine] nut pine; the edible piñon nut of this tree.

piñonada, *f.* [<Sp. *piñón*] large quantity of piñon nuts; season for harvesting piñon nuts.

piñonero, *m.* [<Sp. *piñón* ornith., blue-jay; blue crow; *adj.*, said of the person who gathers or sells piñon nuts.

piojo, *m.* [<Sp. *piojo,* louse] louse; weevil; *piojo amarillo,* bean weevil; *piojo resucitado,* upstart; Johnny-come-lately; parvenu.

pipa, *f.* [<Sp. *pipa,* pipe] pipe, iron pipe; drunkard; *darle a alguno en la pipa,* to give someone a beating.

pipino, *m.* [<Sp. *pepinos*] pickled cucumber.

pipirín, *m.* [<Mex. Sp. slang *pipirín*] food; lunch (slang).

pipirisqui, *adj.* [<Mex. Sp. *pipisqui*] said of the person with thin eyelashes.

piquinique, *m.* [<Eng. picnic] picnic; outing.

piquipiqui, *vb.* [<N.M. Sp. *pica y pica*] a continuous teasing or irritating. (¡*No estés ahi piquipiqui!* Quit your constant teasing!)

piquito, *m.* [<N.M. Sp. *pico,* kiss] a little kiss (especially, a child's kiss).

pirujo, -a, *m.* and *f.* [<Mex. Sp. *pirujo,* fond of women] male or female homosexual.

pisado, *m.* [<Sp. *pisar,* to tread] a kind of wine made by treading on the grapes in a large vat.

pisito, *m.* [<Sp. dim. of *piso,* floor] small rug; throw rug.

piso, *m.* [<Sp. *piso,* floor] rug; throw rug.

pispireta, *f.* [<Mex. Sp. *pispireta*] liberated woman.

pisquear, *vb.* [<Mex. Sp. *pizcar,* to pick cotton, fruit, etc.] to pick peas, potatoes, etc.

pistear, *vb.* [<Mex. Sp. *pisto*] to drink booze, liquor.

pisto, *m.* [<Mex. Sp. *pisto*] a drink of liquor; liquor; *adj.,* drunk. (*El Silas anda pisto.* Silas is drunk.)

pitajaya, *f.* [<Mex. Sp. *pitahaya,* a plant of the Cactus family] small fruit of the *huevo de indio* cactus; bot., a plant of the Cactus family.

pitarrilla, *f.* [<Sp. dim. of *pitarra,* bleari-

ness] a kind of tic-tac-toe game in which one of the players tries to be the first to place three of his chips (pebbles, marbles, grains, etc.) at consecutive points where lines intersect.

pitazo, *m.* [<Mex. Sp. *pitazo* <Sp. aug. of *pito,* horn, whistle] telephone call; ring (telephone); honk.

pitear, *vb.* [<Sp. *pitar*] to honk (car, train, etc.).

pitero, *m.* [<Sp. *pito*] Penitente player of the *pito.*

pitijuyo, *m.* [<unknown origin] a kind of weevil that attacks the leaves of plants, such as beans and corn.

pito, *m.* [<Sp. *pito,* small flute] fife or flute used by the Penitente brothers; spout; valve stem; male organ. *¡Come pitos!* Go to blazes!

pizquear, *vb.* [<Mex. Sp. *pizcar,* to pick cotton, fruit, etc.] to pick fruit, vegetable gardens, etc.

placita, *f.* [<Col. N.M. Sp. *plaza,* fortified place] settlement; small town, village; court, patio.

plan, *m.* [<Sp. *plan*] bottom or basin of a river, valley, etc. *Jugarle un plan a alguno,* to play a trick on someone.

plancha, *f.* [<Sp. *plancha*] flatiron; slowpoke; *tirar la plancha,* to throw in the towel; to fail.

planchada, *f.* [<Sp. *plancha,* flatiron] ironing; work of ironing.

planchazo, *m.* [<Sp. aug. of *plancha*] blow with a flatiron; *dar planchazo,* to get even.

planta, *f.* [<Sp. *planta*] introductory quatrain to a *décima glosada,* a forty-four line poem. See *décima.*

plantarse, *vb.* [<Sp. *plantarse,* to balk] to dress up. (*La Senaida llegó aquí muy plantada.* Senaida got here all dressed up.)

plasta, *f.* [<Sp. *plasta,* anything soft] cow chip or dung; excrement.

plata, *f.* [<Sp. *plata,* silver] money; silver; Mexican currency. *Cien pesos plata,* a

hundred pesos (Mexican currency). See *oro*.

plática, *f.* [<Sp. *plática*] conversation; *revolver la plática,* to change the subject in a conversation.

platicón, *m.* [<Sp. aug. of *plática*, conversation] long conversation; *adj.*, said of one who likes to converse a great deal.

platillo, *m.* [<Sp. dim. of *plato*, dish] auto license plate; phonograph record (platter).

plato, *m.* [<Sp. *plato*] dish; *colmarle el plato a alguno,* to aggravate a person. See also *jarro* (*colmarle el jarro a alguno*).

platón, *m.* [<Sp. aug. of *plato*, large dish] washbasin.

plaza, *f.* [<Sp. *plaza*, square] town; downtown; Col. N.M. Sp., stronghold, fortified place; *plaza de armas,* army campsite where troops of a garrison drilled.

plebe, *f.* [<Sp. *plebe*, populace] children, kids; small fry; the gang. (*¿Dónde dejaron a la plebe?* Where did you leave the kids?)

ploga, *f.* [<Eng. plug] plug, as of tobacco, gas, water, etc.; electric light plug. Also, *plogue*.

ploguear, *vb.* [<Eng. to plug] to plug (a gap, hole, outlet, etc.).

plomo, -ma, *adj.* [<Sp. *plomo*, lead] lazy; applied to a slowpoke (rare).

pluma, *f.* [<Sp. *pluma*, feather] loose woman; prostitute.

plumajillo, *m.* [<Mex. Sp. *plumajillo*] bot., Plumajillo or Sneezeweed, a plant of the Aster family.

población, *f.* [<Sp. *población*] Col. N.M. Sp., a group of ranches (*ranchos*); town; settlement. See also *presidio, ranchería*.

In New Mexico, except for the village, the loosely grouped *ranchos* were generally referred to as *poblaciones,* or, if the population consolidated for mutual defense, as *plazas.* (E. Adams and F.A. Chávez, *The Missions of New Mexico, 1776*)

poca, *f.* [<Eng. poker] poker, a card game. Also, *pócar*.

pocillo, *m.* [<Sp. *pocillo*, chocolate cup] mug, especially for serving Mexican-style cocoa.

In the *trastero,* built in the wall and closed with hand-carved doors, was kept Aunt Dolores' set of fine china, little *pocillos* (mugs), and her copper *jarra* imported from Mexico. These were brought out on special occasions, especially when serving the spicy, foamy Mexican chocolate to some distinguished guest, such as the bishops and other dignitaries. (Cleofas M. Jaramillo, *Shadows of the Past*)

poco, -ca, *adj.* [<Sp. *poco*, a small amount] *un poco de café,* a little coffee; *una poca de agua,* a little water.

pochar, *vb.* [<Mex. Sp. *pochi*, cropped or short-tailed] to crop or cut the hair very short. Also, to poach (<Eng. to poach).

pocho, -cha, *m.* and *f.* [<Mex. Sp. *pocho* <Yaqui *pochio*, dull] Mexican American (derogatory); the Spanish language as spoken by *pochos*.

pochote, *m.* [<Mex. Sp. aug. of *pocho*] sissy (slang).

poder, *vb.* [<Mex. Sp. *poder*] *poderlas una persona,* to be equal to a task; to be good at something. (*El sí que las puede.* He is really good.)

polbero, *m.* [<Eng. pallbearer] pallbearer.

poleadas, *f. pl.* [<Sp. *poleadas*] pap; *poleadas de harina blanca,* a kind of paste used in wallpapering; *poleadas de harina tostada,* a kind of pap used medicinally for loose bowels in infants or the very old.

político, -ca, *adj.* [<Sp. *político*, political] in-law; *padre político,* father-in-law.

politiquear, *vb.* [<Sp. *política*, politics] to work in politics.

politiquero, -ra, *adj.* [<N.M. Sp. *politiquear*] political busybody; petty politician.

polvadera, *f.* [<Sp. *polvareda*] cloud of

dust; dust storm; dusty place. Name of a New Mexico village.

polvero, *m.* See *polbero.*

polvillo, *m.* [<Sp. dim. of *polvo*] ground toasted bread; a drink made from toasted flour used for stomach upset.

polvitos, *m. pl.* [<Sp. dim. of *polvo*, powder] magical powders supposedly prepared by witches.

pomilla, *f.* [<Sp. dim. of *pómez*, pumice] pumice; pumice gravel.

pomo, -ma, *adj.* [<Sp. *pómez*, pumice] foamy; pumice-like; spongy.

pompa, *f.* [<Eng. pump] pump. Also, *pompe.*

pompear, *vb.* [<N.M. Sp. *pompe*, pump] to pump.

pompita, *f.* [<N.M. Sp. dim. of *pompa*, pump] eyedropper.

ponchado, -da, *adj.* [<N.M. Sp. *ponchar*, to puncture] flat or punctured, as a tire.

ponchar, *vb.* [<Eng. to puncture] to puncture. (*Se nos ponchó un hule.* We have a flat tire.)

poner, *vb.* [<Sp. *poner*] to place; *ponérselas una persona*, to go on a drunken spree.

ponsión, *f.* [<Sp. *poción*, potion] a kind of very strong cathartic; *ponsión negra*, black potion.

ponso, *m.* [<unknown origin] bot., Tansy.

póñil, *m.* [<unknown origin] bot., Apache plume, a grass used in making homemade brooms and dusters.

popalina, *f.* See *papalina.*

pope, *m.* [<Eng. puppy] dog; puppy. See also *chulo.*

popote, *m.* [<Mex. Sp. *popote*, stalk] a kind of stud for pierced ears.

popotillo, *m.* [<Mex. Sp. dim. of *popote*, stalk] bot., a plant used in making a tea for kidney trouble; Desert or Mormon tea.

popotón, *m.* [<Mex. Sp. aug. of *popote*] bot., Porcupine grass. See also *zacate* (*del burro*).

populación, *f.* [<Eng. population] population. Cf. Sp. *población.*

poquitero, -ra, *adj.* [<Sp. *poquito*, a tiny bit] cheap; stingy, miserly. See also *taite.*

porlos, *adv.* [<unknown origin] *ir a los porlos*, to go half-and-half. Cf. Sp. *a medias.*

poros, *m. pl.* [<Sp. *poros*, pores] nostrils; *conj.* (*poro*), but. Cf. Sp. *pero.*

porra, *f.* [<Sp. *porra*, blackjack] beating, thrashing; *echar una porra*, to toss a coin; to cast or throw lots.

portarse, *vb.* [<Sp. *portarse*, to behave] to appear; to come. (*Ni pajaritos se portan por aquí.* Not even birds come here.)

pos, *adv.* [<Sp. *pues*] well, why, etc. *¡Pos sí!* Of course! Also, *pus.*

posadas, *f. pl.* [<Sp. *posada*] lodging. *Las posadas* (the seeking of lodging), an enactment of Joseph and Mary's journey in search of lodging on the night of Christ's birth.

Las **Posadas** [The Inns]. The visit of Joseph and Mary to various inns at Bethlehem is enacted at a number of homes in the village; Lucifer conceals himself in each home and rejects the wayfarers; then he finally welcomes them at one house where a *nacimiento* or crèche has been prepared for the Christ Child. (T.M. Pearce, "The New Mexican 'Shepherds' Play," *Western Folklore*)

posolada, *f.* [<Mex. Sp. *posolada* <*posole*] a dinner in which the main dish consists of *posole.*

posole, *m.* [<Mex. Sp. *pozole* <Náhuatl *pozolli*] a dish prepared with chili, hominy, pork, and other ingredients; hominy soup.

posta, *f.* [<Sp. *posta*, post] *a la posta*, speedily; with great haste.

potrero, *m.* [<Sp. *potrero*, grazing land] pasture; a gap or narrow ridge between cliffs; *potreros* are also described as "fingers" of lava rock.

It is our only country of **potreros**. It is difficult to diagram, but perhaps the best idea of its ground plan is to be had by laying the two hands side by side upon a table, with every finger spread to its widest. The Rio Grande flows about north and south through the line of the knuckles in a gorge over two thousand feet deep. The spread fingers represent the cañons; the wedge-shaped spaces between them are the tall *potreros*. These vast tongues of volcanic rock—some of trap, some of lava, some of dazzling pumice—a dozen or more miles long, eight to ten in width nearest the mountains, taper to a point at the river, and there break off in columnar cliffs from one thousand to twenty-five-hundred feet in height. (Charles F. Lummis, *The Land of Poco Tiempo*)

pozo, *m.* [<Sp. *pozo,* hole] rut or deep hole in a road or street; pothole. Cf. Sp. *bache.*

prender, *vb.* [<Sp. *prender*] to hitch horses; to light (fires).

prenderse, *vb.* [<Mex. Sp. *prenderse*] to become attached; to tag along. (*Se le prendió su hermanito y siempre no juimos.* Her little brother tagged along and we did not go after all.)

prendido, -da, *adj.* [<N.M. Sp. *prenderse*] addicted to or hooked on (drugs); attached to or spoiled, as a child; hitched, as a team of horses; lighted or turned on. (*Las lámparas estaban prendidas.* The lamps were lit.) In full swing. (*El baile estaba prendido.* The dance was in full swing.)

prendorio, *m.* [<Sp. *prenda,* pledge] engagement ceremony and ensuing reception.

presado, *adj.* [<Fr. *bleu de Prusse*] *azul presado,* dark blue powder used in dyeing.

presidio, *m.* [<Col. N.M. Sp. *presidio* <Sp. *presidio*] a group of citizens armed for defense.
   Whenever *presidios* are mentioned in this *Ojeada* it should be understood that they are armed people grouped together for defense, and not places intended for the punishment of delinquents. (Lansing B. Bloom, "Barreiro's Ojeada Sobre Nuevo Mexico," *New Mexico Historical Review*)

presilla, *f.* [<Sp. dim. of *presa,* dam] small dam built in an unleveled field to get water to higher ground.

pretales, *m. pl.* [<Sp. *pl.* of *pretal,* breastplate] suspenders. Cf. Sp. *tirantes.*

pretensión, *f.* [<Mex. Sp. *pretensión*] arrogance; presumptuousness.

pretensioso, -sa, *adj.* [<Mex. Sp. *pretensioso*] arrogant; conceited; presumptuous.

pretil, *m.* [<Sp. *pretil,* battlement] a low parapet made of adobe, brick, cement, etc., built around a flat roof.

prevalicar, *vb.* [<Sp. *prevaricar*] to derange one's mind; to cause one to act in an incoherent manner and do foolish things.

priesa, *f.* [<Col. N.M. Sp. *priesa*] haste, hurry; promptness; *darse priesa,* to hurry.

primera, *f.* [<Sp. *primera*] first; *de primera,* first class; *de buenas a primeras,* when least expected; *poner un carro en primera,* to get a car in first gear.

primiciero, *m.* [<Sp. *primicias,* first fruits] Col. N.M. Sp., collector of first fruits.
   An official [*primiciero*] is appointed to collect this offering of first fruits, and he brings it in carts or in any way he can. (E. Adams and F.A. Chávez, *The Missions of New Mexico, 1776*)

primor, *m.* [<Sp. *primor,* beauty] richness; neatness. *¡Qué primor!* How wonderful! What an abundance! How beautiful!

príncipa, *f.* [<Sp. *príncipe*] princess (in folktales).

principal, -la, *m.* and *f.* [<Sp. *principal*] elder; an Indian pueblo official; principal of a school or school district; school superintendent.

prisca, *f.* [<Sp. *brizna,* fragment] iota; a

small amount. (*No tiene ni prisca de ver-güenza.* He has no pride whatsoever. He is a shameless rogue.)

prisco, *adj.* [<Mex. Sp. *prisco,* peach] *durazno prisco,* a kind of small, sweet smelling peach.

> *En un vapor de Jalisco*
> *me salí a pasear un día;*
> *de allí me pasé a Sevilla;*
> *llegué a los Ranchos de Atrisco*
> *comprando durazno prisco . . .*
> On a ship bound for Jalisco
> I went out for a walk;
> From there I went on to Seville
> And got to Ranchos de Atrisco
> Buying small local peaches.
> (*La Severiana,* N.M. Sp. folk song)

privado, *m.* [<Sp. *privado,* private] toilet; outhouse.

probe, *adj.* [<Sp. *pobre*] poor. *¡Probecito!* Poor thing!

probeza, *f.* [<Sp. *pobreza*] poverty. (*¡Qué probeza!* What poverty!)

programa, *f.* [<Sp. *programa*] program. (*¡Qué bonita programa!* What a nice program! *¿Cómo estuvo la programa?* How was the program?)

propio, *adj.* [<Sp. *propio,* proper] *al propio,* on purpose.

¡Pucha!, *interj.* [<Mex. Sp. *pucha*] expression of astonishment, disbelief, surprise, etc. Goodness!

puches, *m. pl.* [<Sp. *puches*] a kind of egg and sugar cookies resembling sponge cake in their texture.

puela, *f.* [<Fr. *poêle* (*la poêle*)] frying pan; skillet.

puelada, *f.* [<N.M. Sp. *puela*] frying-panful. (*Hazte una puelada de papas.* Make a frying-panful of potatoes.)

puelar, *m.* [<N.M. Sp. *puela*] assortment of pots and pans. (*¡Hi, qué puelar!* What an assortment of pots and pans!)

puente, *f.* [<Col. N.M. Sp. *la puente*] bridge.

puerta, *f.* [<Sp. *puerta*] door, gate; *dar puerta una mujer,* to sit in an indecent position; *no jallar la puerta una persona,* to be frightened; to be in a bind; to not be able to make ends meet; *puerta de alambre,* screen door; *puerta de gracias,* Col. N.M. Sp., lit. "door of grace," a direct entrance from the refectory to the church proper; *puerta del zaguán,* a large gate (*puertón*).

puerto, *m.* [<Sp. *puerto,* port] military outpost; *puerto del gobierno,* garrison. *Puerto de Luna,* N.M. place-name.

puertón, *m.* [<Sp. *portón*] large gate; also called *puerta del zaguán.*

> A tier of rooms . . . encompass an open *patio* or court, with but one door opening into the street, a huge gate called la **puerta del zaguán,** usually large enough to admit the family coach. (Cleofas M. Jaramillo, *Shadows of the Past*)

pues, *adv.* [<Sp. *prep. pos*] *en pues de,* after; in pursuit of.

puesto, -ta, *adj.* [<Sp. *pt. part.* of *poner,* to place] *bien puesto,* financially well-off.

pueta, *m.* [<Sp. *poeta,* poet] folk poet; versifier.

pujacante, *m.* [<Comanche *pujacante*] witch doctor or medicine man; soothsayer; *hacer una persona su pujacante,* to perform one's magic.

> They [the Comanches] have their diviners to whom they give the name **Pujacantes,** which is the same as if they called them wizards. (Lansing B. Bloom, "Barreiro's Ojeada Sobre Nuevo Mexico," *New Mexico Historical Review*)

pul, *m.* [<Eng. pool and pull] game of pool; political pull.

pulga, *f.* [<Sp. *pulga,* flea] flea; laxative, physic. N.M. Hispanos identify the word *purga* with Sp. *purgación,* gonorrhea, and avoid it.

pulgarse, *vb.* [<N.M. Sp. *pulga,* laxative] to take a laxative.

pulgatorio, *m.* [<Sp. *purgatorio*] Purgatory; *rezar por las ánimas del pulgatorio,* to pray for the souls in Purgatory.

pulgón, *m.* [<Sp. *aug.* of *pulga,* flea] large flea; bean fly; black bedbug-like insect.

pulso, *m.* [<Sp. *pulso,* pulse] bracelet; pulse; *alborotarle el pulso un hombre a una mujer,* to get a woman sexually aroused; *traer el pulso alborotado,* to be sexually aroused.

pulla, *f.* [<Sp. *púa*] barb; fish bone; splinter; tack; *pullas,* sarcastic remarks.

puncha, *f.* [<N.M. Sp. *punche,* low-class tobacco] low-class female (slang).

punche, *m.* [<Indian?] a low-class, homegrown tobacco; tobacco in general. Also, *punche mexicano.*

    Although true tobacco is a Spanish introduced product in the Southwest, the *punche* grown in New Mexico is called native tobacco as much to distinguish it from commercial brands as to indicate its potent qualities. (E. Boyd, "The Use of Tobacco in Spanish New Mexico," *El Palacio*)

punchón, *m.* [<N.M. Sp. aug. of *punche*] bot., Wild tobacco.

punta, *f.* [<Sp. *punta,* edge] bunch; large group; *a punta de,* by dint of; *punta del arado,* plowshare; *una punta de ladrones,* a bunch of thieves.

puntada, *f.* [<Sp. *puntada* (sewing) stitch] hint; absurdity. *¡Qué puntada!* How absurd! How disgraceful! *Agarrar la puntada,* to catch on, to get the hint.

puntilla, *f.* [<Mex. Sp. *puntilla*] tack; thumbnail; shoemakers' nail.

punto, *m.* [<Sp. *punto*] place; point; spot; drawnwork (*trabajo de punto*); *punto de buey,* Col. N.M. Sp., oxgoad.

puñeta, *f.* [<Mex. Sp. *puñeta*] *hacerse un hombre la puñeta,* to masturbate (said of the male).

pupu, *m.* [<child's expression] fear; *enterrarle a uno pupu,* to be afraid, scared.

purga (la purga), *f.* [<Sp. *purgación*] the clap (gonorrhea), syphilis.

pus, *adv., conj.* [<Sp. *pues*] then; well. Also, *pos.*

puta, *f.* [<Sp. *puta,* prostitute] loose woman; *ser una mujer más puta que una gallina,* to be promiscuous as a cat.

Querer es poder.
Desire is power.

quebrada, *f.* [<Sp. *quebrada,* break, ravine, and Eng. slang break, a piece of good luck] break (slang). (*Estos batos no nos dan quebrada.* These guys don't give us a break.)

quebrado, -da, *adj.* [<Sp. *quebrar,* to break] broken; broke (penniless); wavy (hair); stoop-shouldered; *ojos quebrados,* droopy (eyes). See *clisarse* (*ojos clisados*).

quebrar, *vb.* [<Sp. *quebrar,* to break, and Eng. to break in] to break in (an engine, shoes, etc.); to go broke. (*Cuida tu dinero si no te vas a quebrar.* Take care of your money, otherwise you are going to go broke.)

quedada, *f.* [<Mex. Sp. *quedada,* lit., leftover] spinster; old maid.

quedar, *vb.* [<Sp. *quedar,* to remain] to be left or to remain. (*¿Cuántos quedan?* How many are left?) To fit. (*Estas chinelas no me quedan.* These shoes do not fit me.) To look (well/bad). (*¡Qué mal te queda esa leva!* That coat looks bad on you.) *Quedarse,* to remain or stay behind. (*Quédate tú ahi estudiando.* You stay around studying.) *Quedarse como el que chifló en la loma,* to be left in the lurch; to be stood up; to be disappointed; *quedarse una mujer para vestir santos,* said of a woman who apparently will remain unmarried.

quelites, *m. pl.* [<Mex. Sp. *quelite,* wild spinach] greens, particularly those obtained from wild plants such as Dock, Wild mustard, Lamb's quarters, Purslane, etc. *Quelite de burro,* a kind of nonedible (poisonous) *quelite.*

Weeds of New Mexico in their young and tender growth have long been eaten by the native people, but only recently has their food value in regard to vitamins been established. A number of these, called greens, or **quelites,** have been identified and analyzed in both the fresh and canned state. (Beth B. Brady, "Vitamins from Weeds," *New Mexico Magazine*)

quemado, -da, *adj.* [<Mex. Sp. *quemado,*

141

resentful] taught by experience; having learned one's lesson; sunburned. Cf. Sp. *tostado; m.*, finish, as on a cement floor, sidewalk, etc.

quemón, *m.* [<Mex. Sp. *quemón*<Sp. *quemar,* to burn] to burn or cause to become angry; to taunt. (*Lo voy a hacer para dales un quemón.* I am going to do it just to taunt them.)

quemoso, -sa, *adj.* [<Sp. *quemar,* to burn] piquant; highly seasoned; hot, as chili. Cf. Sp. *picante.*

queque, *m.* [<Eng. cake] cake; *queque de casorio,* wedding cake.

queresas, *f. pl.* [<Mex. Sp. *queresas*<Sp. *cresas*] maggots.

querido,-da, *adj.* [<Sp. *querido*<*querer,* desired] *¡Qué querido!* How nice! How neat! M. or f., loved one, kept woman (mistress).

quése, *interr.* [<Sp. *qué es de*] what has become of?; where is? (*¿Quése el Maque?* Where's Mack?)

quesera, *f.* [<Sp. *quesera,* cheese board] a loft suspended from a ceiling. See also *barbacoa.*

quesque, *vb. exp.* [<Sp. var. of *diz,* they say, and *que,* that] is it true that?; they say that. That's what they say. (*¿Quesque te casas?—Quesque.* Is it true you are going to get married? That's what they say.) See also *esque.*

questa [kwésta], *f.* [<Sp. nineteenth-century spelling. Cf. Mod. Sp. *cuesta*] hill; N.M. place-name.

quiebrasol, *m.* [<Sp. *quebrar,* to break,

and *sol,* sun] opening in the sky at twilight.

quimón, *m.* [<Sp. *camón, camones,* fellies of cartwheels] wood rim, as of a wagon wheel. See also *cama.*

quimona, *f.* [<Eng. kimono] kimono; robe.Cf. Sp. *kimono.*

quince, *m.* [<Sp. *quince*] fifteen; *estar* or *ir pal quince,* to be off; to be wrong; *salir pal quince,* to be wrong; to miscalculate. (*Yo mesmo iba a hacer el income tax pero salí todo pal quince.* I was going to prepare my income tax myself, but I was all wrong.)

quiote, *m.* [<Mex. Sp. *quiote*<Náhuatl *quiotl*] stalk, stem; *el quiote,* male organ; *pelarse uno el quiote,* to be idle, to laze around.

quiquiriquear, *vb.* [<Sp. *quiquiriquí* (also, *kikirikí*), onomatopoeic word (cock-a-doodle-doo)] to chatter, prattle; to engage in idle gossip; to brag.

¡Quítate!, *interj.* [<Sp. *quitarse,* to remove oneself] Forget it! (*Ya sentándose éste a la mesa, ¡Quítate!* Once this guy sits at the table, forget it!)

quiut, *adj.* [<Eng. cute] cute; darling; lovely.

quiutito, -ta, *adj.* [<N.M. Sp. dim. of *quiut*<Eng. cute] very cute; very lovely; just wonderful. (*Qué sombrero tan quiutito trae la Ella.* What a cute hat Ella is wearing.)

quiviro, *adv.* [<N.M. Sp. *quiviro*<*La gran Quivira,* a mythical place] brokenly. (*Habla español muy quiviro.* He speaks Spanish brokenly.)

Yo conozco a la Rafela, no me la ponderen tanto.
I know Rafela, don't exaggerate her qualities
   to me.
(When one knows a situation well, there is no
   need for others to exaggerate.)

rabajeño, -ña, *adj.* [<Sp. *río abajo,* down-river] lowlander, said of a person re-siding along the Rio Grande in New Mexico below La Bajada hill, south of Santa Fe.

> *Al pasar por La Cañada*
> *me dijo una* **rabajeña,**
> *—Si me ves con mi marido,*
> *no me hagas ninguna seña.*
> As I passed through La Cañada
> A local belle warned me once:
> "If you see me with my husband,
> Pretend you don't know me."
> (N.M. Sp. *verso popular*)

rabiate, *m.* [<Sp. *rabo,* tail, and *atar,* to tie] file, line or series of things follow-ing one another. (*Vimos vinir un rabiate de indios.* We saw a long line of Indians coming.) See Sp. *rabiatar.*

rabo, *m.* [<Sp. *rabo,* tail] handle, as of a dipper or skillet. The term is also ap-plied to a child born after twins. The *rabo* is believed to have extraordinary powers.

rabullirse, *vb.* [<Sp. *rebullirse*] to stir; to begin to move.

> *Es tan angosta mi cama*
> *que ni* **rabullirme** *puedo,*
> *que para deber de estar*
> *un pie sobre otro tengo.*
> My bed is so narrow
> That I can hardly stir,
> And in order to stay in it
> I have to cross my feet.
> (*Cristo en la cruz,* N.M. and so. Colo. Sp. Penitente *alabado*)

ración, *f.* [<Sp. *ración,* ration, portion] vertebra or segment composing the backbone; *pl.,* a dish in which the meaty part consists of vertebrae or segments of an animal's backbone; beef back-bones. See also *espinacito.*

radio, *m.* [<Sp. *aparato de radio*] radio set; radio receiver. (*Nos compramos un radio en el Mongomer.* We bought a radio set at Montgomery Ward's.)

radiola, *f.* [<Eng. radiola] radio victrola; radio phonograph.

143

raices [ŕáises], *f. pl.* [<Sp. *pl.* of *raíz,* root] red beets; *raiz quemosa,* radish.

> *Son nación agricoltora*
> *que siembran toda semía;*
> *por ser comidas de casa*
> *siembran melón y sandía;*
> *también siembran calabazas*
> ***raices** y de todas yerbas.*
> They are an agricultural people
> Who sow all kinds of seeds;
> Because they are eaten at home,
> They raise cantaloupes and
>   watermelons;
> They also cultivate red beets and
> All kinds of plants [herbs].
> (A. M. Espinosa, "Romancero Nuevo-
> mejicano," *Revue Hispanique*)

raid, *m.* [<Eng. ride] lift, ride. (*Vamos anca 'l colorado que nos dé un raid.* Let's go to Red's so he will give us a ride.) Also, *raite.*

rajas, *f. pl.* [<Sp. *raja,* split] planking or rough boards used as lath for ceilings and roofing. See also *latía.*

rajada, *f.* [<Sp. *rajar,* to split] crack. Cf. Sp. *rajadura.*

rajarse, *vb.* [<Mex. Sp. *rajarse*] to split (as in St. Spanish); fig., to back down. (*¡No te rajes!* Don't back down.) To tattle. (*Se rajó con su papá.* He told his dad.)

rajetas, *adj.* [<N.M. Sp. *rajarse*] said of a person who habitually goes back on his word.

rajón, -na, *adj.* [<N.M. Sp. *rajarse*] said of a person who tattles or goes back on his word; coward; run, as in a stocking. (*La Clorinda trae un rajón en una media.* Clorinda has a run in one of her stockings.)

ramal, *m.* [<Sp. *rama,* branch] a ring (*anillo de ramal*) made up of two or more rings assembled into a single unit, also called *memoria.* A two-tongued or branched whip.

> When the *vaquero* tied or braided together his bridle reins so that the ends furnished him a two-tongued whip, he called it a **ramal** (rah-Mahl)

which has become romal in cow range idiom. (S. Omar Barker, "Sagebrush Spanish," *New Mexico Magazine*)

ramieda, *f.* [<Col. and Terr. N.M. Sp. *ramieda*] a kind of fence, palisade or stockade (< Sp. *rama,* branch). *Ramiedas* were erected around a *plaza* (hamlet) as a protection against Indian attacks.

rana, *f.* [<Sp. *rana*] frog; female organ (taboo); *ranazo,* heavy blow; thud, from a fall.

ranchería, *f.* [<Am. Sp. *ranchería,* a collection of huts] Col. and Terr. N.M. Sp., *población,* group of ranches; Indian settlement.

> It looks like there could be no mistake in the place, but de Vaca continued to tie in his location. It was at the end of his "fifty leagues northward" which would be near the present Artesia that he came to the four *rancherías* where he turned west toward the mountains. The Spanish word *ranchería* does not translate well into English. The reference was to four semi-permanent Indian villages. (Mrs. Tom Charles, *Tales of the Tularosa*)

ranchero, -ra, *adj.* [<Mex. Sp. *ranchero,* rancher] bashful, shy; *m.,* rancher.

ranfla, *f.* [<Eng. rambler (American Rambler)] auto, car (slang).

rango, *m.* [<Sp. *rango,* rank] grimace; gesture; *agarrar rango,* to assume a position (body or face) in a gesture of contempt or ridicule. (*Nomás le dije y lo, lo agarró rango.* As soon as I told him, he made a wry face.)

rapis (*a rapis*), *adv.* [<Sp. *rapar,* to shave] to cut the hair very short; to shave the head. Cf. Sp. *a rapa.*

raspa, *f.* [<Am. Sp. *raspa,* act of scraping] a folk dance of Mexican origin in which the dancers shuffle their feet back and forth in time with the music; snow cone.

raspón, *m.* [<Sp. *raspar,* to scrape] scratch, skinning. Cf. Sp. *rasguño.*

real

rasposo, -sa, *adj.* [<Sp. *raspar,* to scrape] rough; harsh.

rasquera, *f.* [<Sp. *rascar,* to scratch] itch; itching.

rastra, *f.* [<Sp. *rastrear,* to harrow] harrow. Cf. Sp. *rastro.* See also *fresno* and *jaira; adj.,* lazy, shiftless.

rastrillo, *m.* [<Sp. dim. of *rastro,* rake] rake; *entregar el rastrillo,* to die.

rastrojear, *vb.* [<Sp. *rastrojo,* stubble] to scrounge. See also *pelenquear.*

rata, *f.* [<Sp. *rata,* rat] rat; ground squirrel; fink (slang).

ratón, *m.* [<Sp. *ratón,* mouse] mouse; squirrel; *ratón coludo,* ground squirrel; *ratón pardo,* gray squirrel; *ratón rayús,* chipmunk. See also *ardilla. Ratón volador,* bat. See also *murciégalo.*

ratonal, *m.* [<Sp. *ratón,* mouse] mouse nest; bunch of mice; a plague of mice.

ratonera, *f.* [<Sp. *ratón*] rat or squirrel's nest; a number of mice; a junky place. (*El Santiago vive en una ratonera de los diablos.* James lives in a heck of a junky place.)

Flocks of bluejays added their cries of *"pi-ño-nes"* to those of gleeful children making a lucky find of a *ratonera,* a rat or squirrel hole packed full of *piñones.* (Cleofas M. Jaramillo, *Shadows of the Past*)

raya, *f.* [<Mex. Sp. *raya*] payday (*día de raya*).

rayado, -da, *adj.* [<Sp. *raya,* stripe] striped. Col. N.M. Sp. *los rayados,* a name applied by the early Spanish explorers to the Jumano Indians.

rayar, *vb.* [<Mex. Sp. *rayar,* to pay laborers] to draw, to earn. (*¿Cuánto rayas?* How much do you make?) To pay. (*¿Cuándo rayan?* When do they pay?) To curse or tell someone off. (*Nos rayaron.* They cursed us.) *Rayar maíz,* to strip fresh corn from the cob.

rayús, *m.* [<N.M. Sp. *ratón rayús*] chipmunk.

raza, *f.* [<Mex. Sp. *raza,* the Mestizo people] *La raza,* the Mexican-American minority; *adj.,* Mexican-American.

(*¿Qué es gringa la Mary?—No, es raza.* Is Mary Anglo? No, she is Mexican-American.)

La raza is an expression used by Spanish-speaking people in the Southwest to designate their own group. Literally translated, it means "the race." It should be remembered, however, that "*la raza*" has a somewhat different meaning from the English word "race," and that in using it, the Spanish-speaking people intend no implication that they are biologically different from the majority of Anglos.

The real test of affiliation with the Mexican ethnic group, however, is the feeling of belonging to a body which, on the whole, has cultural and "racial" unity. In the case of the Mexican, ethnic consciousness is expressed by his identification with *La Raza,* "The Race," a genetic denomination by which he includes all Mexicans regardless of class differences or place of birth. This ethnic consciousness becomes intensified in those who live in a predominantly Anglo or non-Latin society that regards Mexicans as culturally different and, for the most part, socially inferior. Sociologically, therefore, recognizable physical or cultural characteristics do not per se indicate membership in an ethnic group. It is rather the identification of self with the group or the "we feeling" that is significant. (Lyle Saunders, *Cultural Difference and Medical Care*)

razón, *f.* [<Sp. *razón,* reason] reason; information, news. (*¿Qué razón me dan del Pete?* Do you have any news of Peter?) *¡Con razón!* No wonder! *De razón,* rational; *gente de razón,* the Hispanos or non-Indians whose way of life followed Spanish rather than Indian customs.

real, *m.* [<Sp. *real,* royal] Col. N.M. Sp., royal campsite; headquarters; main body of an expedition; a silver coin worth 12½ *centavos; real caja,* royal

145

strong box; sub treasury; *real de minas,* mining town; *pl.,* money. (*Ella tiene reales.* She's got money. She's loaded.)

realizar, *vb.* [<Sp. *realizar,* to realize a profit, and Eng. to realize or understand fully] to realize. (*No realicé lo que estaba diciendo.* I didn't realize what I was saying.)

reata, *f.* [<Sp. *reata,* a kind of rope] rope; the male sex organ; *ser una persona muy reata,* to be brave or fair in one's dealings. (*El Efrén es muy reata.* Efren is very fair [a man of his word].)

reatazo, *m.* [<Sp. *reata*] blow with a rope or with any other object; thud, as from a fall. (*Se dio un buen reatazo.* He took a hard fall.)

rebansa, *f.* [<Sp. *rebalsar,* to dam water to form a pool] overflow, as of a ditch.

rebansar, *vb.* [<N.M. Sp. *rebansa*] to overflow.

rebilión, *m.* [<Sp. *rebelión,* rebellion] blizzard; sandstorm; storm; *de rebilión,* by surprise; *venta de rebilión,* clearance sale.

reborujar, *vb.* [<Mex. Sp. *reborujar*<Sp. *reburujar*] to move things to and fro in a disorganized manner; to muss up.

reborujo, *m.* [<Sp. *reburujo,* a bundle wrapped up carelessly] a mess of things piled up helter-skelter; altercation, brawl; confusion.

> *Su mujer, como lo vía*
> *que algo le carcomía,*
> *le pregunta con pacencia*
> *que si qué era lo que había.*
> *El, no queriendo contarle*
> *ni que de una vez supiera,*
> *le dice que viene huyendo*
> *de un **reborujo** en Rivera.*
> His wife, sensing that
> Something was wrong,
> Asked him patiently
> What was the matter.
> And not wanting her to know,
> He avoided an answer,
> Saying he had gotten away
> From a brawl in Rivera.
> (N.M. Sp. *Corrido de Rivera*)

recalarse, *vb.* [<Sp. *recalcar,* to seat at ease] to move in with someone. (*Tú vienes y te recalas conmigo.* You come and move in with me.)

recebido, *vb.* [<Col. N.M. Sp. *pt. part.* of *recebir,* to receive] received.

recebir, *vb.* [<Col. N.M. Sp. *recebir*] to receive. Cf. Sp. *recibir.*

recorte, *m.* [<Sp. *recorte,* clipping] a kind of trivet (rare).

rechaz, *m.* [<Sp. *rechazo,* rebound] rebound, recoil; *de rechaz,* indirectly, by rebound or ricochet; grazingly.

rechola, *f.* [<Mex. Sp. *rechola,* gathering of friends] gathering of bums or tramps; gang of hoodlums; *pl.,* friends. (*¡Píntate de aquí con tus recholas!* Get out of here with your bum friends.)

recholear, *vb.* [<Mex. Sp. *arrecholear,* to get together] to loaf, to loiter.

recholero, -ra, *m.* and *f.* [<N.M. Sp. *recholear*] loiterer; bum.

recholiento, -ta, *adj.* [<N.M. Sp. *recholear,* to loiter] loitering; fond of gang gatherings.

redamadero, *m.* [<N.M. Sp. *redamar*<Sp. *derramar,* to spill] drain; slope; spillage.

redamar, *vb.* [<Sp. *derramar,* to spill] to drain; to spill.

redame, *m.* [<Sp. *derramo,* spillage] declivity, slope; drain; spillage.

redepente, *adv.* [<Sp. *de repente,* suddenly] maybe, perhaps. (*Redepente va a llover.* Perhaps it will rain.) Suddenly. (*Nos cayó aquí mu' redepente.* He dropped in on us all of a sudden.)

redetir, *vb.* [<Sp. *derretir*] to melt. Also, *reditir.* (*Ya se reditió la nieve.* The snow has melted away.)

redibar, *vb.* [<Sp. *derribar*] to demolish, to throw down. *Echar abajo* and *tumbar* are more common terms.

redo (a redo), *adv.* [<Col. N.M. Sp. *riedro* <Lat. *retro,* behind] *¡A redo vaya! Interj.* used as a kind of curse against the devil or merely as an exclamation of surprise. Good heavens! Of all things! (*¡Se*

casó la Sofronia! Sí, ¿eh? ¡A redo vaya! Sofronia got married! Oh, yeah? Good heavens!)

reducion, *f.* [<Sp. *reducción*] Col. N.M. Sp., mission center established for the conversion of nomadic Indians.

reflejar, *vb.* [<Sp. *reflejar,* to reflect, as a mirror reflects light, images, etc.] to notice; to realize or understand fully. (*No reflejé que era mana Casimira.* I did not realize it was old lady Casimira.) See also *realizar.*

reforme, *m.* [<Sp. *reformar,* to reform] turning plow.

refrescadora, *f.* [<Sp. *refrescar,* to cool] refrigerator.

refritos, *m. pl.* [<Sp. *re,* over, and *fritos,* fried; fried over] fried over (beans), refried beans.

refusilata, *f.* [<Sp. *re,* over, and *fusilar,* to execute] brawl; free-for-all fight; riot; tumult.

regente, *adj.* [<N.M. Sp. *re,* very, and *gente,* nice] affable; extremely kind; friendly. (*Probecita, es medio feíta pero mu' regente.* Poor little thing, she's somewhat homely but she's very nice.) See also *gente.*

regidor, *m.* [<Sp. *regidor,* magistrate] Col. N.M. Sp., alderman; councilman; member of a *cabildo.*

regla, *f.* [<Sp. *regla,* ruler] stripe or wainscoting painted on the base of a wall. Cf. Sp. *cenefa.*

regoldar, *vb.* [<Sp. *regoldar*] to belch; to take it easy.

regüelcar, *vb.* [<Sp. *revolcar,* to wallow in mud] to get dirty. (*Ten cuidado, no te vayas a regüelcar.* Be careful, don't get dirty.)

regüeldo, *m.* [<Sp. *revuelco,* rolling] whirlpool in a stream or river.

rejiego, -ga, *adj.* [<Mex. Sp. *rejiego,* crafty, cunning] untamed; wild; barren, applied to mules; touchy.

rejunjuñar, *vb.* [<Sp. *refunfuñar*] to grumble.

relación, *f.* [<Sp. *relación,* narrative] account; narrative; a type of folk song dealing with some absurdity as a theme and narrating exploits of animals or insects in an exaggerated manner.

relajar, *vb.* [<Mex. Sp. *relajar*] to embarrass.

relaje, *m.* [<Mex. Sp. *relajo*] embarrassment. *¡Qué relaje!* How embarrassing! How awful! How absurd!

relajo, *m.* See *relaje.*

relativos, *m. pl.* [<Sp. *relativo,* relating to, and Eng. relative, kinsman] relatives, kinsfolk.

relator, *m.* [<Col. N.M. Sp. *relator*] councilor-at-law appointed to make the briefs of cases to be tried.

relís, *m.* [<Mex. Sp. *relís,* declivity] cliff; ledge; landslide.

> *Vuela, vuela, palomita,*
> *párate en aquel relís;*
> *aquí se acaban cantando*
> *los versos de Reyes Ruiz.*
> Fly away, little dove,
> Find your rest on that cliff;
> Here ends with a song
> The ballad of Reyes Ruiz.
> (Mexico, *Corrido de Reyes Ruiz*)

relisar, *vb.* [<N.M. Sp. *relís,* landslide] to slide.

relós (reloses), *m.* [<Col. N.M. Sp. *relox* [r̃elós] clock; watch; timepiece.

remangar, *vb.* [<Sp. *remangar, arremangar,* to tuck up] to pilfer; to steal (slang).

remanse, *m.* [<Sp. *remanso,* stagnant water] backwater, as in a stream.

remolina, *f.* [<Sp. *remolino,* whirlwind] commotion; turmoil. (*Donde no hay harina todo se hace remolina.* A home without means turns into turmoil.)

remolión, *m.* [<N.M. Sp. *remolina,* turmoil] *venta de remolión,* rummage sale; clearance sale.

remolotazo, *m.* [<N.M. Sp. aug. of *remolote*] an out-of-hand brawl or free-for-all fight.

remolote, *m.* [<Mex. Sp. *molote,* disturbance] brawl; free-for-all fight.

rencoristo, -ta, *adj.* [<Sp. *rencor,* grudge] rancorous; spiteful.

rendir, *vb.* [<Sp. *rendir*] to yield; to go far; to stretch; to tip, as one's hat in greeting someone. (*Echale más harina al chile pa que rinda.* Put more flour in the chili so that it will go farther.)

renegado, -da, *adj.* [<Sp. *renegado,* apostate] said of one who curses as a matter of habit.

renganche (*de renganche*), *prep.* phrase [<Sp. *reenganche*] *de renganche,* with someone else. (*Vamos ir de renganche.* We are going with someone else. [Someone else is taking us.])

rengo, -ga, *adj.* [<Mex. Sp. *rengo*<Sp. *renco*] lame; crippled; handicapped.

renguear, *vb.* [<Mex. Sp. *renguear*<Sp. *renquear*] to limp.

renta, *f.* [<Sp. *renta,* income] house rent.

rentar, *vb.* [<Eng. to rent] to rent. See *arrentar.*

reparador, -ra, *adj.* [<Mex. Sp. *reparar,* to buck] said of the mount (donkey, horse, mare, mule, etc.) that bucks or rears on the slightest provocation.

reparar, *vb.* [<Mex. Sp. *reparar*] to buck; to rear on the hind legs, as horses, mules, etc.; to throw a temper tantrum.

reparo, *m.* [<Mex. Sp. *reparo*] act of bucking or rearing; temper fit or tantrum.

repechado, -da, *adj.* [<Mex. Sp. *repechar,* to shelter] protected, sheltered.

repechar, *vb.* [<Mex. Sp. *repechar*] to shelter; *reflex.,* to find or take shelter.

repecho, *m.* [<Mex. Sp. *repecho*<Sp. *repecho,* declivity] shelter; protected place.

repelar, *vb.* [<Mex. Sp. *repelar,* to nag] to grumble; to nag; to scold; to find fault.

repelón, -na, *adj.* [<Mex. Sp. *repelón,* nagger] grumbling; nagging; said of one who finds fault incessantly.

reperiquete, *m.* [<Sp. *re,* repetitive prefix, and *periquete,* instant] temper fit; tantrum.

replantinarse, *vb.* [<Mex. Sp. *replanti-garse*<Sp. *repantigarse*] to lean back in a chair with one's legs stretched out; to stretch out comfortably in a chair. Also, *replantarse.*

reportar, *vb.* [<Eng. to report] to report; to tell on someone; to accuse; *reflex.,* to report; to appear or present oneself at a place. (*Lo llamó el juez y tiene que reportarse a la cas 'e corte el lunes.* He was called in by the judge and has to report to the courthouse on Monday.)

reporte, *m.* [<Eng. report] report; report card; income tax return.

représ, *m.* [<Sp. *represa,* dam] a kind of dam made by damming the lower part of a runoff so that rainwater will collect into a pool. *Represes* are chiefly used for watering livestock.

represón, *m.* [<N.M. Sp. aug. of *représ*] large dam.

repuñar, *vb.* [<Sp. *repugnar*] to cause disgust, to be repugnant or repulsive.

repuñoso, -sa, *adj.* [<Sp. *repugnante*] repugnant, repulsive, hateful, loathsome. Cf. Sp. *antipático.*

reque, *m.* [<Eng. wreck] accident (auto); wreck.

requearse, *vb.* [<N.M. Sp. *reque,* wreck] to have an auto accident; to have a wreck. (*Se requearon.* They had a wreck.)

requera, *f.* [<Eng. wrecker] tow truck; wrecker.

requesitoria, *f.* [<Sp. *requisitoria*] Col. N.M. Sp., requisition.

requesón, *m.* [<Sp. *requesón,* pot cheese] a kind of moist cheese made with whole milk and rennet. After the milk boils it is allowed to simmer; as it does, the whey surfaces and is dumped out. The *requesón* is then ready to serve.

res, *f.* [<Sp. *res,* animal] beef; cow; *carne de res,* beef; *res caida,* a term applied to an easy female.

resacado, -da, *adj.* [<Mex. Sp. *resacado*] cunning, sly.

resbalador, *m.* [<Sp. *resbalar,* to slide] playground slide.

148

rescate, *m.* [<Mex. Sp. *rescate,* a kind of auction in mines] Col. N.M. Sp., sale; a kind of market or fair where Indians and settlers gathered to trade their animals, captives, goods, etc.

reseco, *m.* [<Sp. *reseco,* exsiccation on trees or shrubs] dry spot on the face or other parts of the skin. Also, *reseca.*

resignar, *vb.* [<Sp. *resignarse,* to resign oneself, and Eng. to resign, as from a position] to resign. (*El Cástulo resignó ayer.* Castulo turned in his resignation yesterday.)

resolana, *f.* [<Mex. Sp. *resolana*] sheltered or sunny side of a place; warmth given off by the sun.

resolanear, *vb.* [<Mex. Sp. *resolanear*] to sit in the sunny side of one's house; to be idle.

resolanero, -ra, *adj.* [<N.M. Sp. *resolana*] said of someone who enjoys the sheltered side of his house; lazy, shiftless.

resollar, *vb.* [<Sp. *resollar,* to breathe audibly] to breathe normally. Cf. Sp. *respirar.* (*No sé qué me dio, no puedo resollar.* I don't know what's wrong with me; I can't breathe.)

respetivo, -va, *adj.* [<Sp. *respetar,* to respect or show respect] well-mannered; respectful. Cf. Sp. *respetuoso.*

resquecito, *m.* [<Sp. dim. of *resquicio*] crack, as in a door.

resuello, *m.* [<Sp. *resuello,* audible breathing] breathing; breath. (*No andes tan rieso, ya se me acabó el resuello.* Don't walk so fast; I am out of breath.)

resumidero, *m.* [<Sp. *re* and *sumidero,* drain] drain; leakage. (*Laguna que no tiene desagüe, tiene resumidero.* A lake that has no outlet has a drain. [Where there's a will, there's a way.])

resurarse, *vb.* [<Sp. *rasurarse*] to shave. (*Vale más vivos barbones que muertos resurados.* Better a live coward than a dead hero.)

retablo, *m.* [<Sp. *retablo*] a two-dimensional line painting of a saint or holy person on a flat tablet or board, designed to hang on a wall. See also *tabla.*

retacado, -da, *adj.* [<Mex. Sp. *retacado,* glutted] constipated.

retajila, *f.* See *retejila.*

retaque, *m.* [<Sp. *retacar*] indigestion.

retejila, *f.* [<Mex. Sp. *retejila*] a long line of things; a pile of many things. *Una retejila de ladrones,* a bunch of thieves; *una retejila de carros,* a long line of cars.

retén, *m.* [<Sp. *retén,* reserve] check chain from double tree to front axle of a wagon.

retobado, -da, *adj.* [<Mex. Sp. *retobado,* saucy; stubborn] grumpy; nagging; stubborn.

retranca, *f.* [<Mex. Sp. *retranca,* brake] barnyard gate; brake on a wagon.

retratería, *f.* [<Mex. Sp. *retratería*] photographer's studio. Cf. Sp. *fotografía.*

retratero, -ra, *m.* and *f.* [<Sp. *retratar,* to photograph] photographer. Cf. Sp. *fotógrafo.*

rétulo, *m.* [<Col. Sp. *rétulo*] sign, placard. Cf. Mod. Sp. *rótulo.*

reumos, *m. pl.* [<Sp. *reuma,* rheumatism] arthritis, rheumatism.

revesear, *vb.* [<Sp. *revés*] to strike with the back of the hand. (*¡Cállate o te reveseo!* Shut up or I'll slap you.)

revisadero, *m.* [<Sp. *revisar,* to check or examine] Col. N.M. Sp., peephole or small window in a *torreón,* q.v.

revolver, *vb.* [<Sp. *revolver,* to stir] to stir; *revolver la plática,* to change the subject in a conversation.

rezador, -ra, *m.* and *f.* [<Sp. *rezar,* to pray] prayer leader and reader in a Penitente *morada;* term applied to a person who is paid to pray at burials, funerals or wakes (*velorios*).

riarribeño, -ña, *adj.* [<Sp. *río arribeño,* from upstream] said of a person from Rio Arriba county in New Mexico or of a person living along the Rio Grande north of San Ildefonso to the Colorado line. See also *rabajeño.*

ribete, *m.* [<Sp. *ribete,* cantle] boot; *de ribete,*

149

to boot; in addition to; extra.

rienda, *f.* [<Sp. *rienda,* rein] rein; *dar rienda a un niño,* to control or rear a child; *a media rienda,* at a trot.

rieso, *adv.* [<Sp. *recio,* strong, heavy] hard; loud; fast, rapidly. (*No andes tan rieso.* Don't walk so fast. *Llovió rieso.* It rained hard.)

ril (*riles*), *m.* [<Eng. rail] rail; cattle guard.

rin, *m.* [<Eng. rim] rim; wheel.

rincón, *m.* [<Sp. *rincón,* nook] nook, corner; cul de sac; large basin; cove.

rinconada, *f.* [<Sp. *rinconada,* a kind of corner] dead end; cul de sac.

rinconera, *f.* [<Sp. *rincón,* inner corner] corner shelf; whatnot, an open shelf for bric-a-brac.

risión, *f.* [<Mex. Sp. *risión*<Sp. *irrisión,* mockery] ridicule. *¡Qué risión!* How ridiculous!

rito, *m.* [<Sp. dim. of *río* (*riito*), river] place-name in New Mexico and southern Colorado.

riumos, *m. pl.* See *reumos.*

robabueyes, *m.* [<Sp. *robar,* to steal, and *bueyes,* oxen] cattle rustler; thief.

rodado, -da, *m.* and *f.* [<Sp. *rodar,* to roll, to wander] tramp; wanderer.

rodar, *vb.* [<Sp. *rodar,* to roll] to announce the banns of marriage; to wander.

rodestrado, *m.* [<Sp. *rodete,* a kind of border, and *estrado,* hall] a border or decoration made of cloth or oilcloth which is placed on walls of halls and rooms to keep the whitewash from soiling one's clothes.

rofe, *adj.* [<Eng. rough] rough; boisterous; unrefined, uncouth. (*¡Cómo es rofe este muchito!* This kid is so rough!)

rogón, -na, *adj.* [<Mex. Sp. *rogón*] said of someone who begs insistingly, especially in matters of love.

rolado, -da, *adj.* [<N.M. Sp. *rolar*<Eng. bedroll] asleep; sleeping; in bed.

rolar, *vb.* [<Eng. roll<bedroll] to sleep; *reflex.,* to go to bed; to go to sleep.

romal, *m.* [<Sp. *ramal,* a strand of rope] a kind of rope; a kind of leash attached to the reins of a riding horse.

romerillo, *m.* [<Sp. dim. of *romero,* rosemary] bot., Silver sage. Also, *romerillo del llano.*

romper, *vb.* [<Sp. *romper,* to break] to tear; to take after someone; to attack. (*Me rompió un chulo.* A dog attacked me. *¡Le dije una picardía y rómpeme!* I told him a bad word and did he come after me!)

ronca, *f.* [<Sp. *roncar,* to snore] heavy sleep after a drunken spree.

rondana, *f.* [<Sp. *roldana*] pulley wheel.

rondanilla, *f.* [<N.M. Sp. dim. of *rondana*] pulley wheel.

roña, *f.* [<Sp. *roña,* scab] caked dirt on one's hands; chapping; dirt; *adj.,* *roñoso,* dirty.

ropa, *f.* [<Sp. *ropa,* clothes] clothes; *ropa de abajo,* underwear.

ropón, *m.* [<Sp. *ropón,* a wide, loose gown worn over one's clothes] a gown-like baby dress.

rosa, *f.* [<Sp. *rosa*] rose; *rosa de Castilla,* a wild rose; *echar de rosa a uno,* to use someone as a scapegoat; to blame another for one's actions; Col. N.M. Sp., a prayer said by an Indian official on his knees as he passed the cane of authority to his successor; *pl.,* popcorn.

rosca, *f.* [<Mex. Sp. *rosca,* a kind of sweet roll] anus; buttocks. (*Le dieron una patada en la rosca.* They kicked his ass.) *Hacerse rosca una persona,* to want to be begged or coaxed; to refuse; to fail to cooperate. (*Se hizo rosca.* He said no.)

roscón, -na, *adj.* [<N.M. Sp. aug. of *rosca*] said of a person who fails to cooperate; said of a person who uses others or takes advantage of them (slang).

rosero, *m.* [<N.M. Sp. *rosas,* popcorn] popcorn machine.

roseta, *f.* [<Sp. *roseta*] sandbur; scalloped wheel-design used in decorating colonial furniture.

rosetilla, *f.* [<Sp. dim. of *roseta*] bot., a

plant known also as *yerba del sapo*.

rosillo, *m.* [<Sp. *rosillo*] bot., Shrubby cinquefoil used in early New Mexico in the making of yellow dye; *adj.*, of a bay or sorrel color.

rosita, *f.* [<Sp. *roseta*] tassel, as on corn and other plants; *rosita morada,* bot., Alpine pink.

rosquear, *vb.* [<N.M. Sp. *rosca,* ass] to make a thread, as in a pipe; to have sexual intercourse (taboo).

rostro, *m.* [<Col. N.M. Sp. *rostro,* track, trace, trail] track, trace, trail. Cf. Mod. Sp. *rastro.*

> *Zaldívar andobo setenta leguas la tierra* [Llano Estacado] *hasta el pueblo de las nueve leguas de largo. Topó* **rostro** *de Humayna algunas veces.*

Zaldívar travelled seventy leagues over the land [Llano Estacado] as far as the nine-league long settlement. Occasionally he ran into Humayna's trail. (*Ytinerario* in *Documentos Inéditos*)

> *Por el* **rostro** *de la sangre*
> *que Jesucristo redama*
> *camina la Virgen pura*
> *en una fresca mañana.*

Following the trail of the blood
That Jesus is shedding,
The Immaculate Virgin wanders along
One early cool morning.
(*Por el rostro de la sangre,* N.M. and so. Colo. Penitente *alabado*)

rueditas, *f. pl.* [<Sp. dim. of *rueda,* wheel] round dried slices of summer squash.

ruego, *m.* [<Sp. *ruego,* entreaty] *de ruego y encargo,* at the mercy of others or depending on others, particularly with respect to transportation. (*¿Que todavía están aquí? Sí, andamos de ruego y encargo.* Are you still here? Yes, we are looking for someone to give us a ride.)

rusio, -sia, *m.* and *f.* [<Sp. *ruso*] Russian.

Saber es poder.
Knowledge is power.

sabandija, *f.* [<Sp. *sabandija,* a kind of insect] a small water bug with extremely long legs.

sabanero, -ra, *adj.* [<Mex. Sp. *sabana,* prairie] of or pertaining to the prairie; *m.,* Col. N.M. Sp., person in charge of the mules of a mule train.

sabanilla, *f.* [<Sp. dim. of *sábana*] Terr. N.M. Sp., baize; woolen homespun; also known as *bayeta.*

> *Sabanilla* or plain-weave homespun in natural finespun yarn was made for many purposes. Dyed with indigo, it made men's breeches, women's skirts, and Franciscan habits. Sewn into a sack and stuffed with raw wool, it made a mattress; it was the fabric on which the solid, all over wool embroidery of the *colcha* was done. (E. Boyd, *Popular Arts of Spanish New Mexico*)

saber, *vb.* [<Sp. *saber,* to know] to know. *Déjame saber.* Let me know. *¿Sabes cómo?* Do you know what I mean?

sabidico, -ca, *adj.* [<Sp. *saber,* to know] learned, well-informed; applied to a know-it-all.

sabina, *f.* [<Sp. *sabina,* juniper] cedar; *sabina blanca,* bot., White cedar; *sabina colorada,* bot., (Red) cedar; *almáciga de sabina,* juniper pitch or resin; *bellota de sabina,* bot., Mistletoe.

sabino, *m.* [<Sp. *sabina,* juniper] *sabino macho,* bot., Mule pine; *adj.,* pinto color (horses); *pl.,* peeled small poles of juniper used as lath in ceilings.

sabrosearse, *vb.* [<Mex. Sp. *sabrosearse*] to lick one's chops. Cf. Sp. *saborearse.*

sacarol, *m.* [<Eng. sucker rod] an iron rod from a pump handle to the cylinder in a well.

sacarreal, *adj.* [<Sp. *sacra y real,* sacred and royal] your royal highness, a term used in N.M. and so. Colo. Spanish folktales when addressing the king.

sacatapones, *m.* [<Sp. *sacar,* to pull out, and *tapones,* plugs; lit., cork-puller-

out] corkscrew. Cf. Sp. *tirabuzón.*

sacate, *m.* See *zacate.*

saco, *m.* [<Sp. *saco,* coarse cloth] Col. and Terr. N.M. Sp., a woolen jacket without sleeves much like a Mexican *cotorina* (vest).

They [the Indians of the pueblos west and south of Santa Fe] mostly wear a kind of short breeches and long stockings, the use of which they most probably acquired from the Spaniards. The **saco,** a species of woolen jacket without sleeves, completes their exterior garment. (Josiah Gregg, *Commerce of the Prairies*)

sacre, *m.* [<Fr. *sacré,* damned, cursed] a curse. (*Me echó un sacre.* He cursed me.)

sacristán, *m.* [<Sp. *sacristán,* sexton] sexton; Col. N.M. Sp., Indian boy selected by the priest to assist him in the mass and to receive religious instruction.

saguán, *m.* See *zaguán.*

salado, -da, *adj.* [<Mex. Sp. *salado,* unlucky] insipid (dull); fraught with failure; unlucky. (*¡Gringo salado!* Cursed gringo!)

salarata, *f.* [<Sp. *salerato*<Mod. Lat. *sal aeratus,* aerated salt] bicarbonate of soda. Also referred to as *soda del martillo* (Arm and Hammer soda).

salero, *m.* [<Sp. *salero,* gracefulness] *echar salero,* to show off.

salido, -da, *adj.* [<Sp. *salido,* protruding] aggressive; bold; forward.

salir, *vb.* [<Sp. *salir,* to go out] *salírsele a uno* (*un secreto*), to make a slip; to let the cat out of the bag; *salir pa atrás,* to come out short; to get the short end of a deal.

salitre, *m.* [<Sp. *salitre,* nitre] a salinous compound of several salts including nitre.

salmos, *m. pl.* [<Eng. salmon] jack mackerel; salmon.

salmuera, *f.* [<Sp. *salmuera,* brine] brine; any food with an excess of salt.

salpática, *f.* [<Mex. Sp. *sal hepática*] Epsom salts.

salpiquear, *vb.* [<Sp. *salpicar*] to spatter, to splash.

saltar, *vb.* [<Sp. *saltar,* to jump] to jump; *saltar una cosa,* to fail; to come to an end. (*¡Ahi saltaron los calzones!* That's the end of my trousers!) *Saltar del cascarón,* just hatched, applied to a young upstart.

saltreática, *f.* [<Mex. Sp. *sal hepática*] Epsom salts. Also, *saltrática* and *saltrástica.*

saludes, *f. pl.* [<Sp. *pl.* of *salud,* health] greetings; regards. Cf. Sp. *saludos* (<*saludo*).

salvado, *m.* [<Sp. *salvado,* bran] bran; fig., dandruff.

salvaje, *adj.* [<Sp. *salvaje,* savage] coarse, gross; stupid.

salvar, *vb.* [<Sp. *salvar,* to save (a life)] to save; to save money. Cf. Sp. *ahorrar.*

salvia, *f.* [<Eng. salve] ointment, salve. (*Ella se puso salvia en un hombro que le dolía muncho.* She put some salve on one of her shoulders that was giving her a great deal of pain.)

sanamabiche, *adj.* [<Eng. son of a bitch] caddish; despicable.

sanar, *vb.* [<Sp. *sanar*] to give birth, to get well.

sancochar, *vb.* [<Sp. *sancochar,* to parboil] to boil fresh meat with vegetables, garlic and salt; to scald (corn).

sanefa, *f.* [<Sp. *cenefa*] border or list painted on bottom part of a wall, especially a porch wall.

sangrador, *m.* [<Sp. *sangrar,* to let blood] Penitente brother who scarified novices' backs to allow blood to flow freely from lashes received in Lenten rites.

sangre, *f.* [<Sp. *sangre,* blood] blood; *sangre de Cristo,* bot., Creeping barberry; *sangre de toro,* bull's blood, a synthetic dye; *sangre de venado,* bot., Dragon's blood, rattan palm; *adj., sangre liviana,* compatible, congenial; *sangre pesada,* boring, dull; uncongenial.

sangría, *f.* [<Sp. *sangría,* bleeding] a kind of small ditch perpendicular to and

taking off from a *contraacequia* or counter ditch, which, in turn, takes off from the main ditch.

sangrita, *f.* [<Sp. dim. of *sangre*, blood] *agarrar sangrita*, to improve one's economic situation; to attain a definite degree of security.

sangrón, -na, *adj.* [<Sp. aug. of *sangre*, blood] boring; disagreeable; uncongenial.

sanjuanear, *vb.* [<Mex. Sp. *sanjuanear*, to punish] to thrash or shake a child; to spank.

santería, *f.* [<Sp. *santo*, saint's image] place where sacred images (*santos*) are carved; the art of carving *santos;* collection of *santos.*

santero, -ra, *m.* and *f.* [<Sp. *santo*] woodcarver, particularly one who carves *santos* or images of holy persons.

santo, *m.* [<Sp. *santo*] image or statue of a saint or holy person; *santo de bulto*, statue of a saint. See *bulto. Santo de retablo*, votive picture offering; *santo de talla*, image of a *santo* in the round; statue of a *santo* or holy person; *quedarse una mujer pa vestir santos*, said of a woman who will probably never marry, a spinster.

santo entierro, *m.* [<Sp. *santo entierro*, holy burial] Christ in the holy sepulcher, an image (*santo*) depicting Christ in a coffin.

santopiés, *m.* [<Col. Sp. *ciento pies* (Molina)] centipede.

sapiento, -ta, *adj.* [<N.M. Sp. *sapo*] lucky.

sapo, *m.* [<Sp. *sapo*, toad] toad; lucky shot in the game of basketball; fat, chubby person; *hacer un sapo*, to make a goal, especially by accident; lucky break; *de sapo*, by chance, by a lucky stroke.

sardo, *m.* [<Mex. Sp. slang *sardo*, sentinel] soldier (slang).

sarnoso, -sa, *adj.* [<Sp. *sarnoso*, itchy] dirty; shabby.

sartén, *m.* [<Sp. *sartén* (*f.*)] frying pan; skillet. The word *puela* (<Fr. *poêle*) is more common.

sastifacer, *vb.* [<Sp. *satisfacer*, to satisfy] to satisfy. (*No me sastifació*. It did not satisfy me.)

sastifación, *f.* [<Col. N.M. Sp. *satisfación*] satisfaction.

saxofón, *m.* [<Eng. saxophone] saxophone. Cf. Sp. *saxófono*.

Sebastiana, *f.* [<Sp. *Sebastiana*, woman's given name] name given to a carved image of the death angel. Also called *la comadre Sebastiana*.

sebo, *adj.* [<Sp. *sebo*] tallow; a term applied to a lazy, shiftless person.

seca, *f.* [<Sp. *seca*, dry] a term used to refer to a ewe not taken by the seed ram at a particular mating season.

secina, *f.* See Spanish *cecina.*

¡Séchu!, *interj.* [<onomatopoeic] command to a donkey to stop.

seda, *f.* [<Sp. *seda*, silk] silk; *criado (criada) entre sedas* (brought up in silk garments), pampered; spoiled.

segunda, *f.* [<Sp. *segunda*, second] second gear (auto); *cas' 'e segunda*, secondhand store; *hacer la segunda*, to harmonize in parallel thirds.

seguro, *m.* [<Mex. Sp. *seguro*] safety pin. The term *fistol* (<Mex. Sp. *fistol*, hair pin) is more common.

seigo, *vb.* [<Sp. *ser*, to be] I am. (*¿Quién es el Silas? Yo seigo*. Who is Silas? I am.)

semaneros, *m. pl.* [<Sp. *semana*, week] Col. N.M. Sp., Indian workers furnished by the Indian pueblos to work for the priest and the pueblo mission or church.

semilla, *f.* [<Sp. *semilla*] seed; *aventarle la semilla a alguno*, to tell someone off.

semita, *f.* See *cemita.*

senado, *m.* [<Col. N.M. Sp. *senado*, assembly; audience] audience. Cf. Sp. *concurrencia. Senado ilustre*, illustrious audience.

sencia, *f.* See *cencia.*

sentido, *m.* [<Sp. *sentido*, sense, sense of hearing] ear; inner ear.

señas, *f. pl.* [<Sp. *señas*, signs] obscene

gestures; finger signs.

sepoltura, *f.* [<Col. N.M. Sp. *sepoltura* (Mod. Sp. *sepultura*)] grave.

serruche, *m.* [<Sp. *serrucho*, handsaw] handsaw; saw in general.

serruchear, *vb.* [<N.M. Sp. *serruche*] to saw.

sesenta (a sesenta), *adv.* [<Sp. *sesenta*, sixty] *ir a sesenta*, to be making sixty miles per hour; to go fast, to be speeding.

sesos, *m. pl.* [<Sp. *seso*, brain] common sense; *adj.*, *sesos de borrego*, stubborn; *sesos de burro*, ignorant, stupid (both applied sarcastically).

sestear, *vb.* [<Sp. *sestear*<*siesta*] to rest from work; to take a short break.

seta, *f.* [<Eng. set] *seta de trastes*, set of dishes.

setear, *vb.* [<Eng. to set] *setear la mesa*, to set the table.

setemesino, -na, *adj.* [<Sp. *siete*, seven, and *mesino*<*mes*, pertaining to the month] premature; applied to a baby born prematurely.

sharque, *m.* [<Eng. shark] chiseler, swindler.

sho, *m.* [<Eng. show] movies; show; theatre.

shocoque, *adj.* [<Col. N.M. Sp. *xococ* [*šo-kók*] sour] sour, spoiled; *leche shocoque*, buttermilk.

> *Antenoche jui a tu casa*
> *y me dieron de cenar*
> *unas tortillas* **shocoques**
> *y frijoles sin guisar.*
> Night before last
> I went to your home
> And was served spoiled tortillas
> And beans without salt and
>   shortening.
> (N.M. and so. Colo. Sp. *verso popular*)

shosho, -sha, *adj.* [<Mex. Sp. *chocha*, sow] sloppy; ill-kempt; dirty.

silla, *f.* [<Sp. *silla*, saddle] a sag between two mountain peaks; *silla de manos*, sedan chair; *traer a una persona en silla*

de manos, to wait on someone hand and foot, to cater to or play up to someone.

sillero, -ra, *adj.* [<Sp. *silla*] said of a person who uses a saddle rather than riding a horse bareback.

silleta, *f.* [<Sp. dim. of *silla*] chair; *silleta mecedora*, rocker, rocking chair.

¡Simón!, *adv.* [<Mex. Sp. *¡Simona!*, Yes! (euph.)] Yes! (euph.) (*¿Vas ir? Simón.* Are you coming? Yes.)

simpático, -ca, *adj.* [<Sp. *simpático*, congenial, pleasant] attractive, good-looking.

síncero [sínsero], *adj.* [<Sp. *sincero*] sincere.

síndico, *m.* [<Sp. *síndico*, recorder] caretaker of a cemetery; trustee (both pertaining to the Penitentes).

sinsonte, *m.* [<Mex. Sp. *sinsonte*] ornith., mockingbird. See also *chinchonte* and *chonte*.

sintopié, *m.* See *cintopié*.

sinvergüenzada, *f.* [<Mex. Sp. *sinvergüen-zada*<*sinvergüenza*] base, shameless action.

sinvergüenzo, -za, *adj.* [<Mex. Sp. *sinvergüenzo*] applied to a rascal, rogue. Cf. Sp. *sinvergüenza*.

sipapú, *m.* [<Tewa *sipapú*, cave] cavity in the earth's surface; hole in the ground.

siquear, *vb.* [<Eng. to sic] to sic a dog on someone.

sisaña, *f.* See *cizaña*.

sitio, *m.* [<Mex. Sp. *sitio*] a spread (cattle); Col. N.M. Sp., small farm.

so, *adv.* [<Eng. so] so. (*So, nos juimos.* So, we left.)

sobador, *m.* [<Mex. Sp. *sobador*] folk chiropractor; bonesetter.

sobajar, *vb.* [<Mex. Sp. *sobajar*] to humiliate; to cut someone down to size.

sobaqueras, *f. pl.* [<Sp. *sobaco*, armpit] crutches. Cf. Sp. *muletas*.

sobar, *vb.* [<Mex. Sp. *sobar*] to set dislocated bones; to rub or give someone a rubdown; to massage.

sobrado

sobrado, *m.* [<Sp. *sobrado, pt. part.* of *sobrar,* extra; a kind of garret] floor or story in buildings. Col. N.M. Sp., *casas de cuatro sobrados,* four-story buildings (in reference to Indian pueblos, such as Pecos and Taos).

sobrar, *vb.* [<Sp. *sobrar,* left over] to feel like it (sarcastic). (*¿Ahora te sobró?* Now you felt like it, huh? [It's about time.])

sobrechuses, *m. pl.* [<Sp. *sobre,* over, and Eng. shoes] overshoes; galoshes.

soca, *f.* [<Mex. Sp. *soca,* stubble] *¡Ni soca!* Nothing! Nothing at all! (slang).

social, *m.* [<Eng. social] party or informal gathering of persons for amusement or recreational purposes; *dar un social,* to have a party.

soda, *f.* [<Eng. soda] soda; soda pop; *soda del martillo,* bicarbonate of soda (Arm and Hammer soda). See also *salarata.*

sofás, *m.* [<Sp. *sofá*] couch; sofa; *pl., sofases.*

soflamero, -ra, *adj.* [<Mex. Sp. *soflamero* <Sp. *soflamero,* said of one who uses deceitful language] a term applied to someone who raises a fuss over slight things or who complains in an exaggerated way about petty things; *n.,* a chronic complainer (slang).

soguilla, *f.* [<Sp. dim. of *soga,* a kind of rope] a woman's thin gold or silver necklace, originally made of intertwisted strands like a rope or cord.

sol, *m.* [<Sp. *sol,* sun] sun; *a mete sol,* at sundown.

solamente (*que no solamente*), *adv.* [<Sp. *solamente,* only] only; *que no solamente,* splendid, wonderful. (*¡Hubo una boda que no solamente!* There was [took place] a wonderful wedding!)

solano, -na, *adj.* [<Sp. *solo,* alone] alone, solitary (rare).

solecito, *m.* [<Sp. dim. of *sol,* sun] sunny side; warmth given off by the sun. (*Vamos a sentarnos en el solecito.* Let's sit out in the sunny side [of a house, place, etc.].)

solecitud, *f.* [<Sp. *solicitud*] anxiety, solicitude.

*Toda tu solecitud
se ferea en rigor extraño;
mi vida, hace más de un año
que no sé de tu salud;
esa sí es ingratitud:
no enviarme cuatro letritas
una o dos con tus manitas
con los que vienen y van.
¡Ese sí es crecido afán!
¡Ah, qué ingrata te acreditas!*

All your sweet affection
Is changing strangely,
My beloved. It's over a year now
That I've had no news of you;
Don't be so thoughtless;
Write me a few lines,
One or two with your tiny hands
And send them to me
With travellers that come and go.
This is a most anxious concern;
Please don't disappoint me.
(*¡Ah, qué ingrata te acreditas!,* N.M. Sp. *décima*)

solera, *f.* [<Sp. *solera,* entablature] insulation between beams (*vigas*) of an adobe house.

solevado, -da, *adj.* [<Sp. *solevar,* to incite to revolt] arrogant, haughty; snobbish. Also, having a swollen rectum; suffering from a slight case of shock.

sollame, *m.* [<Sp. *sollamar,* to scorch] an ulcer-like sore in the mouth; cold sore; fever blister. Also, *sollamo.*

sombra, *f.* [<Sp. *sombra,* shadow] shade; lampshade.

sombrear, *vb.* [<Sp. *sombrear,* to shade] to rest in the shade. (*Vamos a sombrear un rato.* Let us rest a while in the shade.)

sombrerazos, *m.* [<Mex. Sp. *sombrerazos*] *a gritos y sombrerazos,* barely; by the skin of one's teeth (rare).

sombrita, *f.* [<Sp. dim. of *sombra,* shade] shade; shady side. (*Vamos a estarnos toda la mañana en la sombrita.* Let's spend the whole morning in the shade.)

sonar, *vb.* [<Sp. *sonar,* to sound] to sound. (*Ya ni suena ni truena.* You don't even hear about him any more. He is all

washed up.) *Sonarse*, to be announced. (*Se sonó en la suidá de que ya el príncipe había jallado mujer.* It was announced that the prince had found a wife.)

sopa, *f.* [<Col. N.M. Sp. *sopa (de pan)* (Molina)] a kind of bread pudding containing toasted bread, cheese, cinnamon, sugar, etc.

sopaipillas, *f. pl.* [<Sp. dim. of *sopaipa,* a kind of fritter] fritters made of bread dough cut in squares and fried brown in deep fat.

In some parts of New Mexico the *sopaipilla* is called the *buñuelo.* Erna Fergusson says it is a *sopaipilla* when cut into a small square shape, a *buñuelo* when cut large and round, with a hole punched in the middle. (Thomas Ewing Dabney, "What's Cooking?," *New Mexico Magazine*)

sopanda, *f.* [<Mex. Sp. *sopanda*] car spring; bedspring. Cf. Sp. *muelles, resorte.*

sopetón, *m.* [<Sp. *sopetón (de sopetón)*, suddenly] *de un sopetón,* in one gulp.

sopitas, *f. pl.* [<Sp. dim. of *sopa,* sop] milk porridge; *sopitas de miel,* fig., kindness, niceness; *sopitas de jiel,* bitterness, hardship, a hard life or hard time. (*Ahora te da sopitas de miel, más tarde te dará sopitas de jiel.* Now he's all kindness; later he will make it hard for you.)

soplar, *vb.* [<Sp. *soplar,* to blow] to blow. (*Ya no sopla.* He hasn't got it in him [physically or sexually]. He's all washed out.) *Reflex.,* to make off with; to gulp down, to swallow.

Hubo una gran fiesta
hubo muncho vino;
suéltanse los gatos,
sóplanse al padrino.
There was quite a celebration
And much wine was drunk;
The cats got loose
And gulped down the best man.
(*El piojo y la pulga,* N.M. Sp. folk song)

soplón, *m.* [<Mex. Sp. *soplón*<Sp. *soplar,* to blow] tattler, fink (slang).

soportar, *vb.* [<Sp. *soportar,* to suffer, and Eng. to support] to support; to back; to maintain financially. Cf. Sp. *apoyar* and *mantener.*

soporte, *m.* [<Eng. support] maintenance; support. Cf. Sp. *sustento.*

soquete, *m.* See *zoquete.*

soroche, *adj.* [<Am. Sp. *soroche,* a kind of illness caused by rarefaction of the air at great heights] filthy, grimy; grouchy; mischievous, roguish. Also, *sorocho, sorocha.*

sospirar, *vb.* [<Col. N.M. Sp. *sospirar*] to sigh.

sospiro, *m.* [<Col. N.M. Sp. *sospiro*] sigh; *pegar un sospiro,* to sigh.

. . . *despidiendo treinta ayes y sesenta* ***sospiros.***
. . . moaning and lamenting and sighing incessantly .
(Miguel de Cervantes Saavedra, *Don Quijote de la Mancha*)

sótano, *m.* [<Sp. *sótano,* cellar] sunken part in a river or stream. See also *jondable.*

soterrano, *m.* [<Col. N.M. Sp. *soterrano*<*soterrar,* to bury; to place underground] underground structure for storing produce (apples, cabbages, carrots, potatoes, etc.) and canned goods.

suadero, *m.* [<N.M. Sp. *subadero*] saddle blanket.

suave, *adj.* [<Sp. *suave,* soft] soft; fine, splendid; *adv.,* alright; very well. (*¿Cómo estuvo el party? Estuvo muy suave.* How was the party? It was very good. *¿Nos vamos?—Suave.* Shall we leave? Very well.)

subadero, *m.* [<Mex. Sp. *sudadero*] saddle blanket.

suceso, *m.* [<Sp. *suceso,* event, and Eng. success] success. Cf. Sp. *éxito.*

sudadero, *m.* [<Sp. *sudadero,* a kind of handkerchief or cloth for wiping off sweat] saddle blanket.

sudario, *m.* [<Sp. *sudario,* shroud] shroud; a kind of prayer, especially one for

the soul of a deceased person. *Sudarios* are usually recited at *velorios* (wakes) or during Easter time at Penitente rites.

suera, *f.* [<Eng. sweater] sweater. Cf. Sp. *suéter* (*m.*).

suerte, *f.* [<Col. N.M. Sp. *suerte*] agricultural plot on which settlers raised corn, beans, wheat, squash, etc.

suertudo, -da, *adj.* [<Sp. *suerte,* luck] fortunate; lucky.

suiche, *m.* [<Eng. switch] switch.

suichear, *vb.* [<N.M. Sp. *suiche*<Eng. switch] to turn on a switch.

suidá, *f.* [<Sp. *ciudad*] city.

sumidero, *m.* [<Sp. *sumidero,* sink] masked well; pitfall; sinkhole.

A very curious and disagreeable freak of nature found in some parts of the Southwest is that treacherous pitfall known as the *sumidero* . . . These characteristic pits are a sort of mud springs with too much mud to flow, and too much water to dry up. They are roundish, about the size of a well-hole, and sometimes as deep—in fact, they are what we might call masked wells. These masked wells occur in bare alkali-covered flats. The mud upon their surface is baked dry, and there is absolutely nothing to distinguish them from the safe ground around. (Charles F. Lummis, *Some Strange Corners of Our Country*)

súpito, -ta, *adj.* [<Mex. Sp. *súpito,* fast asleep] dead; fast asleep; out cold; knocked out.

surumato, -ta, *m.* and *f.* [<Mex. Sp. *Surumuato,* a place-name in Jalisco, Mexico] a term applied by New Mexico Indo-Hispanos to low-class Mexican farm workers.

susirio, *m.* [<Sp. *susidio*] anxiety; restlessness; concern; worry.

susto, *m.* [<Sp. *susto,* fright] fright; shock. Some kinds of *susto,* a type of illness resulting from fright, are of the magical etiology in that they are felt to be caused by the possession of an individual by an evil spirit. And there are, of course, many kinds of bewitchment in which a person with evil intent and magical power can cause illness symptoms in another. Psychological diseases are those in which a strong emotional experience causes the appearance of the disease symptoms. Examples are *susto* when it occurs in young children who have suffered a severe fright, or epilepsy, which is believed to result from strong emotional feelings. (Lyle Saunders, *Cultural Difference and Medical Care*)

sute, *m.* [<Eng. suit] suit (slang). Sp. *vestido* (dress) is a more common term. Sp. *túnico* (tunic), in turn, is the term for dress.

Tanto quiso el diablo a su hijo hasta que le sacó un ojo.
The devil so loved his child that he finally
   plucked out one of his eyes.
(An overindulgent parent often spoils his
   children.)

tabique, *m.* [<Mex. Sp. *tabique,* jail] *el tabique,* the jailhouse (slang).

tabla, *f.* [<Sp. *tabla,* board] board; two-dimensional line painting of a saint or holy person on a flat tablet or board; the board itself. See also *retablo. Estar* or *quedar tablas,* to be even; to break even; to tie.

A *retablo,* sometimes called a *tabla* (board), is a painting in tempera colors on a slab or panel of pine previously coated with one or more layers of *yeso* (gesso). A group of these panels, forming what is known in English as an altar piece, altar screen, retable, or reredos, is also called a *retablo.* (José E. Espinosa, *Saints in the Valleys*)

tablita, *f.* [<Sp. dim. of *tabla,* board] small board; a thin wooden headdress painted in bright colors. The *tablita* is used by Santo Domingo, New Mexico, Indian women in their festive rites.

There are evergreen branches to symbolize life itself, rain gourds that rattle their prayer messages for rain, symbolic rain sashes, and *tablitas* or head boards that bear symbols of sun, moon, and clouds. (Grant Maxwell, "Corn Dance," *New Mexico Magazine*)

tablón, *m.* [<Sp. aug. of *tabla,* board] a large flat log hewn into the shape of a trough. The *tablón* was used as a washtub for woolens.

Erineo cut and pounded the *amole* roots and threw them into the *tablón*—a long log trough—bare footed women knelt around the trough and with bare arms beat the warm water until the foamy *amole* suds filled the *tablón*. Into the suds the blankets and carpets were dipped, beaten, and squeezed, until the fadeless colors were again bright. (Cleofas M. Jaramillo, *Shadows of the Past*)

taconear, *vb.* [<Sp. *tacón,* heel] to dance.

tacuche, *m.* [<Mex. Sp. *tacuche,* a kind of

prisoners' uniform] man's suit (slang), suit of clothes (slang).

taipear, *vb.* [<Eng. to type] to type.

taite, *adj.* [<Eng. tight] tight, miserly.

talco, *m.* [<Sp. *talco,* talc] pulverized mica or micaceous earth.

talegas, *f. pl.* [<Mex. Sp. *talegas,* testicles] testicles.

talián, *m.* [<Eng. Italian (*The Italian*)] a folk dance.

talón, *m.* [<Sp. *talón,* heel] *picarle* or *avisarle a talón* or *talones,* to take off quickly; to flee.

talpa, *f.* [<Mex. Sp. *tlalpa*] a knob of land rising above the mesa; N.M. placename.

talvina, *f.* [<Sp. *talvina,* a kind of milk extracted from seeds] a homemade face bleach.

> **Talvina** was another face bleaching mask made of bran and the crushed red spikes of the *alegría* plant or wild raspberries. (Cleofas M. Jaramillo, *Shadows of the Past*)

talla, *f.* [<Eng. tie] railroad tie.

talludo, -da, *adj.* [<Mex. Sp. *talludo*] rugged; sturdy.

tama, *f.* [<unknown origin] stand, as for a chest or trunk (rare).

> An especially handsome chest sat upon a stand called **tama**, a carved wooden framework not unlike a pair of andirons. (Roland F. Dickey, *New Mexico Village Arts*)

tamaño, -ña, *adj.* [<Sp. *tamaño,* size] size; *interj.,* ¡*Tamaño . . .*! You rascal!

tamborín, *m.* [<Sp. *tamboril,* a kind of tambourine] noise; racket (rare).

tanape, *m.* [<Eng. turnip] turnip; *tanape amarillo,* rutabaga. Also, *tánape.*

tanate, *m.* [<Mex. Sp.<Náhuatl *tanatl*] testicle; Col. N.M. Sp., a rawhide bucket for loading ore in a mine.

> On that day in 1680, an Indian stood on a ledge beside slowly flowing water inside the mine . . . a cry interrupted his moment of rest . . .

Pile the **tanates** high! . . . Steadying the canoe, he loaded ore into two rawhide buckets called **tanates**. (G. F. Shenk, "The First Gold Mine," *New Mexico Magazine*)

tando, *m.* [<Mex. Sp. slang *tando,* hat] hat (slang). See also *chapero, chaperito.*

tano, -na, *adj.* [<Tewa *Tagno,* placename] Indian from Tano, a colonial Indian pueblo on the site of present Galisteo; an inhabitant of Galisteo, New Mexico; the Indian language of the *Tanos* Indians.

tanque, *m.* [<Sp. *tanque,* vat] tank, reservoir; gas tank.

tanre, *adv.* [<Sp. *tan,* so, and prefix *re*] exceptionally. (*Probecito, siempre jue tanre güeno con todos.* Poor dear, he always was so exceptionally good to everyone.)

tansé, *m.* [<Eng. tansy?] bot., Tansy. Cf. Sp. *tanaceto.*

tanteada, *f.* [<Mex. Sp. *tanteada,* guess] rough estimate.

tantear, *vb.* [<Mex. Sp. *tantear,* to guess or calculate approximately] to guess the price or weight of an object; to beat. (*Se lo tantearon.* They beat him.) To spy upon; *tantearse el sombrero,* to tilt one's hat to one side.

tanteo, *m.* [<Mex. Sp. *tanteo,* appraisal] calculation; *echar un tanteo a algo,* to guess or approximate the price, value, etc., of an item or article; *al tanteo,* at sight. (*Al tanteo yo diría que pesa unas diez libras.* Just by looking at it, I'd say it weighs some ten pounds.)

tanto, *adv.* [<Sp. *tanto,* in such a manner] *Por tanto y no* and *vb.,* almost did not and *vb.* (*Por tanto y no vamos.* We almost did not go. Col. N.M. Sp. (Molina)). ¿*Qué tanto?* How much? Cf. Mod. Sp. ¿*Cuánto?*

taoseño, -ña, *adj.* [<Taos (Indian pueblo)] a resident of the town of Taos, New Mexico.

tapa, *f.* [<Sp. *tapa,* lid] crown of a hat; lid; hubcap.

tapadera, *f.* [<Sp. *tapadera,* lid] lid; pimp; conniver; toe guards or taps.

tapado, -da, *adj.* [<Sp. *pt. part.* of *tapar,* to stop up] said of a dunce; ignorant; constipated; plugged up.

tapador, -ra, *adj.* [<Sp. *tapar,* to cover] pimp; conniver.

tapalina, *f.* [<Mex. Sp. *tápalo,* shawl] a kind of homemade sunbonnet; a homemade raincoat made of gunnysack, newspaper, etc.

tápalo, *m.* [<Mex. Sp. *tápalo*] shawl. Cf. Sp. *chal.*

tapanco, *m.* [<Mex. Sp. *tapanco*<Náhuatl *tlapantli,* flat roof] attic; heap or pile; *tapanco de nieve,* snowbank.

tapeiste, *m.* [<Mex. Sp. *tapeste*<Náhuatl *tlapechtli*] a kind of hayloft or bower in which to keep alfalfa, hay, etc., and which also serves as shelter for domestic animals. Also, *tapeste.*

tapeo, *m.* [<Eng. top] act of topping, as sugar beets.

tapón, *m.* [<Sp. *tapón,* stopper] plug; hard, dry mucous plugging up a child's nose.

tapushque, *m.* See *tepushque.*

tarasqueadas, *f. pl.* [<Mex. Sp. *tarascadas* <*tarasquear,* to snap, as in biting] *tarasqueadas de hogado,* said of someone who snaps back or grasps a chance to put a point across in a conversation.

tarima, *f.* [<Sp. *tarima,* a kind of movable platform; bench] adobe ledge built against a wall to serve as a bench; *baile de tarima,* a marathon type of dance in which a couple danced on a narrow pine slab thrown across a shallow ditch. The object of this dance was to see how long the dancers could dance without falling into the water.

tarime, *m.* [<Sp. *tarima,* platform] wooden floor.

tarja, *f.* [<Sp. *taja,* tally] slab, as of salt pork or bacon.

tarjar, *vb.* [<Sp. *tarjar,* to tally] to make sarcastic remarks.

tarpolio, *m.* [<Eng. tarpaulin] canvas; tarpaulin.

tarre, *adv.* [<Sp. *tan,* so, and augmentative prefix *re*] so; extremely. (*Probecito, tarre güeno que era.* Poor dear, he was so nice.)

tarria, *f.* [<Mex. Sp. *tarria*] a kind of cushion placed at the back of a saddle for carrying things.

tarunual, *adj.* [<Mex. Sp. *tarahumara* (Tarahumara Indian)] ignorant; stupid.

> *Este **tarunual** Manuel*
> *jue caus'e mi perdición,*
> *que al hombre Joaquín Terrazas*
> *le ha entregado mi nación;*
> *que al hombre Joaquín Terrazas*
> *le ha entregado mi nación.*
> This stupid Manuel
> Was the cause of my downfall,
> For he surrendered my people
> To that man Joaquin Terrazas;
> For he surrendered my people
> To that man Joaquin Terrazas.
> (N.M. Sp. *Indita del Indio Victorio*)

tasajos, *m. pl.* [<Sp. *tasajo,* jerked beef] twists or strips of melon, pumpkin, etc., dried in the sun.

> From the pile of yellow pumpkins on the back porch, the smallest ones were selected, peeled, cut in half, and hung on the orchard posts to dry and sweeten in the sun for *tasajos.* They were to be used for *empanaditas* and pie fillings mixed with raisins and piñon nuts. These *tasajos* were also made from melons cut in strips and dried. (Cleofas M. Jaramillo, *Shadows of the Past*)

tasol, *m.* See *tazol.*

tasolera, *f.* See *tazolera.*

tata, *m.* [<Mex. Sp. *tata,* old one] dad; grandpa; elder.

tatemar, *vb.* [<Mex. Sp. *tatemar,* to underdo (meat)] to half roast, to cook rare.

taure, *m.* [<Sp. *tahur,* gambler] swindler; gambler.

tazol, *m.* [<Mex. Sp. *tazol,* trash] bean

hulls and other refuse left after thrashing; straw.

tazolera, *f.* [<Mex. Sp. *tazolera*] shed for storage of hay, straw, etc.

tecato, -ta, *m.* and *f.* [<Mex. Sp. *tecata,* drug] drug addict (slang).

teclo, -cla, *adj.* [<Mex. Sp. slang *teclo*] drunk, tipsy.

tecolote, -ta, *adj.* [<Mex. Sp. *tecolote*<Náhuatl *tecolotl,* owl] speckled; *gallina tecolota,* Plymouth Rock (hen).

tecoloteño, -ña, *adj.* [<N.M. Sp. *Tecolote,* place-name] a resident of Tecolote, New Mexico.

tecomblate, *m.* [<Mex. Sp. *tecomblate*] bot., Caltrops.

techagüiste, *m.* [<Mex. Sp. *zacahuistle*<Náhuatl *zacatl,* grass, and *huitztli,* thorn] bot., a kind of wild grass with thorns.

techo, *m.* [<Sp. *techo,* roof] ceiling; roof; *techo de chingles,* shingle roof; *techo de latón,* galvanized or "tin" roof; *techo de manta,* unbleached muslin ceiling tacked on to roof beams; *techo de tejamanil,* shingle roof.

tegua, *f.* [<Opata *begua*] leather Indian sandal; the Tewa language or nation; *pisarle a la tegua,* to step on it; to hurry.

teja, *f.* [<Sp. *teja,* roof tile] a small flat stone used in the game of *teja.* The game itself is a horseshoe-type of contest in which *tejas* (stones, silver dollars, iron washers, etc.) are thrown from a distance into a small hole in the ground.

> When not engaged in sports or exciting games, the men played *el hoyo* and moved with the sun to snow-cleared patios. Two small, round holes were dug in the ground about thirty feet apart. Each player, standing by one of the holes, took two turns at throwing his *tejas* (a flat round stone about three inches in diameter), into the opposite hole. Three points were won with each *teja* that fell inside the hole, one or two points by the ones that fell on the edge or touched the hole. Some-

times the next player knocked his opponent's *teja* into the hole, counting three points for him. Twelve points won the game. (Cleofas M. Jaramillo, *Shadows of the Past*)

tejamanil, *m.* [<Mex. Sp. *tejamanil*<Náhuatl *tlaxamanilli,* small boards] shingle; *techo de tejamanil,* shingle roof.

tejano, -na, *adj.* [<Sp. *tejano,* from *Tejas* (Texas)] a term applied disparagingly to a white stranger coming into the area from Texas or from the eastern states; a *gringo.*

> Old people, in my youth, used to recount what they remembered of the terrible *Tejanos.* Huge men they were, red and hairy, uttering incomprehensible noises instead of words, frightening babies, stealing cattle, breaching wine and brandy casks, and, when drunk, even desecrating chapels. My grandfather claimed that the unequaled size of our cottonwood tree was due to fertilization the *Tejanos* gave it when they butchered in the patio where it grew. Quite naturally to simple Mexican people, "*Tejano*" was a name of loathing and fright. (Erna Fergusson, *Our Southwest*)

tejaván, *m.* [<Sp. *teja vana* (*a tejavana,* with no more roof than the tiles)] attic; loft; gabled roof.

tejendero, -ra, *m.* and *f.* [<Sp. *tejer,* to weave] weaver (rare).

tela, *f.* [<Sp. *tela,* cloth] cloth; film that forms on boiled milk; *tela de alambre,* wire screen; *tela de cien hilos,* baize (*bayeta*); tela de primavera, flowered silk.

telefón, *m.* [<Eng. telephone] telephone.

telefoneada, *f.* [<Mex. Sp. *telefoneada*] telephone call, ring. (*Dame una telefoneada.* Give me a ring.)

tembladora, *f.* [<Sp. *tembladora,* a kind of pin] hairpin-like ornament on a spiral.

temolada, *f.* [<Mex. Sp. *temole*<Náhuatl *tetl,* fire, and *molli,* stew] ragout; fricassee; goulash.

tender, *vb.* [<Sp. *tender*] *tender el día,* to dawn.

tenga, *interr.* [<Sp. *tener?*] Do you understand? Will you? (*Aquí le dejo a la plebe, la cuida, ¿en tenga?* I am leaving the children with you; you take care of them, do you understand?) Okay? All right?

tenis, *m. pl.* [<Eng. tennis shoes; tennis] tennis; tennis shoes; *colgar los tenis,* to die (slang).

teno, -na, *adj.* [<Col. N.M. Sp. *tenuo*] tenuous; delicate; subtle. Cf. Sp. *tenue.*

> *Gracia juera que conmigo*
> *dijieras, Gracia, soy güeno,*
> *que en este punto tan teno*
> *cantaras con eficacia.*
> It would be something if to me
> You would say, "Gracia, I am good,"
> And of this subtle subject
> You would sing successfully.
> (*Trovos del Viejo Vilmas,* N.M. Sp. folk poetry)

teóriga, *f.* [<Sp. *teórica,* theory] talk; *echar la teóriga,* to chat, to converse.

tepocate, *m.* [<Mex. Sp. *tepocate*<Náhuatl *tepocatl*] tadpole. Cf. Sp. *renacuajo.*

tepopote, *m.* [<Mex. Sp. *tepopote*<Náhuatl *tepetl,* hill, and *popotl,* stem] bot., Mormon tea. See also *cañutillo.*

tepushque, *m.* [<Mex. Sp. *tepuzque*<Náhuatl *tepuzqui,* copper] a pile of things; a lot; a great number. (*Tengo un tepushque de trastes que fregar.* I have a big pile of dishes to wash.) Also, a concoction; a casserole.

tequesquite, *m.* [<Mex. Sp. *tequesquite*<Náhuatl *tetl,* stone, and *quizquitl,* efflorescent] a crude bicarbonate of soda; bicarbonate of soda; *prenderse uno como hierba 'e tequesquite,* to be a nuisance.

> *Tequesquite* is a crude sodium bicarbonate which forms on the borders of mineral springs in New Mexico, and which is also found near several lakes of the state. (Leonora S. M. Curtin, *Healing Herbs of the Upper Rio Grande*)

tequitato, *m.* [<Náhuatl *tequihuaque?*, warrior] Col. N.M. Sp., a kind of town crier in an Indian pueblo; a kind of constable.

> These *caciques* have under them . . . *tequitatos,* who are like *alguaciles* [constables], and who execute in the pueblo the *cacique's* orders, just exactly like the Mexican people. And when the Spaniards ask the *caciques* of the pueblos for anything, they call the *tequitatos,* who cry it out through the pueblo in a loud voice, whereupon they bring with great haste what is ordered. (H. E. Bolton, *Spanish Explorers in the Southwest*)

tercera, *f.* [<Sp. *tercera,* third] third gear (auto).

terciar, *vb.* [<Mex. Sp. *terciar,* to carry an object on one's back] to throw a serape over one's shoulder.

tercio, *m.* [<Mex. Sp. *tercio,* bale] bale of hay; *a tercios,* by thirds. In a land worked *a tercios,* the farmer kept two thirds of the produce and turned over one third to the owner of the farm.

teretón, *adj.* [<Am. Sp. *terete,* robust] *carnero teretón,* seed ram. See *carnero.*

terquear, *vb.* [<Sp. *terco,* obstinate] to insist; to bother.

terregal, *m.* [<Sp. *tierra,* earth] dusty place; excessive dust; loose dirt.

terrenazo, *m.* [<Sp. *tierra,* earth] hometown. See also *pais.*

terrero, *m.* [<Sp. *tierra,* earth] cloud of dust; dusty place.

terribloso, -sa, *adj.* [<Sp. aug. of *terrible*] terribly mischievous.

terromote, *m.* [<Sp. *terremoto,* earthquake] whirlwind.

terrón (terrones), *m.* [<Sp. *tierra,* earth] sod squares held together by plant roots. *Terrones* are used as adobes in house construction.

tesgüín, *m.* [<Mex. Sp. *tesgüino,* alcoholic beverage] a kind of homemade corn liquor. Also, *tesgüino, tisgüín.*

testa, *f.* [<Sp. *testa,* forehead] head.

testear, *vb.* [<Eng. to taste] to taste; to try. (*Testea esta birria a ver si ya esta fría suficiente.* Try this beer to see if it is cold enough.)

testiga, *f.* [<Sp. *f.* of *testigo,* witness] female witness.

teta, *f.* [<Sp. *teta,* teat] nursing bottle; pacifier; *hecho teta,* sulking; *prendido de la teta,* feeding from the public trough.

tetera, *f.* [<Am. Sp. *tetero*] nursing bottle.

tetones, *m. pl.* [<Sp. aug. of *teta,* teat] young green pods of the female cottonwood.

tichear, *vb.* [<Eng. to teach] to teach; to instruct.

tiempo, *m.* [<Sp. *tiempo,* time; weather] time in general; menstrual period. (*Le vino su tiempo.* She is menstruating.) *Tener un buen tiempo,* to have a good time; *tiempo santo,* Holy Week; *sacar uno su tiempo,* to draw one's pay upon dismissal.

tienda, *f.* [<Mex. Sp. *tienda,* store] *tienda de daime,* ten-cent store; *tienda de quince,* fifteen-cent store; *tienda de segunda,* secondhand store.

tiendajón, *m.* [<Sp. *tendajón,* tent] grocery store.

tiendero, -ra, *m.* and *f.* [<N.M. Sp. *tienda,* grocery store] grocery-store keeper.

tiento, *m.* [<Sp. *tiento,* maulstick] a kind of bundle carried on the back of a saddle.

tierra, *f.* [<Sp. *tierra,* land] earth, ground; land; *tierra amarilla,* yellow stained mica; a kind of beige yellow clay used on the lower quarter of a wall, as a wainscot; *tierra bayita* (same as *tierra amarilla*); *tierra blanca,* white clay used in whitewashing walls; *tierra negra,* black earth; *tierra de oro* (same as *tierra amarilla*); *tierra de rata* or *de tuza,* earth dug up by gophers; *tierras de pan llevar,* arable lands; *poner tierras por medio,* to make tracks, to get away.

tíguere, *m.* [<Sp. *tigre*] tiger (also, jaguar, wildcat).

tildío, *m.* [<Mex. Sp. *tildío,* sandpiper] a kind of waterbug. See *sabandija.*

tiliches, *m. pl.* [<Mex. Sp. *tiliches*] odds and ends; trifles.

tilma, *f.* [<Mex. Sp. *tilma*<Náhuatl *tilmatli,* cape] Col. and Terr. N.M. Sp., a kind of poncho; a short Indian saddle blanket.

timbrero, *m.* [<Eng. timberman] lumberjack.

tinaja, *f.* [<Sp. *tinaja,* a large earthen jar] a kind of natural rock tank.

They [Rocky Mountain bighorn or *carnero cimarrón*] are more dependent on water than many desert creatures, and one of the best places to observe them is at a spring or one of those natural rock tanks called *tinajas* (tih-NAH-hahs) by the Spanish. (George Olin, *Animals of the Southwest Deserts*)

tinamaiste, *m.* [<Mex. Sp. *tinamaste* or *tenamaste*<Náhuatl *tenamaxtli*<*tetl,* stone, and *namictia,* to level] trivet. Also, *tinamaishte.*

Cooling was done in three places: in outdoor barbecue pits, in outdoor beehive-shaped adobe ovens, and in the fireplace. Because there was no space for a crane or roasting spit or dripping pan, the pot that was to boil stood over a plain iron trivet or *tinamaiste* while things to be kept warm stood on raked-out coals or merely on the warm adobe hearth. (E. Boyd, *Popular Arts of Spanish New Mexico*)

tinieblas, *f. pl.* [<Sp. *tinieblas,* utter darkness] a portion of the Penitente Lenten service which is held in complete darkness.

When midnight comes, a very dramatic ceremony—*las tinieblas* (the tenebrae), commemorates the three hours of darkness that prevailed over the earth when our Lord died. At the beginning of the ceremony, all candles on a tenebrae candelabrum are lighted. These are of yellow wax, with the exception of the candle at the top, which is white. Two singers chant a strophe from the *Miserere* and, immediately after, another pair of singers answers with a stanza from some hymn dealing with the Passion at the end of which two candles on the tenebrae candelabrum are extinguished. A second stanza is sung by each pair of singers, and two more candles are extinguished. This continues until there remains only one, the white candle at the top. The ceremony symbolizes the manner in which the apostles abandoned Jesus. The white candle, which represents Jesus, is removed to another room so that there remains no light in the church. When the church is dark, the *rezador* (prayer leader) shouts: *"Salgan, vivos y difuntos a acompañarnos por el amor de Dios"* ("All ye living and dead persons come forth to join us, for the love of God"). Immediately after, the *rezador* recites the Apostles' Creed three times in a low voice while the members of the congregation make all kinds of noises with wooden clappers, chains, drums, and flutes to symbolize the disturbances of nature when Our Lord died. (Juan B. Rael, *The New Mexican Alabado*)

tinta, *f.* [<Sp. *tinta,* ink] ink; house paint. Cf. Sp. *pintura.*

tinto, -ta, *m.* and *f.* [<Sp. *tinto,* dyed] a Black.

tipleoso, -sa, *adj.* [<Sp. *tiple,* treble; high-pitched] bothersome.

tipo, *adj.* [<Sp. *tipo,* type] well-dressed; good-looking; *echar tipo,* to show off one's clothes.

tíquete, *m.* [<Eng. ticket] ticket (railroad, bus, etc.); traffic ticket or fine. (*Vas mu' rieso, te van a dar un tíquete.* You are going too fast; you are going to get a ticket.)

tira, *f.* [<Mex. Sp. *tiras,* rags] rags; shreds; *hacer tiras y correas de uno,* to give one a sound beating; *hecho tiras,* raggedy, in shreds.

tirada, *f.* [<Mex. Sp. *tirada,* sly action]

social date; rendezvous. Also, *tirón.*

tirado, -da, *adj.* [<Sp. *tirar,* to toss] ugly; useless, worthless; in disarray, as a room (messy).

tirante, *adj.* [<Sp. *tirante,* tense] passed out, as from drinking too much liquor.

tirar, *vb.* [<Sp. *tirar,* to cast] to cast; to shoot; to throw down; *tirar la vuelta,* to die; *tirar la toalla* (<Eng. to throw in the towel), to give up; *tirarse un hombre a una mujer,* to "lay" a woman.

tirili, *adj.* [<Mex. Sp. slang *tirilongo,* zoot-suiter] in the know. (*Es un bato tirili.* He is a dude in the know [slang].)

tiro, *m.* [<Sp. *tiro,* team of oxen] team (basketball, football, etc.). *De a tiro (deatiro),* awful, terrible; mischievous.

tirón, *m.* [<Sp. *tirón,* pull] hard pull; social date. Also, *tirada.*

tis, *m.* [<Mex. Sp. *tis*<Sp. *tisis*] tuberculosis.

tisgüín, *m.* [<Mex. Sp. *tisgüino*] corn liquor; homemade booze.

titiritear, *vb.* [<Sp. *tiritar*] to shiver, as from cold or fear.

tlaco, *m.* [<Mex. Sp. *tlaco*] Col. N.M. Sp., a copper coin worth one and a half *centavos.*

tlazole, *m.* [<Mex. Sp. *tlazole*] straw.

toallita, *f.* [<Sp. dim. of *toalla,* towel] small towel; *toallita de la cara,* washcloth.

tobazo, *m.* [<Sp. *tobazo,* cotton thistle] bot., Johnson grass.

toca, *f.* [<Sp. *toca,* a kind of hood] hood; covering; *hacer tocas pa que tapen bocas,* to try to put a rumor down because rumors fly.

tocar, *vb.* [<Sp. *tocar,* to touch, etc.] to happen. (*Tocó que ya no se murió.* It so happened that he did not die after all.) To have the occasion to. (*Me tocó ver el eclís.* I had the occasion to see the eclipse.)

tocayo, -ya, *m.* and *f.* [<Mex. Sp. *tocayo* <Náhuatl *tocaitl,* alter ego] namesake.

tofe, *adj.* [<Eng. tough] tough. Also, *tofote.*

toga, *f.* [<Sp. *toga,* dignity (of a judge)] false pride; snobbishness. (*De esa toga murió mi gato.* How snobbish can you get! [An expression used to put down a snobbish person.])

togado, -da, *adj.* [<N.M. Sp. *toga,* snobbishness] snobbish; haughty.

toloache, *m.* [<Mex. Sp. *toloache*<Náhuatl *toloa,* and *tzin*] bot., Thorn apple, Mad apple, Jimson weed.

tolvache, *m.* [<Mex. Sp. *tolvache*] bot., a plant used in curing body sores.

tolvonudo, -da, *adj.* [<unknown origin] fat; bulging.

tomado, -da, *adj.* [<Mex. Sp. *pt. part.* of *tomar,* to imbibe] drunk, tipsy.

tomar, *vb.* [<Mex. Sp. *tomar,* to imbibe] to imbibe; to succeed. (*Tomé escapar.* I succeeded in escaping.) To feel obligated or forced to. (*Tomo estarme aquí fregando los trastes.* I have to stay here washing the dishes.) *Tomar efecto,* to take effect; *tomar lugar,* to take place; *tomar uno su tiempo,* to take one's time.

tomatillo, *m.* [<Mex. Sp. dim. of *tomate*] a kind of green tomato; bot., Ground cherry; *tomatillo chico,* bot., Chico bush; *tomatillo del campo,* bot., Bull nettle.

tombé, *m.* [<Indian *tombé*] a kind of Indian drum.

tomisto, -ta, *adj.* [<Mex. Sp. *tomar,* to imbibe] addicted to drinking; applied to a habitual drinker.

tompeate, *m.* [<Mex. Sp. *tompeate*] a kind of basket; pannier.

ton, *m.* [<Eng. ton] ton. Cf. Sp. *tonelada.*

tonel, *m.* [<Sp. *tonel,* barrel] ton; ton truck; racklike sideboard put on wagons or trucks; tunnel; hay-loader.

tonses, *m. pl.* [<Eng. tonsils] tonsils.

tontear, *vb.* [<Mex. Sp. *tontear*<*tonto,* stupid] to miss an opportunity through sheer stupidity.

tontera, *f.* [<Mex. Sp. *tontera*] foolish act; stupidity. Cf. Sp. *tontería.*

topadero, *m.* [<Sp. *topar,* to meet by chance] goal in the game of *chueco,* q.v.

topil, *m.* [<Indian *topil*] rod of justice; mayor of an Indian pueblo; constable.
　　In New Mexican Spanish, **topil** has usually the meaning of *alcalde, alguacil,* hence applied to the cane or club which he carried, then to the club in general. (A. M. Espinosa, "New Mexican Spanish Folklore," *The Journal of American Folklore*)

toque, *m.* [<Sp. *toque,* touch] puff of a marihuana cigarette (slang).

torcer, *vb.* [<Sp. *torcer,* to twist] to nab (slang); *torcer el rabo,* to die; *torcer el pico,* to die (applied to birds); *torcerse una persona,* to act bashful or shy; to wince, as from a blow or from pain.

torcha, *f.* [<Eng. torch] torch; welding torch.

torchero, *m.* [<Sp. *antorcha,* torch] tall tin candelabra.
　　She fashioned a pair of tall tin candelabra or **torcheros,** holding seven candles in each, a very striking design of bird wings and plant forms which decorate a nook just off the entrance hall. (Ina Sizer Cassidy, "Art and Artists of New Mexico," *New Mexico Magazine*)

toreado, -da, *adj.* [<Sp. *toreado,* mocked <*toro,* bull] sly, cunning; hard to fool or to deceive; experienced. (*Esa güisa está muy toreada.* That chick has been around [is experienced].) Also, *toreadito, toreadita.*

torear, *vb.* [<Sp. *torear,* to mock] to tease; to nettle; *torearse,* to frustrate oneself.

toriquear, *vb.* [<N.M. Sp. *toro*<Eng. bull (idle talk)] to shoot the bull (slang).

torito, *m.* [<Sp. dim. of *toro,* bull] a kind of cocklebur; *torito de la virgen,* ant lion.

tornaboda, *f.* [<Mex. Sp. *tornaboda*] celebration that takes place the day after a wedding.

tornillo, *m.* [<Sp. *tornillo,* screw] screw; bot., Screw bean; *faltarle un tornillo a una persona,* to be "nuts" or off one's rocker.

torote, *m.* [<Mex. Sp. *torote*] a shrub

with enlarged or thickened bark which holds a supply of water.

torque, *m.* [<Eng. turkey] tom turkey. See also *ganso*.

torre, *f.* [<Sp. *torre*, tower] *darle a uno en la torre*, to give someone a sound beating.

torrejas, *f. pl.* [<Sp. *torrejas*, fritters] egg fritters; *torrejas con chile*, egg fritters with chile.

torreón, *m.* [<Sp. aug. of *torre*, tower] Col. N.M. Sp., a round-shaped tower built for defense; *pl.*, round flat stones found in streams. See Sp. *lajas*.

torta, *f.* [<Sp. *torta*, loaf] loaf of bread; *estar prendido de la torta*, to be feeding from the public trough. See also *teta*.

tortera, *f.* [<Sp. *torta*] a kind of bread pan; tin or wood cover for adobe ovens.

tosayes, *m. pl.* [<Tewa *tosayes*] strips of dry pumpkin.

tostadas, *f. pl.* [<Mex. Sp. *tostadas*<*tortillas tostadas*] fried tortilla chips.

tostón, *m.* [<Mex. Sp. *tostón*, a coin worth fifty *centavos*] fifty cents; bot., cultivated Cosmos, a plant of the Aster family.

totacho, *m.* [<Mex. Sp. *totache*<Náhuatl *to*, our, and *tatli*, father] our language, i.e., the Spanish language spoken in the American Southwest.

trabajar, *vb.* [<Sp. *trabajar* and Eng. to work] to work; to function. (*Mi relós no trabaja.* My watch is not running [working].)

trabán, *m.* [<Sp. *truhán*, knave] gambler; rogue.

trabar, *vb.* [<Sp. *trabar*, to join] to irritate; to contradict. (*No le trabes.* Don't contradict him. *Nos trabaron los dedos.* They turned us down.)

trácalas, *f. pl.* [<Mex. Sp. *trácalas*] schemes; debts (rare).

tracalero, -ra, *adj.* [<Mex. Sp. *tracalero*, schemer] said of one who owes many bills (rare).

tragedia, *f.* [<Mex. Sp. *tragedia*] ballad dealing with some tragic theme; ballad

in general. Also, *corrido, indita, versos*.

trago, *m.* [<Sp. *trago*, swallow (of liquid)] a drink, especially of liquor. (*Vamos a echarnos un trago.* Let's have a drink.)

traidas y llevadas, *f. pl.* [<Col. N.M. Sp. *traidas y llevadas*] loose women; prostitutes.

> . . . *y al desarmarle, como él se imaginaba que aquellas* **traidas y llevadas** *que le desarmaban eran algunas principales señoras* . . .
> . . . and as they took off his arms, for he imagined that these loose women were some important ladies, . . .
> (Miguel de Cervantes Saavedra, *Don Quijote de la Mancha*)

tramitar, *vb.* [<Sp. *trámite*, procedure] to plot, to plan. Cf. Sp. *tramar*.

tramos, *m. pl.* [<Mex. Sp. slang *tramos*] trousers, pants (slang).

trampa, *f.* [<Sp. *trampa*, trap] trap; spring catch, as on a cigarette case; *pl.*, clothespins. See also *mordaz* and *palito* (*palitos de la ropa*).

trampar, *vb.* [<Sp. *trampa*, trap] to trap; to catch, as a finger. (*Se trampó un dedo.* He caught one of his fingers.) To pin under; to run over, to trample; *trampar oreja*, to retire, to go to bed.

> *Adiós, adiós,*
> *que te vaya bien;*
> *que te* **trampe** *el tren*
> *que te machuque bien.*
> Good-bye, good-bye,
> May you fare well;
> May a train run over you;
> And mangle you well.
> (N.M. and so. Colo. Sp. rhyme)

trampe, *m.* [<Eng. tramp] hobo, tramp; parvenu.

trampear, *vb.* [<Eng. to tramp] to lead the life of a tramp; *trampear el tren*, to ride the rods.

tranca, *f.* [<Sp. *tranca*, bar placed across a door from within] crossbar; lock. (*Échale tranca al carro.* Lock the car.) See *atrancar*.

trancadera, *f.* [<N.M. Sp. *tranca*, lock]

door latch.

trancar, *vb.* [<N.M. Sp. *tranca*, lock] to close; to lock. (*Tranca la puerta.* Close [or lock] the door.) See also *atrancar.*

trancazo, *m.* [<N.M. Sp. *tranca*, crossbar] blow with a *tranca;* blow in general. (*Se dio un trancazo.* He bumped his head.)

tranchete, *m.* [<Sp. *tranchete*, shoemaker's heel knife] meat carver; *mirar de tranchete*, to look out of the corner of one's eye. See also *ganchete.*

traque, *m.* [<Eng. track] railroad track; racetrack; *estar juera del traque*, to be "nuts"; to be goofy.

traqueado, -da, *adj.* [<N.M. Sp. *traque* (*juera del traque*)] goofy; "nuts."

traquear, *vb.* [<Sp. *traquear*, to crack] to burst; to explode. (*La Elisa está que ya traquea.* Elisa is so large [fat with child] that she is about to burst.) To hit with a loud sound (like a slap). (*¡Cállate o te traqueo!* Shut up or I'll slap you good.)

trasbocar, *vb.* [<Mex. Sp. *trasbocar*, to vomit] to breathe one's last breath; to vomit.

trasbocadera, *f.* [<N.M. Sp. *trasbocar*, to vomit] vomiting spell.

traspasado, -da, *adj.* [<Sp. *traspasar*, to transfix] famished; weak from lack of nourishment.

trasquila, *f.* [<Sp. *trasquilar*, to shear] Col. N.M. Sp., a form of branding; shearing season (sheep); work of shearing sheep.

trastes, *m. pl.* [<Mex. Sp. *trastes*, dishes] *trastes de barro*, pottery; *trastes de concha*, china dishes; *fregar los trastes*, to wash the dishes. Cf. Sp. *lavar los platos.*

trastear, *vb.* [<Mex. Sp. *trastear*, to search] to go through or search carelessly through a drawer; to reel, to stagger; to pry into (drawers, trunks, etc.). See also *josear.*

trastero, *m.* [<N.M. Sp. *trastes*, dishes] cupboard; china closet.

trato, *m.* [<Mex. Sp. *trato*, small store or stand] business. (*Esta tienda tiene mucho trato.* This store has a lot of business.)

travesía, *f.* [<Sp. *travesía*, crossing] shortcut.

tray, *m.* [<Eng. try] try; *hacer el tray*, to try, to attempt.

treato, *m.* [<Sp. met. of *teatro*] theatre.

treila, *m.* [<Eng. trailer] trailer. Also, *tréilar.*

treinta-treinta, *m.* [<Eng. thirty-thirty (.30-30) rifle] a .30-30 rifle.

tren, *m.* [<Sp. *tren*, series of things] belongings; furniture; things. (*Aquí llegó la Senaida con su tren.* Senaida just got here with her furniture and belongings.)

tresquilar, *vb.* [<Col. N.M. Sp. *tresquilar*] to shear (sheep).

tripa, *f.* [<Sp. *tripa*, gut] garden hose.

triques, *m. pl.* [<Mex. Sp. *triques*, kitchen utensils] articles of furniture; household goods.

tritear, *vb.* [<Eng. to treat] to treat.

trítico, -ca, *adj.* [<Sp. *crítico*, critical] said of someone who makes fun of or ridicules others' opinions, customs, views, etc.; faultfinding.

tritiquear, *vb.* [<Sp. *criticar*, to criticize] to criticize; to find fault. (*Al Max le gusta mucho tritiquear.* Max sure likes to criticize.)

troca, *f.* [<Eng. truck] truck; *troca de los lumbreros*, fire engine; *troca de dompe*, dump truck.

trocada, *f.* [<N.M. Sp. *troca*, truck] truckload.

trocado, -da, *adj.* [<Sp. *trocar*, to exchange] distorted. (*Habla inglés todo trocado.* He speaks English badly [in a distorted way]. *Trae los zapatos trocados.* He's got his shoes on wrong.)

trocón, *m.* [<N.M. Sp. aug. of *troca*, truck] large truck; semitrailer.

trochil, *m.* [<Col. N.M. Sp. *troxil*, dim. of *trox* [*tróš*], granary] small enclosure; hogpen, pigsty. Cf. Mod. Sp. *troj.*

trochimochi, *adv.* [<Sp. *troche moche*] hel-

ter-skelter; in a confused manner.

troja, *f.* [<Sp. *troj*] granary.

They filled mud **trojas** to the ceiling with rich grain, for these great, big houses were built for abundance and to be self-sustaining. In those years Taos county had become the granary of New Mexico. (Cleofas M. Jaramillo, *Shadows of the Past*)

trojero, -ra, *m.* and *f.* [<N.M. Sp. *troja,* granary] keeper of the *troja* or granary in the game of *cañute.*

Three small earthen pots were then brought into the room. The largest one was given to Tomás, making him the **trojero** of the *Troja Mayor* (the holder of the main granary). One hundred and one kernels were then put into his pot—his *troja.* (Reginaldo Espinosa, "Cañute," *New Mexico Magazine*)

trola, *f.* [<Eng. trowel, trowel for plastering<Mex. Sp. *trola,* match, light] match, light (slang).

trompa, *f.* [<Mex. Sp. *trompa,* snout] snout; thick, protruding lips; *darle a alguien en la trompa,* to hit someone in the mouth; *poner tamaña trompa,* to sulk.

trompada, *f.* [<Mex. Sp. *trompada*] a blow on the face (mouth or nose) with one's hand.

trompeta, *adj.* [<Mex. Sp. *trompeta*] drunk; merry, especially from drinking.

trompezar, *vb.* [<Sp. *tropezar*] to stumble; to trip.

trompezón, *m.* [<Sp. *tropezón*] act of tripping or stumbling.

trompillo, *m.* [<Sp. dim. of *trompo,* top] bot., Morning glory.

trompitas, *f. pl.* [<N.M. Sp. *trompa,* snout] *hacer trompitas,* to pucker the lips.

trompudo, -da, *adj.* [<Mex. Sp. *trompudo*] having a long snout or thick, protruding lips.

troncha, *f.* [<Mex. Sp. *troncha,* food] largest piece, slice or portion of anything. (*La Rafela quiere toda la troncha par' ella.*

Rafela wants the biggest piece for herself.)

troque, *m.* [<Eng. truck] truck. See also *troca.*

troquear, *vb.* [<N.M. Sp. *troque*] to truck.

troquero, -ra, *m.* and *f.* [<N.M. Sp. *troque*] truck driver.

troquita, *f.* [<N.M. Sp. dim. of *troca*] small truck; pickup truck; fancy or brand-new truck.

trotear, *vb.* [<Sp. *trotear,* to trot; to get a person to move quickly] to set on; to incite, to urge on. (*La trotearon que viniera a echarme mis papas.* They set her on to come and tell me off.)

trovo, *m.* [<Sp. *trova,* verse] a kind of poetic composition in which two or more folk poets engage in dialogue covering a wide variety of subjects (philosophy, Biblical themes, etc.). The most popular New Mexico *trovos* are those of old man Vilmas (*El Viejo Vilmas*), Chicoria, Cienfuegos, and other bards; poetic joust.

trucha, *f.* [<Sp. *trucha*] trout; *trucha rosilla,* rainbow trout; *ir a la trucha,* to go fishing; *adj.,* sly, not easily deceived. *¡Truchas!* Look out! Watch it! (slang). *Ponerse trucha,* to be on the lookout (slang).

trusco, *m.* [<Mex. Sp. *trusco*<Sp. *trocisco?,* piece] stool (turd). *¡Come truscos!* Go to blazes! Skip it! Forget it!

tubo, *m.* [<Eng. tube] inner tube.

tucero, *m.* [<Mex. Sp. *tucero*<*tuza,* prairie dog] prairie-dog hole or mound.

tule, *m.* [<Mex. Sp. *tule*<Náhuatl *tullin*] bot., Cattail. See also *aguapá.*

tumbaga, *f.* [<Mex. Sp. *tumbaga,* gold ring] a large ring made of an alloy of copper and gold.

tunel [tunél], *m.* [<Sp. *túnel*<Eng. tunnel] cave; tunnel.

túnico, *m.* [<Sp. *túnico,* a kind of gown] woman's dress; *túnico de cola,* gown with a long train.

tuniquera, *f.* [<N.M. Sp. *túnico,* dress]

169

turco

dressmaker; seamstress.

turco, -ca, *m.* and *f.* [<Col. N.M. Sp. *turco,* Turk, gypsy] gypsy; fortune-teller. Also, *húngaro.*

turra, *f.* [<Sp. *zurra* [Өúřa], flogging] flogging; whipping.

tusa, tusero. See *tuza, tucero.*

tusado, -da, *adj.* [<N.M. Sp. *tusar*] bobbed hair; a style of haircut.

tusar, *vb.* [<Sp. *atusar,* to cut hair evenly] to bob (hair).

tútano, *m.* [<Sp. *tuétano*] bone marrow.

tuza, *f.* [<Mex. Sp. *tuza*<Náhuatl *tuzan*] prairie dog.

Un grito a tiempo saca un cimarrón del monte.
A shout in time gets a stray animal out of the
woods.
(A stitch in time saves nine.)

ubrada, *adj.* [<Sp. *ubre,* udder] applied
to a cow with a swollen udder.

ubre, *m.* [<Sp. *ubre (f.),* udder] udder.

ulcera [*ulséra*], *f.* [<Sp. *úlcera*] ulcer.

¡Újule!, *interj.* [<Mex. Sp. *¡Újule!*] excl.
denoting surprise or ridicule.

úlsuras, *f. pl.* [<Sp. *úlceras*] ulcers.

ullar, *vb.* [<Sp. *aullar*] to howl.

ullido, *m.* [<Sp. *aullido*] howl.

umento, *m.* [<Sp. *aumento*] sideboard
placed on the box of a wagon or truck.

ungüente, *m.* [<Sp. *ungüento*] ointment,
salve. See also *ingüente, salvia.*

uniones, *f. pl.* [<Eng. union suit] heavy
winter underwear.

uno, *m.* [<Sp. *uno,* one] one; *El uno,* name
of one of the four batons used in the
game of *cañute.*
  Another of the *cañutes* was striped
only one fourth part of its surface—
the burnt stripes running to the hol-
low end. At the other end, the closed
end, it had one line drawn. This *cañute* was called *el Uno* (The One).
(Reginaldo Espinosa, "Cañute," *New
Mexico Magazine*)

unto, *m.* [<Sp. *unto,* grease] axle grease.

uñas, *f. pl.* [<Sp. *uñas,* fingernails, toe-
nails] claws, fingernails, talons, toe-
nails. *Uñas largas* (long fingernails), a
term applied to a person known to be
a cleptomaniac; *enseñar* (or *sacar*) *las
uñas,* to show one's teeth; to show one's
true colors; *echar las cinco uñas a una
cosa* or *clavarle la uña a una cosa,* to
steal, to swipe.

Uropa, *f.* [<Sp. *Europa*] Europe.

usía, *m.* and *f.* [<Sp. *usía<vuestra señoría*]
your lordship, sir; ma'am; *un usía,* a
certain someone.

¡Uta!, *interj.* [<Sp. euph. of *¡Puta!*] Damn!
(euph.).

Vale más adorada de viejo que esclava de joven.
Better be an old man's darling than a young
man's slave.

vaca, *f.* [<Sp. *vaca,* cow] cow; female elk; Col. N.M. Sp., *vacas de Cíbola,* buffalo. Also, *cíbolos. Vaca orra,* sterile cow. See *orra.*

vaciar, *vb.* [<Sp. *vaciar,* to empty] to deflate a tire; to empty; *reflex.,* to reach an orgasm.

vaciero, *m.* [<Sp. *vaciero,* a kind of shepherd] Col. N.M. Sp., assistant to a *caporal* (foreman) in a sheep ranch.

vacil, *m.* [<Mex. Sp. *vacilón,* fun] fun, good time; binge.

vacilada, *f.* [<Mex. Sp. *vacilada*] raillery; teasing; noisy mirth.

vacilar, *vb.* [<Mex. Sp. *vacilar*] to kid; to make fun of. (*Te están vacilando.* They are kidding you [pulling your leg].) To deceive or two-time a person. (*Su güisa lo está vacilando.* His girl friend is two-timing him.)

vacilón, *m.* [<Mex. Sp. *vacilón*] good time, fun; binge, carousal, spree.

vagamunda, *f.* [<Sp. *vagamunda,* vaga-

bond] loose woman, prostitute, whore.

vagamundo, *m.* [<Sp. *vagabundo*] irresponsible bum.

vaina, *f.* [<Mex. Sp. *vaina,* lie] *echar vainas,* to cast sarcastic remarks or aspersions.

valer, *vb.* [<Sp. *valer,* to be worth] to be worth. (*No me valió.* I couldn't get away with it.) *Valerse a la comadre,* to swear eternal friendship (one woman to another).

> *Chiquigüitito de flores*
> *no te redames,*
> *que en esta vida y en l'otra*
> *siempre seremos comadres.*
> *Redondito, redondón,*
> *la que **se vale a la comadre***
> *se le parte el corazón.*
> Little flower basket
> Do not spill over,
> For in this life and the next
> We will always be good friends.
> Round and round and round again
> Whoever swears eternal friendship
> Will be brokenhearted.

(N.M. and so. Colo. Sp. *verso popular*)

valorista, *adj.* [<Sp. *valor,* courage] brave, courageous, daring.

valse, *m.* [<Sp. *vals,* waltz] waltz; *valse chiquiao* (or *versiao*), a dance during which dancing partners compliment each other in poetic quatrains.

Eres linda entre las lindas
linda sin comparación
lindos tu padre y tu madre
y linda tu generación.

You are beautiful among the beautiful
Beautiful beyond compare;
Your parents are wonderful
And so is all your lineage.
(N.M. and so. Colo. Sp. *verso popular*)

vallero, *m.* [<N.M. Sp. *del valle*] a kind of blanket with a complicated pattern of stars. The *vallero* is said to have originated in El Valle, near Trampas, New Mexico.

vaqueta, *f.* [<Sp. *vaqueta,* tanned cowhide] leather in general; leather strap.

vaquetón, -na, *adj.* [<Mex. Sp. *vaquetón,* lazy person] impudent; brazen; rude, shameless; *m.* and *f.,* rascal, rogue.

vara, *f.* [<Sp. *vara,* a variable unit of length about 2.8 ft.] *vara de San José,* bot., Hollyhock.

várbula (várvula), *f.* [<Sp. *válvula*] valve.

vargueño, *m.* [<Sp. *vargueño*<Vargas] a kind of desk; a chest-secretary. Also, *bargueño.*

The Spanish clerk worked at a *vargueño,* a sort of chest filled with drawers, from which the lid was let down as a writing surface. (Roland F. Dickey, *New Mexico Village Arts*)

varilla, *f.* [<Sp. *varilla,* small rod] iron rod; pole; fence post; wooden log; beam; *pl.,* rods on a baby's nose.

When a baby was born the first thing the midwife attended to was to *subirle las varias de la nariz,* raise the rods on the baby's nose by pressing with her thumb the roof of the palate so the baby would not grow up *chato,* flat-nosed. (Cleofas M. Jaramillo, *Shadows of the Past*)

varillero, *m.* [<Sp. *varilla,* rod] peddler; hawker. The term *varillero* was applied early in the twentieth century to peddlers in New Mexico (mostly Syrians, Lebanese, etc., who rode the rods under railroad boxcars and went from town to town selling pins, needles, thread, etc.).

varjel, *m.* [<Sp. *verjel,* flower garden] garden (rare).

Hizo que Adán se durmiera
en un hermoso varjel
y le dio una compañera
pa que estuviera con él.

He caused Adam to slumber
In a beautiful flower garden
And gave him a female companion
To live with him there.
(N.M. and so. Colo. Sp. *Entriega de novios*)

varseliana, *f.* [<Mex. Sp. *varsoviana*<Varsovia,* Warsaw] a kind of folk ballroom dance known in New Mexico and southern Colorado as the "put-your-little-foot-forward" dance.

vecino, -na, *m.* and *f.* [<Sp. *vecino,* neighbor] neighbor (friend); citizen; inhabitant; head of a household; Col. N.M. Sp., taxpayer.

vedera, *f.* [<Sp. *vereda*] path; shortcut; *agarrar la vedera,* to take the shortcut.

vega, *f.* [<Sp. *vega*] grassland; meadow; pastureland.

With Mexican independence came a new policy. Lands were granted to individuals for their own use and to groups that were founding colonies. Grants to settlements included farming lands which were later apportioned to individual settlers and pasture lands (*vegas*) which were common grazing lands available to all. (Beatrice Chauvenet, "Titles from the King of Spain," *New Mexico Magazine*)

veigo, *vb.* [<Sp. *veo*<*ver,* to see] I see.

veintidós, *m.* [<Eng. 22 rifle] 22-caliber rifle.

vejentorio, *m.* [<Sp. *vejestorio*] group of old people. Also, *viejestorio.*

vela, *f.* [<Sp. *vela,* candle] candle; *vela 'e sebo,* tallow candle; *vela 'e espelma* or *vela 'e cera,* paraffin or wax candle; *velas de coyote,* coyote candles or cholla stems; *velas de Dios* (candles of our Lord), bot., Yucca.

velados, *m. pl.* [<Sp. *velar,* to keep watch over] newlyweds.

At the first opportunity the newly-married had to be *velados*—that is, they must kneel with the *padrinos* before the sanctuary rail, holding lighted candles, from the Gospel to the end of the Mass services, in order to receive the nuptial blessing. (Cleofas M. Jaramillo, *Shadows of the Past*)

velís, *m.* [<Eng. valise] suitcase. *¡Águila con los velises!* Heads up! Be on the lookout!

velorio, *m.* [<Mex. Sp. *velorio*<Sp. *velatorio*] wake; *velorio de angelito,* vigil for a deceased child. See *angelito. Velorio de santo,* vigil for a saint.

venado, *m.* [<Sp. *venado,* deer] deer; *venado alazán* (or, simply, *alazán*), elk (also known as *bura*). *Venado alanés,* stag.

vender, *vb.* [<Sp. *vender,* to sell] to sell; *venderse una persona,* an expression applied to a person who breaks an object at a store. (*No vayas a quebrar ese pichel porque te vendes.* Don't break that pitcher, because you'll have to pay for it.) *Vender a una mujer,* an expression applied when a man walks along with a woman and she is on the side next to the curb.

vendible, *m.* [<Sp. *vendible,* salable] roadside food stand, as fruit stand, hamburger stand, etc. Cf. Sp. *puesto.*

venia, *f.* [<Col. N.M. Sp. *venia*] permission; *con la venia,* excuse me (said upon taking leave of someone in a group).

Cf. Sp. *con su permiso.*

venida, *f.* [<Sp. *venir,* to come] an intermittent stream sometimes carrying water; a flash flood.

venir, *vb.* [<Sp. *venir,* to come] *venir pa atrás,* to come back, to return; *venirle su tiempo a una mujer,* to menstruate.

venta, *f.* [<Sp. *venta,* sale] sale; Col. N.M. Sp., branding iron or brand with which an animal was rebranded upon being sold. The *venta* or new brand obliterated the brand of the previous owner; quitclaim brand; *venta de remolión,* clearance sale, rummage sale.

venteado, -da, *adj.* [<N.M. Sp. *venta,* quitclaim brand] said of the animal whose brand was tampered with, especially by rebranding.

ventear, *vb.* [<N.M. Sp. *venta,* quitclaim brand] to rebrand with a *venta* or branding iron.

ventosa, *f.* [<Sp. *ventosa*] a kind of laxative suppository.

ver, *vb.* [<Sp. *ver,* to see] to see. (*Ahi veraste tú.* You'll see. You'll find out. [A kind of threat.])

verdolaga, *f.* [<Sp. *verdolaga,* bot., Purslane] bot., Pigweed.

vergüero, *m.* [<Sp. *gargüero*] gullet, windpipe. See also *guargüero.*

verijas, *f. pl.* [<Sp. *verija,* lower abdomen] pubic region; the region of the genitals.

verónicas, *f. pl.* [<Sp. *Verónica,* woman's name] name given to small girls who followed the Penitentes and wiped the brows of those who were flagellating themselves during Easter rites.

verruga, *f.* [<Sp. *verruga,* wart] chafing; scar or scarred tissue; *verruga de borrego,* fold in sheep's skin.

verso, *m.* [<Sp. *verso,* line of poetry] riming couplet; *verso popular,* riming couplet used in Southwest Spanish folk poetry.

vestido, *m.* [<Sp. *vestido,* dress] suit; men's suit of clothes. See *túnico* and Sp. *traje*

(suit).

vía, *f.* [<Sp. *vida,* life] *¡Por vía tuya!* Please! (For your life's sake!)

vía, *vb.* [<Col. N.M. Sp. *vía (veía)*] used to see, was seeing. (*¡Ah, cómo hacía que no lo vía!* I hadn't seen you in ages!)

viaje, *m.* [<Sp. *viaje,* trip] *viaje redondo,* round trip. Cf. Sp. *viaje de ida y vuelta.*

víbora, *f.* [<Sp. *víbora,* viper] rattlesnake.

viborón, *m.* [<N.M. Sp. aug. of *víbora,* rattlesnake] large snake; mythical monster snake principally in Taos and Picurís Indian folklore.

Beyond La Glorieta, the picnic grounds of the Taos people, the Indians forbade white people to enter the river canyon. Stories were told about the Indians having an enchanted gold mine in the mountains; others about the Indians having a *viborón* (monster rattlesnake), to which they fed infant babies on certain feast days, and this was the reason for the non-increase of the Pueblo's population. (Cleofas M. Jaramillo, *Shadows of the Past*)

vicio, *m.* [<Sp. *vicio,* vice, addiction] bad habit; *vicio inocente,* petty vice, bad habit.

Of all the petty vices practiced by the New Mexicans, the *vicio inocente* of smoking is the most intolerable; and yet it is a habit of which the loveliest and the most refined equally partake. (Josiah Gregg, *Commerce of the Prairies*)

vida, *f.* [<Sp. *vida,* life] life; *a vida y contento,* completely pleased; overjoyed; to one's full enjoyment and satisfaction.

vide, *vb.* [<Col. N.M. Sp. *vide*] I saw (*vide, vites, vido, vimos, ——, vieron*). Cf. Mod. Sp. *vi.*

vidrio, *m.* [<Sp. *vidrio,* glass] crystal; glass; windshield (car). Also, *virdio.*

viejacondo, *adj.* See *viejo (viejondo).*

viejestorio, *m.* [<Sp. *vejestorio,* petulant old man] group or gathering of old people.

viejitos (Los viejitos), *m. pl.* [<Sp. dim. of *viejo,* old man] the old men; the old folks; one's aged parents; *Los viejitos,* a folk dance of Mexican provenience.

viejo, -ja, *m.* and *f.* [<Sp. *viejo,* old man] old man, old woman; husband, wife, a term of endearment; *viejondo,* old with respect to others of a young group; *el viejo,* the boss. Also, *el patrón.*

vieneván, *m.* [<Sp. *viene, van*] Col. and Terr. N.M. Sp., spelling primer, so-called because children spelled a word, then recited it: *v-i-e-n-e (viene), v-a-n (van).*

viernes (de los morrodos), *m.* [<Sp. *viernes,* Friday] *Viernes de los morrodos,* Dunce Friday. Col. and Terr. N.M. Sp., tag applied to the last school day of the week when slow learners were kept after school. On Fridays, school children could go home once they had recited their lessons correctly. The *morrodos* (Sp. *modorros*) or slow learners many times had to stay after school and do special chores for the *mestro* or master (teacher). See also *morrodo.* (This information was supplied by Mr. Amador Abeyta of Sabinal, New Mexico.)

viga, *f.* [<Sp. *viga,* beam, log] roof beam; *cargarle la viga a alguno,* to tell someone off. (*Mano 'Pimenio me cargó la viga.* Old man Epimenio told me off.)

villa, *f.* [<Sp. *villa,* town] Col. N.M. Sp., a town with special privileges.

The word *villa* [*veé-yah*] cannot properly be translated into English, for it meant not a mere town or village, but a special settlement with royal prerogatives as a capital, which when grown bigger, would be given the title of Ciudad Real or royal city. (Fray Angélico Chávez, "The Kingdom of New Mexico," *New Mexico Magazine*)

villero, -ra, *adj.* [<Sp. *villa,* town] townspeople; *pl.,* the people of Santa Fe, New Mexico.

Santa Fe never developed enough

175

in Spanish times to become a city; it stayed a *villa* . . . Its inhabitants were not called 'Santa Féans' but *villeros*, even within my memory. (Fray Angélico Chávez, "The Kingdom of New Mexico," *New Mexico Magazine*)

villita, *f.* [<Sp. dim. of *villa*, town] settlement; suburb; village.

vinatero, *m.* [<Sp. *vinatero*, vintner] Col. and Terr. N.M. Sp., distillery.

According to local tradition supplied by Mr. Pascual Martínez of Taos, a "John Rawlins" lived at Taos in the early [18]30's. He and a brother were engaged in the fur trade and later established a distillery, or *vinatero* about three miles up the little Rio Grande cañon in charge of one Pedro Antonio Gallegos. (Lansing B. Bloom, "Barreiro's Ojeada Sobre Nuevo México," *New Mexico Historical Review*)

violín, *m.* [<Sp. *violín*] *de violín*, free, gratis; at someone else's expense.

virdio, *m.* [<Sp. met. of *vidrio*, glass] glass; crystal; windshield (car).

virgüela, *f.* [<Sp. *viruela*] pock; smallpox; *virgüela de gallina*, chicken pox.

visita, *f.* [<Sp. *visita*, visit] subordinate mission administered by a priest in residence at a neighboring parish.

vistas, *f. pl.* [<Sp. *vista*, view] movies; show.

vítores, *m. pl.* [<Sp. *vítor*, shout of joy] Hurrah! Good news!

vitrola, *f.* [<Eng. Victrola] Victrola; phonograph.

vivas, *f. pl.* [<Sp. ¡*Viva!*, Long live . . . !] excl. of joy; compliments; a kind of toast honoring a guest.

vivén, *m.* [<Sp. *vaivén*] fluctuation; vicissitude, turn of events, change.

Recuerdo que me rogaban
los que ahora apenas me ven,
y mirando tal vivén
dándoles consejo estoy . . .
de que hay una gran distancia
la que va de ayer a hoy.

I remember being begged
By those who now hardly see me,
And seeing this turn of events
I am giving you this advice:
There's quite an interval of time
Between yesterday and today.
(N.M. Sp. folk poetry)

volada, *f.* See *bolada*.

volado, -da, *adj.* [<Sp. *volarse*, to become irritated or exasperated] said of the person who gets annoyed or angry on the slightest provocation; flighty; touchy; immature.

volante, *m.* [<Am. Sp. *volante*, a two-wheeled covered vehicle] Col. and Terr. N.M. Sp., a kind of two-wheeled carriage lighter than a *carreta* (oxcart). The latter [the Ecclesiastical Judge don Lorenzo Rivera] is insolvent on the one hand, and on the other, it is known that he keeps a *volante* with which he furnishes the presidios with seeds, etc., and that he is a very wealthy father. (Eleanor B. Adams and Fray Angelico Chávez, *The Missions of New Mexico, 1776*)

volantín, *m.* [<Mex. Sp. *volantín*, somersault] merry-go-round. See *caballito* (*Los caballitos*).

voltear, *vb.* [<Mex. Sp. *voltear*] to turn (a page, a corner, etc.); *voltear pa atrás*, to turn back, to look back.

Entré a la iglesia
y pisé una grada,
voltié pa atrás
y no vide nada.
I went into the church
And stepped upon a step;
I then looked back
And didn't see a thing.
(*La granada*, The Pomegranate, N.M. Sp. riddle)

vuelo, *m.* [<Sp. *vuelo*, flight] flight; *darse vuelo*, to have a good time.

vuelta, *f.* [<Sp. *vuelta*, stroll] stroll; turn; *poner a uno de vuelta y media*, to tell someone off; *tirar la vuelta* (or *tirar la última vuelta*), to die.

Ya está muy viejo Pedro pa cabrero.
Peter is much too old for a goatherd.
(The old gray mare is not what she used to be.)

yagual, *m.* [<Mex. Sp. *yagual*<Náhuatl *yahualli*] a kind of pad or bolster placed on the head to cushion the weight of objects carried on one's head.

yantén, *m.* [<Indian?] bot., Common plantain.

yarda, *f.* [<Eng. yard] yard; yardstick; enclosure; backyard; railroad yard; *yarda de madera,* lumberyard.

yela, *f.* [<Eng. jelly] jelly; *yela de champe,* rosehip jelly.

yema, *f.* [<Sp. *yema,* bud] hangnail.

yerba, *f.* [<Sp. *yerba,* herb; grass] herbs; weeds. (*Cortaron la yerba.* They cut the weeds.) Cf. Sp. *mala yerba. Yerbabuena,* bot., Mint; *yerba de Alonso García,* bot., Feather dalea, a medicinal plant; *yerba de la golondrina,* bot., Spurge; *yerba de la miel virgen,* bot., Indian paintbrush or Painted cup; *yerba de la negrita,* bot., Bristly mallow; *yerba de la peña* or *de la piedra,* bot., Gray lichen, Moss; *yerba de la sangre,* bot., Creeping barberry, Oregon grape; *yerba de la virgen,* bot., Scar-let gaura; *yerba de la víbora,* bot., Snake or Rattlesnake weed; *yerba del apache,* bot., Indian paintbrush or Painted cup (same as *yerba de la miel virgen*); *yerba del buey,* bot., Gum plant; *yerba del caballo,* bot., Groundsel; *yerba del chivato,* bot., Jerusalem oak; *yerba del lobo,* bot., Orange sneezeweed; *yerba del manso,* bot., a plant of the Lizard's tail family; *yerba del negro,* bot., Globe mallow; *yerba del oso,* bot., Cow parsnip; *yerba del pasmo,* bot., Chill weed; *yerba del peco,* bot., Baneberry; *yerba del pescado,* bot., Pennsylvania smartweed; *yerba del pujo,* a plant used in the curing of tenesmus; *yerba parda,* bot., Blueweed; *yerba santa,* bot., Mountain balm.

yerbal, *m.* [<Sp. *yerba,* weeds] a pile of weeds; a place covered with weeds.

yesquera, *f.* [<Sp. *yesquero,* tinderbox] tinderbox.

> If the tinder box, or **yesquera,** ever was common in New Mexico, it has survived only in one example in the collection of the Historical Society.

This one is of German silver and is therefore easily dated in the later 19th century. It is marked "Josefa Valdez" making it the property of a lady. (E. Boyd, "The Use of Tobacco in Spanish New Mexico," *El Palacio*)

yonque, *m.* [<Eng. junk] junk; junkyard. (*Los muchitos jueron al yonque y de allá llegaron con todo este garrero.* The kids went to the junkyard and brought back all this worthless stuff.)

yugo, *m.* [<Mex. Sp. slang *yugo*<Sp. *yugo,* yoke] work (slang); a job. (*¿Quése el Félix?—Todavía en el yugo. Cae aquí como a las cinco de la tarde.* Where's Felix? Still working. He gets here about five o'clock.) See also *jale* and *chamba* (slang).

Zorra vieja no cae en la trampa.
You can't catch old birds with chaff.

zacate, *m.* [<Mex. Sp. *zacate,* grass] grass; hay; straw; *zacate del burro,* cut and dried sagebrush used in the making of brooms (also called *popotón*).

zacatera, *f.* [<N.M. Sp. *zacate,* grass] shed or barn in which hay, straw, etc., are stored.

zacatito, *m.* [<N.M. Sp. dim. of *zacate*] tender grass; lawn; lawn grass. (*Vamos a sentarnos en el zacatito.* Let's sit out on the lawn.)

zacatón, *m.* [<N.M. Sp. aug. of *zacate,* grass] bot., Bunch grass; Porcupine grass.

zacatonal, *m.* [<N.M. Sp. *zacatón,* Bunch grass] spots covered with *zacatón* or Bunch grass.

zafado, -da, *adj.* [<Mex. Sp. *zafado*] crazy, "nuts"; silly.

zafarse, *vb.* [<Mex. Sp. *zafarse,* to become dislocated] to become dislocated (joints, etc.). (*Se le zafó un hombro.* He suffered a shoulder separation.)

zafón, *m.* [<N.M. Sp. *zafarse*] a sudden jerk. (*Pegó un zafón y se nos soltó.* He jerked suddenly and got away from us.)

zaguán, *m.* [<Sp. *zaguán,* entrance hall] entrance; vestibule; a sort of wide outside sheltered entrance or gate; breezeway.

zalea, *f.* [<Sp. *zalea,* sheepskin mat] sheepskin; goatskin; *tender la zalea,* to die.

zampar, *vb.* [<Sp. *zampar*] to thrust one thing into another; to enter; to hit, to strike.

zancajoso, -sa, *adj.* [<Sp. *zancajoso,* clumsy] gawky.

zapatero, *m.* [<Sp. *zapatero,* shoemaker] *quedarse uno zapatero,* to be left without making a single point in a game.

zapato, *m.* [<Sp. *zapato,* shoe] shoe; *zapatos de hule,* rubbers; galoshes; overshoes.

zapeta, *f.* [<Mex. Sp. *zapeta*] diaper.

zarcillo, *m.* [<Sp. *zarcillo,* tendril of a vine or other climbing plant] bot., Fuchsia,

a plant of the Evening primrose family; Bleeding heart.

zoquetal, *m.* [<Mex. Sp. *zoquete,* mud] muddy place; mudhole.

zoquete, *m.* [<Mex. Sp. *zoquete*<Náhuatl *zoquitl*] mud; plaster.

zoquetero, -ra, *m.* and *f.* [<N.M. Sp. *zoquete,* mud, plaster] plasterer, especially one who uses mud to plaster adobe walls.

zoquetoso, -sa, *adj.* [<N.M. Sp. *zoquete,* mud] muddy. *¡Zoquete!* Like heck!

zorra, *f.* [<Sp. *zorra,* fox] fox; *hacer la zorra,* to take time off on the job; to loaf; to goldbrick.

zorrera, *f.* [<N.M. Sp. *zorrero,* loafer] a term applied to a sheep that insists on straying from the flock.

zotea, *f.* [<Sp. *azotea,* flat roof] roof. (*Que no se suban los muchitos a la zotea porque se caen.* Don't let the kids get on the roof because they'll fall.)

zumbado, -da, *adj.* [<Mex. Sp. *zumba,* drunken spree] drunk; tramp.

BIBLIOGRAPHY

Abert, Lt. J.W. *Report of Lieutenant J.W. Abert of His Examination of New Mexico in the Years 1846–47*. House Exec. Doc. No. 41, 30th Cong., 1st sess. Washington: Wendell and Van Benthuysen, 1848.

Abreu, Margaret. "In the New Mexico Kitchen." *New Mexico Magazine* 17, no. 6 (1939)–18, no. 3 (1940).

Adams, Eleanor B., and Chávez, Fray Angélico. *The Missions of New Mexico, 1776*. Albuquerque: University of New Mexico Press, 1956.

Adams, Ramon F. *Western Words: A Dictionary of the American West*. Norman: University of Oklahoma Press, 1968.

Allwell, Patrick J. *Mexican Immigration into the United States*. Master's thesis, University of Missouri, 1928.

Amor, Ricardo. *Diccionario del hampa*. México: Editorial Sol, 1947.

Anonymous. "What Do We Speak?" *El Palacio* 13, no. 10 (1922): 130–31.

Arreola, José María. "Tres vocabularios dialectales del mexicano." *Investigaciones Lingüísticas*, vol. 2. México, 1934.

Austin, Mary. "New Mexican Spanish." *Saturday Review of Literature* 7 (1931): 930.

Bancroft, Hubert Howe. *History of Arizona and New Mexico 1530–1888*. San Francisco: The History Co., Publishers, 1889.

Barker, George Carpenter. *Pachuco: An American Spanish Argot and Its Social Functions in Tucson, Arizona*. Tucson: University of Arizona Press, 1970.

Benavides, Fray Alonso de. *Memorial 1630*. Translated and edited by Mrs. Edward E. Ayer. Albuquerque: Horn and Wallace, 1965.

Bentley, Harold W. *A Dictionary of Spanish Terms in English*. New York: Columbia University Press, 1933.

Bloom, Lansing B. "Barreiro's 'Ojeada Sobre Nuevo México.'" *New Mexico Historical Review* 3, nos. 1 and 2 (1928): 73–96, 145–78.

Bourke, John Gregory. "Customs of the Rio Grande." *Land of Sunshine* 5 (1896): 168–69.

———. "Notes on the Language and Folk Usages of the Rio Grande Valley." *Journal of American Folklore* 9 (1896): 81–115.

Bowen, J. Donald. *The Spanish of San Antonito, New Mexico*. Ph.D. dissertation, University of New Mexico, 1952.

Boyd, E. "Fireplaces and Stoves in Colonial New Mexico." *El Palacio* 65, no. 6 (1958): 219–24.

———. "New Mexican Filigree Jewelry." *El Palacio* 65, no. 4 (1958): 151–53.

———. *Popular Arts of Spanish New Mexico*. Santa Fe: Museum of New Mexico Press, 1974.

———. "Rio Grande Blankets Containing Hand Spun Cotton Yarns." *El Palacio* 71, no. 4 (1964): 22–28.

———. "The Use of Tobacco in Spanish New Mexico." *El Palacio* 65, no. 3 (1958): 103–06.

Brewster, Mela Sedillo. *A Practical Study of the Use of the Natural Vegetable Dyes in New Mexico*. Albuquerque: University of New Mexico Bulletin No. 306, May, 1937.

Brown, Frances R. "The Spanish Had a Name for Them." *New Mexico Magazine* 20 (1942): 14, 29–30.

Brown, Lawrence K. *A Thesaurus of Spanish Idioms and Everyday Language*. New York: The Marcel Rodd Co., 1945.

Brown, Lorin W. *Folktales*. Manuscript in files of New Mexico Writers' Project. Santa Fe, n.d.

———. *Se volcó la olla*. Manuscript in files of New Mexico Writers' Project. Santa Fe, n.d.

Bunting, Bainbridge. *Taos Adobes*. Santa Fe: Museum of New Mexico Press, 1964.

Bursey, Joseph A. "Horses of the Southwest." *New Mexico Magazine* 11 (1933): 10–12, 36–37.

———. "Minerals of New Mexico." *New Mexico Magazine* 11 (1933): 22–25.

Campa, Arthur León. "Religious Spanish Folk Drama in New Mexico." *New Mexico Quarterly* 2 (1932): 3–13.

———. *Sayings and Riddles in New Mexico*. University of New Mexico Bulletin, Language Series 6, no. 2, 1937.

———. *Spanish Folk Poetry in New Mexico*. Albuquerque: University of New Mexico Press, 1946.

Calderón de la Barca, Pedro. *Teatro*. Colección Austral. Buenos Aires, n.d.

Cárdenas, Freddie. "Décimas." *Compendio de folklore nuevomejicano*. Santa Fe: Sociedad Folklórica, n.d.

Carlisle, Rose Jeanne. *A Southwestern Dictionary*. Master's thesis, University of New Mexico, 1939.

182

Carreño, Alberto María. "El habla popular de México." *Revista de la Facultad de Letras y Ciencias Sociales* 33. Universidad de la Habana, 1916.

Castañeda, Pedro de. *The Journey of Coronado, 1540–1542.* Translated and edited by George Parker Winship. New York: A.S. Barnes, 1904.

Cerda, Gilberto; Cabaza, Berta; and Farías, Julieta. *Vocabulario español de Texas.* Austin: University of Texas Press, 1953.

Cervantes Saavedra, Miguel de. *Don Quijote de la Mancha.* 8 vols. Madrid: Espasa Calpe, S.A., 1964.

Chabat, Carlos G. *Diccionario de caló. El lenguaje del hampa en México.* México: Librería de Medicina, 1964.

Chacón, Herminia B. "The Christ Child Comes to New Mexico." *New Mexico Magazine* 10 (1932): 7–9, 45–56.

Chávez, Fray Angélico. *My Penitente Land: Reflections on Spanish New Mexico.* Albuquerque: University of New Mexico Press, 1974.

———. "Neo-Mexicanisms in New Mexico Place Names." *El Palacio* 57, no. 3 (1950): 67–69.

———. *Origins of New Mexico Families.* Santa Fe: Historical Society of New Mexico, 1954.

Cobos, Rubén. "Canciones españolas que todavía se cantan en Nuevo México." *El Nuevo Mexicano.* Santa Fe, November 9, 1950.

———. "Desarrollo de la canción nuevomexicana." *El Nuevo Mexicano.* Santa Fe, August 3, 1950.

———. "Despedida de novios." *El Nuevo Mexicano.* Santa Fe, November 10, 1949.

———. "Despedimentos y cuándos." *El Nuevo Mexicano.* Santa Fe, April 27, 1950.

———. "El corrido nuevomexicano." *El Nuevo Mexicano.* Santa Fe, January 26, 1950.

———. "El cuándo narrativo." *El Nuevo Mexicano.* Santa Fe, June 1, 1950.

———. "El folklore nuevomexicano." *El Nuevo Mexicano.* Santa Fe, October 6, 1949.

———. "Entriega de bautismo." *El Nuevo Mexicano.* Santa Fe, November 10, 1949.

———. "Entriega de novios." *El Nuevo Mexicano.* Santa Fe, October 20, 1949.

———. "Five New Mexico Spanish Folktales." *New Mexico Folklore Record* 13. Albuquerque, n.d.

———. *Guides to the Rubén Cobos Collection of New Mexican Indo-Hispanic Folklore.* 2 vols. Manuscript in Tutt Library, The Colorado College. Colorado Springs, 1975–76.

———. "La copla popular como planta de la décima." *El Nuevo Mexicano.* Santa Fe, October 13, 1949.

———. "La indita nuevomexicana." *El Nuevo Mexicano.* Santa Fe, March 30, 1950.

———. "New Mexico Luminarias." *The New Mexican,* Santa Fe, December 23, 1962.

———. *Refranes españoles del sudoeste. Southwest Spanish Proverbs.* Cerrillos, New Mexico: San Marcos Press, 1973.

————. "The New Mexican Game of Valse Chiquiao." *Western Folklore* 15, no. 2 (1956).

————. "The New Mexican Memoria or In Memoriam Poem." *Western Folklore* 18, no. 1 (1959).

————. "Trovo entre el Viejo Vilmas y Gracia." *El Nuevo Mexicano.* Santa Fe, January 26, 1950.

————, ed. *Recopilación de las leyes de los reynos de las Indias.* Bureau of Indian Affairs. Albuquerque, 1967.

Cooke, Lt. Col. P. St. George. *Report of Lt. Col. P. St. George Cooke of His March from Santa Fe, New Mexico, to San Diego, Upper California, 1846–47.* House Exec. Doc. No. 41, 30th Cong., 1st sess. Washington: Wendell and Van Benthuysen, 1848.

Córdova, Gilberto Benito. "Certain Curious Colonial Chicano Cosmetological Customs." *El Cuaderno* 3, no. 2 (1974): 19–27.

Costales, Dionisio. *Spanish Games in New Mexico.* Master's thesis, University of New Mexico, 1937.

Crook, Alice M. *Cowboy Dictionary.* Manuscript in files of New Mexico Writers' Project. Santa Fe, n.d.

Curtin, Leonora S.M. *Healing Herbs of the Upper Rio Grande.* Santa Fe: The Rydal Press, 1947.

Cuyás, Arturo. *Appleton's New Cuyás English-Spanish, Spanish-English Dictionary.* Englewood Cliffs: Prentice-Hall, 1972.

Darley, Alex M. *The Passionists of the Southwest, or The Holy Brotherhood.* Glorieta, New Mexico: Rio Grande Press, 1968.

Davidson, Levette J., and Koehler, Olga Hazel. "The Naming of Colorado's Towns and Cities." *American Speech* 7, no. 3: 180–87.

Davis, W.W.H. *El Gringo, or New Mexico and Her People.* New York: Harper, 1857.

De León, Aurelio. *Barbarismos comunes en México.* México, 1936.

Dickey, Roland F. *New Mexico Village Arts.* Albuquerque: University of New Mexico Press, 1949.

Dunton, Nellie. *The Spanish Colonial Ornament.* Philadelphia: H.C. Perleberg, 1935.

Edmonson, Munro S. *Los Manitos: A Study of Institutional Values.* New Orleans: Middle American Research Institute, Tulane University, 1957.

El Cuaderno. Edited by Estevan Arellano. Dixon, New Mexico: La Academia de la Nueva Raza, 1974.

El Espejo: Selected Mexican-American Literature. Edited by Octavio I. Romano V. Berkeley: Quinto Sol, 1969.

El Grito. A Journal of Contemporary Mexican-American Thought. Edited by Herminio C. Ríos. Berkeley: Quinto Sol, 1972.

Emory, W.H. *Notes of a Military Reconaissance from Fort Leavenworth, in Missouri, to San Diego, in California, Including Part of the Arkansas, Del Norte, and Gila Rivers, 1846–47.* House Exec. Doc. No. 41, 30th Cong., 1st sess. Washington: Wendell and Van Benthuysen, 1848.

Entre Verde y Seco. Edited by Estevan Arellano. Dixon: La Academia de la Nueva Raza, 1972.

Espinosa, Aurelio M. "Apuntaciones para un diccionario de nuevomejicanismos; algunas formas verbales, raras y curiosas." *Estudios Eruditos in Memoriam de Adolfo Bonilla y San Martín* 2 (1930): 615–25.

———. "Cuentitos populares nuevo-mejicanos y su transcripción fonética." *Bulletin de Dialectologie Romane* 4 (1912): 97–105.

———. "El desarrollo fonético de las palabras 'todo' 'y' en la frase 'con todo y + substantivo' en el español de Nuevo Méjico." *Investigaciones Lingüísticas* 2, nos. 3 and 4: 195–99.

———. *Estudios sobre el Español de Nuevo México. Parte I, Fonética.* Buenos Aires: Instituto de Filología, Biblioteca de Dialectología Hispanoamericana, 1930.

———. *Estudios sobre el Español de Nuevo México. Parte II, Morfología.* (Translation of *Studies in New Mexican Spanish, Part II, Morphology,* with comparative notes by Angel Rosenblat.) Buenos Aires: Instituto de Filología, Biblioteca de Dialectología Hispanoamericana, 1930.

———. "Los 'Agüelos' de Nuevo Méjico." Santander, Spain. Reprint from the *Boletín de la Biblioteca de Menéndez Pelayo,* 1945.

———. *Los Comanches.* University of New Mexico Bulletin, Language Series 1, no. 1, 1907.

———. "New Mexican Spanish Coplas Populares." *Hispania* 18, no. 1 (1935): 135–50.

———. "New Mexican Spanish Folklore." *Journal of American Folklore* 23 (1910): 395–481; 24 (1911): 397–444; 25 (1912): 395–418; 26 (1913): 97–122; 27 (1914): 105–47; 28 (1915): 315–52; 29 (1916): 505–35.

———. "Nombres de bautismo nuevomejicanos." *Revue de Dialectologie Romane* 5 (1913): 356–73.

———. *Romancero de Nuevo Méjico.* Madrid: Revista de Filología Española, 1953.

———. "Spanish Folklore in New Mexico." *New Mexico Historical Review* 1, no. 2 (1926): 135–55.

———. "Speech Mixture in New Mexico." In *The Pacific Ocean in History,* edited by H. Morse Stephens and Herbert Bolton. New York: MacMillan and Co., 1917.

———. *The Spanish Language in New Mexico and Southern Colorado.* Historical Society of New Mexico, Publication 16. Santa Fe, 1911.

Espinosa, Carmen. "Color for Mi Casa." *New Mexico Magazine* 17, no. 5 (1939): 18, 41–42.

———. "Fashions in Filigree." *New Mexico Magazine* 17, no. 9 (1939): 22–23, 43.

Espinosa, Gilberto. "Los Comanches." *New Mexico Quarterly* 1, no. 2 (1931): 133–46.

———. "New Mexico Santos." *New Mexico Magazine* 13, no. 3 (1935): 9–11, 43; no. 4 (1935): 22–23, 36–37; no. 5 (1935): 24–25.

———. "New Mexico Santos." *New Mexico Quarterly* 6, no. 3 (1936): 181–89.

Espinosa, José E. *Saints in the Valleys.* Albuquerque: University of New Mexico Press, 1960.

Espinosa, Reginaldo. "Cañute." *New Mexico Magazine* 11, no. 5 (1933): 16–17, 46–48.

Federal Writers' Project, W.P.A. *New Mexico: A Guide to the Colorful State.* New York: Hastings House, 1940.

Fergusson, Erna. *Our Southwest.* New York: Alfred Knopf, 1940.

Freire-Marreco, Barbara. "New Mexican Spanish Folklore." *Journal of American Folklore* 29, no. 114 (1916): 536–46.

Gamio, Manuel. *Mexican Immigration to the United States: A Study of Human Migration and Adjustment.* Chicago: University of Chicago Press, 1930.

Gilbert, Fabiola C. de Baca. *The Good Life.* 1949. Reprint. Santa Fe: Museum of New Mexico Press, 1982.

———. *We Fed Them Cactus.* Albuquerque: University of New Mexico Press, 1954.

González, Dolores, ed. *Canciones y juegos de Nuevo México. Songs and Games of New Mexico.* Cranbury: A.S. Barnes and Co., 1974.

González, Nancie L. *Spanish-Americans of New Mexico: A Heritage of Pride.* Albuquerque: University of New Mexico Press, 1967.

Gray, Edward D. McQueen. *Spanish Language in New Mexico: A National Resource.* University of New Mexico Bulletin, Sociological Series 1, no. 2, 1912.

Greene, E.L. "Rambles of a Botanist in New Mexico." *American Naturalist* 12 (1878): 172–208.

Gregg, Josiah. *Commerce of the Prairies.* Edited by Max L. Moorhead. Norman: University of Oklahoma Press, 1954.

Hardman, Martha James. *The Phonology of the Spanish of El Prado, New Mexico.* Master's thesis, University of New Mexico, 1956.

Haught, B.F. "The Language Difficulty of Spanish-American Children." *Journal of Applied Psychology* 15 (1931): 92–95.

Hills, E.C. "New Mexican Spanish." *Modern Language Association Publications* 21, no. 3, 1906.

Horka-Follick, Lorayne Ann. *Los Hermanos Penitentes.* Los Angeles: Westernlore Press, 1969.

Hughes, John T. *Doniphan's Expedition; Containing an Account of the Conquest of New Mexico.* Cincinnati: J.A. Co., 1848.

Jaramillo, Cleofas M. *Shadows of the Past.* 1941. Reprint. Santa Fe: Ancient City Press, 1980.

Johnston, Capt. A.R. *Journal of Captain A.R. Johnston, First Dragoons, 1846–47.* House Exec. Doc. No. 41, 30th Cong., 1st sess. Washington: Wendell and Benthuysen, 1848.

Keleher, William Aloysius. *Memoirs, 1892–1969: A New Mexico Item.* Santa Fe: Rydal Press, 1969.

Kercheville, F.M. *A Preliminary Glossary of New Mexican Spanish.* University of New Mexico Bulletin, Language Series 5, no. 3, 1934.

———. "Dialogues of Don Plácido." *New Mexico Magazine* 14, no. 7 (1936)–20, no. 7 (1942); 24, no. 1 (1946)–24, no. 12 (1948).

———. "Spanish and English in the American Southwest." *New Mexico School Review* 16 (1936): 24–25.

Kiddle, Lawrence B. "Los nombres del pavo en el dialecto nuevomejicano." *Hispania* 24 (1941): 213–16.

———. " 'Turkey' in New Mexican Spanish." *Romance Philology* 5 (1951–52): 190–97.

Kittle, J.L. "An Authentic Form of Folk Music in Colorado." *Colorado Magazine* 22, no. 2 (1945): 59–63.

———. "Folk Music of the Upper Rio Grande." *Southwest Review* 30, no. 2 (1945): 192–95.

———. *Leyes del Estado de Nuevo México.* Translated by Imelda E. Chávez. Albuquerque: Valliant, 1925.

———. *Leyes del Estado de Nuevo México.* Translated by Juan A.A. Sedillo, Ireneo L. Chaves, and Juan D. Kavanaugh. Santa Fe (?), 1927.

Lucero White Lea, Aurora. "Folkways and Fiestas." *New Mexico Magazine* 18, no. 3 (1940): 18–19, 44.

———. *Literary Folklore of the Hispanic Southwest.* San Antonio: The Naylor Co., 1955.

———. *Los Hispanos.* Denver: Sage Books, 1947.

Lummis, Charles F. *Land of Poco Tiempo.* New York: Scribners, 1913.

———. *Mesa, Cañon, and Pueblo.* New York: Century, 1925.

———. *Some Strange Corners of Our Country.* New York: Century, 1906.

Magoffin, Susan Shelby. *Down the Santa Fe Trail, 1846–47.* New Haven: Yale University Press, 1926.

Malaret, Augusto. *Diccionario de Americanismos.* Buenos Aires: Academia Argentina de Letras, 1942.

Martínez, Filemón. "Conservation and Purification of the Spanish Language." *Lulac News* 5 (1938): 13–18.

Martínez, Reyes N. *The First Phonograph.* Manuscript in files of New Mexico Writers' Project. Santa Fe, n.d.

———. *The Weaver of Talpa.* Manuscript in files of New Mexico Writers' Project. Santa Fe, n.d.

McSpadden, George. *Some Semantic and Philological Facts of the Spanish Spoken in Chilili, New Mexico.* University of New Mexico Bulletin, Language Series 5, no. 3, 1934.

Molina, Flavio M. *Nombres indígenas de Sonora y su traducción al Español.* Hermosillo, Sonora: Impresora y Editorial, S.A. de C.V., n.d.

Molina, Fray Alonso de. *Vocabulario en lengua Castellana y Mexicana y Mexicana y Castellana.* 1571. Reprint. México: Editorial Porrúa, 1970.

Neuman and Baretti. *Dictionary of the Spanish and English Languages.* 2 vols. Boston: Wilkins, Carter, and Co., 1847.

Northrop, Stuart A. *Minerals of New Mexico.* University of New Mexico Bulletin, Geological Series 6, no. 1, 1942.

Pearce, Thomas M., ed. *New Mexico Place Names: A Geographical Dictionary.* Albuquerque: University of New Mexico Press, 1965.

———. *Southwest Heritage: A Literary History with Bibliography.* Albuquerque: University of New Mexico Press, 1938.

Pearce, Thomas M., and Thomason, A.P. *Southwesterners Write.* Albuquerque: University of New Mexico, 1946.

Pino, Pedro B. *Exposición sucinta y sencilla de la provincia del Nuevo México; hecha por su diputado en cortes don Pedro Baptista Pino, con arreglo á sus instrucciones.* Cádiz: Imprenta del Estado Mayor General, 1812.

187

Place, Edwin B. *Group of Mystery Plays Found in a Spanish-Speaking Region of Southern Colorado.* University of Colorado Studies 18, no. 1 (1930): 1–8.

Pooler, Lolita H. *Cuentos populares de Nuevo Méjico, recogidos.* Bachelor's thesis, University of New Mexico, 1930.

Rael, Juan B. "Alternate Forms in Speech of the Individual." *Studies in Philology* 36, no. 4 (1939): 664–70.

———. *A Study of the Phonology and Morphology of New Mexico Spanish Based on a Collection of 400 Folktales.* Ph.D. dissertation, Stanford University, 1937.

———. " 'Cosa nada' en el español nuevomejicano." *Modern Language Notes* 69, no. 1 (1934): 31–32.

———. *Cuentos Españoles de Colorado y de Nuevo México.* 2 vols. Stanford: Stanford University Press, n.d.

———. "New Mexican Spanish Feasts." *California Folklore Quarterly* 1, no. 1 (1942): 83–90.

———. "New Mexico Wedding Songs." *Southern Folklore Quarterly* 4, no. 2 (1940): 55–72.

———. *The New Mexican Alabado.* Stanford: Stanford University Press, 1951.

———. *The Sources and Diffusion of the Mexican Shepherds' Plays.* Guadalajara: Librería La Joyita, 1965.

Raillière, Father J.B. *Colección de cantos espirituales.* Las Vegas, New Mexico. Revised edition. El Paso, 1956.

Raines, Lester. *The Laxative of the Strangers.* Manuscript in files of New Mexico Writers' Project. Santa Fe, n.d.

Ramos Duarte, Félix. *Diccionario de mexicanismos.* México, 1898.

Real Academia Española. *Diccionario de la lengua.* Madrid: Real Academia Española, 1949.

Reindorp, Reginald. *The New Mexican Décima.* Master's thesis, University of New Mexico, 1933.

Rendón, Gabino. *Hand on my Shoulder.* New York: Board of National Missions, The United Presbyterian Church in the U.S.A., n.d.

Ribera Ortega, Peter. *Christmas in Old Santa Fe.* Santa Fe: Piñón Publishing Co., 1961.

Richie, Eleanor L. "Spanish Place Names in Colorado." *American Speech* 10, no. 2 (1935): 88–92.

Robb, J.D. *Spanish Folk Songs of New Mexico.* Albuquerque: University of New Mexico Press, 1957.

Robelo, Cecilio A. *Diccionario de aztequismos.* México: Ediciones Fuente Cultural, n.d.

Romancero español. Colección Austral. Buenos Aires, n.d.

Romero, Cecil V. "A Unique American Chronicle." *El Palacio* 24, no. 19 (1938): 154–65.

———. "Notes on New Mexican Spanish." *El Palacio* 24, no. 16 (1928): 290–95.

———. "Spanish in New Mexico." *El Palacio* 24, no. 15 (1928): 286–87.

Rubio, Darío. *La anarquía del lenguaje en la América española.* México, 1925.

Santamaría, Francisco J. *Diccionario de mejicanismos.* México: Editorial Porrúa, 1959.

Saunders, Lyle. *Cultural Difference and Medical Care.* New York: Russell Sage Foundation, 1954.

Scholes, France V. "The Supply Service of the New Mexico Missions in the Seventeenth Century." *New Mexico Historical Review* 5 (1930): 93–155, 186–209, 386–404.

Sinclair, John L. "Vaquero Lingo." *New Mexico Magazine* 15, no. 12 (1937): 20–21, 38–39.

Sociedad Folklórica. *Compendio de folklore nuevomejicano. Conjunto de las tradiciones y costumbres.* Santa Fe: La Sociedad Folklórica, n.d.

Standley, Paul C. "Some Useful Plants of New Mexico." *Smithsonian Annual Report* 19, no. 11 (1912): 447–62.

Stark, Richard B. *Music of the Spanish Folk Plays in New Mexico.* Santa Fe: Museum of New Mexico Press, 1969.

Swadesh, Frances Leon. *Los Primeros Pobladores. Hispanic Americans of the Ute Frontier.* Notre Dame: University of Notre Dame Press, 1974.

Thomas, Alfred B. *Forgotten Frontiers.* Norman: University of Oklahoma Press, 1932.

Tidestron, Ivar, and Kittell, Sister Teresita. *A Flora of Arizona and New Mexico.* Washington: Catholic University of America, 1942.

Vigil, Ella M. *Guide to the Ella M. Vigil Collection of Southern Colorado Indo-Hispanic Folklore.* Manuscript in possession of the author. Colorado Springs, 1975.

Villagrá, Gaspar de. *Historia de la Nuevo México.* México: Museo Nacional, 1900.

Weigle, Marta. *Brothers of Light, Brothers of Blood: The Penitentes of the Southwest.* Albuquerque: University of New Mexico Press, 1976.

Winship, George Parker. "The Coronado Expedition, 1540–42." In *14th Annual Report, Bureau of American Ethnology, 1892–93.* Washington: Government Printing Office, 1896.